Java J2SE 1.4 Core Platform Update

James Hart

Wrox Press Ltd. ®

Java J2SE 1.4 Core Platform Update

Printing History

Some material first published in *Early Adopter J2SE 1.4*, September 2001

This edition, fully revised and updated, with additional material, first published March 2002

Published by Wrox Press Ltd,
Arden House, 1102 Warwick Road, Acocks Green,
Birmingham, B27 6BH, UK
Printed in the United States
ISBN 1-861007-27-2

Trademark Acknowledgments

Credits

Author
James Hart

Technical Reviewers
Richard Bonneau
Andrej Gabara
Craig McQueen
Phil Powers-DeGeorge

Managing Editor
Jan Kolasinski

Technical Editor
Ismail Bhana

Project Manager
Beckie Stones

Production Coordinator
Natalie O'Donnell

Index
Bill Johncocks

Proof Reader
Chris Smith

Cover
Chris Morris

Previous Edition Credits
Vishwajit Aklecha, Kapil Apshankar, Christianne Bailey, Mankee Cheng

About the Author

James Hart

James Hart is a writer, programmer, and technical communicator employed by Wrox Press in Birmingham, England. As a member of Wrox's editorial team he has been helping other authors teach programming concepts for three years. As well as Java, his technical interests include Mac OS X, web programming, and XML, and he has written about IBM's Java web services platform for the Wrox books *Professional Java XML* and *Java XML Programmer's Reference.* James is a keen follower of developments in the Java platform, and has been developing with J2SE 1.4 since the first beta release. He wrote *Early Adopter J2SE 1.4* in 2001 and has been lucky enough to have the opportunity of updating and revising that book now that J2SE 1.4 has finally been released. James has also contributed to books on the JSP Standard Tag Library, and Java programming on Mac OS X.

I have to thank everyone who's worked on this book, both the original manuscript and the new material in this edition. Ish, Mankee, Beckie, Christianne, Jan, Vishwajit, Kapil, Richard, Phil, Craig, Andrej, Natalie, Chris, and Bill – you've all helped make this book far better than it could otherwise have been.

Java J2SE 1.4 Core Platform Update

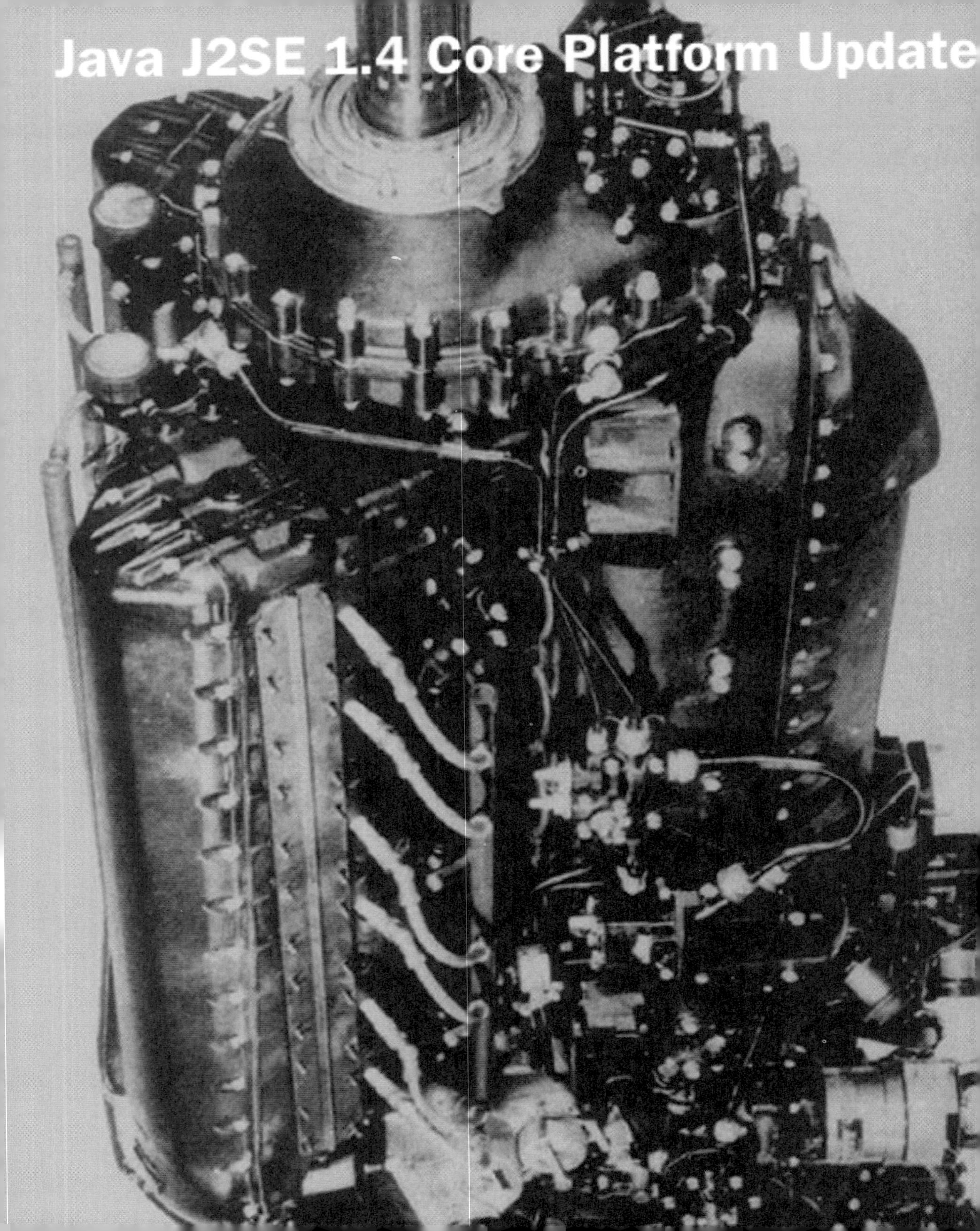

Table of Contents

Java J2SE 1.4 Core Platform Update

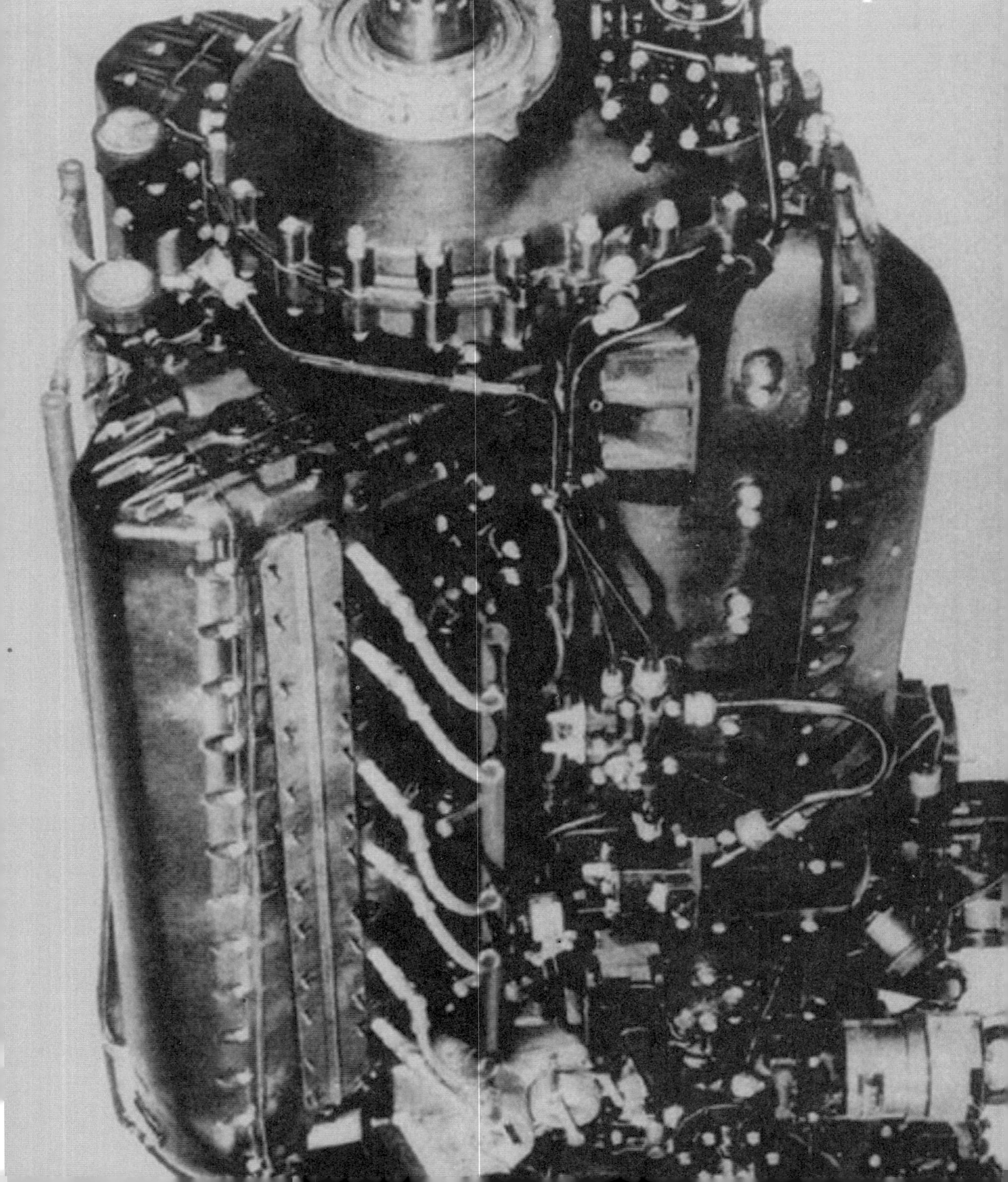

J2SE 1.4: An Introduction

The 1.4 release of the **Java 2 Platform, Standard Edition** is the biggest upgrade to the functionality of the basic Java platform since Java 2 was released over two years ago. The new version, known before its release by the codename **Merlin**, represents a real commitment by Sun and the Java community to make Java a viable client platform, after several years of concentrating on the server. The changes to the platform are far-reaching, and in many cases, represent steps very different from the simple addition of a few more classes that we've normally come to expect from a Java platform roll out.

This book presents an assessment of the significance of the changes to the Java 2 platform that Merlin introduces. We will look at the new facilities that have been added, and the upgrades that have been provided, and try to examine what the overall effect of the changes is on application development with Java. We'll try to demonstrate some of the platform's capabilities, and shine a light on its most useful new facilities. First, we will look at how J2SE 1.4 fits into the Java story.

From Applets to Servlets and Back Again

Back in 1996, Java was good for one thing: making geometric shapes move around on a web page. **Applets** were the first breakthrough for Sun's memory-managed, object-oriented language, and while like every web technology from frames to Flash Applets suffered their share of abuse, earning them a bit of a bad reputation, they represented a unique and still compelling proposition: downloadable applications, which run inside a secure sandbox environment, accessible via the Web. No installation, no hassle, just functionality on demand.

The browser wars ensured that no client-side technology could dominate for the next few years, while ActiveX controls fought plug-ins, and applets fought JavaScript, JScript, and ECMAScript therefore, the demand grew for more powerful server-side technologies, which could enable complex interactive applications to be delivered using plain old HTML, avoiding the mess of different browser standards completely. Applets, while still just about the second most popular client-side technology after JavaScript, are no longer Java's main deployment environment. Server-side enterprise Java – **servlets** and **Enterprise JavaBeans (EJBs)** – turned out to be the environment in which the cross-platform nature of Java would thrive.

Now though, things are changing once again. The **thin client** of HTML-based web applications is a limiting factor in the development of more complex services. New software distribution models that have recently been proposed, such as the software rental model of **application service providers (ASPs)**, and the service-oriented architecture of **web services**, are much more interesting if clients can run more complex and customizable applications, rather than simply rendering HTML. Indeed, two of the killer apps of the modern Internet have turned out to be rich client interfaces to online services: Napster, and instant messaging clients. While most instant messaging software, and file-sharing clients such as Napster, are native applications rather than Java ones, Java's sandbox model is perfectly suited to this sort of task.

However, even applets are limited, being totally dependent on the web browser for their lifecycle. Large applications can't be deployed as easily as applets since they might, depending on the browser's cache, have to be downloaded every time the client accessed the application. In addition, all the problems associated with ensuring the applet is compatible with the client's installed Java environment make applets awkward for serious applications.

The latest Java technology to answer these problems is the **Java Network Launch Protocol (JNLP)**, which is one of the main subjects of Chapter 4, *Clients and GUIs* . The JNLP basically defines the format of an XML document, which a client downloads from a web server, and reads in order to discover the URL from which it can download JAR files containing a particular application. In addition, the file provides details of the version of Java required and the standard extensions the application requires in order to run. The practical upshot of this is that it is possible for clients to click on a hyperlink pointing to one of these files, and for the browser to pass the file on to a helper application that can start up an independent JVM outside the browser, download the JAR file of the application (or check it against a previously downloaded version and update it if it has changed), and execute the program as a desktop application. The Java 2 security model enables this application to be sandboxed just as effectively as an applet, but its independence from the browser enables it to be re-launched, having once been installed in this manner, simply by using the helper application.

Thick Clients Are Back

So, if the time is right for thick clients, how does J2SE 1.4 address the needs of client development? Well, almost all of the changes in 1.4 will either directly or indirectly make it easier to develop more powerful client applications in 100% pure Java.

GUI Power

Java's GUI support has had a turbulent past. The **Abstract Windowing Toolkit (AWT)** provided in early Java run-time environments was a bit of a kludge. It used the native user interface components of the underlying operating system to provide windows, buttons, scrollbars, menus, and so on. Unfortunately, different platforms have very different components, and their behavior is idiosyncratic. This meant writing consistent user interfaces using one single codebase was pretty tricky. Java 2's **Java Foundation Classes**, **JFC**, used a different approach. One of the libraries in AWT was Java2D, a screen drawing API. This was used by the Swing classes to draw native 100% Java GUI components, removing the reliance on the operating system by drawing components itself. Using pluggable look-and-feel modules, the Swing user interface could be modified to mimic the behavior of different operating systems, or it could use a completely different look and feel, such as Swing's native metal components.

This reliance on Java2D, however, means that Swing has been dogged by performance problems. Swing components themselves are 100% pure Java – they have no operating system native code. To make Swing perform, you need to make Java2D perform. To that end, J2SE 1.4 ships with an enhanced **HotSpot virtual machine** optimized for client-side computing, and a vastly improved Java2D library, which provides better access to operating system drawing primitives and graphics acceleration, as well as getting rid of some bottlenecks in the graphics pipeline. For example, operations that cause a Java2D object to repaint itself (that is, work out from first principles exactly what pixels should appear on the screen to represent it) have been minimized, so that repaints occur less frequently.

What this really means is that a lot of the speed problems Swing used to suffer from are gone. On a modern desktop computer (or even a modern portable computer), the J2SE 1.4 run-time environment should easily provide enough performance for most GUI applications. The change, even with the beta version of the platform, is noticeable – the NetBeans IDE, for example, is probably one of the most complex GUI applications to run in pure Java, and its performance under 1.4 is visibly improved. Menus feel more responsive, and window resize and drag operations are smooth and reactive. It feels pretty much like a native OS application.

Matching the GUI performance of native applications isn't all that is required though. Java applications need to match the user interface. Swing's Windows look-and-feel (Windows, regardless of anybody's personal preferences, being probably the most important client platform most developers need to consider) has been further improved to match Windows 2000's appearance more closely (too bad Windows XP shipped during the beta cycle), to follow user color and style preference settings, and to ensure that Swing applications are harder to distinguish from Windows native applications. With Web Start providing the ability to create desktop and Start menu shortcuts to your applications, it is going to become possible to give people a Java application to run, without them ever needing to know.

Networked Clients

The applet sandbox, while limiting applets' ability to affect the machine on which they are running, has always allowed applets to open network connections back to the server they came from. For this reason, they've always encouraged development of client code that is connected back to the server. This ability is also present in the JNLP sandbox that Web Start applications live in. Reaching back to the server for updated data, or to activate services, is a key feature in networked client applications, such as those in the application service provider model, or for web service-based solutions. However, Java's network capabilities have lagged behind developer needs somewhat in this regard, most notably in its lack of native support for the most important network data interchange format of the moment, **XML**. J2SE 1.4 solves the XML problem with support for **XML parsing and transformation** using XSLT. It also makes some significant advances in the networking field with support for the **secure socket layer connections** (**SSL**), necessary for encrypted data transmission. There is also future-proofing, in the form of **IPv6 support**, which will enable Java programs to access addresses in the next-generation Internet, and some fundamental changes to the way threads work in order to enable the more graceful handling of threaded I/O operations, typical of networking applications. In addition, the new I/O APIs provide a completely new approach to handling data from network sockets as well as files, including asynchronous I/O operations, instead of synchronous (blocking) I/O.

IPv6

IPv6 is the upgrade to the Internet protocol, IP, which handles basic addressing for all Internet traffic. The four billion (well, more precisely, 4,294,967,296) IP addresses that can be described using the familiar dotted quad IP address – that's every address from `0.0.0.0` to `255.255.255.255` – are not sufficient for the needs of the modern Internet. IPv6 is a completely re-architected protocol, with new delivery systems and tunneling models, but its most important addition is a new addressing scheme, which provides some 7,9228,162,514,264 million billion possible addresses – according to a University of Hawaii estimate, that would be more than enough to give a billion IP addresses to every grain of sand on every beach on Earth (http://www2.hawaii.edu/suremath/jsand.html) – and still have plenty left over. While it's unlikely that we'd need to address grains of sand individually, this does open up the possibility for IP addresses to be assigned to almost any device, such as mobile phones, washing machines, light bulbs, and so on. An IPv6 address is written out as six groups of four hexadecimal digits, like this:

34A1:GE23:190E:BBFA:267A:004F

That's 24 hexadecimal digits, which is equivalent to a 96-bit binary number.

IPv6 protocol stacks are being developed for most operating systems. Linux has an experimental kernel module that implements IPv6, and Solaris has something similar. An early access IPv6 stack is available for Windows. Java is keeping pace by offering enhanced support for IPv6 addressing in J2SE 1.4, although it only supports the experimental UNIX IPv6 stacks, and not the Windows technology preview. This support will enable Java to operate on IPv6 networks when they begin to develop.

Encryption and Security

Three existing, complementary Java APIs have been incorporated into the J2SE:

- **Java Authentication and Authorization Service – JAAS**
- **Java Cryptography Extension – JCE**
- **Java Secure Sockets Extension – JSSE**

JAAS handles the management of users, identification, and trust in a secure environment. JCE provides encryption and decryption of data using a variety of algorithms for both digital data security and for data signing and verification. It provides a means to programmatically access and manage public-key infrastructure (PKI) systems, with public and private keys, and key signing and certification to establish webs of trust and mistrust.

Building on top of these systems is the JSSE. JSSE provides socket implementations that transparently perform encryption of on-the-wire data using SSL over TCP/IP. SSL allows for authentication of a connecting party, using PKI certificates, and reliable encryption of data over the wire between the two parties. Connecting all of these pieces together into a secure architecture where only trusted parties (vouched for by certificate authorities, and identified by their private key) can execute sensitive code or access sensitive data (either locally or over a secure, authenticated network connection) is the challenge of secure programming. We'll look at a lot of the basic functionality of the Java Security Architecture in Chapter 3, *Security*. For a thorough grounding in developing secure applications using these APIs, you might want to look at *Professional Java Security*, published by Wrox Press, ISBN 1-861004-25-7.

An Enriched Platform

So, the platform has been enriched by some new APIs; Java developers are used to this. But at the same time, there are two things that are changing in this version of the platform that haven't really been attempted before, and they represent a change in the character of Java platform releases. For a start, there's a change to Java syntax. It's not a far-reaching one, but it is source-code incompatible, which may upset developers of a conservative disposition. On the other hand, it shows how such changes can be handled sensitively and smoothly, and opens the door for further syntax changes in the future. Secondly, the incorporation of the JAXP XML processing API into the platform has brought an incipient problem to the fore – that of the incorporation into Java of programming standards external to Java itself.

The Java 2 platform consists of a number of components. In the past, when you installed Sun's run-time environment, either alone or as part of the SDK, you got the set of classes that make up the platform API, plus you also got a set of classes that support that implementation internally. These classes weren't part of the platform API, but they were included in the run-time library, `rt.jar`.

Now, in J2SE 1.4, things have got a lot more complicated. Instead of just these two types of class existing in the run-time library, classes fall into four categories:

- Classes and interfaces from the platform API
- Classes and interfaces from third-party standards endorsed by the platform API
- Classes providing the underlying Sun implementation of the platform API
- Classes from third parties providing the underlying implementation of the platform API

In fact, Java has incorporated classes from a third-party standard for a long time in the `org.omg` hierarchy. But in this version, with the inclusion of the two large XML APIs, DOM and SAX, and the IETF's GSS Kerberos library, it has become clear that this isn't just a limited part of the API any more. These classes have all been given the term **Endorsed Standards**, and they have a special status among the classes in `rt.jar`, in that they can be replaced, by dropping a JAR file containing a newer version into the `jre/lib/endorsed` directory.

In addition, Sun has taken the bold step of including two open source products in its distribution (Crimson and Xalan, the XML and XSLT processors in J2SE 1.4, which are released under the Apache Software License). These products exist independently of Sun's product release cycle, and again, Sun has allowed them to be overridden by newer versions in the endorsed directory.

As web services become more important (and their impact on Java seems certain), we'll see more and more standards impacting on the Java class library, such as SOAP, ebXML, and so on. The introduction of a smooth mechanism for dealing with issues like this is significant, and shows that Java is maturing as an API structure.

The Competitive Landscape

It's impossible to ignore that J2SE 1.4 is coming out at a crucial time in Java's history. Microsoft's .NET platform has just been released, and its presence in the development marketplace is bound to have an effect on Java programmers. .NET is a very direct competitor to Java, an alternative run-time built on similar founding principles. At the most basic level, it offers a new language, C#, that Java developers will find offers few surprises, and some interesting (maybe even tempting) features. The .NET platform itself bears more than a passing resemblance to Java, full of namespaces (.NET packages) with names like `System.IO`, `System.Net`, and `System.Security`. But it's been able to learn from some of Java's mistakes, and does have some compelling features. In particular, its support for XML is deep-grained and powerful, and it has an interesting trust and security model. The ASP.NET web programming model is, it must be said, a way ahead of what JSP can offer.

In addition, .NET represents a commitment on Microsoft's part to a new networked application architecture of rich client systems (in Microsoft's vision, Windows systems, naturally), which will integrate seamlessly, even invisibly, with online services. Instead of licensing software, in this world you rent features. The key enabling technologies are XML web services, and ubiquitous broadband net access. Clearly one of these is in its infancy, and the other is some way off. But a lot of energy is being invested (by Sun, IBM, Oracle, and others, as well as Microsoft) in building the architecture to enable this sort of service-oriented software market.

In this environment, it is important for those of us who want to continue to develop in Java that the platform at the very least keeps up. So it's great to see XML support at the core of the platform, even if it is somewhat less integrated into the platform than it is in .NET. But it's more important to see established, tried-and-tested APIs like JAAS, the Java Security Architecture's Authentication and Authorization Service, which provides a powerful trust model for secure programming. It's also good to see old APIs getting overhauled, like the new NIO I/O architecture. Just as Microsoft gets round to copying Java's byte and character stream architecture, Java moves on to higher-level channels and lower-level buffers.

At the same time, Microsoft's real strength has always lain in its tightly integrated development tools. Visual Studio .NET represents a continuation of this trend. It's good to see Sun, then, pushing its development tool, Forte for Java, alongside the J2SE 1.4 download, giving more of an impression of integration between Forte and the SDK. And if usage of Forte increases, then it has to have a positive effect on the development of NetBeans as an IDE platform, and Forte as a tool.

This Book

So, over the course of this book, we will be taking a look at the technologies J2SE 1.4 has added and improved in order to capitalize on this thick-client opportunity. JNLP, I/O, security, and XML are four major themes, but in investigating all of these facilities, we shall also see a number of other smaller functional improvements that have been added.

The intention of the coverage in these pages is to give you a sense of what possibilities each new capability offers, provide a summary of the architectures and the most useful APIs, and to give you some example code that shows it in action. This book doesn't intend to provide comprehensive reference material – this is, after all, available in the documentation that can be accessed and downloaded from the Sun web site. Instead, we have tried to draw together the important elements, and provide warnings about the hidden dangers and pitfalls we've encountered that the documentation doesn't tell you about, into a book that will hopefully act as a useful companion as you explore the new functionality of J2SE 1.4. Take what is here as a starting point for your own explorations, and hopefully you will find that we have helped you over some early hurdles. In addition, we will have pointed out a few hidden gems in the new platform that don't make the headlines, but are well worth knowing about. One great example is the expanded capabilities of Javadoc – take a look at Chapter 7 for details.

The book is structured not strictly around single API changes, but more around development themes. We'll be looking at the following:

- I/O: the new socket and file I/O capabilities of J2SE 1.4, and the Image I/O API
- Security: cryptography, secure socket communications, authentication and authorization, and digital signatures

- Clients and GUIs: new graphics rendering capabilities, GUI component functionality, and the new JNLP client environment
- XML: parsing, transforming, and generating XML data from Java programs
- Utilities: logging, preferences, and regular expressions
- Language and Tools: the new `assert` keyword, and changes to `javac` and `javadoc`
- The Future: a look at what's coming in J2SE, including the early access previews of Java XML Binding and generics

Installing and Using J2SE 1.4

Installing the latest release of the J2SE 1.4 SDK is very simple, and pretty much the same as installing any other version of the Java 2 Platform. It's worth thinking about briefly, however, since you may well want to keep your existing JRE installation alongside the new release. First of all, you can find the J2SE page on the Sun web site by locating this URL in your browser: http://java.sun.com/j2se/. Here, you will be able to get hold of older versions of the J2SE environment, as well as the latest 1.4 releases.

While you are on this page, one thing to point out is that the documentation is available here for browsing online, and also for download (a package of around 30 MB). Take heed of Sun's warning about the content of both the online documentation and the downloadable bundle though:

> *"The website-browsable version and downloadable version of the Java 2 SDK documentation may not always be in perfect sync. For expediency, we may make changes to the website version that we do not make immediately in the downloadable version."*

Now, back to installing. By clicking the relevant links, you can download a suitable version of the SDK for your platform, which is around 40 MB, depending on the version you have selected. If you can't download that much data because of bandwidth limitations, you can get a CD from Sun containing the SDK by purchasing the Java Jumpstart pack (although at time of writing, Jumpstart had not been updated to contain the final release of J2SE 1.4). Jumpstart can be found at http://www.sun.com/developers/devessentials/jumpstart.html. Once the download has finished, all you need to do is unpack the contents of the file into a suitable directory. You now have a working Java 2 platform 1.4 SDK set up on your machine, which will happily sit alongside your present Java runtime installation(s), without their interfering with each other.

Running Multiple JREs

We can easily switch between different versions of the Java runtime existing on the same machine, and make sure that we are not compiling and executing code with just any old runtime the command shell finds on the system. The easiest solution is to configure yourself several **batch files** that switch the necessary environment variables over for you.

If you intend to use early access release versions of up-and-coming Java technologies (as we will be doing in the final chapter of this book), batch files can also help you to store them in a specific place and let your runtime know of this location, as and when you need to. We can achieve this kind of flexibility very simply by using a batch file. On Windows, this might be something like the following:

```
@echo off
set JAVA_HOME=C:\j2sdk1.4.0
set JNLP_HOME=C:\Program Files\Java Web Start
set JAXB_HOME=C:\jaxb-1.0-ea
set JSR14DISTR=C:\jsr14_adding_generics-1_0-ea
set PATH=.;%JAVA_HOME%\bin;%PATH%
set CLASSPATH=.;%JNLP_HOME%\javaws.jar
```

I have named this particular file `jdk1.4.bat`, and dropped it into the `WINNT` directory. Now, whenever I open a new, fresh command window, I just need to run this batch file by typing `jdk1.4`, and it will set up the shell to look for the correct locations of my 1.4.0 versions of `javac.exe`, `java.exe`, and other relevant files. I can run an alternative batch file to switch to a different JRE version.

A UNIX system might use a batch file like this, although the precise format will depend on your preferred shell:

```
#!/bin/sh
export JAVA_HOME=/usr/local/jdk1.4_beta2
export JNLP_HOME=/usr/local/javaws
export JAXB_HOME=/etc/java/jaxb-1.0-ea
export JSR14DISTR=/etc/java/jsr14_adding_generics-1_0-ea
export J2SE13=/usr/local/jdk1.4_beta2
export PATH=.:$JAVA_HOME/bin:$PATH
export CLASSPATH=.:$JNLP_HOME/javaws.jar
```

The advantage of using a method such as this to set up your environment is the flexibility and control it allows. This also gives you the security of knowing exactly which program is going to run when you type `java` at the command prompt. It saves having to hardcode paths and environment variables on your system, which can cause all kinds of problems when you want to override them in order to use a beta.

Forte for Java

Sun is now pushing a combined download of J2SE 1.4 and Forte for Java 3.0. Forte is a 100% pure Java integrated development environment, which supports GUI editing, debugging, and a range of advanced development systems for web and enterprise development. The community edition, included in the free download, doesn't offer full enterprise support, but is nonetheless a powerful and flexible Java tool. The code editor is excellent, and its project management and compilation support is very good indeed.

The combined download is about 66 MB, and installation is very smooth. It's worth noting that at this stage Forte for Java 3.0 does not fully support the new language features of J2SE 1.4, such as the `assert` keyword. However, it's a very modular IDE, and supports dynamic updates, so if you install it now, this functionality will be added at a later date when it becomes available.

Forte can also support multiple compilation and execution environments. You configure Forte's default JRE on installation, and this is used for all projects by default. We can, however, launch Forte using another JRE, which will execute the IDE based on a different Java home. To do so, we need to run the IDE from the command line. From the `forte4j/bin/` directory, run the following command, substituting your desired Java home directory:

```
> runide -jdkhome C:\jdk1.3.1_02
```

In addition, we can set up additional compilers or runtimes for a particular project.

From the Project menu, select Settings....

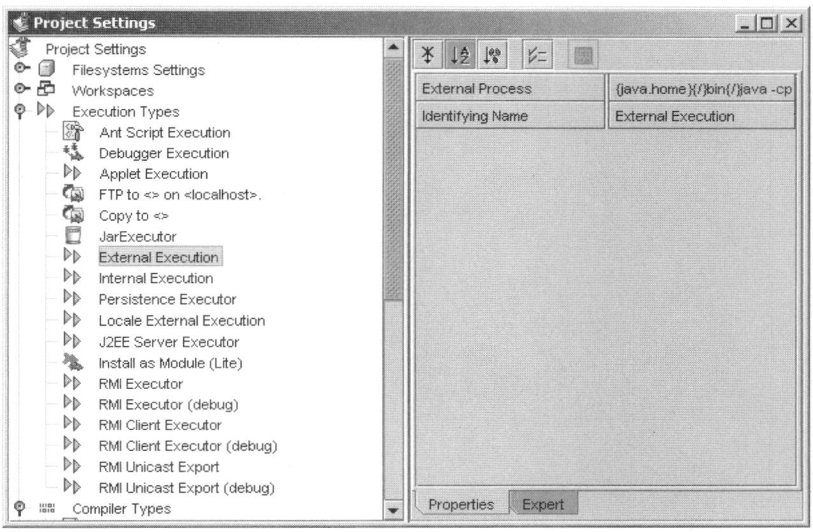

You can add a new execution type by right-clicking on Execution Types:

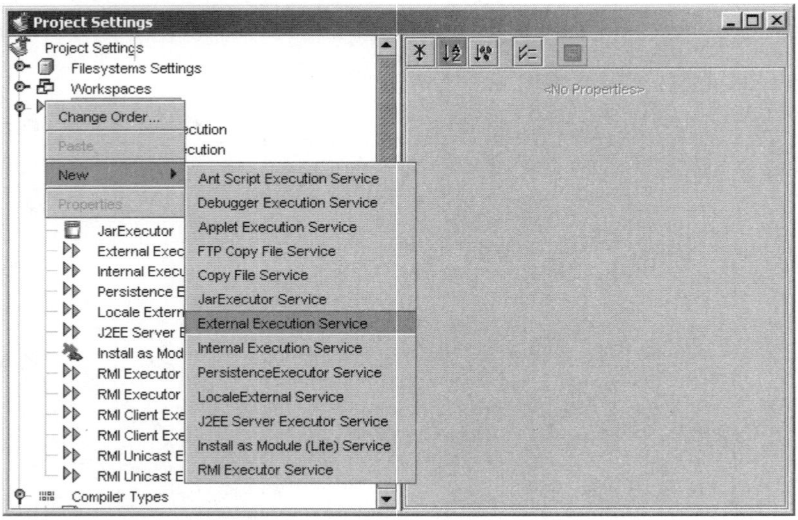

The new execution service can be configured by selecting it, and then double-clicking the External Process property. We can then edit the command line for another JRE:

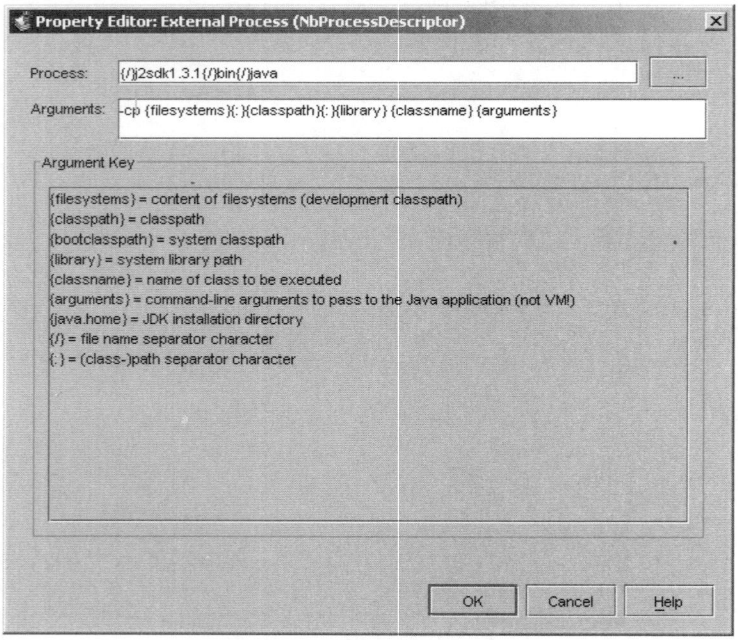

We can configure a new external compiler in a similar way. Now, for each class file in the project, we can set the execution properties, and select the alternative environment:

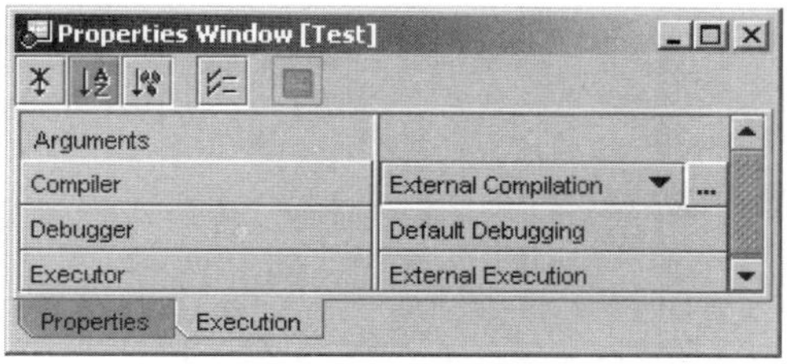

There's no space here to go into the detailed configuration and usage of Forte for Java; check out the online documentation and the included online tutorial for further information.

Java J2SE 1.4 Core Platform Update

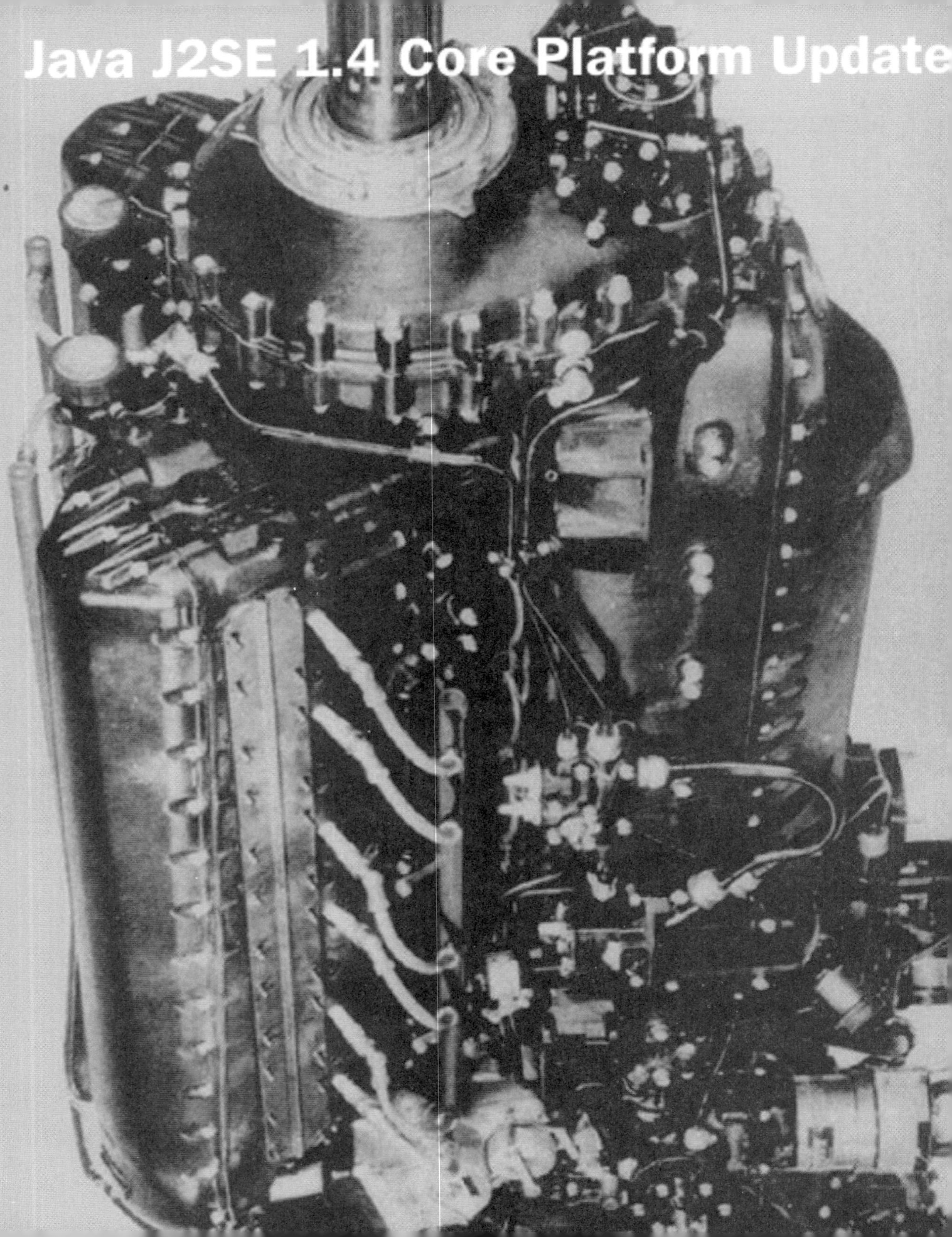

I/O

Java I/O is probably just about due for a real shakeup. The `java.io` package's byte streams have been a part of the platform since the 1.0 release, and character streams (readers and writers) came along with Java 1.1. Similarly, the `java.net` socket `system` has been in place since Java began. Not that age is an indication of obsolescence, but it is true that the Java platform is now used in ways that were not envisaged at the time those parts of the platform were designed.

J2SE 1.4 includes an overhaul of I/O and networking so fundamental that much of it has been placed in a new separate package tree, `java.nio`. At the same time, these changes have also had far-reaching implications in the rest of Java. Fundamental classes have been altered in order to allow for new functionality: `Thread` and `String`, to name two. This chapter is a quick tour of this new functionality. We'll look at how the underlying architecture of the new system works, how it interoperates with existing I/O, and how it changes the way we deal with files and sockets.

In addition, J2SE 1.4 incorporates a new API for reading and writing images in a number of common formats, and we'll take a look at that functionality at the end of the chapter.

Secure communications are an important facility in J2SE 1.4, and since this is a huge topic, we'll look at cryptographic support for I/O operations in the next chapter.

New I/O – NIO

Streams alone don't really provide all the functionality developers need to perform I/O operations. Java's basic byte and character streams perform simplistic I/O operations, which allow you to read data from a stream into an array of bytes or characters, or write data from an array to a stream. These operations will always block; a read request on an `InputStream` will always try to return at least one byte, waiting until data is available if necessary (unless an end-of-file is reached), and possibly blocking until sufficient data is available for it to provide exactly as many bytes as were requested. Similarly, write operations will always write all the data passed to them.

Sometimes this isn't the behavior we want. We might want to read what data is available now, but otherwise to just continue with whatever we're doing. We don't always want to wait for data to arrive if it's not here already, as our code may have far more important things to be doing. For example, rather than waiting for a busy server to get back to it with a packet of music data, a media player might be better off playing a bit of the music that it has already downloaded, before going back again and seeing if the data has arrived.

Processing raw arrays of bytes and characters is also pretty difficult; there aren't easy ways to convert byte array data into Java primitives, for example, and analyzing a character array isn't easy until you turn it into a `String`.

The buffered and data stream classes are supposed to overcome these limitations, but reading Java primitives one at a time from the data stream is not an easy way to program image decoders, for example, that have to read numerical data for each pixel in a file. Buffering provides a means to read data more than one character or byte at a time, and to provide more concrete guarantees about when read requests will be serviced, but the buffer is hidden from us, meaning we can only obtain data from the line in a form the buffer provides – a byte array, or a `String`.

In other words, we're stuck between two extremes: having to program our own buffer-processing logic around a byte array, or using the buffer behind a `BufferedReader`, and only being able to extract `Strings` from it.

Buffers and Channels

The new I/O framework, NIO, is in part an attempt to make up for these shortcomings. It does so in the first instance by providing a set of `Buffer` classes, that are essentially rich object wrappers around arrays of bytes – with the added advantage that the JRE can implement them using high-performance, OS-specific memory-buffer routines. They are able to take advantage of facilities common in modern operating systems, such as mapping the bytes of a file into an in-memory buffer, so that random accesses can be performed extremely fast – and again, can make use of native operating system libraries that perform just this task. This sort of facility makes it almost transparent whether a file is being accessed on disk, or via an in-memory clone. In fact, `Buffers` make up the bulk of the `java.nio` package. The core buffer interface and functionality is defined in the abstract class `java.nio.Buffer`, and other abstract classes extend this to provide specific data buffer interfaces, such as `java.nio.ByteBuffer`, `java.nio.CharBuffer`, and so on. Concrete implementations of these classes are provided by a vast number of supporting (package-private) classes that Sun uses to deliver buffers that use native functionality, the Java heap, or Java arrays to provide their backing data. We don't access these classes directly, but rather through the abstract API classes.

The transfer of data into and out of buffers is performed by NIO `Channels`. A channel represents a source and/or a destination for data, so, for example, we have `SocketChannels` and `FileChannels`. We also have `Pipes`, which are internal channels to move data between different parts of the same program.

What's the difference between a channel and a stream? Well, for a start, channels can be readable and writable at the same time – almost like an `InputStream` and an `OutputStream` combined. They also embody the connection to the data store, just as `Socket` or `File` does. In fact, the `java.nio.channels.Channel` interface itself only defines two methods: `close()`, and `isOpen()`, which embody the channel's status as representing a *connection*. The channel interface hierarchy steadily adds to these methods in a complex series of inheritance relationships. The two most important interfaces, `java.nio.channels.WritableByteChannel` and `java.nio.channels.ReadableByteChannel`, add the key `write()` and `read()` methods, both of which take a `ByteBuffer` as an argument, and return an `int` (the number of bytes read or written). Actual concrete channels are instances of classes that extend the abstract classes `java.nio.channels.FileChannel`, `java.nio.channels.SocketChannel`, and so on. The exact nature of these channels, and the operations they support, is defined by the set of interfaces they implement. So a `FileChannel`, for example, implements `GatheringByteChannel`, `ScatteringByteChannel`, `InterruptibleChannel`, and `ByteChannel`. These interfaces are extensions of other interfaces, so `FileChannel` also implements `ReadableByteChannel`, `WritableByteChannel`, and `Channel`. We'll see the whole of this hierarchy a little later in the chapter when we look at channels in detail, as well as discovering just what scattering and gathering means.

2

I/O

Blocking and Non-Blocking I/O

A key difference between channels and streams is that channels are able to be either blocking or non-blocking. In the case of file channels, their I/O operations are always carried out in blocking mode. In the case of a socket, their blocking status is customizable. If we activate non-blocking transfers, then we have the option of asking whether a particular operation can be performed without blocking, and attempt to write or read as much data as possible before the channel runs out of data, or backs up. This means that a read operation may not fill the buffer it is given, and a write operation may not write all the provided data. This might sound like a recipe for anarchy, but in performance-sensitive applications it can be very useful indeed. If we are running a live video streaming server, for example, it might be very helpful; we can continue to sample and write video data into the server's video buffer, and the socket connections will write as much of this data as they can – but not at the expense of holding up video processing. The process of finding out if a non-blocking channel is ready to perform an operation without blocking is called **selection**, and channels that can be used in a non-blocking manner are identified by the fact that they implement the `java.nio.channels.SelectableChannel` interface.

The `SocketChannel` class implements all the same interfaces as the `FileChannel` we mentioned above, but also implements `SelectableChannel`, allowing it to provide non-blocking operations. On the other hand, the `ServerSocketChannel` class doesn't implement either `ReadableByteChannel` or `WritableByteChannnel`, but does implement `SelectableChannel`.

What About Old I/O?

Basically, the functionality we have always expected to get via `InputStream` and `OutputStream` is now provided via channels, albeit in a modified form. Indeed, the `java.nio.channels.Channels` class provides a set of static utility methods that enable us to interoperate with old style I/O APIs:

- `static ReadableByteChannel newChannel(InputStream in)`
- `static WritableByteChannel newChannel(OutputStream out)`
- `static InputStream newInputStream(ReadableByteChannel ch)`
- `static OutputStream newOutputStream(WritableByteChannel ch)`
- ```
  static Reader newReader(ReadableByteChannel ch,
                          CharsetDecoder dec,
                          int minBufferCap)
  ```
- ```
  static Reader newReader(ReadableByteChannel ch,
                          String csName)
  ```
- ```
  static Writer newWriter(WritableByteChannel ch,
                          CharsetEncoder enc, int
                          minBufferCap)
  ```
  ```

- static Writer newWriter(WritableByteChannel ch, String csName)

We'll look at the functionality of ReadableByteChannel and WritableByteChannel, and the successive levels of functionality added by scattering and gathering, and selectability later in this chapter, after first looking at buffers in a bit more depth.

At the same time, J2SE 1.4 hasn't given up on the old I/O frameworks. There are a couple of improvements to the existing systems as well. Most notably, old style blocking I/O operations have been made to behave in a more thread-friendly manner, and threads themselves have been altered to make this possible. Blocked I/O calls can now be interrupted safely by a call to the blocking thread's interrupt() method, where before, the only real way to abort a blocking read or write in progress was to close the underlying socket or file. Since closing a resource like that is a pretty drastic course to take just to pull a thread out of a dead-end, this is a real improvement. In addition, the old closing technique has been made an "official" way to shut down a blocking I/O method, since closing a port underneath a blocking operation will now lead to the thread being interrupted, rather than an IOException being thrown.

In addition, as we mentioned in the opening chapter of the book, support for the next generation Internet protocol, IPv6, has been rolled in. This is great future-proofing, but with a lack of stable IPv6 stacks on any platform, it is not really a production feature at this stage.

Buffers

As we've already said, Buffers are basically powerful wrappers around what are simply arrays of bytes. Indeed, it is possible to construct a ByteBuffer by calling the static ByteBuffer.wrap(byte[] a) method. They can also represent a directly mapped region of memory though, with all the performance benefits that implies. To obtain a direct byte buffer, we call ByteBuffer.allocateDirect(int a), specifying the number of bytes we want.

We add data to buffers by either using the buffer's own put() methods, or by passing the buffer to a channel's read() method. We read data by using the buffer's get() methods, or by passing the buffer to a channel's write() method.

All buffers have four basic properties:

1. A **capacity**
2. A **limit**
3. A **position**
4. A **mark**

A buffer's **capacity** cannot be changed once the buffer has been allocated. It's the total number of bytes the buffer can store. The **limit** is a movable end-marker within the allocated buffer that allows us to dynamically change the size of the usable part of the buffer. By default, the limit of a newly allocated buffer is the same as its capacity. We can't read or write data beyond the buffer's current limit, and we can never move the limit beyond the buffer's capacity (obviously).

The **position** of a buffer is the location at which the next *relative* put, get, read, or write will take place. All of these operations can be performed as relative (to the current position) or absolute (specifying an offset from the start of the buffer) operations. Relative operations have the side effect of changing the position to the index immediately after the last piece of data modified or read. The position is always lower than the buffer's limit. It is analogous to a file pointer, or cursor.

The **mark** is a labeled position in the buffer, which is always earlier in the buffer than the current position. The position can be rolled back to the mark simply by calling the `reset()` method on the buffer. By default, no mark is defined, which is effectively like having the buffer marked at position zero. The region of the buffer between the mark and the limit is the region in which we are interested at any given time.

Buffers all have the following methods to manage and query their capacity, position, limit, and mark, and these methods are defined in the abstract class `Buffer`:

Buffer method	Effect
`int capacity()`	Returns the buffer's capacity.
`Buffer clear()`	Sets the buffer's limit to its capacity, clears any mark, and sets the position to zero.
`Buffer flip()`	Sets the buffer's limit to its position, clears any mark, and sets the position to zero – preparing a buffer that has just been written to for reading.
`boolean hasRemaining()`	Returns `true` if the position is less than the limit.
`int limit()`	Returns the current limit.
`Buffer limit( int newLimit)`	Sets the limit.
`Buffer mark()`	Sets the mark to the current position.
`int position()`	Returns the current position.
`Buffer position( int newPosition)`	Sets the position. The mark or limit will be adjusted if the position is set outside the range they define.
`int remaining()`	Returns the buffer's limit minus its position.
`Buffer reset()`	Sets the position back to the mark.
`Buffer rewind()`	Sets the position to zero, clearing any mark.

Buffer doesn't provide any functionality beyond this. The ByteBuffer class defines the following methods for writing and reading bytes and byte arrays:

- byte get()
- ByteBuffer get(byte[] dst)
- ByteBuffer get(byte[] dst, int offset, int length)
- byte get(int index)
- ByteBuffer put(byte b)
- ByteBuffer put(byte[] src)
- ByteBuffer put(byte[] src, int offset, int length)
- ByteBuffer put(ByteBuffer src)
- ByteBuffer put(int index, byte b)

The two methods specifying the index parameter are absolute, as they get or set the value of the byte at that position in the buffer. All the other methods operate as relative operations, since they take place at the buffer's current position.

You'll notice that many buffer methods that would normally be expected to have a return type void actually return a buffer. This will always be a reference to the buffer on which the method was called, so that the operations can be chained together. For example, to set a buffer's limit, perform a relative write, and then mark the buffer at the end of the written data, we could write one line:

```
ByteBuffer bb = ByteBuffer.allocate(16);
bb.limit(8).put((byte) 42).mark();
```

Buffers and Primitive Data

One problem with traditional Java I/O was its inability to interact with streams of encoded binary data from non-Java sources. Character handling (thanks to character streams) was generally adequate for text-based applications (such as HTTP serving), but when it comes to reading in or writing out binary structures representing image, sound, video, or even numerical data, Java has always been difficult to control. For example, there's the issue of byte ordering. When you have a short integer consisting of two bytes, does the first byte represent the most significant or the least significant eight bits? If you follow the **big-endian** policy it's the most significant bits, but for **little-endians** it's the opposite. Java, as a platform, is fundamentally big-endian. If your code has to read a file-format designed on little-endian principles, then you're forced to calculate the values yourself. This situation does arise in real-world file formats. For example, the BMP and GIF formats are little-endian, while JPEG is big-endian; RIFF files (such as WAV and AVI) can be either, depending on the information contained in the file header.

NIO offers a solution to this. Its buffers have a byte-ordering property, which we can set to either `ByteOrder.BIG_ENDIAN` or `ByteOrder.LITTLE_ENDIAN` as the need arises (the default is the Java platform default, big-endian). As data is written or extracted, this property is used to work out the correct mapping from a Java type to a raw byte representation.

One thing missing from this handling of different byte-to-value mappings is any way of reading or writing unsigned integers. While Java doesn't have the concept of a `uint`, `ulong`, *or* `ushort`, *there are plenty of languages out there that do. They are therefore able to make use of the extra bit gained by not specifying whether a value is positive or negative and use it to double the maximum positive value that can be represented using the same number of bits. Values in file formats are often encoded in the form of unsigned values. For example, the width and height of an image are always going to be positive. Unsigned values are rarely used within programs, however, because they can't support standard arithmetic, which is why they are absent from Java. To interpret unsigned values correctly, you'll still have to do some work yourself.*

To actually extract multi-byte values from a byte buffer, we can use these methods:

- `char getChar()`
- `double getDouble()`
- `float getFloat()`
- `int getInt()`
- `long getLong()`
- `short getShort()`

These are the relative get variants; absolute versions of all of them exist, which take an `int` as an argument, and start reading from that position.

In addition to calling these methods directly upon a `ByteBuffer`, we can also obtain **view buffers**. These are buffers that see the same data as the byte buffer contains, but as an array of Java primitives, rather than as an array of bytes. These view buffers all extend the `Buffer` class, like `ByteBuffer`, providing type-specific put and get methods to alter the buffer's content. They are obtained using the following methods of a `ByteBuffer`:

- `CharBuffer asCharBuffer()`
- `DoubleBuffer asDoubleBuffer()`
- `FloatBuffer asFloatBuffer()`
- `IntBuffer asIntBuffer()`
- `LongBuffer asLongBuffer()`

- ByteBuffer asReadOnlyBuffer()
- ShortBuffer asShortBuffer()

The returned buffer will be mapped onto the portion of the byte buffer after the current position, up to the limit. It will have a capacity equal to the number of primitives of the type that can fit into this sub-array of bytes. Changes to the data in the buffer made through this view will be reflected in the data that can be seen through the byte buffer view, and vice versa. However, the two buffers will have completely independent positions, limits, and marks.

Here's an example of view buffers in action:

```
import java.nio.*;

public class Buffers {

  public static void main(String[] args) {
    try {
      float[] floats = {
        6.612297E-39F, 9.918385E-39F, 1.0193785E-38F, 1.092858E-38F,
        1.0469398E-38F, 9.183596E-39F
      };

      ByteBuffer bb = ByteBuffer.allocate(floats.length * 4);

      FloatBuffer fb = bb.asFloatBuffer();
      fb.put(floats);

      CharBuffer cb = bb.asCharBuffer();
      System.out.println(cb.toString());

    } catch (Exception e) {
      System.out.println(e.getMessage());
      e.printStackTrace();
    }
  }
}
```

We initially create an array of `float` values (the reason for the obscure values will become clear), and initialize it with six floating-point numbers. A Java `float` is four bytes, so in order to make a byte buffer big enough to hold them, we allocate a buffer four times as long as the array.

We then obtain a `FloatBuffer` view of the `ByteBuffer`, and use a relative bulk `put` operation to populate it with our `floats` array. This will be reflected directly in the data content of the byte buffer.

Next we obtain a `CharBuffer` view of the same `ByteBuffer`. A `CharBuffer's toString()` method can be used to easily obtain a `String` consisting of the characters remaining (after the current position) in the buffer.

It so happens that the bytes in the buffer map to printable characters:

```
> java Buffers
Hello world!
```

Here's an illustration of the different views involved in the example:

Figure 1

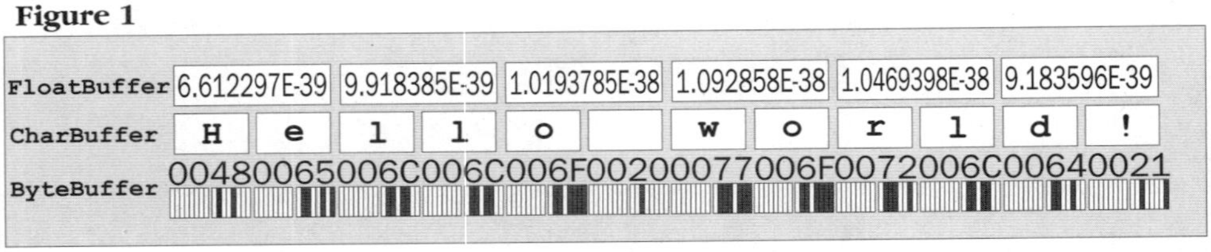

This shows the 24 bytes in the byte buffer, as a sequence of bits, and written out as hexadecimal values. At the top are the six floating-point numbers we originally entered. As you can see, they map onto four-byte sequences in the underlying buffer. Below them, we have the two-byte characters. The pairs of bytes are interpreted as big-endian 16-bit Unicode values.

CharBuffers, Strings, and StringBuffers

`CharBuffer` implements a new interface in J2SE 1.4: `java.lang.CharSequence`. In addition, `Strings` and `StringBuffers` also now both implement this interface. It defines four methods:

- `char charAt(int index)`
- `int length()`
- `CharSequence subSequence(int start, int end)`
- `String toString()`

`String` and `StringBuffer` both already contained the `charAt()`, `length()`, and `toString()` methods, and also `substring()` methods with identical signature and semantics to the `subSequence()` method, except with a return-type of `String`. However, defining this almost as a marker interface does allow some methods that would normally be forced to either choose whether to accept a `String`, `StringBuffer`, or now `CharBuffer` (or, possibly, to overload them all), to accept and return a `CharSequence` instead. A case in point is the regular expression package, which we'll take a look at in Chapter 6, *Utilities*.

Obviously, this interface is brand new now. The possibility exists for a lot of classes that currently work with `Strings` to be modified in a manner that won't break existing code, in order to handle arbitrary character sequence objects.

Channels

As was mentioned earlier, channels derive their interfaces by implementing one or more interfaces from the `java.nio.channels` package. The root `Channel` interface is extremely simple, and declares two methods:

- `void close()`
- `boolean isOpen()`

A channel is open once it has been created, and can never be re-opened once closed.

Then, we have the method defined by the `ReadableByteChannel` interface:

- `int read(ByteBuffer bb)`

This returns, as we discussed before, the number of bytes read from the channel into the byte buffer.

And the `WritableByteChannel` interface defines the reciprocal method:

- `int write(ByteBuffer bb)`

This gets bytes from the buffer, and writes them to the channel. Again, the return value is the number of bytes written.

Both methods advance the position of the buffer to the point following the last byte read or written.

A convenience interface, `ByteChannel`, consolidates these two interfaces, but adds nothing of its own. It is this interface that is implemented by the channels that most interests us: `SocketChannel` and `FileChannel`.

The `java.nio.channels` package is a mess of inheritance, interfaces, and abstract classes. Here's a diagram that might serve as a useful reference to how things fit together. The arrows represent inheritance/implementation relationships:

Figure 2

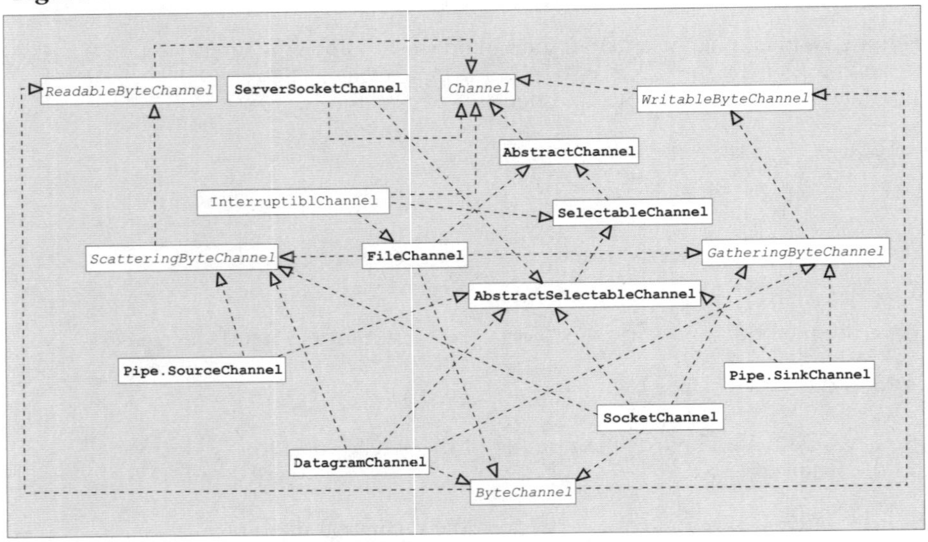

`AbstractChannel` and `AbstractSelectableChannel` are classes defined in the `java.nio.channels.spi` sub-package. Italic names refer to interfaces. All the other classes are in fact abstract, and concrete instances of subclasses are obtained via static methods, or from factory methods on other classes. The actual instances returned are native implementations, from the `sun.nio` packages, but you don't need to concern yourself with that.

We can get hold of concrete channel instances in the following ways:

Channel Type	Obtained By
`ServerSocketChannel`	Call to `ServerSocketChannel.open()`
`FileChannel`	Call to `getChannel()` method on an existing `java.io.RandomAccessFile`, `java.io.FileInputStream`, or `java.io.FileOutputStream` instance
`SocketChannel`	Call to `SocketChannel.open()`, or call `getChannel()` method on an existing `java.net.Socket` created by a `ServerSocketChannel`
`DatagramChannel`	Call to `DatagramChannel.open()`

File Channels

A `FileChannel` is a readable and writable channel, although whether it is possible to use both functionalities depends on the way the `FileChannel` was created. It will be writable if it was created from a `FileOutputStream` or a `RandomAccessFile` that was opened read-write. It will be readable if it was opened from a `FileInputStream`, or from a `RandomAccessFile`. In addition to the basic channel-buffer interactions, it also supports some advanced file operations:

- File locks can be obtained on a portion of a file.
- File data can be mapped to an in-memory buffer.
- Data can be transferred to any writable channel, or from any readable one, using a method optimized to use hardware and operating system functionality.
- Random-access reads and writes can take place on the channel itself (not just on the buffer). Think of the file channel as a reel-to-reel tape. You can record data onto it, or play data from it, anywhere, but you have to wind the tape back and forth to find the right spot.

The file's size is available from the channel via the `size()` method. The size will be increased if data is written to the channel beyond its current size. A file's size can be reduced to a certain length by calling the `truncate()` method.

The channel also has a file pointer, the location of which can be found and set using the `position()` method. This is the location from which data will next be read, or at which the next write operation will begin.

This little example performs a straightforward copy operation. When you run it, specify the name of the file to copy as the first command-line argument, then the name of the file to copy to:

```
import java.io.*;
import java.nio.*;
import java.nio.channels.*;

public class Copy {

  public static void main(String[] args) {
    FileChannel in = null;
    FileChannel out = null;

    if (args.length < 2) {
      System.out.println("Usage: java Copy <from> <to>");
      System.exit(1);
    }

    try {
      in = new FileInputStream(args[0]).getChannel();
      out = new FileOutputStream(args[1]).getChannel();

      out.transferFrom(in, 0L, (int) in.size());

    } catch (Exception e) {
```

```
      e.printStackTrace();
    }
    finally {
      try {
        if (in != null) {
          in.close();
        }
        if (out != null) {
          out.close();
        }
      } catch (IOException e) {}
    }
  }
}
```

The core of this class is the `transferFrom()` method call, which performs an optimized transfer of bytes between two channels. We pass in the channel to read, the offset within the channel to start reading (in our case, zero), and the number of bytes to transfer (in our case, the same number of bytes that the source file contains).

This should hopefully show that the new I/O system is at least as easy to use as the old system, and in some ways easier; writing the above application with traditional I/O functionality would be much more complex, and would not benefit from the performance of the `transferFrom()` method.

Let's look at how we can use a `FileChannel` to read in and modify a file. The following program implements the king of all encryption mechanisms, the **Rot13 cipher** (Ok so it's not exactly strong encryption. We're coming to that in the next chapter, though).

Rot13, for those who don't know, simply involves taking every alphabetic character in the text to be encoded and rolling it on by thirteen characters, wrapping back to the start of the alphabet if you go over the end. The neat thing about the algorithm is, of course, that if you run it twice, you get back your original text.

We'll load the file we want to process into an in-memory buffer before we process it. To do so, we simply call the `FileChannel`'s `map()` method:

- `MappedByteBuffer map(int mode, long position, int size)`

We first pass in the type of mapping we want, chosen from the following instances of `FileChannel.MapMode`:

Mapping Type Constant	Meaning	Effect
`FileChannel.MapMode.READ_WRITE`	read-write	Changes to the data in the buffer will be reflected in the file. Changes may propagate at any time, depending on the operating system's file-mapping behavior. Changes made by other processes to the file may be made visible.
`FileChannel.MapMode.READ_ONLY`	read-only	The resulting buffer will be a read-only buffer: changes to the content will not be permitted. Changes made by other processes to the file may be made visible.
`FileChannel.MapMode.PRIVATE`	copy-on-write	Open the channel read only. If a change is made to the buffer, a private copy will be made. Subsequent changes are made using this private copy. The copy's version will not subsequently be propagated to the original file. This provides a means to open a file as read-only, but be able to make alterations to it. The buffer can subsequently be written out to another file, or even the same one.

We'll want our changes to propagate to the original file, so we'll choose the read-write mapping, `FileChannel.MapMode.READ_WRITE`.

The next parameter is the index of the first byte in the file we want to map, and the last is the number of bytes we want in our map. This returns a `MappedByteBuffer`, which is an extension of an ordinary `ByteBuffer`, with three additional methods:

- `MappedByteBuffer force()`
- `boolean isLoaded()`
- `MappedByteBuffer load()`

These allow us to manage the status of the mapping between the in-memory data, and the physical storage. `load()` loads the bytes from the file into the map, synchronizing the buffer with the file. `force()` forces the buffered changes to be written out to the file synchronizing the file with the buffer. We can check to see if the file has been loaded using the `isLoaded()` method.

Once we've mapped the buffer, we simply iterate through the bytes in the buffer, performing a Rot13 operation on them. We do, however, make the assumption here that the input document is encoded in a plain 8-bit encoding format based on ASCII, such as UTF-8, since Rot13 is only intended as an encryption system for the basic Latin alphabet. This assumption lets us treat each byte as a separate character.

Here's the code for Rot13.java:

```
import java.io.*;
import java.nio.*;
import java.nio.channels.*;

public class Rot13 {

  public static void main(String[] args) {
    FileChannel in = null;

    if (args.length < 1) {
      System.exit(1);
    }

    try {
      in = new RandomAccessFile(args[0], "rw").getChannel();

      MappedByteBuffer mbb =
        in.map(FileChannel.MapMode.READ_WRITE, 0L,(int) in.size());
      mbb.load();
```

Now we've mapped and loaded the buffer, we need to iterate through the buffer. The hasRemaining() method provides a useful condition for a condition loop:

```
      while (mbb.hasRemaining()) {
        byte c = mbb.get(mbb.position());
```

We use the absolute get() operation here, passing in the parameter of our current position, because we don't want our position to be changed by this operation – we still have to write back the modified character yet.

Now we perform the Rot13 operation. We need to treat uppercase and lowercase characters separately. In each case, if the character is in the first half of the alphabet, we add thirteen to it; if it's in the second half, we subtract 13 – exactly the same as adding 13, mod 26, relative to the start of the alphabet.

```
        if (('a' <= c) && (c <= 'z')) {
          if (c < 'n') {
            c += 13;
          } else {
            c -= 13;
          }
        } else if (('A' <= c) && (c <= 'Z')) {
          if (c < 'N') {
            c += 13;
```

```
          } else {
            c -= 13;
          }
        }
        mbb.put(c);
      }

      mbb.force();

    } catch (Exception e) {
      e.printStackTrace();
    }
    finally {
      try {
        if (in != null) {
          in.close();
        }
      } catch (IOException e) {}
    }
  }
}
```

The Rot13 program will encode any alphabetic characters in a file you pass to it, but won't touch characters outside that range. To get your original data back, just Rot13 it again.

Scattering and Gathering

Scattering and gathering operations are supported by all the main channels in the NIO system, including file and socket channels. The `ScatteringByteChannel` interface extends the `ReadableByteChannel` interface, providing methods that perform **scattering reads**. Similarly, the `GatheringByteChannel` interface extends `WritableByteChannel` and supports **gathering write** operations. Basically, whereas normal read and write operations use a single `ByteBuffer`, scattering is the process of reading in bytes from one channel into a sequence of buffers, and gathering is the process of writing out the content of a series of buffers sequentially into a channel.

Why would you want to do this? Well, if you are reading from a file that follows a certain byte format (perhaps it begins with a three-character identifier, then a two-byte version number, then an integer size, then some data), then rather than reading the whole file into a `ByteBuffer` and pulling out the data piece by piece, we can define a sequence of buffers that the data should be read into in sequence. So, for example, if we were to read in the byte sequence we generated earlier, into a series of three buffers (one five-character buffer, one two-digit integer buffer, and one three-digit short integer buffer), the three buffers would contain the following information:

Figure 3

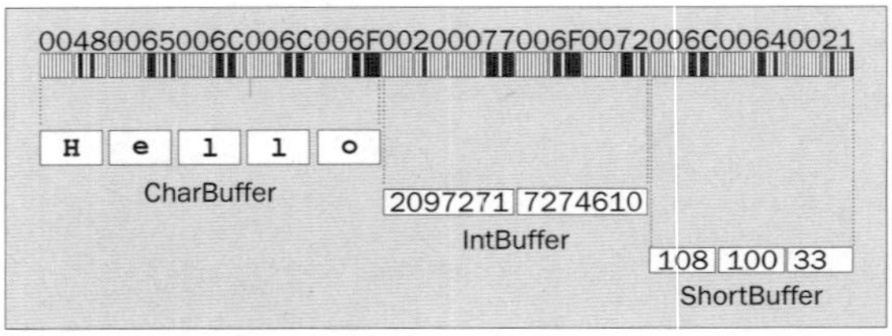

This is a scattering-read – the data is scattered, as it is read, into a series of containers.

Scattering operations can be performed by any class that implements the `ScatteringByteChannel` interface, which defines two methods:

- `int read(ByteBuffer[] dsts)`
- `int read(ByteBuffer[] dsts, int offset, int length)`

Each of these takes an array of `ByteBuffers`, but remember we can view a byte buffer as any other kind of buffer we want to. The second variant specifies an offset within the virtual super-buffer created by lining up the array of buffers, and a number of bytes to read in.

A gathering-write operation is the inverse. This gathers together a series of byte buffers, and outputs their content as if they were one contiguous buffer.

These techniques are ideal for handling byte-level file formats and wire-protocols. For example, we could design a simple format for exchanging messages like this:

- The first four bytes are an integer representing the message ID
- The next eight bytes are four Unicode characters identifying the message type
- The next eight bytes are a long integer representing the length of the message, *n*
- The next *n* bytes are the message, encoded as Unicode characters

To help with designing classes that handle this protocol, we can create an interface like this one:

```
public interface ByteSizes {
  public static final int BYTE_SIZE   = 1;
  public static final int CHAR_SIZE   = 2;
  public static final int SHORT_SIZE  = 2;
  public static final int INT_SIZE    = 4;
  public static final int FLOAT_SIZE  = 4;
  public static final int LONG_SIZE   = 8;
  public static final int DOUBLE_SIZE = 8;
}
```

This specifies constants for the number of bytes taken up by each Java primitive (incredibly, there is no class in the Java platform that provides these constants). Now, we just implement or extend this interface wherever we need to use these constants. We can now specify another interface that identifies the components of one of our formatted messages:

```
public interface MessageProtocol extends ByteSizes {
  public static final int MESSAGE_ID_LENGTH      = 1 * INT_SIZE;
  public static final int MESSAGE_TYPE_LENGTH    = 4 * CHAR_SIZE;
  public static final int MESSAGE_LENGTH_LENGTH = 1 * LONG_SIZE;
}
```

So, having specified the elements of the protocol, we can build a gathering writer that will build a message and write it to a `GatheringByteChannel`:

```
import java.nio.channels.*;
import java.nio.*;
import java.io.*;

public class MessageSender implements MessageProtocol {

  public void send(GatheringByteChannel out, int messageId,
                   String messageType,
                   String message) throws IOException {
```

Our first task is to create a byte buffer to store each of the elements of the message. The lengths of these are all constant, except for the message itself, for which we calculate the length in bytes.

```
    ByteBuffer messageIdBytes = ByteBuffer.allocate(MESSAGE_ID_LENGTH);
    ByteBuffer messageTypeBytes =
      ByteBuffer.allocate(MESSAGE_TYPE_LENGTH);
    ByteBuffer messageLengthBytes =
      ByteBuffer.allocate(MESSAGE_LENGTH_LENGTH);
    ByteBuffer messageBytes = ByteBuffer.allocate(message.length()
                                                  * CHAR_SIZE);
```

The next task is to write each piece of data to its buffer:

```
    messageIdBytes.asIntBuffer().put(messageId);
    messageTypeBytes.asCharBuffer().put(messageType);
    messageLengthBytes.asLongBuffer().put((long) message.length());
    messageBytes.asCharBuffer().put(message);
```

Finally, we perform the gathering-write operation, passing an array containing all the buffers, in order:

```
    out.write(new ByteBuffer[] {
      messageIdBytes, messageTypeBytes,
      messageLengthBytes, messageBytes
```

```
    });
  }
```

Now, while this method is intended to be used from other classes, we can add a quick `main()` method to this class that creates a simple `FileChannel` from an output stream, which we can use to generate a test message.

```
  public static void main(String[] args) {
    if (args.length < 1) {
      System.exit(1);
    }

    try {
      FileChannel fc = new FileOutputStream(args[0]).getChannel();
      new MessageSender().send(fc, 0, "TEXT", "hello world");
    } catch (Exception e) {
      System.out.println(e.getMessage());
      e.printStackTrace();
    }
  }
}
```

Next, we need to write a `MessageReceiver` that can understand the messages:

```
import java.nio.channels.*;
import java.nio.*;
import java.io.*;

public class MessageReceiver implements MessageProtocol {

  public void receive(ScatteringByteChannel in) throws IOException {
```

Again, the first task is to allocate appropriately sized byte buffers. At this stage, of course, we have no idea how big the message part is going to be. While it is possible to find the size of a file, this method deals with the more general type of `ScatteringByteChannel`, which could be supplying us with data from a socket, a pipe to another piece of code, or a file – so we can't find out the size by asking the channel. We'll allocate that buffer later.

```
    ByteBuffer messageIdBytes = ByteBuffer.allocate(MESSAGE_ID_LENGTH);
    ByteBuffer messageTypeBytes =
      ByteBuffer.allocate(MESSAGE_TYPE_LENGTH);
    ByteBuffer messageLengthBytes =
      ByteBuffer.allocate(MESSAGE_LENGTH_LENGTH);
```

Now we can perform a scattering read, pulling data into all three of these buffers:

```
    in.read(new ByteBuffer[] {
      messageIdBytes, messageTypeBytes, messageLengthBytes
    });
```

We must rewind all of the buffers, having written data to them, so that we can get data out from them starting at the beginning:

```
    messageIdBytes.rewind();
    messageTypeBytes.rewind();
    messageLengthBytes.rewind();
```

Now we can obtain a view of each of the buffers, and read the appropriate information:

```
    int messageId      = messageIdBytes.asIntBuffer().get();
    String messageType = messageTypeBytes.asCharBuffer().toString();
    long messageLength = messageLengthBytes.asLongBuffer().get();
```

Now we know how many characters are in the message, we can allocate a buffer for it, perform a normal (non-scattering) read, and then read out the data as a string. Finally, we can print the message out to the screen:

```
    ByteBuffer messageBytes = ByteBuffer.allocate((int) messageLength
                                                  * CHAR_SIZE);
    in.read(messageBytes);
    messageBytes.rewind();
    String message = messageBytes.asCharBuffer().toString();

    System.out.println("Msg: " + messageId);
    System.out.println("Type: " + messageType);
    System.out.println(message);
  }
```

As before, we can provide a simple test method here, that reads in a file containing a single message, and calls the `receive()` method.

```
  public static void main(String[] args) {
    if (args.length < 1) {
      System.exit(1);
    }

    try {
      FileChannel fc = new FileInputStream(args[0]).getChannel();

      new MessageReceiver().receive(fc);

    } catch (Exception e) {
      System.out.println(e.getMessage());
```

```
      e.printStackTrace();
    }
  }
}
```

Running the two pieces of code one after another should allow us to generate the following output:

```
> java MessageSender test.txt

> java MessageReceiver test.txt
Msg: 0
Type: TEXT
hello world
```

We'll revisit `MessageSender` and `MessageReceiver` later on, when we've covered the basics of the NIO networking architecture.

Buffer Splicing

Another potential application for gathering writes is to perform virtual slicing and dicing of an existing buffer. For example, we can use the `ByteBuffer`'s `slice()` method to obtain a `ByteBuffer` view of a sub-sequence of the original buffer. By then gathering these views of different parts of a buffer in a different sequence, we can splice together the original buffer into a completely different order, without actually copying or moving any data around. For example:

```
import java.io.*;
import java.nio.*;
import java.nio.channels.*;

public class Splicer {

  private static int BYTES_PER_SLICE = 4;

  public static void main(String[] args) {
    FileChannel in = null;
    FileChannel out = null;

    if (args.length < 2) {
      System.exit(1);

    }

    try {
      in = new FileInputStream(args[0]).getChannel();
      out = new FileOutputStream(args[1]).getChannel();
```

```
    int byteCount = (int) in.size();
    ByteBuffer bb = ByteBuffer.allocate(byteCount);
    in.read(bb);

    int subBufferCount = (int) (byteCount / BYTES_PER_SLICE);

    ByteBuffer[] subBuffers = new ByteBuffer[subBufferCount];
```

Here's the magic part: we populate an array of `ByteBuffers` with sequences that are just lightweight views of the underlying buffer. These sequences are arranged in the reverse order to their original buffer sequence:

```
    for (int a = 0; a < subBufferCount; a++) {
      bb.limit((a + 1) * BYTES_PER_SLICE);
      bb.position(a * BYTES_PER_SLICE);
      ByteBuffer buf = bb.slice();
      subBuffers[subBufferCount - a - 1] = buf;
    }
```

Now we perform a gathering write, using the array of virtual buffers:

```
    out.write(subBuffers);
  } catch (Exception e) {
    e.printStackTrace();
  }
  finally {
    try {
      if (in != null) {
        in.close();
      }
      if (out != null) {
        out.close();
      }
    } catch (IOException e) {}
  }
 }
}
```

Now, put in a file containing the text:

```
abcdefghijklmnopqrstuvwxyz
```

And out comes a file containing:

```
uvwxqrstmnopijklefghabcd
```

Note that the program always returns an exact multiple of `BYTES_PER_SLICE` bytes, so only 24 characters are processed.

Socket Channels

Socket channels, just like file channels, implement the scattering and gathering byte channel interfaces. They also implement `ByteChannel`, meaning that they support reading and writing operations.

Unlike `FileChannels`, they can only be created directly, by calling the static `open()` method:

```
SocketChannel sc = SocketChannel.open();
```

You can also obtain a `SocketChannel` from a `Socket`. If we had a `Socket` in the variable `sock`, we could obtain a channel as follows:

```
SocketChannel sc = sock.getChannel();
```

Note that this only works if the socket was originally created with a channel, either by the above method, or by a `ServerSocketChannel`.

More importantly, they differ from `FileChannels` in one important respect: they indirectly extend the `SelectableChannel` class.

A **selectable channel** has the ability to participate in what is termed **multiplexed asynchronous non-blocking I/O**. This is essentially a long-winded way of saying "scalable server I/O". To break down the meanings, this form of I/O is:

- **Non-blocking** – Operations will not block waiting for an I/O channel to accept or provide data
- **Asynchronous** – Operations are performed outside the thread that calls them
- **Multiplexed** – Multiple channels can participate in multiple operations simultaneously

The first ability, then, that selectable channels have, is the ability to perform non-blocking operations. A `SelectableChannel` has the following two methods:

- `void configureBlocking(boolean block)`
- `boolean isBlocking()`

So, we can tell the channel whether to use non-blocking or blocking behavior, and we can query its current blocking status.

There are four operations that can be performed in an asynchronous manner:

- Accepting connections
- Initiating connections
- Reading from a channel
- Writing to a channel

In order to do so, we make use of a `Selector`. A `Selector` is a manager of multiplexed channels; it keeps a reference to a set of channels, and can be queried to provide a group of those channels that are ready to perform a particular operation. First, we create a selectable channel and put it into non-blocking mode. Then we obtain or create a selector. We register the channel with the selector, specifying which operations we are planning on performing with that channel.

A channel can be registered with multiple selectors, and a selector can have multiple channels registered with it. That's why this kind of I/O is described as multiplexing.

When we wish to perform an I/O operation that we have earlier registered a channel for, we call the selector's `select()`, `select(long timeout)`, or `selectNow()` method. These operations all perform the same task, but differ in how they return. When any of these methods is called, a **selection operation** is initiated: the selector examines the channels that have been registered, to see if any of them is ready to perform an operation for which it was registered. Any that are ready are placed into a pool of "selected" channels. The first method blocks until at least one registered channel is available to perform an operation. The second blocks until a channel is available, or until the timeout elapses, whichever occurs sooner. The last doesn't block at all – the selector examines all the channels it has, transfers any that are ready to the selected pool, and then returns, whether any were ready or not.

All of the selection methods return an `int`, representing the number of channels that were selected during the operation.

If any channels were selected, we can then obtain the set of selected channels, choose one, and be assured that we can perform the operation the channel is ready for, without any risk of it blocking. Indeed, if we attempt to perform an operation on a channel, and it is not ready to comply, then an exception is thrown, telling us that it was not able to perform a non-blocking operation.

So, it is possible to have a number of threads operating in a loop, using selectors to poll a large number of channels to see which ones are free. For a video multi-casting server, for example, that has a large number of simultaneously connected clients, a pool of threads could have the dedicated task of polling for which connections are ready to accept a write operation, ensuring that so long as there is a connection there that can be written to, data is being written.

Let's take a look first at how we can use our message sender and message receiver in a client-server application, using new-style socket I/O. Once we've developed a simple, blocking version, we'll adapt it to use asynchronous, multiplexing, non-blocking I/O.

First, we need to add another attribute to our `MessageProtocol`:

```
public interface MessageProtocol extends ByteSizes {
  public static final int MESSAGE_ID_LENGTH     = 1 * INT_SIZE;
  public static final int MESSAGE_TYPE_LENGTH   = 4 * CHAR_SIZE;
  public static final int MESSAGE_LENGTH_LENGTH = 1 * LONG_SIZE;
  public static final int DEFAULT_PORT          = 2000;
}
```

This specifies the port the server will listen on, and the port the client will try to connect to. Let's look at the client:

```
import java.nio.channels.*;
import java.nio.*;
import java.io.*;
import java.net.*;

public class Client implements MessageProtocol {

  public static void main(String[] args) {
    if (args.length < 1) {
      System.exit(1);
    }

    try {
      SocketChannel sock = SocketChannel.open();
      sock.connect(new InetSocketAddress(args[0], DEFAULT_PORT));
```

To open a connection, we first create the socket channel, then we call its `connect()` method. `InetSocketAddress` is a new class in `java.net` for J2SE 1.4 – it is basically the same as an `InetAddress`, but incorporates port information as well.

Now, we can create a message sender and use it to build and send the message using the socket channel. Once the call to the message sender returns, we know the message has been sent, so we can call the message receiver, and tell it to read the socket channel, looking for a response from the server:

```
      new MessageSender().send(sock, 0, "TEXT",
                               "testing, testing, 1, 2, 3");
      new MessageReceiver().receive(sock);
    } catch (Exception e) {
      System.out.println(e.getMessage());
```

```
      e.printStackTrace();
    }
  }
}
```

That's our simple client. Now, here's a simple server:

```
import java.nio.channels.*;
import java.nio.*;
import java.io.*;
import java.net.*;

public class Server implements MessageProtocol {

  private static int id = 0;

  public static void main(String[] args) {
    MessageReceiver messageReceiver = new MessageReceiver();
    MessageSender messageSender = new MessageSender();

    try {
      ServerSocketChannel ssc = ServerSocketChannel.open();
      ServerSocket server = ssc.socket();
      server.bind(new InetSocketAddress(DEFAULT_PORT));
```

For a `ServerSocketChannel`, there is a three-step process. We must first open a `ServerSocketChannel`, and then obtain the underlying `ServerSocket` object. We can then call that `ServerSocket's bind()` method to attach it to a particular port.

We have a simple service loop here on the server:

```
      while (true) {
        SocketChannel sock = ssc.accept();
```

The `ServerSocketChannel` has an `accept()` method, which returns a `SocketChannel` object.

We can now read the message, using the message receiver, and reply, using the message sender.

```
        messageReceiver.receive(sock);
        messageSender.send(sock, id++, "TEXT",
                        "Message Received and understood");
      }
    } catch (Exception e) {
      System.out.println(e.getMessage());
      e.printStackTrace();
    }
  }
}
```

2

I/O

Run the server, then the client (using a separate command prompt). You should see this in the server window:

```
> java Server
Msg: 0
Type: TEXT
testing, testing, 1, 2, 3
```

And this in the client:

```
> java Client 127.0.0.1
Msg: 0
Type: TEXT
Message Received and understood
```

The message IDs of subsequent responses from the server will steadily increase.

This server has its problems. For a start, it is blocked in a read, then write operation, every time it receives a connection, which we could address easily using the standard approach to server I/O – spawning a thread to handle each request as and when it arrives. But spawning large numbers of threads causes contention problems, and ultimately can lead to difficulties with scalability. With NIO, instead of having one thread for each simultaneous request, we are going to have one thread, using a `Selector` to discover exactly what operations need performing, and then perform each operation in turn. On a single processor system, no matter how many threads are executing at a time, the computer is still only doing one thing at once. Using a single thread reduces the number of context switches the processor has to perform in order to execute code in different threads, so, with a large number of simultaneous connections, should be more efficient.

Asynchronous I/O

`Server2` will perform accept, read, and write operations with multiple connections, all on the main thread.

```
import java.nio.channels.*;
import java.nio.*;
import java.io.*;
import java.net.*;
import java.util.*;

public class Server2 implements MessageProtocol {

  public static void main(String[] args) {
    MessageReceiver messageReceiver = new MessageReceiver();
    MessageSender messageSender = new MessageSender();

    try {
      int id = 0;
```

Here's where we begin the asynchronous coding. First, we create a selector that will tell us if there are connections that need serving. Then we create a `ServerSocketChannel`, as before, but configure it as non-blocking.

Again, we bind it to the appropriate port on the machine.

```
    Selector selector = Selector.open();

    ServerSocketChannel ssc = ServerSocketChannel.open();
    ssc.configureBlocking(false);

    ServerSocket server = ssc.socket();
    server.bind(new InetSocketAddress(DEFAULT_PORT));
```

Now we need to register the `ServerSocketChannel` with the selector. We specify that we want to be informed about this channel whenever it is ready to accept a connection without blocking, so we specify that using the `OP_ACCEPT` selection key value.

```
    ssc.register(selector, SelectionKey.OP_ACCEPT);
```

Now, the main loop of the application performs a selection operation. This operation will block until one of the registered selectable channels is ready to perform some action. Now, at this stage we've only registered one channel, but we'll be adding channels as we process connections. This means we're not blocking a whole thread just waiting for connections to arrive – the thread will be woken up if a connection is ready to be read or written to as well. The server will *only* be blocked here when there is literally nothing for it to do.

If our server needs to get on with something else when there are no connections to process, we could replace this `select()` operation with a `selectNow()` operation. Then, after processing any available connections, we can insert the code that should be executed each time round the loop.

```
    int a;

    while (true) {
      a = selector.select();
```

If the selection operation returns any connections, we need to process all the selected connections. We extract an iterator and handle each supplied connection.

```
      if (a > 0) {
        try {
          Set keys = selector.selectedKeys();

          Iterator i = keys.iterator();
```

```
      while (i.hasNext()) {
```

For each connection, we need to determine what state it's in. Our first job is to remove it from the set of selected keys (if we don't, it will still be there the next time we call `select`). We then find out what operations the key was registered for. We'll use this to determine what we should do with it.

```
        SelectionKey selectedChannelKey =
          (SelectionKey) i.next();

        i.remove();

        int purpose = selectedChannelKey.interestOps();
```

If the key is for a connection registered for accept operations, it must be our `ServerSocketChannel`. We extract the channel, and perform an `accept()` operation on it, knowing that we can definitely do so without it blocking.

The returned `SocketChannel` needs to be configured as non-blocking, and then registered with the `Selector`. Our first task is to read in the message sent by the client, so we register that interest.

```
        if ((purpose & SelectionKey.OP_ACCEPT) > 0) {

          ServerSocketChannel selectedChannel =
            (ServerSocketChannel) selectedChannelKey.channel();
          SocketChannel sock = selectedChannel.accept();
          sock.configureBlocking(false);

          sock.register(selector, SelectionKey.OP_READ);
```

If the connection returned was registered for reading, then it's a `SocketChannel` freshly registered by the accept handler. We extract the channel, and use the message receiver to interpret what it has to say. Once that's finished, we register the same socket to be written to.

```
        } else if ((purpose & SelectionKey.OP_READ) > 0) {

          SocketChannel sock =
            (SocketChannel) selectedChannelKey.channel();
          messageReceiver.receive(sock);

          sock.register(selector, SelectionKey.OP_WRITE);
```

If the channel was registered for writing, then it must have just been read from, so it is now ready for the server's reply. Again, we extract the channel, and use the message sender to send it a response. We've now finished with the channel, so we can close it.

```
        } else if ((purpose & SelectionKey.OP_WRITE) > 0) {

          SocketChannel sock =
            (SocketChannel) selectedChannelKey.channel();

          messageSender.send(sock, id++, "TEXT",
                             "Message received and understood");

          sock.close();
```

To finish up, there's the usual IO error handling. We handle errors inside the loop, so that a single connection failure doesn't crash the server.

```
        }
      }
    } catch (Exception e) {
      System.out.println(e.getMessage());
      e.printStackTrace();
    }
   }
  }
 } catch (Exception e) {
   System.out.println(e.getMessage());
   e.printStackTrace();
 }
}
}
```

This server should be able to handle many simultaneous connections, even though it is single threaded. We could improve its scalability by introducing a producer/consumer thread model, centered on the selector.

NIO Conclusions

The new I/O framework is a revolutionary addition to the Java platform. As we've seen, the kind of code we write using the new system doesn't have to be all that different from what we're used to. Making proper use of channels though, particularly their scattering and gathering modes, and of multiplexers, allows us to build completely different kinds of code. A whole new range of I/O idioms have been introduced, and the system has implications far beyond the basic functionality of reading and writing to and from files and the network. Buffers, for example, look as if they could find plenty of uses as arbitrary in-memory data stores (particularly since they can be so easily transferred to and from a file). As a safe, managed environment in which it is possible for us to play around with data at the byte level, they could provide the backing for any number of performance-sensitive, data-heavy tasks. This could open the door for writing high-performance 100% pure Java implementations of multi-dimensional collection classes, with fast sorting algorithms (one of the basic requirements for developing a performance database system). Another application that would really test buffering would be a dynamic DOM parser that mapped parts of a large on-disk XML file into memory buffers, then into DOM objects, on demand, rather than all at once.

Multiplexed I/O feels very powerful. The 100% pure Java application servers out there would really benefit from re-architecting to take advantage of it. Although implementation is tricky, the results should be worth the difficulty encountered.

Image I/O

To round off this chapter, let's take a brief look at another new I/O framework that's been added with J2SE 1.4. The Image I/O system takes the principles of the old `java.io` framework and applies them to images. In short, it is a quick way to read and write image files, in formats such as GIF, PNG, and JPEG. So, we have the `javax.imageio.streams.ImageInputStream` and `ImageOutputStream` interfaces, and `javax.imageio.ImageReader` and `ImageWriter` classes. In a parallel attempt to overcome some of the limitations of the old I/O system that we have already seen solved earlier in this chapter, there is even a `javax.imageio.streams.IIOByteBuffer` class, which is basically an object wrapper around a byte array (definitely evidence of a lack of co-operation between some of the JSR expert groups).

The power of this system, however, is in its provider-based architecture, which allows readers and writers for different file formats to be created relatively easily, and accessed even more simply.

This power is demonstrated by the simplicity exposed via five static methods in the `javax.imageio.ImageIO` class:

- `static java.awt.image.BufferedImage read(File input)`
- `static java.awt.image.BufferedImage read(InputStream input)`
- `static java.awt.image.BufferedImage read(URL input)`

- `static boolean write(java.awt.image.RenderedImage im, String formatName, File output)`
- `static boolean write(java.awt.image.RenderedImage im, String formatName, OutputStream output)`

These methods hide away so much functionality, that they only throw `IOExceptions` or `IllegalArgumentExceptions`. The read methods use a number of techniques to identify a service provider capable of reading the supplied image – providers can be selected based on the image's MIME type (where known), file extension, or on the basis of the opening few bytes of the file. The write methods, however, require you to specify the format you want your image written in.

JPEG, GIF, and PNG providers ship with the J2SE 1.4 platform. Here's an example of how the image I/O framework can be used:

```
import javax.swing.JFrame;
import java.awt.Graphics;
import java.awt.image.BufferedImage;
import javax.imageio.ImageIO;
import java.io.File;

public class IIO extends JFrame {

  private BufferedImage bi;

  public static void main(String[] args) {
    if (args.length > 0) {
      new IIO(args[0]).show();
    } else {
      System.out.println("Usage: java IIO <picture filename>");
    }
  }

  public IIO(String filename) {
    setDefaultCloseOperation(EXIT_ON_CLOSE);
    setTitle(filename);

    try {
      bi = ImageIO.read(new File(filename));
    } catch (Exception e) {
      e.printStackTrace();
    }

    setSize(bi.getWidth(), bi.getHeight());
```

```
  }

  public void paint(Graphics g) {
    g.drawImage(bi, 0, 0, getWidth(), getHeight(), this);
  }
}
```

This code results in this sort of display:

In addition to this simple API, there are more complex systems available for the management and translation of image format metadata, allowing applications to benefit from the support of any image I/O service providers present on a system, and to take advantage of whatever features each format has to offer, without having to know anything about the actual underlying format. We'll put Image I/O to the test a little more in Chapter 4.

Conclusions

The new I/O APIs will revolutionize Java file and network programming – no question about it. The problem with such a big change as this is that it leaves a lot of other systems behind, and it will be some time before systems like the Image I/O and JSSE frameworks take advantage of the possibilities offered by the NIO API. It will certainly be interesting to see how buffers and channels are exploited in other parts of the Java platform in the future.

Java J2SE 1.4 Core Platform Update

Security

Security has always been a key concern in the design of the Java platform. From its origins in the sandboxed applet environment of the browser, one of the main driving forces behind Java's architecture has been the need to establish secure and trusted code.

J2SE 1.4 incorporates several new components into its security model that enhance and extend the measures available in the standard edition since the advent of Java 2. While these additions have, for the most part, been available as optional extensions to the Java standard platform for some time, their inclusion in the standard edition is an endorsement of their use in general Java applications, and an encouragement to Java coders to familiarize themselves with these facilities. So, for those of you who haven't experimented in the past with the Java Cryptography Extensions (JCE), or Java Authentication and Authorization Services (JAAS), and the Java Secure Sockets Extension (JSSE), this chapter will introduce the principles behind them, and demonstrate how and when each of them should be used. Since this is an introductory overview of these technologies, we won't be able to go into much depth about the specific differences between the previous, separately distributed versions, and those versions included in the J2SE 1.4.

In this chapter, we'll take a look at the disparate technologies that are grouped under the umbrella heading of the "Java Security Architecture". In reality, they all serve quite different purposes, which are conveniently grouped under the heading of security. Several of them were already a part of J2SE prior to 1.4.

The JSA consists of the following components:

1. The **Java Platform Security Architecture**, which is the system that enables a JVM to grant permissions to code selectively, based on its origin, and therefore enables such things as applet sandboxes and safe RMI. Sandboxing has been a core component of Java since its creation, but the platform security architecture is the new model introduced in Java 2.

2. The **Java Cryptography Architecture**, again a core component of Java since version 1.1, has provided basic support for digital signatures and message digests. It is this functionality that underlies, for example, Java's JAR-signing process.

3. J2SE 1.4 adds to the cryptography architecture with a new **Certificate Chain API**. This allows a signature or key to be analyzed on the basis of its certification. A certificate chain verifies the authenticity of a particular document by providing a secure set of guaranteed statements of authenticity, generally leading back to a central, universally recognized certificate authority.

4. The **Java Cryptography Extensions (JCE)** included in J2SE with version 1.4 for the first time, provide full cryptographic functionality – encryption and decryption – and enhanced cryptographic algorithms that augment the functionality of the core Java Cryptography Architecture.

5. The **Java Authentication and Authorization Services (JAAS)**, also new to the J2SE in version 1.4, extend the core platform security architecture, providing the ability to grant permissions to code on the basis of who is running it.

6. The **Java Generic Secure Services (GSS) API binding** is an endorsed standard (in the sense described in Chapter 1), which consists of an Internet standard API for accessing certain security systems, such as Kerberos authentication and single-sign-on. More information about Kerberos can be found at http://web.mit.edu/kerberos/www/.

7. The **Java Secure Sockets Extension (JSSE)**, which implements the Internet standard TLS (transport layer security) and SSL (secure sockets layer) cryptographic protocols transparently within the standard Java socket I/O framework.

So, with J2SE 1.4, the whole of the Java security architecture has been integrated into the standard edition. This is clearly an extensive set of APIs, designed to address almost any possible security requirement, so in this chapter we will concentrate on how we can use them to achieve some core security-related tasks:

- Data encryption and decryption
- Secure communication with SSL/TLS
- User login security

- Cryptographic message signing and authentication

This set of tasks touches on the core classes in each of the frameworks, and covers the most common tasks a developer is likely to encounter.

Cryptography Basics

Cryptography forms a fundamental component in the security architecture, underlying all the other components. It therefore makes sense for Java developers to have a firm grasp of the basic principles of cryptography. In this section, we'll introduce and define a lot of terms, which we're going to make much use of throughout the chapter.

The core purpose of cryptography is to take some meaningful data (usually referred to as the **plaintext**) and convert it into some seemingly meaningless data (referred to as the **ciphertext**), and back again. An algorithm that accomplishes these two tasks (respectively, **encryption** and **decryption**) is known as a **cipher**.

Cryptography as a science is historically concerned with the manipulation of textual data. Hence, the terms "plaintext" and "ciphertext" are now used even when the values being discussed aren't textual. In fact, the principles described here can be applied to any kind of data.

Whenever we talk about a cipher, we often refer to its strength. A cipher is **strong** if, when we encrypt a message using it, an attacker (that is, a malicious third party we don't want to see the original plaintext, but who might have gained access to the ciphertext) can't figure out the plaintext of the message using the information they have (the process of analyzing a message to decrypt it without having the key or encryption cipher is called **cryptanalysis**). We need to clarify this a little. It is possible to break almost any cipher, given enough time and resources. So, in cryptography we often talk about the **intrinsic value** of the data being encrypted. A cipher is then regarded as strong if it will take an attacker more time and resources to break it than is considered worthwhile, given the intrinsic value of the encrypted data. The value of data often decreases with time, so it is often regarded as sufficient to encrypt data with a cipher that can be broken only after a long time, after which the data may no longer have much intrinsic value.

For example, information about an upcoming product announcement only has intrinsic value before the public announcement. Once it is public, decrypting the data would be a waste of time. So, during the pre-release period, it should be encrypted with a cipher that will take at least until the announcement date to crack using current cryptanalytical techniques. As we'll see, there are ciphers in use that were once regarded as strong, but have recently been cracked in less than 24 hours, albeit by a determined and coordinated effort by the Internet community (so perhaps if you are transmitting data that might be of interest to a large body of Internet users, such as the trailer for the next Star Wars movie, you should take extra precautions).

Much published work in cryptanalysis is in the field of calculating how long it will take a person, with certain resources available to them, to crack a particular code. In addition, you need to be aware of physical and human security issues, as it makes little difference how strong your encryption is if someone can read your key from a piece of paper on your desk.

Ciphers turn out to have many applications and uses, which are all essentially beneficial side effects of their core purpose – encryption and decryption. For the purposes of our initial discussion, though, we'll concern ourselves with the problem that ciphers were first developed to solve – transmitting information from one place to another, securely, in the hope that nobody other than the intended recipient can access the information.

In order to securely communicate a message to one intended recipient, it is necessary to agree on how the encryption and decryption will be performed. For example, I could agree with a friend that I'll always send them messages written in pig Latin (a child's code that renders the first sentence of this paragraph as *Inay orderay otay ecurelysay ommunicatecay ayay essagemay otay unway intendeday ecipientray, tiay siay ecessarynay otay agreeay onay owhay ethay encryptionay anday ecryptionday illway ebay erformedpay*). My friend will, knowing the basic rules of the cipher (the cipher **algorithm**), be able to rapidly read my messages. It might take a malicious third party a little longer (not knowing in advance how we were planning on encoding our messages), but once they had worked out the algorithm, they would be able to decrypt the messages just as rapidly as the intended recipient. An issue also arises when I want to communicate with another friend, without the first one knowing. I have to come up with a different set of encryption/decryption rules, so that I can communicate with them without the first friend being able to understand my messages too. Pretty soon, I'm going to run out of silly little codes.

What's needed is a cipher that produces an output that is not simply a product of the plaintext input, but which requires a second piece of information as well. This allows the same cipher to be used to generate different output on different occasions, even when given the same plaintext input. Now I don't need to come up with a different cipher for each new friend, I just have to use a different value for this second piece of information. In fact, I can use different values each time I use the cipher. I just need to make sure that the intended recipient knows the value I used when I encrypted the message. We usually call this second piece of information a **key**.

Strong cryptographic systems all employ keys. Until recently, all such systems employed, in one form or another, a **secret key** – it is necessary in such systems for both the sender and the recipient to know the same secret key, and the value used in encryption is also employed in decryption.

Secret Key Cryptography

Secret key ciphers all rely on the two communicating parties being the only two people in the world who know the secret key being employed for the communication. Alternatively, you can use secret key ciphers to encrypt data for your eyes only, in which case the secret key need only be known to you. Because the same key needs to be known both at encryption and decryption time, secret-key ciphers are sometimes called **symmetric ciphers**.

A classic secret-key cipher, widely employed in pre-digital communications by military and governmental organizations, is one that uses a code book. Each page in the code book is a key for use in the cipher. Typically, you would encrypt a message using the code book by selecting a page from the book (possibly at random, possibly based on some rule about the time of day, or the day of the month, or who the recipient is), and applying a transformation on each letter of your message, using each letter of the page in the code book. When you reach the end of the page, you start using the page again from the beginning. The recipient, who has a copy of the same code book (or at least the code page), then applies the reverse transformation. Only somebody else who has the code book can easily decrypt the message. However, if somebody collects enough ciphertext sent using the same code page, then they can begin to infer the messages from the ciphertext, especially if they are able to guess at the structure of one of the messages, know that it contains a particular word, or, worst of all, have a copy of a plaintext message encrypted using that code page – they can immediately ascertain the whole page and decrypt any message encrypted using it.

Consider the obvious code book cipher, where each letter in the message is transformed into a number from 1 to 26, and the same is done for the letters in the code page, then the message is encrypted by adding the number for each letter in the message to the corresponding number in the codepage, and subtracting 26 if the number is greater than 26. The number is then turned back into a letter. Here's an example:

Plaintext	H	E	L	L	O	W	O	R	L	D
Plaintext values	08	05	12	12	15	23	15	18	12	04
Code page	J	E	I	P	N	E	D	K	A	Q
Code page values	10	05	09	16	14	05	04	11	01	17

Summed values	18	10	21	28	29	28	19	29	13	21
Sums mod 26	18	10	21	02	03	02	19	03	13	21
Ciphertext	R	J	U	B	C	B	S	C	M	U

A simple attack on this cipher involves taking two messages encoded with the same page, converting them to numbers using the same rule, and subtracting one from the other. For example, here's a second message encrypted using the same cipher:

Plaintext	G	O	O	D	B	Y	E	E	E	E
Plaintext values	07	14	14	04	02	25	05	05	05	05
Code page	J	E	I	P	N	E	D	K	A	Q
Code page values	10	05	09	16	14	05	04	11	01	17

Summed values	17	19	23	20	16	30	09	16	06	22
Sums mod 26	17	19	23	20	16	04	09	16	06	22
Ciphertext	Q	S	W	T	P	D	I	P	F	V

Ciphertext A	Q	S	W	T	P	D	I	P	F	V
Ciphertext B	R	J	U	B	C	B	S	C	M	U
CipherText A Values	17	19	23	20	16	04	09	16	06	22
Ciphertext B Values	18	10	21	02	03	02	19	03	13	21
A - B	-01	09	02	18	13	02	-10	13	-07	01

The resulting numbers represent the offsets between the corresponding letters in the two original plaintexts – the random component of the code page has been completely eliminated. Analysis of the message consisting of two combined plaintext messages is then relatively trivial (well, perhaps trivial is the wrong word – it's a little like solving a double-sided jigsaw puzzle – difficult, but possible).

The most secure cryptographic system (in that no purely cryptanalytical attack on it will ever succeed without additional information obtained from either communicating party) is one based on a truly random **one-time-pad**. It too is a secret key system, and uses streams of characters, like code pages, but the "pads" used in one-time-pad cryptography are not repeated like code pages, and each page is only ever used once. Thus no duplicate-keyed messages exist to compare the randomized ciphertext to, so it isn't possible to extract the plaintext without a copy of the pad used. In fact, the only cryptanalytical approach that can yield results is to attack the mechanism used to generate the random entries in the pads themselves. The mechanism for generating the numbers really has to be truly random for the one time pad to be completely secure, but finding a truly random source of data is a real challenge for cryptography. Computers are fundamentally deterministic machines – their output depends solely on their input. This makes them very bad random number generators, since anything they produce can theoretically be reproduced by putting the same data in. To generate random data with a computer, you need an external source of random, irreproducible data. Techniques employed for ultra-secure key generation include measuring the incidence of cosmic rays in the atmosphere, or radioactive particle decay. Less well-equipped computers often make use of external sources of "random" data such as the timing of keystrokes, measuring mouse movement, or network packets. Some systems, such as Linux, collect data about external events and use it to top up what is termed an "entropy pool". By using data from the entropy pool, such a system can to some extent guarantee that it is using data that can't be reproduced exactly by another computer, since it depends on external events. For the most part, computers generate what appear to be random numbers using pseudo-random number generators, which are algorithms that generate values that seem random, but in fact form a mathematically related sequence – a sequence that could be reproduced exactly by running the same pseudo-random number generator again. The sequence can be altered by providing a key, which affects where the sequence begins. A good pseudo-random number generator can be a source for reasonably strong one-time-pad-like ciphers, as we'll see a little later on.

The main weakness of either of these systems, and of secret key systems in general, is **key management**. How do you make sure that the only person who knows the key to decrypt the message is the person you're sending the message to? Well, normally, it's a case of distributing the key via some other secure method – face-to-face, or over some previously agreed secure communications mechanism. When the number of secure connections required is large (such as for an entire diplomatic corps, navy, or global corporation), managing a large number of keys becomes very difficult. Managing fewer keys opens you up to vulnerabilities, as discussed above. Nonetheless, secret key cryptography has its advantages – chiefly speed and simplicity. And, as we'll see, the key management problem has, to a large extent, been solved over modern communications networks.

Digital encryption – that is, the automated encryption of data in computer systems – initially developed techniques based on existing non-digital cryptographic systems, such as code books. The modern descendents of code book ciphers are **block ciphers**.

Block Ciphers

A block cipher allows you to use a fixed length key to encrypt a message of any length. Typically, such a cipher takes a plaintext message, and divides it into fixed length chunks, called blocks, then encodes each block. Obviously, there are a number of algorithms you can use to combine a key with a block to generate a ciphertext version of the block. Additionally, you don't have to simply use the same key with each block in turn. There are several ways of encrypting the blocks, which are called block cipher modes. One mode, known as **Electronic Code Book (ECB)** mode, uses the obvious approach of encrypting each block using the original key. Other modes, such as **Cipher Feedback (CFB)** and **Cipher Block Chaining (CBC)** use the result of each block encryption, combined with the initial key, to generate a new key for encoding the next block. These techniques ensure, for example, that if the same plaintext occurs in more than one block in the message, or in more than one message encoded with the same initial key, the ciphertext will be different, making it harder for an attacker to work out the key by collecting messages (ECB mode encodings are slightly more vulnerable to this process, but have the advantage that they can be carried out blisteringly fast using dedicated hardware).

You can strengthen the action of some block ciphers by using an iterative process that effectively applies the cipher several times.

While it's not necessary, it's normal for the block size to be the same as the key length, or shorter. This is a result of a simple mathematical property of such systems: imagine the block length was one byte (8 bits). There are 256 possible messages such a block can represent. So, for any of these plaintext messages, there are 255 possible ciphertext interpretations that the cipher can generate. So for a given cipher, 255 keys are enough to be able to generate every possible ciphertext message from a plaintext message. So, you can describe all those keys using just 8 bits.

In practice, block ciphers use much larger blocks and keys – 64 or even 128 bits. If that doesn't sound like a lot, remember, a 64-bit key isn't only 8 times more complex than an 8-bit key – it's 2^{56} times more complicated.

The widely adopted standard DES (for Digital Encryption Standard) is a 64-bit iterated block cipher, developed in the 1970s from an algorithm called Lucifer, created by IBM. DES was developed and standardized by the US Government, and is codified in Federal Information Processing Standard 46-3. DES can be applied in several standard modes, including ECB, CFB, and CBC.

DES actually uses only a 56-bit key, although eight parity bits are normally provided, making keys appear to be 64 bits in length.

DES is getting long in the tooth, and modern hardware makes DES vulnerable to brute-force decryption (a brute-force approach is one which makes no intelligent guesses about the key from the encrypted message, but rather keeps trying keys until it finds one that works. Consider it the equivalent of a safecracker trying every possible combination until the safe opens). A systematic DES cracking effort mounted by the Electronic Frontier Foundation, using Distributed.net's distributed client-base to harness the idle processing power of desktop computers around the world, cracked a DES key in only 22 hours. Dedicated DES-cracking hardware exists, and, with large resources such as those at the disposal of the US government, it is certainly possible to break DES keys as a matter of course in very short timeframes.

Triple DES is a kludge to make DES more secure, which involves applying DES three times (sometimes using two, sometimes three different keys), and is currently the approved method of encryption for the US Government. Although you can employ triple DES by encrypting a message three times with three different keys (encrypt, encrypt, encrypt, known as DES-EEE), a more common approach is to encrypt with one key, decrypt with a different key, then encrypt, either with a third key, or the first again. This approach is known as DES-EDE (encrypt, decrypt, encrypt). Triple DES has really been a stopgap effort since just using two 56-bit keys doesn't really mean you get 2^{112} different keys to play with – it still turns out that ultimately, you get caught out by the fact that there are only 2^{64}-1 ways of encrypting a 64 bit block, and for a given block, several key combinations turn out to be equivalent. Searching the keyspace is harder, and requires more computer resources (typically it requires more storage, rather than more time), but it can still be done, so ultimately triple DES will fall to a bruteforce approach as well.

AES, the Advanced Encryption Standard, is the result of a US government search for a 128-bit block cipher. The selected candidate is the Rijndael algorithm, developed by two independent Belgian cryptographers (from a field which included entries from IBM and RSA). Rijndael's official home is http://www.esat.kuleuven.ac.be/~rijmen/rijndael, but it also has an excellent fan page at http://rijndael.com. Not yet that widely adopted, AES is expected to gradually replace DES and Triple DES as the standard symmetric secret key cipher.

What difference will 128-bit blocks make? Well, to support 128-bit blocks, Rijndael uses 128-bit, 192-bit, or even 256-bit keys (and can also support blocks of these lengths), and a 128-bit key will take 2^{72} times as long to search out by brute force as a 56-bit key. At the rate the EFF/Distributed.net program cracked the DES key, it would take 10 billion, billion years to search this keyspace. Even if they made advances in processing that reduced the search time for a DES key to a second, a 128-bit Rijndael key would take 150 million billion years to find. Similar calculations for 256 bit keys are left as an exercise for the reader, but given that the Universe is only believed to have existed for 13-16 billion years, the timescales involved are hardly relevant to most people's cryptographic concerns.

Other block ciphers include RSA's RC2 and RC5 (widely used in internet cryptography), and Bruce Schneier's Blowfish algorithm (which is fast, but is not so widely used, so has not been subjected to as much analysis as some other ciphers). Variants of these algorithms were both candidates for the AES, and should offer equivalent levels of security to Rijndael.

RC2, RC5, Blowfish, DES, Triple DES EDE, and AES Rijndael are all implemented in the JCE.

Stream Ciphers

If you are encrypting data that is in a stream, rather than a buffer, then you need a cipher that can be applied byte-by-byte, even bit-by-bit on the data as it streams through. What you really need to accomplish this is a long stream of random bits that you can combine with the stream of data in a reversible way (usually using an exclusive-or operation), then to decrypt the message, you need to use the same stream of random bits to recover the plaintext. This stream of random bits is called a keystream. Using a strong pseudo-random number generator, seeded with a secret key, you can generate keystreams that exhibit similar properties to the one-time-pad discussed above.

A common stream cipher is RSA's RC4. However, if you are prepared to buffer bits in the stream until you have enough to make up a block, then you can apply a block cipher in CFB or CBC mode, for example, as if it were a stream cipher. The resulting cipher is just as strong as the block cipher, and is particularly hard to decrypt if you only intercept part of the stream.

JCE supports RC4, and block ciphers in stream modes, as stream ciphers.

Password-Based Encryption

It's difficult for users to be reliably expected to come up with good, secure 56 or 128-bit keys. Experience shows that, if you ask someone to come up with a memorable 4-digit number (for use as a PIN), they tend to pick from a very limited selection of those on offer (in particular, they'll tend to pick numbers that start with 19). Ask someone to choose a number between 1 and 2^{128}, and you're not likely to get much further.

Password-based encryption is the name for a set of techniques that allow a user's secret key to be a password or passphrase, that they will remember, and that generate a usable 56 or 128-bit key from the password or passphrase, such that a good password generates a good, seemingly random key. Not surprisingly, the approach taken is basically to encrypt the password.

Usually, you use a cryptographic hashing algorithm (which we'll come to in a moment), to derive a key from the password. Unfortunately (as is often the case in cryptography), a naive approach to this has problems. If two people choose the same password, then the hashed values will be the same, and the encryption key will be the same. If you have a lot of users, it's almost certain that someone will be using an obvious password like, say, "`password`". An attacker who knows the hashing algorithm you use will be able to generate the keys for any number of likely passwords and try them to see if they match (using a dictionary and a number of algorithms for combining words from it, you can in fact generate enough possible keys almost to be guaranteed success, and the number of simple word combinations is nowhere near the order of magnitude of the number of possible 128-bit keys). So, to ensure that such an attack isn't trivial, a random component is introduced into the hashing algorithm. This random value is called a **salt**. The role of the salt is not to be secret, but to defeat pre-prepared dictionary attacks, and make such an attack take considerably longer.

To password protect a file, for example, you might encrypt it with DES-EDE, and a password-derived key. The salt used to calculate that key, though, is needed when it comes to decrypt the file, so it really needs to be stored in the encrypted file as well. So, a malicious party can extract the salt, and calculate the key that would be generated with that salt for every likely password, then try to decrypt the file using each key in turn. What they can't do is take a dictionary of pre-prepared password-based keys and throw them at the problem. But a party who knows the password can enter it, and an algorithm can extract the salt from the file, generate the key, and decrypt the file.

There are any number of ways you can generate a key from a password, and then, obviously, you can use it as the key for any block or stream cipher you choose. One standard is the RSA's Public Key Cryptography Standard Number 5 (PKCS#5), which specifies standard combinations of hashing algorithms and encryption ciphers. These are fully supported by JCE.

Public Key Cryptography

In 1976 something amazing happened – somebody published a practical application for an obscure branch of pure mathematics. This really doesn't happen very often. Whitfield Diffie and Martin Hellman became the first people to publicly describe a system of public key cryptography.

The mathematical foundation of public key cryptography is the development of "one-way trapdoor functions", which are themselves part of a broader subject within cryptographic applications, namely, one-way functions. A one-way function reliably and repeatably maps an input value to a particular output value, but there exists no reverse function that can take the output and generate the input (or at least, none that works any more efficiently than an exhaustive search of all possible input values, looking for the one which gives the same output). One-way functions make useful cryptographic hash-functions, which we'll come to in a moment.

A one-way trapdoor function is a one-way function with a twist. There is no general function that will map back in the opposite direction. However, there is a function (the trapdoor) that will provide such a mapping, but it relies on knowing a secret piece of information.

Public key cryptography starts off with that secret piece of information, which is called a **private key**. Using a special one-way function, we generate a value from the private key. This is called the **public key**. Because we used a one-way function, it's not possible to obtain the private key from the public key, so you can give the public key out to anybody, and the secret remains secure. The crucial property of this public key is that when we use it in combination with another one-way function to encrypt a message, it leaves a trapdoor that only someone who knows the private key can open.

A secret key and a private key are not the same thing at all. A secret key is the shared key in a symmetric cipher that is known by all parties to the communication (it's sometimes called a shared secret). A private key is the private part of a public-private key pair, and is known only to the key owner. You can share a secret, but you don't share what's private.

It's a little like this: I want to send you a message in secret, so I ask you to send me a lockable suitcase. You keep the suitcase's key, and send me the suitcase. I put the message into the suitcase, lock it using the simple push-to-close lock, and send it back to you. You receive the suitcase, unlock it using your key, and read the message. The information on how to open the suitcase – the key – never leaves your hands, so you can be assured that the message will arrive safely.

By distributing your public key to anyone who wants to contact you, you're doing the equivalent of widely distributing those suitcases, so anyone who wants to can lock a message in it and send it to you.

Public key cryptography "solves" the biggest problem in cryptography – key management. The public key reveals no secrets, so it can be freely distributed. The private key is kept secret, and never transmitted anywhere. The disadvantage is that the one-way and trapdoor functions (the encryption and decryption algorithms) are much slower than typical secret-key cryptographic algorithms, such as block ciphers. However, it's perfectly possible for two parties to agree a secret key using public key cryptography as a secure mechanism, then exchange messages using fast, efficient secret key cryptography.

What about cryptanalysis? Well, one-way functions rest on the idea of **hard problems** – essentially, problems in mathematics that can't be solved via a shortcut. Take multiplication. If we multiply x by y, and get z, the inverse operation is to divide z by y to get x. So, the inverse of the function "multiply by 7" is "divide by 7". Put five into the "multiply by 7" function, and we get 35 out. Put 35 into the "divide by seven" function, and we get 5 back. Now, imagine that the only way to divide 35 by 7 was actually to keep trying to multiply numbers by seven, until we got 35, then to return that number as the answer. If that was true, division by seven would be a hard problem, and we could safely call multiplication a one-way function. For sufficiently large values, multiplication would effectively be a cryptographic hashing function. Obviously, that isn't the case with division, where there are shortcuts. But there are some functions for which it is believed there are no shortcuts. These hard problems, which include the factoring problem we'll look at in a moment, are what guarantee that nobody can take a public key, and derive the private key from it. This guarantee should pretty well hold, unless there are any more revolutionary developments in number theory. As we've said, they don't happen often. It's worth noting, though, that nobody has yet proven that these problems really are hard.

The factoring problem is the problem of taking a number, and calculating its prime factors. Every positive integer has a unique set of prime factors, that is, a set of prime numbers which, when multiplied together, produce the number. The only known way to find all the prime factors of a number is to systematically try dividing it by all of the prime numbers less than its square root. For a large number, naturally, this can take some time. It can take longer still if the number has no small prime factors, only large ones. The extreme case is to take a number that is the product of two large prime numbers. Finding those two prime numbers is the same as finding the number's prime factors, so the only way to do so is to perform the exhaustive search of primes below the square root. When we're dealing with truly large prime numbers this is a massive search space (for example, there are about 2 billion billion 20 digit prime numbers, according to the Prime Number Theorem), and just locating the prime numbers is a challenge.

The RSA algorithm is the best-known public key cryptography algorithm. It is based around the factoring problem, and was developed in 1977. It is fully supported by JCE. One of the main driving forces behind its wide adoption was its use by Netscape as the foundation for the Secure Sockets Layer, SSL, used to encrypt communication between a web browser and web server. Typical RSA keys are 1024 or 2048 bits in length, in order to provide large enough numbers that they are difficult to factor in a reasonable time. A 512-bit RSA key was factored in 7 months in 1999, using 300 networked machines, so the larger key sizes are normally used (even though a concerted effort like that to crack a public key is actually a massive amount of resources to devote to obtaining a limited quantity of data, and would not enable systematic cracking of keys). Note that public keys have to be much larger than secret keys in order to be secure. In particular, very valuable keys such as those used by certificate authorities can be very large indeed, and 4096 bits are common.

Digital Signatures

The RSA algorithm exhibits an interesting property. Not only does it ensure that if you encrypt a message using the public key, it can only be decrypted using the private key, but the opposite is also true: a message encrypted using a private key can only be decrypted using the matching public key. This allows for digital signing: if you receive a message that can be decrypted with a particular public key, then it must have been encrypted by the owner of the matching private key, since private keys are not shared. So, a message encrypted with a private key can be authenticated as originating with the owner of that particular private key. Again, the use of one-way functions prevents the private key from being revealed by this process.

Imagine the inverse suitcase analogy. As well as the suitcases that only you can unlock, you have suitcases that can only be locked with your key, but that just have a push button to open them. If you send me a document locked in one of these suitcases, if the suitcase is locked when it arrives, I know the document must have been the one you put in it, since if someone else opened it and tampered with it, they wouldn't be able to lock the suitcase again.

In fact the one key management problem that is inherent to public key cryptography is that you have to be absolutely sure that the public key you are using to encrypt or decrypt data really originated with the person to whom you are trying to send encrypted data, or who sent you the signed data. If you can't be certain of this, then the system isn't secure. The solution to this is to use certification, which is the key component of what is called **Public Key Infrastructure**, or **PKI**.

Public Key Infrastructure

If I want to communicate with my friend Bob securely, I need Bob's public key. But Bob and I can't meet up physically, and he doesn't want to read out his public key over the phone (it's 1024 bits long) and we can't trust a medium like e-mail, because someone could easily intercept the public key and replace it with a different one. So how can Bob send me his public key securely? We could encrypt the e-mail with a secret key, but I have just the same problem obtaining the secret key from Bob as I do obtaining his public key, with the added disadvantage that if someone intercepts the secret key, they can use it to replace Bob's public key with their own, and we're back to square one.

But if I know somebody else, let's call her Catherine, who can physically go and meet Bob and get his public key, and I already have her public key, she could sign a message containing Bob's public key, to say that she believes that it does indeed correspond to a private key that only Bob has. Catherine can **certify** Bob's public key as belonging to Bob. So, Bob can e-mail me his key, signed by someone I trust, and no third party can step in and replace it with another key, because their key won't be signed by Catherine. I can verify that the message I received was signed by Catherine, using her public key. Then I have Bob's public key, and I can communicate with him securely. If the evidence is convincing enough for me, I can also assert to others that the key is Bob's, so if someone I know wants to communicate with Bob, I can sign his key with my private key and send it to them, too, so they know that I believe this really is Bob's key.

PKI allows for informal networks of trust such as this to be established, but it also allows for more formal structures. If a single central authority is prepared to perform the real-world validation required to be certain that a particular public key was generated from the private key of a particular individual, then they can vouch for anybody. All that's required is for everybody to know that organization's public key, then anybody who wants to pay this organization for the privilege can obtain a signed proof of identity, in the form of that organization's stamp on their public key.

Such central organizations are called **certificate authorities**, and the best-known example is Verisign (http://www.verisign.com). Verisign specializes in certifying that particular public keys belong to certain companies, so, for example, they can be used by those companies in web transactions. So, if you want to buy something from Acme Tools Inc. of Ames Iowa, you might go to www.acmetoolsofamesiowa.com. But before you tap in your credit card number to buy a number-5 widget extractor, you want to be certain that your credit card details really are going to Acme Tools Inc., not some teenage kid's bedroom. Well, if Acme's site uses HTTP over SSL (S/HTTP), which is the case if its site URL starts with https://, then the first thing that your web browser will obtain from the site will be Acme Tools Inc.'s digital certificate, which is their public key, signed by a certificate authority. And unless a reputable certificate authority certifies that the key belongs to Acme Tools Inc., you should take your credit card details elsewhere. If you have a certified public key certificate, though, your browser can go ahead and generate a secret key, encrypt it with the public key, and send it to the site, and you can begin conversing with them over a secure channel, using the secret key with a fast cipher like DES-EDE.

Now all you have to worry about is the trustworthiness of Acme Tools Inc., and of their certificate authority, and of your web browser, when it claimed the certificate was genuine. What you don't have to worry about is a malicious third party in between, which is just as well, since certificate authorities, real-world companies, and browser manufacturers are all people you can track down and hold to real laws, and you have some comeback if any of them let you down.

Cryptographic Hashing

We're all familiar with the basic idea of a hash function, such as the one required by Java's `hashvalue()` method. Java uses these hash values to calculate numbers that represent objects, which are dependent on those objects' states. Two objects, with different states, should (but do not have to) have different hash values, but if their states are equal, they must have the same hash value. The rules are well known.

Java uses hash values to implement hash maps and hash sets. The subtly different art of cryptographic hashing is the process of taking a value (usually a string), and generating a number from it in such a way that it follows the normal hashing rules (equal strings generate equal codes), but most importantly, that you cannot infer anything about the original string from the hash value. For cryptographic purposes, it is important that generated hash values are very different for only subtly different input values. In this way, cryptographic hashes are like sophisticated checksums, and, like checksums, often make use of modular arithmetic to provide this property.

As we said earlier, cryptographic hash functions can be used for generating keys from passwords. But they have other functions.

Because a hash function generates a short value that is derived from the input string, hash values are sometimes known as message digests. You can compare two files for differences with a reasonable degree of accuracy by calculating hash values for them, and comparing the values. If the hash values differ, the files are different (the hashing system can't prove a positive in the same way, because there's the possibility of there being two different files that generate the same message digest).

A particularly useful application of message digests in cryptography is in relation to message signing. Rather than encrypting an entire message using a private key, we can calculate a message digest, and encrypt that using the private key (it will take a lot less time, since we are encrypting less data). Now, the recipient of the message can calculate its hash value, decrypt the digest using the public key, and check for a match. Obviously, if the results differ, then the message that was signed isn't the one you received; someone's been tampering.

Well known cryptographic hashing algorithms include the RSA-developed Message Digest (MD) series (MD2, MD4, MD5), and the US Government's Secure Hashing Algorithm (SHA) series (SHA and SHA-1). MD5 and SHA-1 are available in the JCE.

Politics of Cryptography

Ever since private individuals and organizations began to develop cryptographic techniques, governments have made efforts to control and restrict access to cryptographic tools. For a long time the United States regarded cryptographic software as a weapon, and prohibited export of strong cryptographic tools. Arbitrary limitations, such as restricting key sizes to 40 bits, were imposed to prevent such software being used to encrypt data that might be of interest to the US government (all in the interests of national security, of course).

Other governments have also restricted the use of cryptography by their citizens, and there are many complex export and import regulations in place around the world that prevent software with particular cryptographic capabilities being freely distributed. The rise of e-commerce as an economic power, however, has meant that most of the world now allows strong cryptography, the economic benefits being seen to outweigh national security issues (although changes in the nature of global politics can have a powerful impact on these priorities).

The upshot of this is that Sun ships its cryptographic software with a "crippled" cryptography policy that allows limited, but still strong, cryptography, which can be freely exported to most countries of the world (Sun is, of course, a US company). A separate policy file can be downloaded that enables the use of unrestricted strength ciphers. For details of the legal status of these two downloads you should refer to the JCE documentation.

All of the code in this chapter, including code that uses strong secret and public key cryptography, will run on the restricted policy files, but if you want to use larger keys, you will need to obtain the unrestricted policy files from Sun. If you develop software that uses cryptography, you must make sure you are doing so within the legal framework in place in the country where you live, and in particular you must exercise extreme caution if you intend to export the software, whether via public distribution, or privately, and ensure you comply with any local export or import legislation. Again, the JCE documentation contains detailed notes and onward links.

Cryptography – Further Reading

Cryptography is a massive and fascinating subject. If you're interested in learning more, here are some references you may wish to look into.

General Cryptography

- The RSA web site has an excellent cryptography FAQ at:
  http://www.rsasecurity.com/rsalabs/faq
- A list of other FAQs can be found at:
  http://www.faqs.org/faqs/cryptography-faq
- A very readable account of cryptographic history can be found in Simon Singh's *The Code Book* (Anchor, 0-38549-532-3).
- A more thorough work on the same subject is David Kahn's *The Codebreakers* (Scribner, 0-68483-130-9).
- An up-to-date account of current cryptographic politics can be found in Steven Levy's *Crypto* (Viking, 0-67085-950-8).
- Bruce Schneier has a superb essay on cryptography at:
  http://www.counterpane.com/whycrypto.html
- A selection of cryptographic links can be found at:
  http://world.std.com/~franl/crypto.html

Algorithms

- US Government encryption standards, such as DES, DES-EDE and AES, are codified in Federal Information Processing Standards, FIPS. The FIPS homepage is: http://www.itl.nist.gov/fipspubs
- DES is described in FIPS 46-3: http://csrc.nist.gov/publications/fips/fips46-3/fips46-3.pdf
- DES modes of operation are described in FIPS 81: http://www.itl.nist.gov/fipspubs/fip81.htm
- SHA hashing algorithms are defined by FIPS 180-1: http://www.itl.nist.gov/fipspubs/fip180-1.htm
- AES is described in FIPS 197: http://csrc.nist.gov/publications/fips/fips197/fips-197.pdf
- RSA defines commercial cryptographic standards, such as the Public Key Cryptography Standard (PKCS) and RSA algorithms. These can be found at the RSA Laboratories home page: http://www.rsasecurity.com/rsalabs
- Rijndael, the AES algorithm: http://www.esat.kuleuven.ac.be/%7Erijmen/rijndael/index.html
- Bruce Schneier's Blowfish: http://www.counterpane.com/blowfish.html
- RSA co-founder Ronald Rivest's MD5 hashing algorithm is defined by Internet RFC 1321: http://www.ietf.org/rfc/rfc1321.txt
- Bruce Schneier (creator of the Blowfish algorithm mentioned earlier) has written an excellent work on digital cryptographic techniques, *Applied Cryptography: Protocols, Algorithms, and Source Code in C, 2nd Edition* (Wiley, 0-47111-709-9).

Encryption and Decryption

Let's look at how we can use the JCE to perform some basic encryption and decryption operations. First of all, let's look at how we can use a simple block cipher to encrypt and decrypt data. We'll build a simple command-line utility that takes data from standard in, encrypts it, and outputs the ciphertext to standard out.

JCE is built around a service-provider architecture. Any algorithms that we want to use we specify using plain text parameters, and the JCE architecture finds a suitable provider of that functionality. The full list of names of algorithms supported by Sun's reference implementation is in Appendix A of the JCE documentation, which comes with the J2SE documentation download, or can be found online at:

- http://java.sun.com/j2se/1.4/docs/guide/security/jce/JCERefGuide.html

But we'll use a few of the more common algorithms here.

Encryption

Our first program will use triple DES-EDE, known to the JCE by the string `DESede`. We'll use some of NIO's functionality (which we met in the previous chapter) to buffer content for encryption.

Here's what our encryption program does:

- Obtains a key generator for DES-EDE keys
- Uses it to create a new DES-EDE key
- Creates a DES-EDE encryption cipher initialized with the key
- Allocates a byte buffer for the plaintext
- Reads in the plaintext from standard in
- Uses the cipher to encrypt the plaintext into a ciphertext buffer
- Writes the ciphertext buffer out to standard out
- Outputs the key to a key file (so we can decrypt the ciphertext later)

The program just takes the name of the key file as an argument.

Let's run through the code for `Encrypt.java`:

```
import javax.crypto.*;
import javax.crypto.spec.*;
import java.io.*;
import java.nio.*;
import java.nio.channels.*;

public class Encrypt {

   public static void main(String[] args) {
      FileOutputStream keyOut = null; // so we can close it
                                      // in the finally block

      try {
         String algorithm = "DESede";
         String keyfile   = args[0];
```

Now we get to the first bit of cryptographic code. javax.crypto.KeyGenerator is a source of secret (symmetric) keys. It uses a pseudo-random number generator (provided by the JCE, although we can provide it with our own if we don't trust it) to generate keys for a particular algorithm. In this case, we're telling it to generate DES-EDE keys, and we'll get the default key size for that job (a combination of three 56-bit DES keys) – although for some algorithms, we can also specify the key size that we're after.

We call the generateKey() method, which can take some time to return while the random number generator does its work. It returns a javax.crypto.SecretKey, which is an "opaque" key – that is, an internal representation of a key, not suitable for distribution. We'll see how to turn an opaque key into a proper description of a key we can share in a moment.

```
KeyGenerator keyGen = KeyGenerator.getInstance(algorithm);
SecretKey key       = keyGen.generateKey();
```

Next we create an instance of a javax.crypto.Cipher object. Ciphers are objects that can apply a particular algorithm to perform some cryptographic operation – typically encryption or decryption. Before performing such an operation, the cipher needs to know what operation we want to perform (what mode it will operate in), and which key to use when doing it. We set these properties using the init() method.

```
Cipher cipher = Cipher.getInstance(algorithm);
cipher.init(Cipher.ENCRYPT_MODE, key);
```

JCE uses confusing terminology here, and refers to encryption and decryption as 'modes' of operation for a cipher. Of course, as we discussed earlier, DES and other block ciphers can be applied in a number of modes, such as cipher block chaining, and so on. These modes are specified in JCE as part of the algorithm name, not the cipher mode.

Now we break out the NIO operations. We create channel wrappers around standard in and out, and allocate a fixed-size input buffer. This sets a limit on the size of files we can handle, but because we're going to have to maintain the entire file in RAM, then encrypt it into a separate buffer of equal or greater size, it makes sense for us to control how much data we read in this way, so we don't unexpectedly run out of RAM. Then we keep reading bytes until the number of bytes read is -1, which signifies end of data.

```
ReadableByteChannel in  = Channels.newChannel(System.in);
WritableByteChannel out = Channels.newChannel(System.out);

ByteBuffer plaintext    = ByteBuffer.allocate(4096);

int a = 0;
while (a >= 0) {
   a = in.read(plaintext);
}
```

After reading into the buffer, we call the buffer's `flip()` method, which sets the limit to the current position, then sets the position to zero, resetting the buffer so that subsequent read operations will operate on the data we just read in. We find out where the limit is, which tells us how many bytes were read in all.

Next, we extract the underlying byte array from the plaintext buffer, since ciphers act on byte arrays. Using the underlying array doesn't allocate any more memory to data storage, it just gives us a reference to the same array the buffer is built around.

```
plaintext.flip();

int inSize = plaintext.limit();

byte[] plaintextBytes = plaintext.array();
```

At last, here's the encryption operation. `Ciphers` can be used in two ways: continuously, or all in one. Continuous use of a `Cipher` allows us to hand the `Cipher` the message for encryption in chunks, one chunk at a time. It will then generate the appropriate chunk of ciphertext for us to append to our encrypted message. This allows us to use the cipher on a stream of data as it arrives, rather than on a completely loaded buffer. All in one encryption is just what it sounds like – the cipher operates on the whole message at once.

JCE's `Cipher` class implements both of these by having two encryption/decryption method types: `update()` and `doFinal()`. A continuous cryptographic operation consists of one or more calls to `update()`, followed by a call to `doFinal()` with the last chunk. A single all-in-one operation uses a single call to `doFinal()`. That's what we're doing here. We specify which portion of the input byte array we want to be encrypted, and the ciphertext comes out as a byte array. We then wrap this using a NIO `ByteBuffer`, and write it out to the output stream.

```
byte[] ciphertextBytes = cipher.doFinal(plaintextBytes, 0,
                                        inSize);

ByteBuffer ciphertext  = ByteBuffer.wrap(ciphertextBytes);
out.write(ciphertext);
```

Now, it's all very well outputting the ciphertext but, since the key was randomly generated, it's not going to be much use to anyone unless we store the key you need to decrypt the ciphertext somewhere. We're going to write it out to a file, whose name is supplied on the command line. Rather than wrapping this code in NIO channels, we'll use the shorter syntax of classic IO.

We need to use a JCE `SecretKeyFactory` to turn our opaque internal key into something we can store outside the application. The key specifications that `SecretKeyFactory` generates contain enough information to accurately reconstruct the key used in encryption, and, indeed, the `SecretKeyFactory` is capable of converting a key specification back into an opaque secret key.

Key specifications have different properties depending on the algorithm they specify, so each is represented by a different type. Annoyingly, they don't share a common mechanism for extracting a written representation of the key for storage or transmission, so we can't write polymorphic code here that will work with other algorithms.

```
         keyOut = new FileOutputStream(keyfile);

         SecretKeyFactory skf =
           SecretKeyFactory.getInstance(algorithm);
         DESedeKeySpec keyspec =
           (DESedeKeySpec) skf.getKeySpec(key, DESedeKeySpec.class);

         keyOut.write(keyspec.getKey());
```

Finally, we have some cleaning up to do. We're ignoring many of the things that might go wrong here – in particular, buffer overrun exceptions, which mean the file is too large, and any problems that occur in the key writing operation. In the encryption process, there's little that can really go wrong, except if our algorithm requests aren't supported by the particular provider we're using. In this case, we're using the Sun provider's most basic options, so that's not an issue.

```
      } catch (Exception e) {
         e.printStackTrace();
      } finally {
         if (keyOut != null) {
            try {
               keyOut.close();
            } catch (Exception e) {
               e.printStackTrace();
            }
         }
      }
   }
}
```

Disposing of Secure Data

Truly security-conscious code of this sort would make sure it zeroed all of the sensitive values stored in arrays in that finally clause. The key and the plaintext need to be removed from memory as soon as we're done with them, so nobody can bring down the system and access them in the program's memory. There are a couple of holes it's hard even for a really paranoid programmer to plug though. The key specification object will hang around in memory until the garbage collector collects it (a rather direct real-world analogy: your bank sends you a new account pin number, and after memorizing it, rather than shredding it, you throw it in the trash and leave it out to be collected next week). We have to assume that the implementation of the cipher hasn't left any private arrays floating around with keys or plaintext in.

This is a reason why byte arrays rather than strings are preferred for secure applications. String objects can be more persistent than you'd like. Being immutable, a string maintains a set of characters that won't be garbage-collected until the string is, and even when a string has been garbage-collected, the memory containing it isn't necessarily zeroed out until something else is stored there. If a string gets interned (added to the internal string pool) for any reason, it will persist until the program exits. Byte arrays, on the other hand, can be changed, and we can overwrite their contents with zeroes or some other arbitrary, non-sensitive information. Even if the array reference persists until the garbage collector collects, it doesn't contain anything dangerous.

So, now we can run this code. Let's encrypt the program's own sourcecode. Here's the command line:

```
> javac Encrypt.java

> java Encrypt test.key < Encrypt.java > Encrypt.java.cipher
```

This command is using redirection to take input from one file and pipe output to another. The result: we now have a triple-DES encrypted file in `Encrypt.java.cipher`, and a triple-DES key in `test.key`. Now for the next challenge: how do we decrypt the file?

Decryption

As you might expect, the inverse operation is pretty much the same, just in reverse order. Let's run through what we have to do:

- Load the key specification from a specified key file
- Generate an opaque key from the key specification
- Create a DES-EDE decryption cipher initialized with the key
- Allocate a byte buffer for the ciphertext
- Read in the ciphertext from standard in
- Use the cipher to decrypt the ciphertext into a plaintext buffer
- Write the plaintext buffer out to standard out

Here's the code walkthrough for `Decrypt.java`:

```
import javax.crypto.*;
import javax.crypto.spec.*;
import java.io.*;
import java.nio.*;
import java.nio.channels.*;
```

```
public class Decrypt {

   public static void main(String[] args) {
      FileInputStream keyIn = null;

      try {
         String algorithm = "DESede";
         String keyfile   = args[0];
```

First we're going to read in that key file. Open up a `FileInputStream`, find out how many bytes there are, and allocate an array that big. Then we read from the input stream until it's full.

```
         keyIn = new FileInputStream(keyfile);
         byte[] keyspecBytes = new byte[keyIn.available()];
         keyIn.read(keyspecBytes);
```

Now we have to use this array of bytes to construct a `SecretKey` object. The `SecretKeyFactory` class comes in again here:

```
         SecretKeyFactory skf =
             SecretKeyFactory.getInstance(algorithm);
         DESedeKeySpec keyspec = new DESedeKeySpec(keyspecBytes);
         SecretKey key         = skf.generateSecret(keyspec);
```

Now, just like before, we need to obtain a cipher for the DES-EDE algorithm, and initialize it with a mode (decryption this time), and a key.

```
         Cipher cipher = Cipher.getInstance(algorithm);
         cipher.init(Cipher.DECRYPT_MODE, key);
```

The I/O and decryption code is then exactly the same as before.

```
         ReadableByteChannel in  = Channels.newChannel(System.in);
         WritableByteChannel out = Channels.newChannel(System.out);

         ByteBuffer ciphertext = ByteBuffer.allocate(4096);

         int a = 0;
         while (a >= 0) {
            System.err.print(".");
            a = in.read(ciphertext);
         }

         ciphertext.flip();
         int inSize = ciphertext.limit();

         byte[] ciphertextBytes = ciphertext.array();
```

3

Security

```
        byte[] plaintextBytes  = cipher.doFinal(ciphertextBytes, 0,
                                              inSize);
        ByteBuffer plaintext   = ByteBuffer.wrap(plaintextBytes);

        out.write(plaintext);

      } catch (Exception e) {
        e.printStackTrace();
      } finally {
        if (keyIn != null) {
          try {
            keyIn.close();
          } catch (Exception e) {
            e.printStackTrace();
          }
        }
      }
    }
}
```

Now, let's get our code back. We can type:

> javac Decrypt.java

> java Decrypt test.key < Encrypt.java.cipher > Encrypt.java.plain

Now, we can take a look in `Encrypt.java.plain`, and should find a perfect copy of our original source.

So, we've made a generic DES-EDE encryption/decryption tool. Converting this to run with any of JCE's other block ciphers (Blowfish, AES, RC4) is fairly simple. Unfortunately, the existence of cipher-specific key specification classes prevents us from easily writing a single generic program to handle all the block ciphers.

Stream Ciphers

JCE provides some useful classes for building stream-based encryption and decryption systems. We'll build a program now that uses a block cipher in stream mode – a simple terminal-based chat program, which allows users to connect to one another and communicate.

To ease key management, we'll use password-based encryption, so you just need to telephone one another, agree a one-time password key, and hook the connection up. Once the connections are established, everything you type is encrypted and sent to the other machine to be displayed. This will let us look at how to configure a more complex cipher.

With JCE, this is a pretty trivial program to implement. JCE provides `CipherInputStream` and `CipherOutputStream` classes, which we'll use here to layer cryptographic functionality into our application. Unfortunately, because JCE's streams are based around old-style-I/O, yet again we're forced to stick with old streams, rather than new channels.

Architecturally, it's a simple single-connection socket server, and a simple socket client, built into the same program. Here's how it works. The main thread first starts off a second thread. This second thread creates a server socket listening on a known port (we're using 9999, for no particular reason), and blocks waiting for someone to connect to it. Meanwhile, the main thread carries on, trying to connect to the same port number on the remote host using a client socket. Each time it fails, it waits for a bit, before trying again.

The effect of running two such programs on different hosts, pointed at each other, is as follows: First, host A starts its server socket on port 9999, then tries to connect to port 9999 on host B from its client thread. There's nothing there yet, so it pauses, then tries again. When host B starts up, it starts its server socket on port 9999, and then tries to connect to port 9999 on host A. This succeeds, and host B now has an outbound connection to host A. the next time host A's client socket retries port 9999, it succeeds, and it now has an outbound connection to host B.

So, we only use the client sockets to write data to, and the server sockets to read data from, even though they could be used two-way.

Now, here's how we layer the cryptographic capabilities onto this. Both users run the same program on their own machine, and supply the same password. Both programs independently generate a salt at random, and use it to generate a secure key from the password. These are the keys they will use for encrypting outbound data from each client. Before sending any encrypted data at all down the wire, the first thing they send is the salt value. Then, when the server sockets receive a connection, they simply look at the first few bytes, looking for a salt, and use it to construct the key they will use for decrypting inbound data. So, in the end, data going in each direction is encrypted using a different key, even though both connections use the same password.

```
import java.net.*;
import java.io.*;
import javax.crypto.*;
import javax.crypto.spec.*;
import java.security.*;

public class SecureChat extends Thread {
```

The first task is to set out a few constant values that need to be shared by both the client and server threads. The password-based encryption algorithm we're using is `PBEWithMD5AndDES`, which means that MD5 will be used to generate a DES key, and encryption of the live data will be done with DES. The randomness algorithm SHA1 Pseudo-random number generator (`SHA1PRNG`) is used to come up with cryptographically random numbers for the salt. As always, the exact string names for these algorithms can be found in the JCE Guide's Appendix A.

```
public static final String PBE_ALGO  = "PBEWithMD5AndDES";
public static final String RAND_ALGO = "SHA1PRNG";
public static final int SALT_SIZE    = 8;
public static final int PBE_ITER     = 10;

private static int port = 9999;

// Milliseconds to wait between connection attempts
private static int retryDelay = 5000;
```

Now, here's the main method, which contains the common initialization, and then the client logic (the client is the part of the program that takes data you type, and sends it to the remote host). We print quite a bit of progress information out to the console, because the cryptographic initialization takes time, and it's as well to keep the user informed.

```
public static void main(String[] args) {
   if (args.length != 2) {
      System.out.println(
        "Usage: java SecureChat <password> <host>");
      System.exit(1);
   }

   char[] password = args[0].toCharArray();
   String host = args[1];

   System.out.println("Starting up crypto engine");

   try {
```

First off, we need a key factory to turn the password into a key.

```
      SecretKeyFactory keyFactory =
        SecretKeyFactory.getInstance(PBE_ALGO);

      PBEKeySpec keyspec = new PBEKeySpec(password);
      SecretKey key = keyFactory.generateSecret(keyspec);

      System.out.println("Key specification generated");
```

Now we have all the information the server needs to start. It uses the same basic key specification, but obviously uses a different salt, so we pass it the key specification, and start it up.

```
      SecureChat server = new SecureChat(key);
      server.start();
```

Now we generate the client salt. `java.security.SecureRandom` is a subclass of `java.util.Random`, which is cryptographically strong in the sequences of numbers it generates.

```
        SecureRandom rand = SecureRandom.getInstance(RAND_ALGO);

        byte[] salt = new byte[SALT_SIZE];
        rand.nextBytes(salt);

        System.out.println("Salt generated");
```

We now construct our encryption cipher, from the salt and the key specification.

```
        PBEParameterSpec params =
          new PBEParameterSpec(salt, PBE_ITER);

        Cipher encrypter = Cipher.getInstance(PBE_ALGO);
        encrypter.init(Cipher.ENCRYPT_MODE, key, params);
```

The client will keep trying to connect to the server for as long as its own server is running, so even if it connects, then loses a connection, it will try to connect back. You'll have to break out of operation to stop it running.

The client tries to connect to the target port on the remote host. On success, it extracts an `OutputStream` that can be used to talk to the server, and sends it the salt straight away.

```
        while (true) {
           Socket s = null;

           try {
              System.out.println("Trying to connect...");

              s = new Socket(host, port);

              OutputStream rawOut = s.getOutputStream();
              rawOut.write(salt);
              rawOut.flush();
```

Now, here's the clever part. We wrap an encrypting filter around the raw output stream. This object will now encrypt every byte that passes through it, according to the password-based key we have made.

```
              CipherOutputStream secureOut =
                new CipherOutputStream(rawOut, encrypter);

              System.out.println("Outbound connection secured");
```

All that remains now is to loop, waiting for the user to type in any data. Any line they do enter gets dropped straight into our encryption stream to the server.

```
            BufferedReader rawIn =
              new BufferedReader(new InputStreamReader(System.in));

            while (true) {
               byte[] line = rawIn.readLine().getBytes();
               secureOut.write(line);
               secureOut.flush();
            }
```

As usual, there's the clearing up to do at the end of the client code. If anything goes wrong in the course of a connection, we just try to connect again, after a short delay.

```
         } catch (Exception e) {

            if (s != null) {
               s.close();
               s = null;
            }

            synchronized (e) {
               e.wait(retryDelay);
            }
         }
      }
   } catch (Exception e) {
      e.printStackTrace();
      System.exit(1);
   }
}
```

Now, instances of this class are separate threads that do the server part of the job. Here's the code for this part of the operation. As you'd expect, a lot of it is as above, only backwards. The constructor puts away the key spec in a safe place so the thread's `run()` method can get at it.

```
SecretKey key;

public SecureChat(SecretKey key) {
   this.key = key;
}

public void run() {
```

```
    // runs the server

    try {
      System.out.println("Starting up server");
```

Now, we start a server socket on the appropriate port, and block, waiting for the remote host to connect.

```
      ServerSocket ss = new ServerSocket(port);

      Socket s = ss.accept();

      System.out.println("Foreign host connected");
```

The first job is to obtain the input stream, and read the salt that the client will have sent us. Old blocking I/O helps us here, since this call won't return until it has read as many bytes as we tell it to.

```
      InputStream rawIn = s.getInputStream();

      byte[] salt = new byte[SALT_SIZE];
      rawIn.read(salt);
```

We could implement a verification mechanism here to ensure that the salt that arrives is valid, perhaps calculating and transmitting a checksum for the salt – but we can usually confidently rely on TCP/IP's error checking to guarantee this for us. Having obtained the salt the client is using, we should have all the information needed to build our decryption cipher.

```
      PBEParameterSpec params =
        new PBEParameterSpec(salt, PBE_ITER);

      Cipher decrypter = Cipher.getInstance(PBE_ALGO);
      decrypter.init(Cipher.DECRYPT_MODE, key, params);
```

The `CipherInputStream` wraps the raw input stream in a filter that allows us to decrypt every byte that comes through.

```
      CipherInputStream secureIn =
        new CipherInputStream(rawIn, decrypter);

      System.out.println("Inbound connection secured");
```

Now, we just iterate round, waiting for data from the client, and when we receive it, we print it out.

```
      while (true) {
        byte[] bytes = new byte[secureIn.available()];
        secureIn.read(bytes);
```

```
            System.out.print(new String(bytes));
         }
      } catch (Exception e) {
         e.printStackTrace();
         System.exit(1);
      }
   }
}
```

So, now we're finished, we can run the client on two machines. If the two computers are on a LAN, and one is called George and the other Mildred, we need to type the following commands:

```
George> java SecureChat password Mildred
```

And

```
Mildred> java SecureChat password George
```

substituting a less obvious password for the word `password` in both cases (making sure it's the same password in both machines, though). After each machine has started up (it takes some time to do the key generation steps), you'll hopefully see both computers announce that they have connected. Type something in one of the command prompts, and hit return. Now type some more. You'll notice that data doesn't filter through immediately, but it does make its way through, and arrives at the other end in blocks of clear text.

Key Storage and Administration

Secret keys and private keys are sensitive pieces of data. If you need to keep them in persistent storage between invocations of a program, we need somewhere safe to do so. Java comes with a basic key management system that revolves around objects called `KeyStores`.

`java.security.KeyStore` is not a new class to JDK 1.4, but it does take on more significance in the context of the new cryptographic capabilities. Keystores are designed to be securely persisted somewhere, such as to a file, using a password-based cryptographic algorithm. At the same time, all the keys they contain are stored encrypted within the store, again by a password-based algorithm. Keystores were used in prior versions of J2SE to manage security information for the signing and verification of JAR files.

Like all of Java's cryptography architecture, keystore implementations are selected at run time, using the provider architecture. Sun has always provided the `JKS` (Java Keystore) implementation, but this was relatively weak, from a cryptographic point of view. A password-based Triple-DES provider comes with JCE, called `JCEKS`, and provides considerably more cryptographic strength.

The easiest way to administer keystores located in files is to use the `keytool` command-line utility that comes with Java. This tool allows you to generate public-private key pairs, export public keys, and so on, all using a few command line options.

You create a keystore by performing an operation with the keytool that requires a keystore to store the result in, such as generating a new key. If the specified keystore doesn't exist, then it will be created. Each key in a keystore is stored under a name, called its alias.

Here's the basic syntax to generate a key:

```
> keytool -genkey -alias mykey -keystore keys.key
Enter keystore password:  passwd
What is your first and last name?
  [Unknown]:  James Hart
What is the name of your organizational unit?
  [Unknown]:  Rapid
What is the name of your organization?
  [Unknown]:  Wrox Press
What is the name of your City or Locality?
  [Unknown]:  Birmingham
What is the name of your State or Province?
  [Unknown]:  West Midlands
What is the two-letter country code for this unit?
  [Unknown]:  uk
Is CN=James Hart, OU=Rapid, O=Wrox Press, L=Birmingham,
ST=West Midlands, C=uk correct?
  [no]:  y

Enter key password for <mykey>
        (RETURN if same as keystore password):
```

The series of prompts asking for personal information provides the key tool with information about the person who owns the key, information which is stored within the key itself. When a client authenticates a key, they will know that the person they are communicating with is the key owner. Now, at this stage, the only person asserting that this is true is you, but you can have the key signed by a certification authority, which will back up your claim. Then, when the client examines your key, they'll see it not as simply you claiming to be who you are, but a certification authority claiming you are who you say you are. Platform-dependent details of obtaining a certified key and importing it using `keytool` can be found in the `keytool` documentation at:

- http://java.sun.com/j2se/1.4/docs/tooldocs/win32/keytool.html
- http://java.sun.com/j2se/1.4/docs/tooldocs/solaris/keytool.html

Now, by default, you'll get a 512-bit DSA (Digital Signature Algorithm) key, stored in a JKS keystore. To generate a custom key, we can use some of the more advanced options. To generate a key suitable for commercial encryption use, we really need to use at least a 1024-bit RSA key, and we should store it using the secure `JCEKS` keystore provider. Here's how:

```
> keytool -genkey -alias serverkey -keyalg RSA -keysize
1024 -keystore serverkey.key -storetype JCEKS
```

So, that gives us a public-private key pair for the server side. But for a client to connect to an authenticated secure server, the client needs the server's public key. We need to export the public key in a form the client can understand. Keytool can be used to generate digital certificates in two standard forms. Here's how we can export the key we just created:

```
> keytool -export -alias serverkey -keystore serverkey.key
-storetype JCEKS -rfc -file servercert.crt
```

This exports the public key as a "self-certified" certificate – that is, a certificate which claims that you are who you say you are. If you receive such a certificate from somebody in person, then it is probably adequate.

Now, Java clients need to be able to access certificates so they will know which servers to trust. Conveniently, keystores can also store certificates. A keystore used to store just certificates of trusted parties is known as a **truststore**. We can create such a truststore containing the certificate we just made like this:

```
> keytool -import -alias servercert -keystore
servercert.trust -storetype JCEKS -file servercert.crt
```

This time, we're creating a new keystore (called `servercert.trust`), by importing the server certificate.

A truststore needn't, of course, contain all of the certificates for all of the servers you are likely to contact; it only needs to contain the certificates of root authorities – that is, of organizations or individuals that you trust to vouch for the validity of others. Java comes with a truststore full of root certificates from certification authorities, in `jre/lib/security/cacerts`.

Programmatically, we can manipulate keystores using the `java.security.KeyStore` class. New keystores can be created using its `getInstance()` methods, and we can load existing keystores from a file, or any other stream source, using the `load()` method. Keystores can be written to a stream, using the `store()` method. Both loading and storing operations take a password as an encryption key.

Secure Sockets

JSSE, the Java Secure Sockets Extension builds on JCE to provide the cryptographic tools needed to implement the standard Internet encryption and authentication layers, SSL (Secure Sockets Layer) and TLS (Transaction-Level Security). These standards use public key cryptography to initiate a connection and agree a secret key, which can then be used for secure communication. SSL and TLS are widely applied in the following protocols:

- Secure HTTP (plain HTTP over an SSL connection)
- SSH secure shell (similar to Telnet over an SSL connection)
- Secure SMTP (plain SMTP over an SSL connection)
- IPSEC (Secure IP – used to tunnel IP packets securely across the internet, as, for example, in Virtual Private Networks (VPNs))

SSL, like any socket connection, requires a server and a client. The server has to have a private-public key pair, so that, when a client connects, it can send the client its public key. Using key certification as decribed above the client can, if required, verify the key against a database of certificates to see if it's genuine. The client now has the ability to communicate securely with the server – but the server can't do the same to the client. The client now typically generates a secret key, and sends it to the server, encrypted with the server's public key. If the server wants, it can also require that the client send a certified public key, so that the server can authenticate the client's identity too.

If both parties are satisfied with the supplied credentials, then the sockets are configured to encrypt all data using the agreed secret key. We're now in the position our secure chat application was in before – able to use standard I/O operations to send encrypted data between the client and server.

SSL is typically used to negotiate keys of three different strengths: 40-bit (nowadays, about as secure as a wet paper bag), 56-bit (DES-level security) or 128-bit (strong encryption). Naturally, we generally want to use 128-bit keys.

The purpose of JSSE is to provide a framework that builds on Java's standard networking API, so the code we can write using JSSE should look familiar if you've ever written socket programs in Java.

Let's build a quick client and server that use JSSE to establish a secure connection. This will let us see the basic structure of a JSSE client and server.

Here's our `SecureServer.java` file, which contains the server code:

```
import java.net.*;
import java.io.*;
import javax.net.*;
import java.security.*;
```

```
import javax.net.ssl.*;
import javax.crypto.*;

public class SecureServer {

   public static final int PORT = 10000;

   public static void main(String[] args) {

      try {
```

The first job is to use the default `javax.net.ssl.SSLServerSocketFactory` to obtain a `javax.net.ssl.SSLServerSocket`. This class extends `java.net.ServerSocket`, so it has all of the methods we're used to.

```
         System.out.println("Initializing crypto system");

         ServerSocketFactory ssf =
           SSLServerSocketFactory.getDefault();

         SSLServerSocket ss =
           (SSLServerSocket) ssf.createServerSocket(PORT);
```

From here, it starts to look a lot like regular socket programming. We just block waiting for a connection, and when we receive one, obtain an output stream from it, and write the current date to it. The only difference is that, the data we write to this output stream is getting transmitted down a negotiated secure connection.

```
         System.out.println("Accepting connections on port " + PORT);
         Socket sock = ss.accept();

         System.out.println("User connected");
         ss.close();

         OutputStream rawOut = sock.getOutputStream();
         PrintWriter out =
           new PrintWriter(new OutputStreamWriter(rawOut));
         out.println(new java.util.Date().toString());
         out.flush();
         sock.close();

      } catch (Exception e) {
         e.printStackTrace();
      }
   }
}
```

Now, here's the client, SecureClient.java. The client takes the host to connect to as a command-line argument:

```
import java.net.*;
import java.io.*;
import javax.net.*;
import java.security.*;
import javax.net.ssl.*;
import javax.crypto.*;

public class SecureClient  {

   public static final int PORT = 10000;

   public static void main(String[] args) {
```

First, we check the argument list and make sure a host has been specified.

```
      if (args.length != 1) {
         System.out.println("Usage: java SecureClient <host>");
         System.exit(1);
      }

      String host = args[0];

      try {
```

The client uses a javax.net.ssl.SSLSocketFactory to obtain a socket.

```
         System.out.println("Initializing crypto system");

         SocketFactory sf = SSLSocketFactory.getDefault();
         SSLSocket sock = (SSLSocket) sf.createSocket(host, PORT);
         System.out.println("Server connected");
```

Yet again, the code now takes on the flavor of normal socket programming. We obtain the socket's input stream, and read a line from it.

```
         InputStream rawIn = sock.getInputStream();
         BufferedReader in =
                new BufferedReader(new InputStreamReader(rawIn));
         System.out.println(in.readLine());
         sock.close();

      } catch (Exception e) {
         e.printStackTrace();
      }
```

```
    }
}
```

So, we can now start up a command prompt and run the server. We need to tell it where to find a keystore containing a suitable private-public key pair (such as the 1024-bit RSA key we generated earlier). We do this by defining three system properties:

```
> javac SecureServer.java

> java -Djavax.net.ssl.keyStore=serverkey.key
-Djavax.net.ssl.keyStoreType=JCEKS
-Djavax.net.ssl.keyStorePassword=passwd SecureServer
Initializing crypto system
Accepting connections on port 10000
```

Now, on a second command prompt, run the client. Using similar properties, we need to tell it where to find a truststore that contains a certificate that will validate the server:

```
> javac SecureClient.java

> java -Djavax.net.ssl.trustStore=servercert.trust
-Djavax.net.ssl.trustStoreType=JCEKS
-Djavax.net.ssl.trustStorePassword=passwd SecureClient
localhost
Initializing crypto system
Server connected
Wed Feb 13 17:09:24 GMT 2002
```

You'll almost certainly experience some noticeable delays in the process, while the ciphers do their work. As you should see, when we talk about some ciphers being slower than others, this isn't just idle discussion of insignificant little performance tweaks – there's a real effect on user-experience. Choosing a cipher strength and algorithm is always a case of compromising with a cipher strong enough to protect the data, yet fast enough to be useful.

If you need convincing that the connection is secure and authenticated, try running the client without specifying the truststore:

```
> java SecureClient localhost
Initializing crypto system
Server connected
javax.net.ssl.SSLHandshakeException: Couldn't find trusted certificate
        at com.sun.net.ssl.internal.ssl.SSLSocketImpl.b(DashoA6275)
        at com.sun.net.ssl.internal.ssl.SSLSocketImpl.a(DashoA6275)
        at com.sun.net.ssl.internal.ssl.ClientHandshaker.a(DashoA6275)
        at com.sun.net.ssl.internal.ssl.ClientHandshaker.
```

```
    processMessage(DashoA6275)
  at com.sun.net.ssl.internal.ssl.Handshaker.
    process_record(DashoA6275)
  at com.sun.net.ssl.internal.ssl.SSLSocketImpl.a(DashoA6275)
  at com.sun.net.ssl.internal.ssl.SSLSocketImpl.a(DashoA6275)
  at com.sun.net.ssl.internal.ssl.AppInputStream.read(DashoA6275)
  at sun.nio.cs.StreamDecoder$CharsetSD.
    readBytes(StreamDecoder.java:404)
  at sun.nio.cs.StreamDecoder$CharsetSD.
    implRead(StreamDecoder.java:442)
  at sun.nio.cs.StreamDecoder.read(StreamDecoder.java:179)
  at java.io.InputStreamReader.read(InputStreamReader.java:167)
  at java.io.BufferedReader.fill(BufferedReader.java:136)
  at java.io.BufferedReader.readLine(BufferedReader.java:299)
  at java.io.BufferedReader.readLine(BufferedReader.java:362)
  at SecureClient.main(secureClient.java:43)
```

Clearly, there's a lot going on beneath the surface in a successful interaction.

The system parameters we use to specify the location of trust and key information are employed, in fact, by the default SSL context, to initialize the default SSL socket factories we've been using, with keys. We can create SSL contexts programmatically if we wish to, just by calling the static `getInstance()` methods of the `javax.net.ssl.SSLContext` class. Instances obtained in this way can be configured with custom keystores, truststores, and a random number generator (using the `init()` method), and we can then obtain `SSLSocketFactory` and `SSLServerSocketFactory` instances from them using the `getSocketFactory()` and `getServerSocketFactory()` methods.

Authentication and Authorization

One common task in a wide variety of programs is determining who the current user is, and what they should be allowed to do. While the mechanism for obtaining identification information from the user will often depend on the application (for example, prompt for a password, show a login dialog, send the user a login web page, request a thumbprint, retina scan, or DNA sample), once identity is established, we need to have a mechanism for granting that user privileges, or preventing them from accessing certain data or functionality.

JAAS provides a pluggable authentication system for Java applications. Using JAAS as your authentication and authorization model allows you to configure your application to use any number of authentication modules to confirm user identity. In addition, it provides a uniform model for representing the current user within an application, and low-level security-manager support for granting and revoking permissions.

Logging In

A login consists of obtaining some information from the outside world about who the user of the program is. There are two ways of finding this out: ask the computer, to see if it already knows anything about the user (so, for example, we can obtain Windows NT or UNIX user login information), or ask the user themselves.

We perform a login operation in these steps:

- Obtain a `javax.security.auth.login.LoginContext` object for the application or component
- Call its `login()` method to trigger the process of finding out who the user is
- Call its `subject()` method to obtain a `javax.security.auth.Subject` object representing the user
- Perform operations that require the user information in the `Subject`
- Call the `LoginContext's logout()` method to dispose of the subject information

When we request a `LoginContext` object, one is constructed using information found in a configuration file, which is found by reading the system security property `login.config.url.`*n*, where *n* is a number from 1 upwards. These properties are specified in the `lib/security/java.security` properties file. In the absence of any of these settings (which specify URLs of files in login configuration format, which we'll look at in a moment), the configuration will be loaded from the file specified in the `java.security.auth.login.config` system property.

The login configuration file or files that are loaded contain application configurations, in the following format (this is the configuration file `login.config` that goes with an example we'll code up in a moment):

```
AuthTest {
  com.sun.security.auth.module.KeyStoreLoginModule requisite
    keyStoreURL="file:///private.key" keyStoreType=JCEKS;
  com.sun.security.auth.module.NTLoginModule optional;
  //com.sun.security.auth.module.UnixLoginModule optional;
};
```

Note that you should only use either the `NTLoginModule` or the `UnixLoginModule` line (or neither if your system isn't either, such as a Windows ME machine) – the classes are platform-specific, and are only available on the relevant platform.

The name, `AuthTest`, is the name of the application, which we specify when we request a `LoginContext` object. The content of the block between the braces is then a series of login module specifications, which state that when the application requests that someone be logged in, the login module or modules specified will be used.

The format of each line is simply a fully qualified class name (always of an implementation of `javax.security.auth.spi.LoginModule`), followed by a keyword that specifies the significance of the module, followed by any options the module needs in order to function.

The possible keywords for module significance are:

- `Required` – the module must successfully log in. Even if log in fails, however, subsequent modules will be executed (which hides the source of error).
- `Requisite` – the module must successfully log in. Subsequent modules will not be executed if login of this module fails.
- `Sufficient` – the module is not required to succeed, but if it does, no further modules are executed.
- `Optional` – the module does not have to succeed.

Why would you want an optional module? It may be that we don't want to prevent a user logging in if they don't have certain login privileges – we just want to open up additional capabilities if they do. For example, if a user has a Windows login, they may get access to certain networked facilities, but the program will still run in reduced functionality mode if they don't. Alternatively, we might be implementing a software licensing system, and if the user can provide a particular key (which they might get by purchasing it) they unlock extra application facilities. In these cases, we don't have a problem if the user can't provide these credentials, but when we analyze those credentials later on, we can use them to decide which features to grant access to.

In the example file above, we are requiring that a keystore login succeed, but operating system login is optional. What this means is that login will only succeed if the user is able to log into the specified keystore, but that if they do succeed, we should try a platform-specific login as well. The platform-specific modules don't require any interaction with the user at all; they simply gather information about the user already logged into the operating system. So if they succeed, we gather additional information about the logged-in user, but if they fail we've lost nothing because we still know the user logged in to the keystore successfully.

The login modules provided with Sun's JAAS implementation are as follows (all in the package `com.sun.security.auth.module`):

- `JndiLoginModule` supports user lookup in a JNDI directory system
- `KeyStoreLoginModule` supports user login using a key alias and password to a keystore

- Krb5LoginModule supports Kerberos 5 login
- NTLoginModule obtains information about the current Windows NT user (the NT user system is the same as that used on Windows 2000 and XP Professional)
- SolarisLoginModule (deprecated) obtains information about the current Solaris user
- UnixLoginModule obtains information about the current Solaris or Linux user

Active logins that require user interaction, such as the KeyStoreLoginModule, need a way to communicate with the user that fits with the user interface of the application. In order to allow us to design our own user interface, but support pluggable authentication modules, we supply the LoginContext with a class that implements javax.security.auth.callback.CallbackHandler. A CallbackHandler has to take an array of javax.security.auth.callback.Callback objects and populate each one with the required information, interacting with the user wherever necessary. The callback system is designed to be compatible with different UI strategies, although I can see it being problematic in a web context. Here's a class that provides a command-line console callback interface:

```
import javax.security.auth.callback.*;
import java.io.*;

public class ConsoleHandler implements CallbackHandler {

   public void handle(Callback[] callbacks) throws IOException,
    UnsupportedCallbackException {

      BufferedReader in = new BufferedReader(
                           new InputStreamReader(System.in));

      for (int a = 0; a < callbacks.length; a++) {

         Callback callback = callbacks[a];

         if (callback instanceof NameCallback) {

            // a name callback requests a username

            NameCallback ncb = (NameCallback) callback;
            System.out.print(ncb.getPrompt());
            ncb.setName(in.readLine());
            System.out.println();
```

```
} else if (callback instanceof PasswordCallback) {

    // a password callback requests a password

    PasswordCallback pcb = (PasswordCallback) callback;
    System.out.print(pcb.getPrompt());
    pcb.setPassword(in.readLine().toCharArray());
    System.out.println();
} else if (callback instanceof TextInputCallback) {

    // a text input callback requests arbitrary textual input

    TextInputCallback ticb = (TextInputCallback) callback;
    System.out.print(ticb.getPrompt());
    ticb.setText(in.readLine());
    System.out.println();
} else if (callback instanceof TextOutputCallback) {

    // a text output callback is just a message for the user

    TextOutputCallback tocb = (TextOutputCallback) callback;
    switch (tocb.getMessageType()) {
       case TextOutputCallback.ERROR:
          System.out.print("ERROR ");
          break;
       case TextOutputCallback.WARNING:
          System.out.print("WARNING ");
    }
    System.out.println(tocb.getMessage());
} else if (callback instanceof ConfirmationCallback) {

    // a confirmation callback is really intended
    // for a GUI to show a set of buttons. We'll present
    // it as a multiple-choice list

    ConfirmationCallback ccb =
                       (ConfirmationCallback) callback;
    switch (ccb.getMessageType()) {
       case ConfirmationCallback.ERROR:
          System.out.print("ERROR ");
          break;
       case ConfirmationCallback.WARNING:
          System.out.print("WARNING ");
    }
    String[] options  = new String[] {};
    int defaultOption = ccb.getDefaultOption();
```

```
            switch (ccb.getOptionType()) {
               case ConfirmationCallback.YES_NO_OPTION:
                  options = new String[] {"Yes", "No"};
                  break;
               case ConfirmationCallback.YES_NO_CANCEL_OPTION:
                  options = new String[] {"Yes", "No", "Cancel"};
                  break;
               case ConfirmationCallback.OK_CANCEL_OPTION:
                  options = new String[] {"OK", "Cancel"};
                  break;
               default:
                  options = ccb.getOptions();
            }
            int selectedOption = -1;
            while (selectedOption < 0) {
               String prompt = ccb.getPrompt();
               if (prompt != null) System.out.println(ccb.getPrompt());
               for (int b = 0; b < options.length; b++) {
                  System.out.print("   " + b + ") " + options[b]);
                  if (b == defaultOption) System.out.print(" *");
                  System.out.println();
               }
               String input = in.readLine();
               if (input.equals("")) selectedOption = defaultOption;
               try {
                  selectedOption = Integer.parseInt(input);
               } catch (NumberFormatException e) { }
            }
            ccb.setSelectedIndex(selectedOption);
         } else {

            // any other kind of callback, we don't support

            throw new UnsupportedCallbackException(callback);
         }
      }
   }
}
```

Notice how each callback type is a different kind of JavaBean, some properties of which we read; others of which we set to return data to the login module.

Once we return from this method, the module will continue the login process using the information we have submitted.

Let's build a simple class that lets us log in using this handler.

```
import javax.security.auth.*;
import javax.security.auth.login.*;
import java.util.*;

public class AuthTest {

   public static void main(String[] args) {

      try {
         LoginContext lc =
           new LoginContext("AuthTest", new ConsoleHandler());

         lc.login();
         System.out.println("Login succeeded");
         lc.logout();
      } catch (LoginException e) {
         System.err.println("Couldn't log in");
         e.printStackTrace();
         System.exit(1);
      }
   }
}
```

Well, I said it would be simple. We request a login context, supplying the name of the application for which we want a valid user (as specified in the `login.config` file) and an instance of the console-based login handler. Then we call `login()`, print a message on success, and `logout()`. On failure to log in, an exception will be thrown, which we'll catch and display.

Before we can run this code, we need a keystore to log into. Effectively, a keystore login is used to provide a user with access to a particular private-public key pair. You should create a keystore, containing a key with an alias matching each user's name, and a key password specified by the user. You can specify the keystore password as an option to the login module in the `login.config` file, using the `keyStorePasswordURL` option to specify a file containing the password. If you don't, a callback will be generated requesting the keystore password.

Here's how this code is run:

```
> javac AuthTest.java

> java -Djava.security.auth.login.config=login.config
  AuthTest
```

We specify the login configuration file using the system property method. The login module should now call back to our handler to request a key alias, and key password (and a keystore password if you didn't specify one). It will also call back to ask us to choose OK or Cancel. If we enter the right password(s), we'll see the login succeess message.

Subjects, Principals, and Credentials

When a user is logged in by a particular module, that module may supply information about the user. For example, the `KeyStoreLoginModule` will extract the distinguished name information (that's the user name and location information you supply when you create a key) from the keystore and attach it to the logged in user, so we can access it. The system login modules will supply information about the user's account on the local system or network they're logged onto.

Similarly, logging in via a certain module may provide you with certain credentials, such as a private or public key. Obviously, once you've logged in to a `KeyStoreLoginModule`, it populates your credential sets with your private-public key pair.

We can access this information, which is stored in what are called `Principals` and `Credentials`, by asking the `LoginContext` to give us the currently logged in `Subject`, by calling its `subject()` method.

In JAAS, a principal is something that the logged in user *is*. A credential is something that only they *have*. For example, a particular user might be David Jones, an employee of Acme Tools Inc. of Ames Iowa, employee number 4728629, the person who can be accessed via phone extension 539, and the person whose e-mail address is `davidj@acmetoolsofamesiowa.com`. These would all be encoded as principals describing the logged in user. At the same time, he might have the key to the intranet site, a public-private key pair for e-mail encryption, and a signed document certifying his status as an employee of the company. These could all be encoded as credentials.

Using JAAS we can restrict access to certain code to people who match certain principals. In particular, we can limit access to a user's private credentials to that user, or other users with certain principals. This enables a user to load their private key into a multi-user program, with a reasonable assurance that the key won't be accessible to other logged in users.

Once we have a `Subject`, we can call the following methods to access information about them:

- `public Set getPrincipals()`
- `public Set getPrincipals(Class c)`
- `public Set getPrivateCredentials()`
- `public Set getPrivateCredentials(Class c)`
- `public Set getPublicCredentials()`
- `public Set getPublicCredentials(Class c)`

The variants that take a `Class` object return `Set` objects that contain only objects that belong to the specified class.

3

Security

So, the KeyStoreLoginModule will populate a successfully logged-in subject with the following:

- ❑ A javax.security.auth.x500.X500Principal principal, representing the distinguished name of the key record
- ❑ A javax.security.auth.x500.X500PrivateCredential private credential, representing the private key
- ❑ A java.security.cert.CertPath public credential, representing the public key's certificate chain

We can add some code to our class that will extract some of this information and use it. This is a little program that allows us to use a key pair in a keystore to produce signed document digests, and to verify them against the original key. This program uses the same core authentication code as AuthTest.java, but we'll call it AuthSign.java:

```
import java.security.*;
import java.security.cert.*;
import javax.security.auth.*;
import javax.security.auth.login.*;
import javax.security.auth.x500.*;
import java.io.*;
import java.nio.*;
import java.nio.channels.*;

public class AuthSign {

   public static void main(String[] args) {

      if (args.length != 3) {
         System.out.println(
           "Usage: java AuthSign <s|v> <file> <sigDest>");
         System.exit(1);
      }

      FileInputStream fis                = null;
      FileOutputStream sigOutputStream = null;
      FileInputStream sigInputStream    = null;

      try {
         boolean verify = args[0].equalsIgnoreCase("v");

         LoginContext lc =
                new LoginContext("AuthTest", new ConsoleHandler());
```

3

Security

```
lc.login();
System.out.println("Login succeeded");
```

The login logic is no different. Now, we need to obtain the current `Subject`, and extract its principals and credentials.

```
Subject s = lc.getSubject();
X500Principal dName =
  (X500Principal) s.getPrincipals(X500Principal.class)
                                            .toArray()[0];
X500PrivateCredential keyRecord =
  (X500PrivateCredential)
    s.getPrivateCredentials(X500PrivateCredential.class)
                                            .toArray()[0];
```

We can obtain the user's distinguished name identity, and print it out:

```
System.out.println("Distinguished identity is: "
                    + dName.getName());
```

Now we need to get their keys so we can sign or verify a document. Both can be obtained from the private key record.

```
PrivateKey privKey = keyRecord.getPrivateKey();
PublicKey pubKey  = keyRecord.getCertificate().getPublicKey();
```

Digital signing is managed by a core component of the JCA (not an extension component, so not new to J2SE 1.4) – the `java.security.Signature` class. This class operates very similarly to `Cipher`, except that it generates digital signatures, not encrypted documents. We initialize it to take an MD5 hash function of the document, and encrypt the result with an RSA key. We'll move the data about using NIO.

```
Signature signer = Signature.getInstance("MD5withRSA");

FileChannel sourceFile = fis.getChannel();
FileChannel sigFile = null;

fis = new FileInputStream(args[1]);
```

If we're verifying, we need a read-only channel to the signature file, and we need to initialize the `Signature` object to verify, using our public key. If we're not verifying, we're signing, so we need a write-only channel to the signature file, and we need to initialize the `Signature` object for signing, with our private key.

```
if (verify) {
  sigInputStream = new FileInputStream(args[2]);
```

```
            sigFile = sigInputStream.getChannel();

            signer.initVerify(pubKey);
        } else {
            sigOutputStream = new FileOutputStream(args[2]);
            sigFile = sigOutputStream.getChannel();

            signer.initSign(privKey);
        }
```

Whatever our intentions, the `Signature` object needs to see the whole file. We pass the file through it using its `update()` method.

```
        ByteBuffer source =
          ByteBuffer.allocate((int) sourceFile.size());

        sourceFile.read(source);

        signer.update(source.array());
```

Now, again, our direction depends on whether we're verifying or signing. To verify a previous signature against the file, we need to read in the signature file, and ask the `Signature` object whether it matches. We print out a message to let the user know what the result was.

```
        if (verify) {
            ByteBuffer sig =
                        ByteBuffer.allocate((int) sigFile.size());
            sigFile.read(sig);

            boolean valid = signer.verify(sig.array());

            System.out.println(valid ?
                               "File matches sig" :
                               "File does not match sig");
```

On the other hand, if it's signing, then the `Signature` object will have calculated the signature as it went through the file, and all we need to do is extract it and write it to the file.

```
        } else {
            ByteBuffer sig = ByteBuffer.wrap(signer.sign());
            sigFile.write(sig);
            System.out.println("Signature completed");
        }
        lc.logout();
```

```
        } catch (Exception e) {
            e.printStackTrace();
            System.exit(1);
        } finally {
            try {
                if (fis != null) fis.close();
                if (sigOutputStream != null) sigOutputStream.close();
                if (sigInputStream != null) sigInputStream.close();
            } catch (IOException ioe) {}
        }
    }
}
```


Code-Level Security and Authorization

Java's security manager enforces policies about which code is allowed to access what functionality. JAAS adds an extension to it, to allow the security manager to discriminate not just on the basis of which code is running, but who is running it.

JAAS extends the basic Java `Policy` class so that it supports granting privileges to principals. So, in a policy file we can now write:

```
grant Principal javax.security.auth.x500.X500Principal
    "CN=James Hart,OU=Rapid,O=Wrox Press,L=Birmingham,ST=West Midlands,
 C=uk"
{
    ... usual security permission grants
};
```

Policy files only have an effect when you are running under a security manager (type `-Djava.security.manager` on a Java command line to enable the default security manager and its default policies). Now, we can carry out actions with the privileges that are granted to a logged-in user by using the static `Subject.doAs()` method. We need to pass in a logged-in subject, and an instance of a class implementing the interface `java.security.PrivilegedAction`. The `PrivilegedAction's run()` method will be invoked with the privileges granted to the user via the policy file.

In addition, you'll need to grant your application code base permission to use authentication:

```
grant codeBase "file:///authtest" {
    permission javax.security.auth.AuthPermission
      "createLoginContext.AuthTest";
    permission javax.security.auth.AuthPermission "doAs";
};
```

Conclusions

This has been a whistle-stop tour of the highlights of the new Java encryption and authentication APIs. The mix of higher-level libraries, such as SSL, and lower-level libraries down at the JCE level, makes this a confusing area to develop in at first. But once you've looked around the packages, and poked through the class libraries thoroughly, you will find there's a class for most things. If Sun doesn't provide one, there are third-party JCE extensions readily available.

We started off with an overview of cryptographic techniques, in particular looking at the different algorithms available for block and stream encoding, and public key cryptography. We then saw how these algorithms can be applied using JCE. We looked at Java's key management tools, and their role in public key cryptography.

We then saw how JSSE builds on those same key management tools to provide SSL socket connections. Finally, we looked at how JAAS authenticates users, and used JAAS to implement a public-key-based document signing utility.

One last reminder; Cryptographic software is subject to global import and export laws in various countries, and if you are developing with cryptographic libraries for global distribution, you should look at Sun's extensive notes on the subject included with the J2SE.

Java J2SE 1.4 Core Platform Update

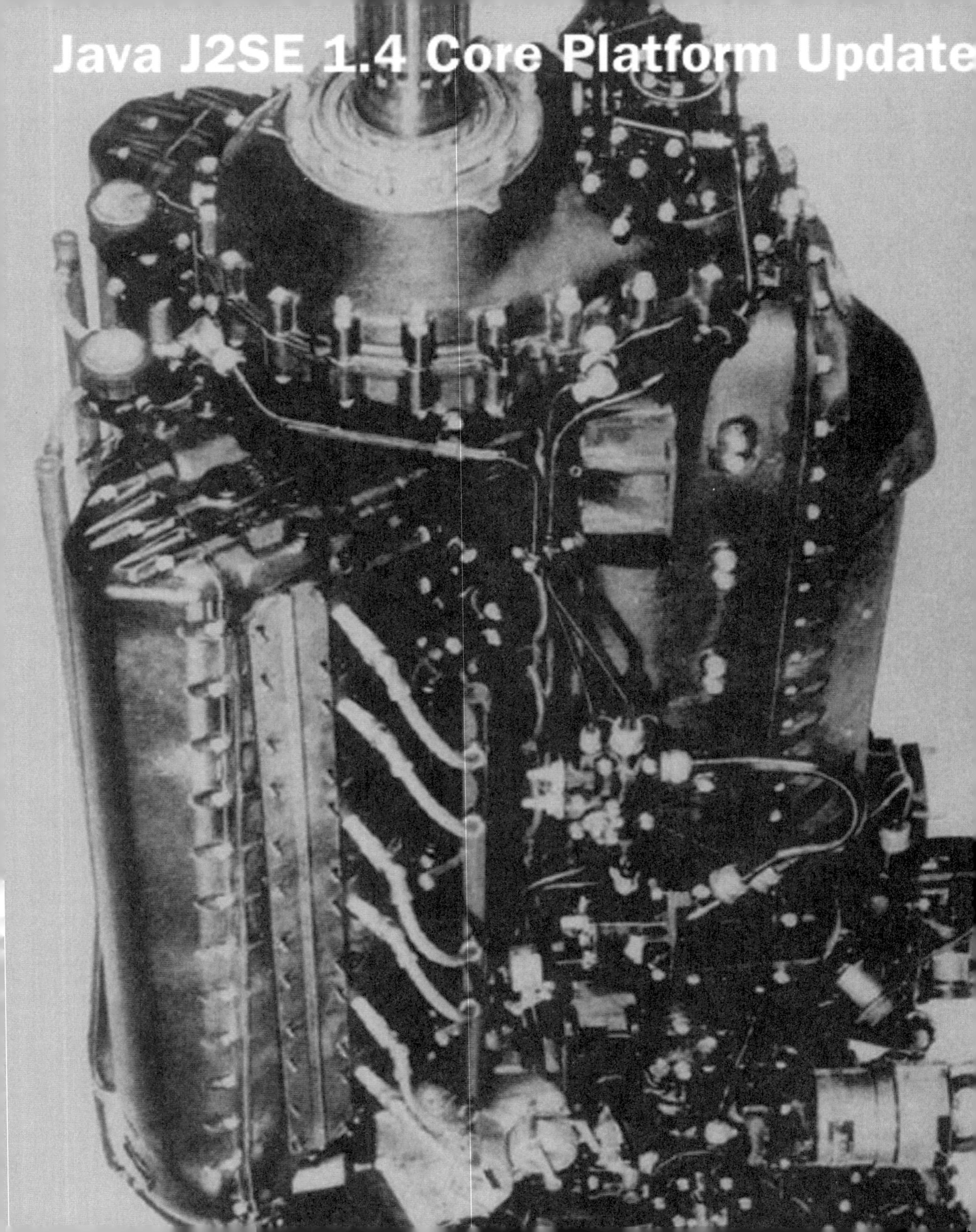

Clients and GUIs

Sun has made some serious performance improvements to Java's client-side application, GUI, and graphics capabilities in J2SE 1.4. In addition, they've introduced some powerful new tools for graphical programs to use, such as an exclusive full screen mode, and access to accelerated hardware.

Beyond the pure graphics APIs, there are improvements to GUI functionality as well, including drag-and-drop, and mousewheel support.

And there are improvements to the client environment, too. Applets get a boost, with some new capabilities (although there are some problems here, as we'll see), and there's the exciting new environment provided by **Java Network Launch Protocol** (**JNLP**). In the second half of this chapter, we're going to focus on this deployment environment, supported by the inclusion of **Java Web Start** in the J2SE 1.4 runtime. We'll be developing a JNLP application – one that can be launched by clicking a hyperlink on a web page – for viewing photographs.

We'll take these topics in that order, effectively starting from the bottom and working up. In this chapter, then, we'll look at:

- Low level graphics
- Full screen mode
- Accelerated graphics
- GUI components
- Mousewheel support
- Drag-and-drop improvements

- Persistence model
- Client environments
- The new Java Plug-in for Applets
- JNLP

Low-Level Graphics

The most significant improvements in the Java2D API for graphics rendering are really both concerned with rationalizing and improving access to graphics-rendering contexts outside the conventional GUI window – so, we have enhanced off-screen rendering (to the point where Java2D will now run even on a system without any graphical support) that allows us to take advantage of accelerated video RAM, and we have the ability to take over the entire screen, bypassing the windowing system altogether.

The new facilities are made available through an enhanced `java.awt.GraphicsEnvironment` object. This class, which has been available in AWT for some time as a means to access fonts on the system, now can be used to find out about the graphics devices connected to the machine.

The singleton `GraphicsEnvironment` is obtained with a call to the static `GraphicsEnvironment.getLocalGraphicsEnvironment()` method. We can then check whether screen rendering is available at all by calling the returned object's `isHeadless()` method.

A headless environment is a program execution environment that doesn't have access to screen rendering, mouse, and keyboard events. For example, a rack-mounted server might not have any video support at all, only allowing access via Telnet or SSH (such an environment doesn't generate key events, it only responds to character streams). Java programs in that context won't be able to draw to the screen, because there is no screen. At the same time, Java programs launched within the context of a Telnet session to a remote host, even though that host may have local video support, will be in a similar situation – unable to display graphics to the screen. These environments are headless.

Before J2SE 1.4, it was not possible for Java code running in a headless context to access graphics functionality at all – a major headache for server-side image generation (for example, automatic generation of graphs for a web site). Now, with J2SE 1.4, we can discover if the environment is headless, in order to decide what interface features to use. Even if the environment is headless, we can still create and draw images in memory.

We can also obtain objects representing the screen or screens attached to the computer by calling `getScreenDevices()` and `getDefaultScreenDevice()`, which return an array of, or a single, `ScreenDevice` object. We can use these objects to access full screen and accelerated rendering.

Full-Screen Mode

Full screen mode is a new feature of J2SE 1.4, and it allows us to obtain direct, priority control over every pixel on the screen; normal windowing is suspended. And it's extremely simple to use – all we have to do is create an AWT `Window` (which also includes `JWindows`, `Frames`, and `JFrames`), obtain a `ScreenDevice` object, and call its `setFullScreenWindow()` method, passing in our window. It really couldn't be simpler. If you've ever programmed the Windows DirectDraw API you may find that this, and the other low-level graphics functionality, seems very familiar. This is likely a result of the implications of modern graphics hardware, and the fact that both APIs are trying to achieve the same thing.

Here's a program that takes a single image file, loads it in using Image I/O (as we saw at the end of Chapter 2), and displays it in full screen.

The class, `FullScreen`, extends `java.awt.Window`, to make it easy for us to provide rendering facilities to draw to the screen. Here's the code in `FullScreen.java`:

```
import java.awt.*;
import java.awt.event.*;
import java.awt.image.*;
import javax.imageio.*;
import java.io.*;

public class FullScreen extends Window {

  private BufferedImage pic;
```

The main method first does a couple of sanity checks – making sure the user provided a filename, and that the system supports full-screen graphics. The magic here is in the two lines that obtain a `GraphicsDevice` object representing the current main screen (on a multi-headed system, you can also obtain separate objects representing each of the screens).

```
  public static void main(String[] args) {
    if (args.length != 1) {
      System.out.println("Usage: java FullScreen <picture>");
      System.exit(1);
    }

    GraphicsEnvironment ge =
      GraphicsEnvironment.getLocalGraphicsEnvironment();
    GraphicsDevice screen = ge.getDefaultScreenDevice();

    if (! screen.isFullScreenSupported()) {
      System.out.println("Full screen mode not supported");
      System.exit(1);
    }
```

Now, we load in the image that the user specified using the Image I/O system. This creates a `BufferedImage` object. A `BufferedImage` is basically an object representing an image stored in an in-memory buffer (stored in main system memory). We can make use of a `BufferedImage` by drawing it onto the screen, or by writing it out to a file, for example.

If loading succeeds, we create an instance of this class, passing the image to its constructor. Since it extends `Window`, we can pass it to the screen's `setfullScreenWindow()` method.

```
    try {
      BufferedImage loadedpic = ImageIO.read(new File(args[0]));
      screen.setFullScreenWindow(new FullScreen(loadedpic));
    } catch (Exception e) {
      System.err.println(e.getMessage());
    }
  }
```

Now, here's the constructor, which we call before passing the window to the screen. Windows always need a parent component, so we have to call `super` with a root frame for the application. This frame will remain invisible, so isn't really going to get in the way.

We store the image away for future use, and add a mouse listener that closes the application when the user clicks on the window.

```
  public FullScreen(BufferedImage pic) {
    super(new Frame());

    this.pic = pic;

    addMouseListener(new MouseAdapter() {
      public void mouseClicked(MouseEvent e) {
        System.exit(0);
      }
    });
  }
```

Finally, we override the window's `paint()` method, to provide custom rendering functionality. This method is called when AWT wants to display our window on the screen, and it passes us a `java.awt.Graphics` object (actually, it will generally be an instance of `java.awt.Graphics2D`, but we don't need any of its specialized functionality, so we don't need to cast it to the newer type), which we can use to draw. We render the buffered image onto the window.

```
  public void paint(Graphics g) {
    g.drawImage(pic, 0, 0, getWidth(), getHeight(), this);
  }
}
```

Now, you call this program, specifying the file you want to view on the command line, like this:

```
> java FullScreen pic.jpg
```

The result should be that the screen goes blank, and is replaced with your selected image (possibly distorted to fit the screen's aspect ratio). I won't provide a screenshot, since your results are likely to depend on the picture you choose!

Accelerated Graphics

Modern computer hardware features capabilities that Java programmers are frequently unable to access. For example, most graphics cards have a large amount of memory on the card, and specialized hardware that can transfer information between different parts of the card's memory (called video RAM, or VRAM) at lightning speeds, far faster than transferring from system memory. The ability to rapidly draw and manipulate in-memory images, and quickly push them onto the screen, allows development of smooth animations and other moving graphics. This is generally what we mean by 2D graphics acceleration (3D acceleration is a different matter, and provides specialized functionality that can only be accessed through APIs like Java3D).

The problem with drawing to the computer screen is typically that the graphics card on a computer has to send to the monitor, 50 to 100 times a second, the image represented by a portion of memory on the graphics card, called the frame buffer. If we are in the process of updating that portion of the graphics card, say because we are halfway through drawing a shape, then we will see the half-drawn shape on the screen. If we are frequently trying to update an image, say because we're displaying an animation, then we'll see flickering, as the half-rendered versions of each frame are displayed.

Let's look at a basic graphics routine (we'll use full-screen graphics, just to see what can be done with them), written first without acceleration, and then we'll add some acceleration functionality using new J2SE 1.4 functionality.

What we want to do is animate a collection of pictures flying around the screen. First of all, let's create a class that can draw a picture in a different place on the screen at different times. `ImageRenderer` keeps track of how long ago it was created, and uses this value as an input to a function, that works out whereabouts on the screen to display an image. We'll use it in each of our attempts to make a smoothly animated system. We're falling back on that staple of animated screensavers, the Lissajous figure, to provide us with smooth, curving paths for our images.

In case you missed that lesson, a Lissajous figure is a path traced by a point over time that is deflected in one direction by one sinusoidal wave, and in the other direction by a different sinusoidal wave. The difference between the periods and phases of the two functions produces graceful curves like these:

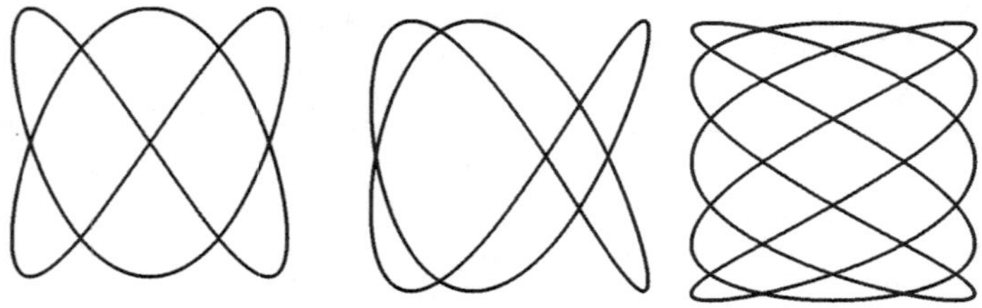

`ImageRenderer` isn't really that interesting a class – it only has two parts: a constructor, which precalculates as much as it can about the path the picture will follow, chooses some random parameters that affect the Lissajous path for the picture, and stores away references to all the objects it will need; and a method, `render()`, which calculates where the image should be at the current time, and then draws it there. A small piece of this functionality is delegated out to a utility method, `getFactor()`. Here is `ImageRenderer.java`:

```
import java.awt.image.*;
import java.util.*;
import java.awt.*;

public class ImageRenderer {

  private static final int MAX_HEIGHT = 300;
  private static final int MAX_WIDTH = 300;

  private static final int MIN_PERIOD = 6000;
  private static final int MAX_PERIOD = 60000;

  private int baseWidth;
  private int baseHeight;
  private int screenWidth;
  private int screenHeight;
  private int maxWidth;
  private int maxHeight;
  private long startTime;
  private BufferedImage pic;

  private int xperiod;
  private int yperiod;
  private int zoomperiod;

  private Random rand;

  private Window window;
```

4

Clients and GUIs

```
ImageRenderer(BufferedImage pic, GraphicsDevice screen,Window
                                        window)
{
  this.pic     = pic;                  // the image we will render
  this.window = window;                // the window we will render to
  baseWidth    = pic.getWidth();       // the width of the picture
  baseHeight   = pic.getHeight();      // the height of the picture
  screenWidth = screen.getDisplayMode().getWidth();
                                       // the width of the screen
  screenHeight = screen.getDisplayMode().getHeight();
                                       // the height of the screen
  startTime = new Date().getTime(); // the current number of
                                       // milliseconds since 1970
  rand = new Random();                 // A source of randomness

  // Calculate the maximum size for this image,
  // preserving aspect ratio

  double aspect = ((double) baseWidth) / ((double) baseHeight);
  maxWidth       = baseWidth;
  maxHeight      = baseHeight;

  if (maxWidth > MAX_WIDTH) {
    maxWidth  = MAX_WIDTH;
    maxHeight = (int) (((double) MAX_WIDTH) / aspect);
  }
  if (maxHeight > MAX_HEIGHT) {
    maxHeight = MAX_HEIGHT;
    maxWidth  = (int) (((double) MAX_HEIGHT) * aspect);
  }

  // choose random periods for movement and size

  xperiod    = rand.nextInt(MAX_PERIOD - MIN_PERIOD) + MIN_PERIOD;
  yperiod    = rand.nextInt(MAX_PERIOD - MIN_PERIOD) + MIN_PERIOD;
  zoomperiod = rand.nextInt(MAX_PERIOD - MIN_PERIOD) + MIN_PERIOD;
}

void render(Graphics2D g) {

  // obtain zoom, horizontal and vertical deflections

  double zoomFactor = getFactor(zoomperiod);
  double xFactor    = getFactor(xperiod);
  double yFactor    = getFactor(yperiod);
```

```
    // calculate image size

    int width  = (int) (maxWidth * zoomFactor);
    int height = (int) (maxHeight * zoomFactor);

    // calculate position

    int maxX = screenWidth - width;
    int x    = (int) (maxX * xFactor);

    int maxY = screenHeight - height;
    int y    = (int) (maxY * yFactor);

    // display the image
    g.drawImage(pic, x, y, width, height, window);
  }

  private double getFactor(int period) {
     long time = new Date().getTime();
     double n  = ((double) time) / ((double) period);
     double s  = Math.sin(n * Math.PI * 2);
     return s * s;
  }
}
```

Now, let's get on and develop an unbuffered application that can display a set of images on the screen using this class. Here's `UnbufferedAnimator.java`:

```
import java.awt.*;
import java.awt.event.*;
import java.awt.image.*;
import javax.imageio.*;
import java.io.*;
import java.util.*;

public class UnbufferedAnimator extends Window {

  private ImageRenderer[] pics;
  private boolean running = true;

  public static void main(String[] args) {
    if (args.length < 1) {
      System.out.println(
        "Usage: java UnbufferedAnimator <picture filename list>");
      System.exit(1);
```

```
    }

    new UnbufferedAnimator(args).animate();
    System.exit(0);
  }
```

The beginning of this program is very similar to that of our `FullScreen` program above. This one reads in multiple files specified on the command-line, so the main method passes the constructor an array of filenames. We leave to the constructor some of the functionality we put in the main method before, so it's here we find the code that obtains the current screen, and checks that full-screen graphics are supported. We need one of our `ImageRenderer` instances for each of the specified files, so we create an array to store them in, and fill it by loading in each image in the same way as we loaded a single image before. Because we won't be filling the screen with an image as before, we set the background color to black, and then switch to full screen mode – this basically clears the screen to black. As before, we set up a mouse listener so you can close the app by clicking.

```
  public UnbufferedAnimator(String[] filenames) {
    super(new Frame());
    GraphicsEnvironment ge =
      GraphicsEnvironment.getLocalGraphicsEnvironment();
    GraphicsDevice screen = ge.getDefaultScreenDevice();

    if (! screen.isFullScreenSupported()) {
     throw new IllegalStateException(
                          "Full screen mode not supported");
    }

    pics = new ImageRenderer[filenames.length];

    for (int a = 0; a < filenames.length; a++) {
      try {
        BufferedImage pic = ImageIO.read(new File(filenames[a]));
        pics[a] = new ImageRenderer(pic, screen, this);
      } catch (Exception e) {
        throw new IllegalArgumentException(e.getMessage());
      }
    }

    setBackground(Color.BLACK);
    screen.setFullScreenWindow(this);

    addMouseListener(new MouseAdapter() {
      public void mouseClicked(MouseEvent e) {
        synchronized(UnbufferedAnimator.this) {
          stop();
```

```
            dispose();
          }
        }
    });
  }
```

There are three methods that manage the window's progress. The `animate()` method is a loop that continuously renders and re-renders the window until the animation is stopped. The `stop()` method stops the animation. Because this may be requested from a different thread (such as the AWT event-handling thread), we synchronize it on the object itself. A similarly synchronized method, `isRunning()`, is called by the loop to check that the animation hasn't been stopped.

```
  public synchronized void stop() {
    running = false;
  }

  public synchronized boolean isRunning() {
    return running;
  }

  public void animate() {
    running = true;
    while (isRunning()) {
      render();
    }
  }
```

The `render()` method simply obtains a `Graphics2D` object for this window, clears it (using the `clearRect()` method), which draws a black rectangle across it, and then passes the same `Graphics2D` object to each of the `ImageRenderer`'s `render()` methods in turn.

The bodies of this method and the mouse click handler are synchronized on the window instance. This prevents the window being disposed of while the rendering operation is halfway through, which would lead to exceptions being thrown.

```
  public synchronized void render() {
    Graphics2D g = (Graphics2D) getGraphics();
    g.clearRect(0, 0, getWidth(), getHeight());
    for (int a = 0; a < pics.length; a++) {
       pics[a].render(g);
    }
  }
}
```

4

Clients and GUIs

Now, put a selection of JPEG files into the application's folder, and type the following at a command prompt:

```
> java UnbufferedAnimator *.jpg
```

The shell will turn the wildcard filename into a list of files, and the program will load all of them in. You should find that you get a screen full of flying pictures, but that they flicker very unpleasantly. We can do better than this.

The main technique for getting around this sort of problem is to use a technique called **double buffering**. We maintain an in-memory image that is the same size as the screen space we are trying to animate. We draw each frame in the in-memory buffer, and then copy the complete buffer to the screen each time it's completed.

Basic Double Buffering

We can implement a naive double buffering strategy on this program, employing existing Java techniques:

```
import java.awt.*;
import java.awt.event.*;
import java.awt.image.*;
import javax.imageio.*;
import java.io.*;
import java.util.*;

public class BadlyBufferedAnimator extends Window {

  private ImageRenderer[] pics;
  private boolean running = true;
  private BufferedImage buffer; //new

  public static void main(String[] args) {
    if (args.length < 1) {
      System.out.println(
        "Usage: java BadlyBufferedAnimator <picture filename list>");
      System.exit(1);
    }

    new BadlyBufferedAnimator(args).animate();

    System.exit(0);
  }

  public BadlyBufferedAnimator(String[] filenames) {
    super(new Frame());
```

4

Clients and GUIs

```
    GraphicsEnvironment ge =
      GraphicsEnvironment.getLocalGraphicsEnvironment();
    GraphicsDevice screen = ge.getDefaultScreenDevice();

    if (! screen.isFullScreenSupported()) {
       throw new IllegalStateException(
         "Full screen mode not supported");
    }

    pics = new ImageRenderer[filenames.length];

    for (int a = 0; a < filenames.length; a++) {
      try {
        BufferedImage pic = ImageIO.read(new File(filenames[a]));
        pics[a] = new ImageRenderer(pic, screen, this);
      } catch (Exception e) {
        throw new IllegalArgumentException(e.getMessage());
      }
    }

    buffer = new BufferedImage(screen.getDisplayMode().getWidth(),
                               screen.getDisplayMode().getHeight(),
                               BufferedImage.TYPE_INT_RGB);

    setBackground(Color.BLACK);
    screen.setFullScreenWindow(this);

    addMouseListener (new MouseAdapter() {
      public void mouseClicked(MouseEvent e) {
        synchronized (BadlyBufferedAnimator.this) {
          stop();
          dispose();
        }
      }
    });
  }

  private synchronized void stop() {
    running = false;
  }

  private synchronized boolean isRunning() {
    return running;
  }
```

```
  public void animate() {
    while (isRunning()) {
      render();
    }
  }

  public synchronized void render() {
    Graphics2D g = buffer.createGraphics();
    g.clearRect(0, 0, getWidth(), getHeight());
    for (int a = 0; a < pics.length; a++) {
       pics[a].render(g);
    }
    getGraphics().drawImage(buffer, 0, 0,
                            getWidth(), getHeight(), this);
  }
}
```

We're using a `BufferedImage` as an off-screen buffer. This seems, given the name, like a logical enough idea. But unfortunately, as you'll find if you run this program, it doesn't work very well. The flickering has mostly gone but rendering, on most machines, is going to be very jerky and not at all smooth. This isn't what we're after.

Accelerated Double Buffering

Now, using J2SE 1.4, we can implement an effective double buffering strategy. The problem with our image buffer was that it is a heavyweight image, stored on the system heap, and passing it to the screen requires an entire screenful of data, that we've just drawn, to be moved over to video RAM. For a 1280 by 1024 pixel screen resolution in 32-bit color, that's 5.2 megabytes of image data. Java's also trying to be helpful, by making things easy for us – it's not just copying the bytes over, it's performing a mapping between the color depth and scale of the buffered image, and the screen colors and pixels. We're doing that for every frame. No wonder it's slow.

J2SE 1.4 introduces a new image class: `VolatileImage`. A `VolatileImage` is an image that, if the hardware supports it, is stored in accelerated video memory (if you don't have accelerated video memory, it will be stored in system memory, just like a `BufferedImage`). As a result, it is subject to the whims of hardware and operating system-level random behavior – the sort of thing we started programming Java to avoid – but the API provides us with a degree of protection.

Essentially, the video memory can be overwritten if the user switches to another application or changes video modes, or if another window takes over the full screen mode. Any data there may be lost, or overwritten, and if we try to render it to screen, the results will not be predictable. The `VolatileImage` class can't protect us from this happening, but it can certainly let us know if we have lost the contents of the buffer, and need to redraw it. In the meantime, we have a buffer that can be copied to the screen blazingly fast, if the hardware supports it.

We can replace our BufferedImage above with a VolatileImage. It's not quite a drop-in replacement, but the changes aren't that comprehensive. Let's make another version of our animator. This one's VolatileBufferedAnimator.java:

```
import java.awt.*;
import java.awt.event.*;
import java.awt.image.*;
import javax.imageio.*;
import java.io.*;
import java.util.*;

public class VolatileBufferedAnimator extends Window {

  private ImageRenderer[] pics;
  private boolean running = true;
  private VolatileImage buffer;

  public static void main(String[] args) {
    if (args.length < 1) {
      System.out.println(
       "Usage: java VolatileBufferedAnimator <picture filename list>");
      System.exit(1);
    }

    new VolatileBufferedAnimator(args).animate();

    System.exit(0);
  }

  public VolatileBufferedAnimator(String[] filenames) {
    super(new Frame());

    GraphicsEnvironment ge =
      GraphicsEnvironment.getLocalGraphicsEnvironment();
    GraphicsDevice screen = ge.getDefaultScreenDevice();

    if (! screen.isFullScreenSupported()) {
       throw new IllegalStateException(
         "Full screen mode not supported");
    }

    pics = new ImageRenderer[filenames.length];

    for (int a = 0; a < filenames.length; a++) {
      try {
```

4

Clients and GUIs

```
        BufferedImage pic = ImageIO.read(new File(filenames[a]));
        pics[a] = new ImageRenderer(pic, screen, this);
      } catch (Exception e) {
        throw new IllegalArgumentException(e.getMessage());
      }
    }

    buffer = screen.getDefaultConfiguration()
                   .createCompatibleVolatileImage(
                               screen.getDisplayMode().getWidth(),
                               screen.getDisplayMode().getHeight());

    setBackground(Color.BLACK);
    screen.setFullScreenWindow(this);

    addMouseListener (new MouseAdapter() {
      public void mouseClicked(MouseEvent e) {
        synchronized (VolatileBufferedAnimator.this) {
          stop();
          dispose();
        }
      }
    });
  }

  private synchronized void stop() {
    running = false;
  }

  private synchronized boolean isRunning() {
    return running;
  }

  public void animate() {
    while (isRunning()) {
      render();
    }
  }

  public synchronized void render() {
    do {
      buffer.validate(getGraphicsConfiguration());
      Graphics2D g = buffer.createGraphics();
      g.setBackground(Color.BLACK);
```

```
      g.clearRect(0, 0, getWidth(), getHeight());
      for (int a = 0; a < pics.length; a++) {
        pics[a].render(g);
      }
    } while (buffer.contentsLost());
    getGraphics().drawImage(buffer, 0, 0,
                            getWidth(), getHeight(), this);
  }
}
```

We obtain a `VolatileImage` from the `GraphicsConfiguration` associated with the screen to which we are rendering. Remember, if we were on a multi-headed system (with more than one monitor), it would most likely have multiple graphics cards, meaning an image stored in video RAM on one of them isn't much use to the other card.

The biggest change is in the `render()` routine. We wrap the entire buffer rendering process in a loop that continually re-renders the buffer until the content sticks. The initial call to `validate()` sets us up for a series of drawing operations. Any data loss in the buffer after that call, and before the call to `contentsLost()`, will result in `contentsLost()` returning `true`. Only if `contentsLost()` returns `false` do we copy the contents of the buffer to the screen, using the same method as before. But this time, it's going to run much more quickly.

This program should (depending on your hardware) actually produce smooth animation, even with quite a large number of images. On a system without specialized video RAM, it should perform similarly to our previous example using system memory buffers. Now, hopefully, we can see the benefit of accelerated double buffering.

Buffering Strategies

Because double buffering is such a common animation strategy, J2SE 1.4 also adds some convenience support for buffered image rendering. This makes use of the volatile image functionality, but also adds some other tricks that are even more efficient. For example, we can make use of page-flipping, where two (or more) buffers are maintained in video RAM, and the video card simply switches between sending one page and the other to the monitor, without moving large amounts of data around in memory at all. We can even make use of multiple buffers to smooth out animation even more (averaging out uneven rendering times across a number of frames) – at the expense of using more storage space in VRAM.

AWT `Windows` and `Canvases` can now have a **buffering strategy** associated with them. A buffering strategy associates one or more back-buffers (off-screen buffers) with the canvas or window, and specifies a process allowing our program to render to those buffers, before it renders the buffers to the screen.

Here's how easily we can modify our original unbuffered animator to use the full buffering system:

```
import java.awt.*;
import java.awt.event.*;
import java.awt.image.*;
import javax.imageio.*;
import java.io.*;
import java.util.*;

public class StrategyBufferedAnimator extends Window {

  private ImageRenderer[] pics;
  private boolean running = true;

  public static void main(String[] args) {
    if (args.length < 1) {
      System.out.println(
       "Usage: java StrategyBufferedAnimator <picture filename
list>");
      System.exit(1);
    }

    new StrategyBufferedAnimator (args).animate();

    System.exit(0);
  }

  public StrategyBufferedAnimator(String[] filenames) {
    super(new Frame());
    GraphicsEnvironment ge =
                 GraphicsEnvironment.getLocalGraphicsEnvironment();
    GraphicsDevice screen = ge.getDefaultScreenDevice();

    if (! screen.isFullScreenSupported()) {
       throw new IllegalStateException(
                    "Full screen mode not supported");
    }

    pics = new ImageRenderer[filenames.length];

    for (int a = 0; a < filenames.length; a++) {
      try {
        BufferedImage pic = ImageIO.read(new File(filenames[a]));
        pics[a] = new ImageRenderer(pic, screen, this);
      } catch (Exception e) {
        throw new IllegalArgumentException(e.getMessage());
```

4

Clients and GUIs

```
      }
    }
    setBackground(Color.BLACK);
    screen.setFullScreenWindow(this);
    createBufferStrategy(3);

    addMouseListener (new MouseAdapter() {
      public void mouseClicked(MouseEvent e) {
        synchronized (StrategyBufferedAnimator.this) {
          stop();
          dispose();
        }
      }
    });
  }

  private synchronized void stop() {
    running = false;
  }

  private synchronized boolean isRunning() {
    return running;
  }

  public void animate() {
    while (isRunning()) {
      render();
    }
  }

  public synchronized void render() {
    BufferStrategy strategy = getBufferStrategy();
    Graphics2D g = (Graphics2D) strategy.getDrawGraphics();
    g.clearRect(0, 0, getWidth(), getHeight());
    for (int a = 0; a < pics.length; a++) {
      pics[a].render(g);
    }
    strategy.show();
  }
}
```

So, outside the changes to the class name, there are a grand total of three modifications. First, we need to create a buffer strategy. `createBufferStrategy()` takes an `int`, which is the number of buffers to create. Then, when we're rendering the window, we don't want to draw onto the window directly. We need to get the graphics context for the current rendering buffer, which we get from the `BufferStrategy` object. We render onto this object, and when we're finished, push the rendered version onto the screen by calling the strategy's `show()` method. It really is that simple.

This version of the application runs, on my test machine, more smoothly than all the others. Of course, all of these applications benefit from J2SE 1.4's improved image scaling algorithms, and overall performance improvements in the 2D rendering pipeline. Certainly on this evidence, Java's getting faster.

GUI Components

Stepping up a level for a moment, J2SE 1.4 has also made some improvements in the GUI libraries, particularly in two regards: there's now support for scroll wheels on mice, and the drag-and-drop system in Swing has been overhauled. In addition, a new serialization mechanism has been introduced to make GUI serialization more robust.

Mousewheels

If you have a Swing application that uses any of Java's standard scrollable components, then you already have scroll wheel support in your application – just run the application, and it works. Scrollable panels, lists, and textboxes all work with wheel mice, without any intervention on the part of the programmer. In addition, we can add scrolling support to our own components and windows, by implementing `MouseWheelListener`. Here's an adaptation of Chapter 2's Image I/O viewer application that uses the scroll wheel to zoom in and out.

```
import javax.swing.JFrame;
import java.awt.Graphics;
import java.awt.event.*;
import java.text.NumberFormat;
import java.awt.image.BufferedImage;
import javax.imageio.ImageIO;
import java.io.File;

public class ZoomingViewer extends JFrame {
```

We track the amount by which we're zoomed in using an integer. Negative integers mean we're zoomed out, positive integers mean we're zoomed in. Zero means we're seeing the image at 100% normal size. We also create and store away a percentage text formatter, for use later on. The constant `ZOOM_AMOUNT` is a number used to decide how much we zoom in or out for each notch on the value of `zoom`. The formula for working out how many times normal size to display the image is simply $\text{ZOOM\_AMOUNT}^{\text{zoom}}$.

```
private BufferedImage bi;
private int zoom = 0;
private String filename;
private NumberFormat perc = NumberFormat.getPercentInstance();

private static final double ZOOM_AMOUNT = 1.1;

public static void main(String[] args) {
  if (args.length > 0) {
    new ZoomingViewer(args[0]).show();
  } else {
    System.out.println(
      "Usage: java ZoomingViewer <picture filename>");
  }
}
```

The `sizeToZoom()` method calculates how far we should zoom, and resizes the window. It also puts the percentage level of zoom in brackets in the window title.

```
private void sizeToZoom() {
  double factor = Math.pow(ZOOM_AMOUNT, zoom);
  setSize((int) (bi.getWidth() * factor),
          (int) (bi.getHeight() * factor));

  setTitle (filename + " (" + perc.format(factor) + ")");
}

public ZoomingViewer(String filename) {

  setDefaultCloseOperation(EXIT_ON_CLOSE);
  this.filename = filename;

  try {
    bi = ImageIO.read(new File(filename));
  } catch (Exception e) {
    e.printStackTrace();
  }
```

Here's where the magic's added. After calling `sizeToZoom()` initially, to set the default size for the window, we register a `MouseWheelListener` on the window itself. This requires us to define one method, `mouseWheelMoved()`, through which we receive a `MouseWheelEvent`. From this, we can find out how far the wheel has been turned. `getWheelRotation()` returns the number of "notches" the wheel was moved, a positive number if it was moved up, a negative number if down. The way our program's implemented, we can just add this number to the zoom level, and call `sizeToZoom()` to have the window resized.

```
    sizeToZoom();

    addMouseWheelListener(new MouseWheelListener() {
      public void mouseWheelMoved(MouseWheelEvent e) {
        int steps = e.getWheelRotation();
        zoom += steps;
        sizeToZoom();
      }
    });
  }

  public void paint(Graphics g) {
    g.drawImage(bi, 0, 0, getWidth(), getHeight(), this);
  }
}
```

That's it. We can now resize our image using the mousewheel:

Drag-and-drop

AWT has supported drag-and-drop since Java 2 first came out. But, while Swing has been able to take advantage of AWT's functionality in this regard, it hasn't been a very easy experience for developers. Now, J2SE 1.4 has added a friendly system over the top of AWT's data transfer system, allowing Swing applications to implement drag-and-drop with the minimum of effort. As a beneficial side effect, since the functionality is related, clipboard data transfers are enabled via the same mechanism, allowing developers to implement both mechanisms in the same section of code.

The implementation hinges around a new property, added to the `JComponent` class, called `TransferHandler`. An instance of the new `TransferHandler` class is passed to a `JComponent` by calling its `setTransferHandler()` method, and any assigned transfer handler is retrieved via `getTransferHandler()`.

We'll take a look at what new functionality these facilities offer. We won't go in depth into the AWT data transfer and drag-and-drop model, since these aren't new – although they are providing the under-the-covers implementation, and clearly are still available if you need the extra power.

Many standard Swing components have been drag-and-drop enabled, allowing us to take advantage of drag-and-drop functionality very easily. Drag support isn't enabled by default, so you won't suddenly find that all the text fields in your delicately crafted application now support drag-and-drop or copy and paste, but drag-and-drop can be turned on in any Swing component that allows it by calling `setDragEnabled(true)`. Here's a quick example to show what's possible:

```
import java.awt.*;
import javax.swing.*;
import java.awt.event.*;

public class DragDropText extends JFrame {

  public static void main(String[] args) {
     new DragDropText().show();
  }

  public DragDropText() {
    super("Drag-and-drop Text Demo");

    setDefaultCloseOperation(JFrame.EXIT_ON_CLOSE);

    JTextField field1 = new JTextField("Life's a drag", 20);
    JTextField field2 = new JTextField("and then you drop", 20);
    field1.setDragEnabled(true);
    field2.setDragEnabled(true);
```

```
    Container content = getContentPane();

    content.setLayout(new BoxLayout(content, BoxLayout.Y_AXIS));
    content.add(field1);
    content.add(field2);

    pack();
  }
}
```

The only specialized code in this class is in the two lines where we turn on drag support on the text fields. Now, when you execute this program, you'll find drag-and-drop editing is available between the text fields. If you run a second instance of the program, you can drag text between fields in both programs. Even more impressively, the system interoperates with the native drag-and-drop mechanisms. On Windows, try dragging text to or from WordPad, to see the system in action.

Enabling Drag-and-drop in Custom Components

Now, let's go one step further, and build a drag-and-drop enabled component. We'll build a color well, which we can drag colors onto or off. Swing's `JColorChooser` supports drag-and-drop, so we'll have a ready source of colors.

Building a drag-and-drop component is very easy with the new tools. First, we need to register a `TransferHandler`. Just doing this enables drop support. To allow drags, we need to detect drag events, and call the transfer handler's `exportAsDrag()` method.

To make things even more trivial, the `TransferHandler` class comes with a default implementation that takes the name of one of the component's public JavaBean properties as a `String` argument. A transfer handler instantiated in this way will use reflection to read this property to service drag events, and to write to it when receiving drop events.

Here's our color well component, `ColoredCircle`. It has one public property, `color`, accessed via `getColor()` and `setColor()`. Apart from those accessors, it has a constructor, which calls many parent methods to set up the kind of component this is, and intializes the object. It has to create a transfer handler for the `color` property, and also sets up a cursor, so that the cursor changes when over the component.

```
import javax.swing.*;
import java.awt.*;
import java.awt.event.*;

public class ColoredCircle extends JPanel {
```

```
  private Color color;

  public ColoredCircle(Color color) {
    super();
    this.color = color;
    setOpaque(false);
    setPreferredSize(new Dimension(32, 32));
    setMinimumSize(new Dimension(32, 32));
    setMaximumSize(new Dimension(32, 32));
    setTransferHandler(new TransferHandler("color"));
    setCursor(Cursor.getPredefinedCursor(Cursor.HAND_CURSOR));
```

We add a mouse listener, to detect when the mouse is pressed. That is sufficient for us to consider a drag has been initiated. It's possible that if you also wish to handle click events, you might want to initiate drag events only when the mouse is dragged out of the component while held down, or moved more than a few pixels from its initial click location.

On detecting a drag gesture, we get the transfer handler, and call its `exportAsDrag()` method. We pass in the component, the mouse event, and a constant indicating that the drag is to take a copy of the value, not move it. Notice we don't specify here that it is the color object we want to transfer – that will be extracted by the transfer handler, which will look for the `color` property.

```
    addMouseListener(new MouseAdapter() {
      public void mousePressed(MouseEvent e) {
        getTransferHandler().exportAsDrag(
          ColoredCircle.this, e,
          TransferHandler.COPY);
      }
    });
  }
```

We now implement the paint method, and the setter and getter methods for the property.

```
  public void paintComponent(Graphics g) {
    super.paintComponent(g);
    g.setColor(color);
    g.fillOval(1, 1, getWidth()-2, getHeight()-2);
    g.setColor(Color.BLACK);
    g.drawOval(1, 1, getWidth()-2, getHeight()-2);
  }

  public Color getColor() {
    return color;
  }
```

```
  public void setColor(Color c) {
    color = c;
    repaint();
  }
}
```

Now, let's build a small application that uses this component. The application will display a window containing five color wells, and a button. The wells will all be drag-and-drop enabled. Clicking the button will bring up a color chooser dialog box, which can be used to drag new colors onto the wells.

```
import java.awt.*;
import javax.swing.*;
import java.awt.event.*;

public class DragDropColor extends JFrame {

  public static void main(String[] args) {
    new DragDropColor().show();
  }

  public DragDropColor() {
    super("Drag-and-drop Color Demo");

    setDefaultCloseOperation(JFrame.EXIT_ON_CLOSE);

    Container content = getContentPane();

    content.setLayout(new BoxLayout(content, BoxLayout.Y_AXIS));
```

We create an array of the initial colors that will be held by our set of color wells. Then, we iterate through them, creating `ColoredCircle` objects from each of them.

```
    Color[] colors = new Color[] {Color.RED, Color.GREEN,
                        Color.BLUE, Color.WHITE, Color.BLACK};

    for (int a = 0; a < colors.length; a++) {
      ColoredCircle circle = new ColoredCircle(colors[a]);
      content.add(circle);
    }
```

We create a second `JFrame` to hold the color, chooser dialog box. We instantiate a color chooser, turn on drag-and-drop support on it, and place it in the frame. The frame remains hidden initially. We configure it so that, on closing, it hides rather than being destroyed.

```
    final JFrame chooserFrame = new JFrame("Color Chooser");
    chooserFrame.setDefaultCloseOperation(JFrame.HIDE_ON_CLOSE);

    JColorChooser colorChoice = new JColorChooser();
    colorChoice.setDragEnabled(true);

    chooserFrame.getContentPane().add(colorChoice);
    chooserFrame.pack();
```

Now we can create a button to show the color chooser, and add it to our main frame.

```
    Button showColors = new Button("Show Colors");
    showColors.addActionListener(new ActionListener() {
                         public void actionPerformed(ActionEvent ae) {
                           chooserFrame.show();
                         }});
    content.add(showColors);

    pack();
  }
}
```

Run the application, and you'll get the following frame:

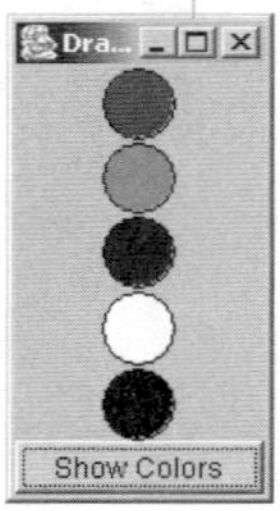

You should find you can drag the colors between the cells. Opening up the color chooser shows a second window like this:

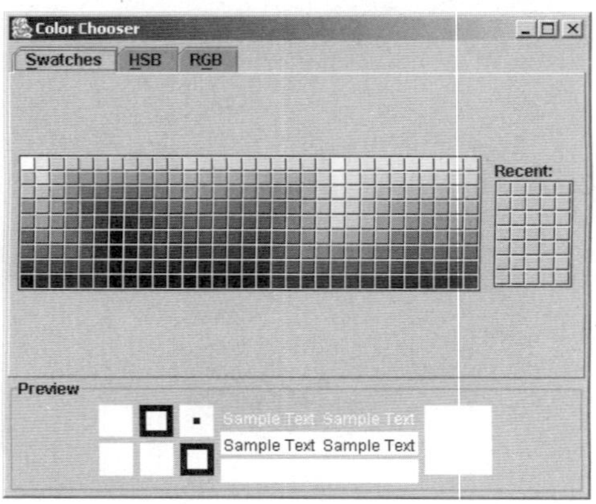

The entire preview area is a drag source and drop destination for colors, and you can drag-and-drop between the two windows. Again, you can drag between instances of the application but, because this isn't a plain text drag, you'll find you can't drag to or from native applications (they don't know what to do with a `java.awt.Color` object).

Long-Term GUI Component Serialization

Browsing the Swing JavaDocs in the J2SE 1.4 distribution, you'll find that every class now carries a health warning:

Warning: Serialized objects of this class will not be compatible with future Swing releases. The current serialization support is appropriate for short-term storage or RMI between applications running the same version of Swing. As of 1.4, support for long-term storage of all JavaBeans has been added to the `java.beans` package. Please see XMLEncoder...

The problem that this warning is trying to address is a simple one: programmers use `ObjectOutputStreams` to write out objects to disk for storage. That's what they're for, after all. `ObjectOutputStreams` rely on Java serialization though, which is a fragile way of representing an object's properties – it depends on the class definition for the object being exactly the same in the JVM that the object is deserialized in. This is generally a safe assumption in short-term storage, or in transfer of the object over RMI. In a long-term storage situation though, serialization is too easily broken by class definition changes, as it depends on the class internal data structure. Since Sun is in the process of seriously re-architecting Swing classes, it makes sense to try to decouple the serialized form from the internal representation. To do this, you need to serialize only the public properties of a class, leaving you free to tear up the class's insides and start again.

The solution offered in J2SE 1.4 is to use an alternative class to the `ObjectOutputStream`, the `java.beans.XMLEncoder`.

This is provided by the new **long-term persistence of JavaBeans API**, which consists of two classes: `XMLEncoder`, and `XMLDecoder`. They really do directly replace the function of the `ObjectOutputStream` and `ObjectInputStream` in a long-term persistence situation, but they have one specific job: to serialize all the readable bean properties of an object to an XML document, and to read such XML documents, instantiate the necessary object, and set all the bean properties back to their original values.

For Swing components, which are all designed around JavaBean principles, this is a useful supplement to the existing serialization technology.

`XMLEncoder` has two methods that are of interest, and one of those is its constructor:

- `public XMLEncoder(OutputStream out)`
- `public void writeObject(Object o)`

4

Clients and GUIs

Similarly, XMLDecoder has a very simple API:

- public XMLDecoder(InputStream in)
- public Object readObject()

The important thing to notice is that none of these methods throw exceptions. Both classes use a setExceptionListener() method to acquire an object that implements the ExceptionListener interface, an interface we can implement by just providing an implementation of the public void exceptionThrown(Exception e) method.

These methods really are that simple, and they easily generate XML data that can be used very simply to repopulate the properties of a JavaBean with the values held previously.

This limited ability to write out and read in XML data is one of a vast number of XML-related APIs that will be arriving in the J2SE over the coming years. The first proper XML API, the Java API for XML Processing (JAXP), is the subject of the next chapter.

Client Environments

Java has two classic application-execution environments: the java executable JVM (and its javaw variant), and the applet environment. In the last part of this chapter, we'll take a look at the updated applet environment, and the new JNLP environment, which is a powerful execution system that combines some of the benefits of applets with the power of the executable JVM.

Java Plug-In

The Java plug-in has undergone some surgery with version 1.4. As well as sporting a new look during applet loading (it shows a progress bar on a grey background), and offering improved applet-caching, it also has support for programmatic access to the underlying Document Object Model of the HTML document in which it is embedded – similar to the functionality afforded to JavaScript scripts embedded in an HTML page.

The functionality is, however, a little sketchy, at least in the current version. The implementation will only be available on browsers that have the Sun J2SE 1.4 plug-in installed, and it is patchy to say the least. The following code compiles and should, according to the limited documentation on the subject, work fine:

```
import java.applet.*;
import org.w3c.dom.*;
import org.w3c.dom.html.*;
import com.sun.java.browser.dom.*;
```

```
public class DomInvestigator extends Applet implements DOMAction {

  public void start() {
    try {
      DOMService plugin = DOMService.getService(this);
      HTMLDocument htDoc = (HTMLDocument) plugin.invokeAndWait(this);
      System.out.println(htDoc.getTitle());
      System.out.println(htDoc.getURL());
      System.out.println(htDoc.getReferrer());
      htDoc.open();
      htDoc.write("This text was added by the applet");
    } catch (Exception e) {
      e.printStackTrace();
    }
  }

  public Object run(DOMAccessor accessor) {
    Document doc = accessor.getDocument(this);

    if (doc instanceof HTMLDocument) {
      return doc;
    } else {
      System.err.println("No HTML document was returned");
      return null;
    }
  }
}
```

Notice the `com.sun...` package in the import list. This contains the proprietary Sun plug-in functionality. The fact that we access these classes means this applet won't even load if the Sun plug-in isn't present. We access the DOM by a convoluted route – first we request an instance of `com.sun.java.browser.dom.DOMService`, then we call its `invokeAndWait()` method, passing in the applet itself. This is because we're implementing `com.sun.java.browser.dom.DomAction`, which requires us to have a `public Object run(com.sun.java.browser.dom.DOMAccessor accessor)` method. Calling `invokeAndWait()` causes the DOM implementation to call in to this `run()` method with a `DOMAccessor` object, allowing us to return the value we pass back. There is an asynchronous variant (`invoke()`), which doesn't allow you to return values from the `run()` method.

As it stands on the current implementation, this code runs fine, except that the methods called on the `HTMLDocument` instance all return `null`, and the `open()` method (which is supposed to open up the document so data can be written to it using the `write()` method we call subsequently) is not yet implemented in the plug-in, so throws an exception.

In short, this functionality appears to be experimental at this stage. Proceed with caution.

JNLP

The most significant introduction to GUI application programming on J2SE 1.4 is the arrival of Java Web Start as a core component of the runtime. Web Start provides an application-execution environment that can download Java application code and resources from a location on the Internet, and execute the code locally as an application. The enabling technology is called the Java Network Launch Protocol, JNLP.

The Java Network Launch Protocol is unusual for an Internet application programming solution, since it requires more specialized software to be deployed on the client than on the server. Most Internet applications are simply based around an ordinary web browser, but with a specialized web server that understands some form of programming language, such as JSP, Perl, or ASP. For a server to serve JNLP applications, all that's needed is a standard HTTP web server. The application is deployed simply by placing any JAR files that make up the application, together with a specially formatted XML file (known as a **JNLP file**) that describes the application, in a directory on the server that can serve files – just like the ordinary HTML files and images that make up a web site.

The client on the other hand, needs to have a JNLP client installed and integrated into its browser, similar to adding a plug-in to the browser for recognizing a particular MIME type. The browser, then, is configured to recognize JNLP files (either by their MIME type, `application/x-java-jnlp-file`, or by its file extension, `jnlp`), and hand them over to the JNLP client for interpretation. If the browser's user then clicks on a link within an HTML page that points to a JNLP file on a web server, it downloads the XML file, then launches the JNLP client, and hands it the content of the JNLP document.

The client parses the file, and extracts the information it needs in order to launch the application – most importantly, the location from which the JAR file(s) containing the application's code and resources should be obtained, and the name of the main class. This allows the client to start up a JVM, and load in the application.

Figure 1

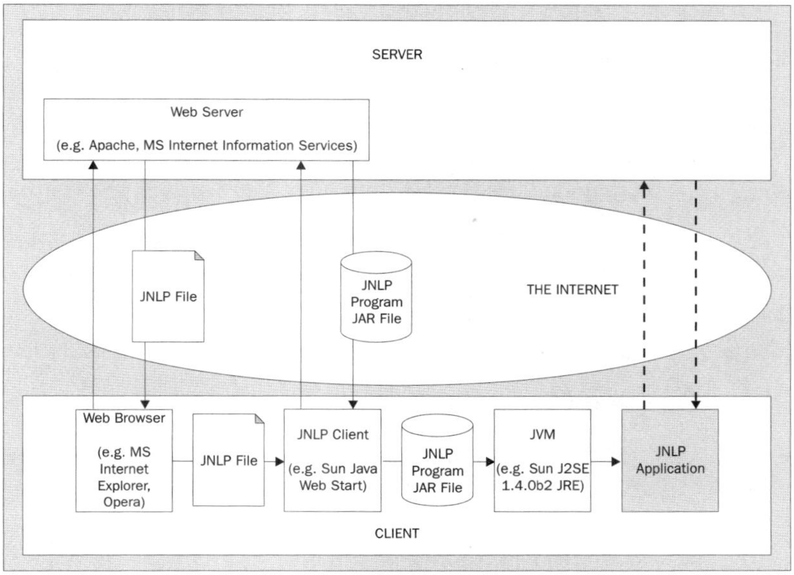

In this diagram, we can see the relationship between the three client programs: the web browser requests a JNLP file from the server, launches the JNLP client, and passes to it the file. The JNLP client parses the file, identifies the JAR file it should download, and does so. It then spawns a JVM, and launches the JAR file it has obtained within that JVM. The JNLP application is then running inside the virtual machine, and is able to communicate, should it wish, with the server from which it originated (the dotted arrows on the right).

There's much more that JNLP clients can do, but their basic functionality is simply to assist a web browser in launching a JVM for a Java application. In addition, they may do any of the following other tasks:

- Downloading and installing the version of the Java runtime required to execute the particular application
- Downloading and installing additional code libraries or Java extensions that might be needed for the application to run
- Caching applications after download, so that a download can be avoided in future, or even so that applications can be run from the cache without the client having to be online
- Comparing a cached version of an application with the version on the server, and downloading and incorporating a partial JAR file update, known as a JARDiff, into the application (this requires the support of the web server)

Whatever functionality the JNLP client provides, it also controls the local system access granted to the downloaded code. In exactly the same manner as the applet sandbox, the JNLP sandbox restricts the ability of downloaded untrusted code to access JRE functionality that could potentially harm the host system. The application has unlimited access to any resources contained within JAR files downloaded as part of the JNLP process, via the class loader system, and is also allowed to open network connections back to the system from which it was downloaded in order to obtain further resources. A JNLP application can't open arbitrary files on the local system though, nor can you open socket connections to machines on the local network, or indeed anywhere else on the Internet other than where the application originated.

As a way to provide a safer means for such code to actually access some of the functionality present on a typical desktop computer, and which normally would be available to an installed application, JNLP clients can provide a set of services, which permit certain operations, but only with the express permission of the user. So, to read data from a local file, we can use the JNLP `FileOpenService` service, which will cause the JNLP client to first ask the user if the application is allowed to open a file, and then show a file-open dialog. Since this file-open dialog is managed by the JNLP client program, all that our application sees is the selected file that the user chose, and the user can therefore be assured that the visiting code can't do anything malicious to or with the rest of the data on the local filesystem.

Figure 2

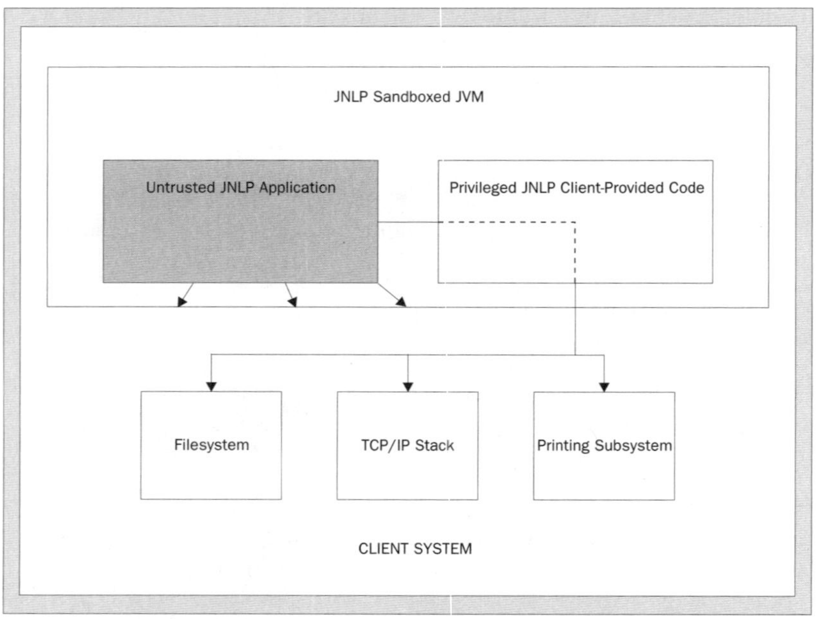

Other facilities accessible through these secure service interfaces include access to the system clipboard, printing, file saving, and access to a limited persistent store (somewhat analogous to the cookies used by web sites to store a small amount of preference information). These services, in the `javax.jnlp` package, make up what is known as the JNLP API.

Of course, if all these sandbox limitations are *too* limiting for your application, you can sign the JAR files of your applications, and give your users the option of choosing to run your code in a trusted context. Trusted JNLP applications have full access to all of the classes in the JRE. We will look at trusted JNLP applications later, in the *Trusted Execution* section.

The Java Web Start JNLP client is included with J2SE 1.4, but is typically not installed in the same location as the SDK (on Windows, it is installed under `Program Files`). It includes the key `javaws.jar` file, which, in addition to containing all the classes that make up the actual Web Start client, incorporates the JNLP API classes, which are needed on the `classpath` at compile time if your code uses the service infrastructure at all (at run time, these classes are provided by the JNLP execution environment, so you don't need to worry about specifying them on the `classpath`). If you don't want to put the `javaws.jar` file on the `classpath` (it is, after all, a complete application, not just the six or seven classes we're interested in), you can download the **JNLP Developer's Pack** from http://java.sun.com/products/javawebstart/download-jnlp.html, which includes the full API documentation, a lightweight `jnlp.jar` file that you can keep on your `classpath` (since it only defines the JNLP API interfaces), and a servlet implementation of the JARDiff protocol.

So, that's the overall architecture of the JNLP system, as implemented by Java Web Start. Let's now look at the elements that we need to use to develop and deploy a JNLP application.

The JNLP File

JNLP files are the key to JNLP as an application technology and, as mentioned earlier, are simply XML files with certain XML elements and attributes (the complete DTD can be found in the JNLP specification at http://java.sun.com/products/javawebstart/download-spec.html). They are the programmatic equivalent of a `README` file, explaining to the JNLP client how to download, install, and run the application. Rather than start off with a laborious discussion of the DTD in depth, here is an example so you can see what sort of data JNLP files include. It is actually the JNLP file, `photoview.jnlp`, for the application we will develop later in this chapter:

```
<?xml version="1.0" encoding="UTF-8"?>
<jnlp codebase="http://rapid.wrox.com/j2se/photoview/">
  <information>
    <title>PhotoView</title>
    <vendor>Wrox Press - J2SE 1.4</vendor>
    <icon href="PhotoView.jpg"/>
  </information>

  <resources>
    <j2se version="1.4.0+"/>
    <jar href="photoview.jar"/>
  </resources>
```

```
  <application-desc
      main-class="com.wrox.rapid.j2se.photoview.PhotoViewer"/>
</jnlp>
```

There's not really a great deal of mystery to these files.

The first piece of information in this file is the codebase for the application. This is the base URL of the directory containing all of the application's resources, in JAR files, used to resolve all relative URLs given in the document. It also identifies the application's home host – the only host it is allowed to speak to.

What follows next is an <information> element, specifying details like the application's name, vendor, and icon image.

A <resources> element specifies the application's prerequisites – in this case, it needs a J2SE 1.4 installation, and it needs the client to download the photoview.jar file from the code base. In addition to jar and j2se elements, the <resources> section can also specify native libraries (JNI extensions incorporating platform-specific binary code), required Java extensions (such as Java3D, JMS, and so on), and also specify which packages can be found in which JAR files (allowing the JNLP client to perform lazy downloading of JAR files – downloading the JAR file containing a particular package *only* when its classloader needs to load a class from that package).

The final element depends on the type of resource that this JNLP file specifies – an application, in our case, but it could also be a specification for an applet, an extension library, or a JRE installer. Most of the time, we'll want this to be an application descriptor. As you can see, what we use this element for is to name the class that needs to be started in order to run the application. JNLP uses the standard public static void main(String[] args) entry point, and we can specify arguments to the method by including <argument>arg</argument> elements inside the application-desc element.

In addition to these elements, there is one kind of element not included in the above example: a <security> element, which is used to request a privileged execution environment. More discussion of this element's usage is shown later in this chapter, under the heading *Trusted Execution.*

The JNLP API

JNLP services are provided by the JNLP client, and are only available to code running inside the context of a JNLP sandbox. Since JNLP is intended to be an implementation-neutral specification, not simply the specification for the Java Web Start client's behavior, not all services have to be provided on all platforms by all implementations. This may be because the particular platform (a set-top box, or a handheld device, perhaps) doesn't have printing functionality, or a local filesystem, or some other feature exposed via the full JNLP API. So, we should always be prepared for the possibility that a particular service won't be available.

To request a service, we call the javax.jnlp.ServiceManager's lookup() method, which takes a String (the fully-qualified name of the service interface we want an implementation for), and returns an Object. It can also throw an UnavailableServiceException, in the event we request a service that doesn't exist. This is the sort of code we can write to look up services:

```
javax.jnlp.FileSaveService f;
javax.jnlp.BasicService b;

try {
  f = (FileSaveService)
      ServiceManager.lookup("javax.jnlp.FileSaveService");
  b = (BasicService) ServiceManager.lookup("javax.jnlp.BasicService");
} catch (UnavailableServiceException e) {
  JOptionPane.showMessageDialog(this, "JNLP Error",
              "Could not obtain required JNLP services",
                                JOptionPane.WARNING_MESSAGE);
  System.exit(1);
}
```

A couple of things to note here, which are a bit of a reminder of the difference between a JNLP application and an applet. We're able to assume Swing is installed (because JNLP is a Java 2 technology, there's no danger of being stuck with AWT-only runtimes. The ability to specify the minimum JRE version using the j2se element in the JNLP file for our application also allows us to make further assumptions about what will be available on the system). And we are also able to call System.exit(). Unlike applets, which can't terminate their JVM, our application has its own exclusive JVM to do with as it pleases. BasicService is a core service, in that it provides us with information about where the JNLP file's codebase is, and also allows us to launch a web browser on the machine, pointing to a particular URL, if the machine supports web browsing.

So, having obtained a service object from the ServiceManager, we can perform some limited interactions with our environment. The available services are as follows:

- javax.jnlp.BasicService
- javax.jnlp.ClipboardService
- javax.jnlp.DownloadService
- javax.jnlp.ExtensionInstallerService
- javax.jnlp.FileOpenService
- javax.jnlp.FileSaveService
- javax.jnlp.PersistenceService
- javax.jnlp.PrintService

Their interfaces are explained in the JNLP API JavaDocs, which can be read online at:

- http://java.sun.com/products/javawebstart/docs/javadoc/

Implementing a JNLP Application

Almost any kind of application can be run as a JNLP application. However, the run-time security configuration of the JNLP sandbox does impose some limitations that make it more suited for applications that are really a client-side extension of some server-side function. Client systems in a centrally controlled peer-to-peer scenario, such as instant messaging clients, or Napster-like file sharers for example, would make excellent JNLP applications – such applications benefit from rich user interfaces that aren't possible within a web browser, and the ability to install and run the client program for the network via a simple click on a web hyperlink provides a seamless transition for users from the browser into the independent client application.

The application we'll build now is along these lines; it provides a rich client-side interface for interacting with server-side resources. In this case, it is a browser for viewing photo galleries on a server. This suits JNLP since it is a network traffic-oriented task, and browsing a selection of pictures benefits from the multiple window interface we'll be able to create with JNLP. We will also be able to give users the option of saving files to disk. The application is called **Photo Viewer**, and it has the following features:

- It will download an index file from the server it is launched from, and download and display thumbnail images for all the files indexed
- Clicking on a thumbnail image will result in the full image being downloaded and displayed in a separate window
- The user will be able to save the file they are viewing to the local filesystem

To whet your appetite, here's a screenshot of the browser window:

`PhotoViewer` consists of the following classes:

Class	Function
`PhotoFrame`	Displays a single `PhotoPanel`
`ThumbnailBox`	Displays a single thumbnail image and the image's name
`PhotoViewer`	The main application class; manages thumbnails, and browser and frame windows
`PhotoBrowser`	Implements a window that shows thumbnails of all the images in a directory
`PhotoPanel`	Displays a photograph

The JNLP application will begin by looking in its `codebase` directory for a file with a particular name (`pv_index.txt`). This file should contain a list of names of image files in that directory. It can also contain pointers to other directories that contain similar files, simply by specifying a relative URL with a slash on the end. Here's a sample file for the above window:

```
m_street.jpg
s_frisco.jpg
s_ggbridge.jpg
s_hill.jpg
s_streets.jpg
scotland/
```

It will then build a browser window, showing thumbnails for each of the images listed, and providing a link to open a new browser for any directories linked from the file. Small, thumbnail versions of the full-sized images are downloaded, by looking for a file with the same name as the full-size image appended with a specific extension. If no thumbnail is provided, we will show a blank thumbnail at first, but replace it with an image when the user requests the download of a full image.

Clicking a thumbnail will open a frame showing the full sized image (although it will be scalable by resizing the window).

Closing all the application's browsers will lead to the application closing down.

We'll start off with `PhotoViewer.java`, since it manages the entire application, and handles resource management.

PhotoViewer

`PhotoViewer` is a Swing `WindowAdapter` – it functions as a controller for all the windows in the application, managing their creation, and releasing resources on their destruction (this is important, since the application can have a large number of images resident in memory at once). It keeps a track of which images have already been downloaded, so that we don't have to spend too much time downloading files.

```
package com.wrox.rapid.j2se.photoview;

import javax.swing.*;
import java.awt.*;
import java.awt.image.*;
import java.awt.event.*;
import java.io.*;
import javax.imageio.*;
import javax.imageio.stream.*;
import java.util.*;
import java.net.*;
import javax.jnlp.*;

public class PhotoViewer extends WindowAdapter {

  public static final String INDEX_FILE_NAME      = "pv_index.txt";
  public static final String THUMBNAIL_EXTENSION = ".thumb.jpg";
```

These two variables define, respectively, the name of the file that will be searched for in any directory the application tries to browse, and the extension that should be added to the name of a file to find the matching thumbnail file (as we explained, we don't have to provide thumbnails on the server – the application will download the full files and calculate thumbnails later on, but the thumbnail files provide a useful hint).

```
  private static HashMap browsers = new HashMap();
  private static HashMap photos   = new HashMap();
  private static HashMap thumbs   = new HashMap();
```

We will store three kinds of instance in three global `HashMaps`, all of them indexed by the URL of the resource they represent; `browsers` indexed by the directory URL; `photos` indexed by their file URL, and `thumbs`, indexed by the URL of the file they represent. Keeping a central store of the open windows means that, as they are closed, we can free up associated resources and also detect when the last window is closed, triggering the application's quitting. It also prevents us from opening multiple browsers or photo frames for the same URL. Indexing our thumbnails provides us with the ability to check if a thumbnail has already been downloaded for a particular image and, if not, to provide one.

```
  private static PhotoViewer windowManager = new PhotoViewer();
```

Finally, for the preliminaries, a single instance of the `PhotoViewer` class will serve as a window event listener for every window in the application.

Now comes the entry point – the `main()` method. I've written this in such a way that it will run on a JNLP system, but will fall back to command-line arguments if it isn't running in a JNLP environment (in other words, if the application is launched from the command line). This is useful for testing. We can simply run the application, specifying a URL to function as the `codebase` as the one command-line argument. In this case, however, it won't be able to use the JNLP functionality that it requires to save images.

The `main()` method's one and only task is to find the starting URL that the first browser should be pointed at. This is either the `codebase` URL for the application (if JNLP is running it), or the first argument passed in on the command line.

```
public static void main(String[] args) {

  URL initialDirectory = null;

  try {
    System.out.println("trying JNLP");
    BasicService bs = (BasicService)
      ServiceManager.lookup("javax.jnlp.BasicService");
    initialDirectory = bs.getCodeBase();
```

We try to locate the `codebase` using the `BasicService` object. If this operation fails, we fall back:

```
  } catch (Throwable jnlpNotFound) {
    System.out.println("JNLP launch failed");
    System.out.println("trying command-line launch");
    if (args.length > 0) {
      try {
        if (args[0].startsWith("http://")&&args[0].endsWith("/")) {
          initialDirectory = new URL(args[0]);
        }
      } catch (Exception e) {
        System.out.println("Could not initialize context");
      }
    }
  }

  if (initialDirectory == null) {
    System.out.println("No initial directory found - exiting");
    System.exit(1);
  } else {
    System.out.println("Starting in directory: "
                       + initialDirectory.toString());
    showBrowser(initialDirectory);
  }
}
```

The final act of the main() method is to call showBrowser(), passing in a URL. This is the next method in the class.

showBrowser()'s job is to display a browser for a given URL. This may mean going to the URL, downloading a pv_index.txt file, and initializing a new browser window. If the URL has already been accessed though, and we already have a window for it, we simply need to show the existing browser. This is where those centralized hash-maps come in, and the first thing we do is check the hash-map:

```
public static void showBrowser(URL directory) {
  PhotoBrowser browser = (PhotoBrowser) browsers.get(directory);

  if (browser == null) {
```

If there was no value returned from the hash-map, we need to download and parse the pv_index.txt file for this directory. We calculate absolute URLs from the relative URLs in the file, and populate a List with them:

```
    java.util.List images = new ArrayList();

    try {
      URL index = new URL(directory, INDEX_FILE_NAME);
      BufferedReader br = new BufferedReader(
         new  InputStreamReader(index.openStream()));

      URI startPoint = URI.create(index.toString());

      String line;
      while ((line = br.readLine()) != null) {
        URI specifiedURI = new URI(line);
        if (specifiedURI.isAbsolute() || specifiedURI.isOpaque()){
          System.out
            .println("found an absolute or opaque URI - discarding");
        } else {
          URI absoluteURI = startPoint.resolve(specifiedURI);
          System.out.println("found relative URI: resolves to "
                             + absoluteURI.toString());
          images.add(absoluteURI.toURL());
        }
      }
    } catch (Exception e) {
      e.printStackTrace();
    }
```

4

Clients and GUIs

We are making use of a new J2SE 1.4 class here, `java.net.URI`. This class is capable of handling arbitrary URI strings, including relative URIs, and performing operations such as resolving them against known URIs. This class, unlike `java.net.URL`, enables us to make sure that the URLs specified in the file aren't absolute, which means they must be referring to files that are on the same server as our codebase, which is a necessary pre-condition to our being able to access them.

Having parsed the `pv_index.txt` file, we can create the new browser window, and register the single global window manager as its window listener. We also store the new object away in the hash-map:

```
      browser = new PhotoBrowser(directory, images);
      browser.setDefaultCloseOperation(JFrame.DISPOSE_ON_CLOSE);
      browser.addWindowListener(windowManager);

      browsers.put(directory, browser);
    }
```

Finally, to live up to the name of the method, we show the browser (this is either the browser that came out of the hash-map, or it's the one we just created):

```
    browser.show();
  }
```

The next method is concerned with creation of photo frames. Notice that it doesn't actually show the frame – that job is done by a separate method. This is because there are some occasions (we'll see exactly which later) when it is useful to download the image before the window needs to be displayed.

The logic is very similar, however, to the previous method's operation: look for an existing frame for this URL, but if there isn't one, create it:

```
  public static PhotoFrame getPhoto(URL location) {
    PhotoFrame photo = (PhotoFrame) photos.get(location);

    if (photo == null) {
      photo = new PhotoFrame(location);
      photo.setDefaultCloseOperation(JFrame.DISPOSE_ON_CLOSE);
      photo.addWindowListener(windowManager);

      photos.put(location, photo);
    }
    return photo;
  }
```

This is the wrapper around the previous method that also shows the resulting frame:

```
public static void showPhoto(URL location) {
  getPhoto(location).show();
}
```

The final factory method of this type creates ThumbnailBoxes. Again, the logic should be familiar.

As we'll see shortly, when a ThumbnailBox is created, it is initialized with a blank icon the same size as the one we will ultimately use for our thumbnail. Having created a ThumbnailBox, we subsequently can pass in a BufferedImage, and it will swap in a new icon. We try to do this immediately after creating the ThumbnailBox, but it doesn't matter if we fail – there is no obligation to have thumbnail files available on the server. Instead, we'll just make sure later that once we've downloaded the image for a particular URL, we pass it in to the setThumb() method of the matching ThumbnailBox, and a thumbnail will then be available.

```
public static ThumbnailBox getThumbnail(URL location) {
  ThumbnailBox thumb = (ThumbnailBox) thumbs.get(location);

  if (thumb == null) {
    thumb = new ThumbnailBox(location);
    try {
      URL thumbnailFile = new URL(location,
                                  location.getFile()
                                  + THUMBNAIL_EXTENSION);
      BufferedImage bi = PhotoViewer.getImage(thumbnailFile);
      thumb.setThumb(bi);
    } catch (IOException e) {
      // no problem - thumbnail file did not exist, so a blank
      // icon is in place
    }
    thumbs.put(location, thumb);
  }
  return thumb;
}
```

This next method is used throughout the application whenever images are needed. It takes a URL as an argument, and returns a BufferedImage.

Basically, this wraps a similar method on the ImageIO class, but it enforces a couple of important policies.

Firstly, it explicitly tells the Image I/O system to use a MemoryCacheImageInputStream. The default is generally to use a FileCacheImageInputStream, which requires the program to create a temporary local file in order to store data while decoding it into a form that fits in a BufferedImage object. Unfortunately, in the JNLP environment, creating files on the client is frowned upon, and a SecurityException is thrown if you try. Using a memory cache avoids this problem, although it does increase the memory requirements of the application.

Secondly, this method checks to see if this image is one for which we don't yet have a thumbnail. If we don't, and there is a thumbnail component registered waiting for one, then the full-sized image is passed to it for use as a thumbnail.

```
public static BufferedImage getImage(URL location)
  throws IOException {
    InputStream imageSource = location.openStream();
    ImageInputStream iis =
      new MemoryCacheImageInputStream(imageSource);
    BufferedImage bi = ImageIO.read(iis);

    ThumbnailBox thumb = (ThumbnailBox) thumbs.get(location);
    if (thumb != null) {
      if (!thumb.hasThumbnail()) {
        thumb.setThumb(bi);
      }
    }
    return bi;
}
```

Finally, we implement the one method we need to employ as a window listener. We are interested in window close events, because we want to remove any related resources from our global hash-tables. Failing to do so would be a great way to run out of RAM, since for the duration of the time we maintain a reference to a `BufferedImage`, it's going to stay with us.

```
public void windowClosed(WindowEvent e) {
    Window w = e.getWindow();

    if (w instanceof PhotoFrame) {
      Iterator i = photos.keySet().iterator();
      while (i.hasNext()) {
        if (photos.get(i.next()) == w) {
          i.remove();
        }
      }
    } else if (w instanceof PhotoBrowser) {
      Iterator i = browsers.keySet().iterator();
      while (i.hasNext()) {
        if (browsers.get(i.next()) == w) {
          i.remove();
          PhotoBrowser pb    = (PhotoBrowser) w;
          Component[] comps = pb.getContentPane().getComponents();
          Object[] urls      = thumbs.keySet().toArray();
          for (int a = 0; a < comps.length; a++) {
            for (int b = 0; b < urls.length; b++) {
```

```
            if (thumbs.get(urls[b]) == comps[a]) {
              thumbs.remove(urls[b]);
            }
          }
        }
      }
    }
```

We also check to see when the last browser is closed, and tidy up completely so we can shut down safely.

```
    if (browsers.size() == 0) {
      Iterator k = photos.keySet().iterator();
      while (k.hasNext()) {
        PhotoFrame pf = (PhotoFrame) photos.get(k.next());
        pf.hide();
        pf.dispose();
      }
      System.exit(0);
    }
  }
 }
}
```

That's it for the main class. Now, let's look at the `ThumbnailBox` class.

ThumbnailBox

`ThumbnailBox` is a vertically arranged box, containing two things: a label with the name of the file in it, and a button with an icon in it. There are two kinds of icon, both of which we've defined as inner classes, blank icons, and thumbnail icons. Clicking the button will lead to the picture being displayed.

```
package com.wrox.rapid.j2se.photoview;

import javax.swing.*;
import java.awt.*;
import java.awt.image.*;
import java.awt.event.*;
import java.io.*;
import javax.imageio.*;
import java.util.*;
import java.net.*;

public class ThumbnailBox extends Box {

  private ThumbnailBox theBox;    // for inner class
```

```
private BufferedImage thumb;
private JButton openButton;

private boolean hasImage = false;

private URL url;
```

A `ThumbnailBox` is tied directly to the URL of the file it represents, so it is a `URL` that is required as a constructor argument:

```
public ThumbnailBox(final URL source) {
  super(BoxLayout.Y_AXIS);

  theBox = this;
  Icon thumbnail = null;
  url = source;

  thumbnail = new BlankIcon();

  JLabel nameLabel =
    new JLabel(source.getFile(), SwingConstants.LEFT);
  openButton = new JButton(thumbnail);
  openButton.addActionListener(new ActionListener() {
    public void actionPerformed(ActionEvent ae) {
      PhotoViewer.showPhoto(source);
    }
  });

  add(nameLabel);
  add(Box.createVerticalStrut(3));
  add(openButton);
}
```

The button is set up with a simple action-event handler, since it hands over the creation and showing of the photo to the `PictureViewer`'s static method.

The following methods allow us to change and view the properties of a thumbnail box once it has been created – most importantly, to set the thumbnail image:

```
public BufferedImage getThumb() {
  return thumb;
}

public void setThumb(BufferedImage bi) {
  thumb = bi;
```

```
    openButton.setIcon(new ThumbnailIcon());
    hasImage = true;
  }

  public boolean hasThumbnail() {
    return hasImage;
  }

  public URL getURL() {
    return url;
  }
```

The inner class `ThumbnailIcon` is used to define a thumbnail image and implements the `Icon` interface – a general-purpose image-drawing interface in Swing.

We define the maximum height and width that a thumbnail can be with constants, but we'll have to calculate a height and width for the icon to be displayed at so the icon fits in this space, but maintains the correct aspect ratio. That's what the `getImageHeight()` and `getImageWidth()` methods below do:

```
  private class ThumbnailIcon implements Icon {

    private static final int MAX_WIDTH = 100;
    private static final int MAX_HEIGHT = 100;

    public int getIconHeight() {
      return MAX_HEIGHT;
    }

    public int getIconWidth() {
      return MAX_WIDTH;
    }

    public int getImageHeight() {
      double height = thumb.getHeight();
      double width  = thumb.getWidth();
      double aspect = width / height;
      if (width > MAX_WIDTH) {
        width  = MAX_WIDTH;
        height = width / aspect;
      }
      if (height > MAX_HEIGHT) {
        height = MAX_HEIGHT;
      }
      return (int) height;
```

```
  }

  public int getImageWidth() {
    double height = thumb.getHeight();
    double width = thumb.getWidth();
    double aspect = width / height;
    if (height > MAX_HEIGHT) {
      height = MAX_HEIGHT;
      width = height * aspect;
    }
    if (width > MAX_WIDTH) {
      width = MAX_WIDTH;
    }
    return (int) width;
  }

  public void paintIcon(Component c, Graphics g, int x, int y) {
    int width      = getImageWidth();
    int height     = getImageHeight();
    int topBorder  = (int) ((MAX_HEIGHT - height) / 2);
    int leftBorder = (int) ((MAX_WIDTH - width) / 2);
    g.drawImage(thumb, x + leftBorder, y + topBorder,
                width, height, theBox);
    g.draw3DRect(x + leftBorder, y + topBorder,
                 width, height, false);
  }
}
```

BlankIcon is a much-simplified version of the previous class. It has a lot less to worry about:

```
private class BlankIcon implements Icon {

  private static final int WIDTH = 100;
  private static final int HEIGHT = 100;

  public int getIconHeight() {
    return HEIGHT;
  }

  public int getIconWidth() {
    return WIDTH;
  }

  public void paintIcon(Component c, Graphics g, int x, int y) {
    // nothing to paint
```

```
    }
  }
}
```

PhotoBrowser

`PhotoBrowser` represents a directory on the server, and presents a thumbnail for each image specified in the `pv_index.txt` file. It also has a **File** menu, which presents a list of any other directories that were listed in the index file.

The layout is a simple flow-layout; the thumbnails are laid out from left to right until the edge of the window is reached, then a new row is started, and so on. This approach makes perfect sense for this sort of data.

```
package com.wrox.rapid.j2se.photoview;

import javax.swing.*;
import java.awt.*;
import java.awt.image.*;
import java.awt.event.*;
import java.io.*;
import javax.imageio.*;
import java.util.*;
import java.net.*;

public class PhotoBrowser extends JFrame {

  private PhotoBrowser theBrowser;    // for inner classes

  public PhotoBrowser(URL root, java.util.List images) {
    theBrowser = this;
    setTitle(root.getPath() + " on " + root.getHost());
    BrowserMenu menuBar = new BrowserMenu();
    setJMenuBar(menuBar);

    getContentPane().setLayout(new FlowLayout(FlowLayout.LEFT));
```

Having configured the window, our next job is to iterate through the list of data parsed out of the index file, and build the appropriate component for each one. If it is a file, then the component is a thumbnail. If it is a directory, it is an item in the **File** menu.

```
    Iterator i = images.iterator();
    while (i.hasNext()) {
      try {
        URL location = (URL) i.next();
```

```
        if (location.toString().endsWith("/")) {
          // directory
          menuBar.addLink(location);
        } else {
          // file
          getContentPane().add(PhotoViewer.getThumbnail(location));
        }
      } catch (Exception e) {
        e.printStackTrace();
      }
    }
    pack();
  }
```

The menu is quite simple: it is initialized with a close item, and then a separator. The URLs to connect to other folders are initialized by a separate method call.

```
  private class BrowserMenu extends JMenuBar {

    private JMenu fileMenu = new JMenu("File");

    public BrowserMenu() {
      JMenuItem closeMenuItem = new JMenuItem("Close");
      closeMenuItem.addActionListener(new ActionListener() {
        public void actionPerformed(ActionEvent ae) {
          theBrowser.hide();
          theBrowser.dispose();
        }
      });
      fileMenu.add(closeMenuItem);
      fileMenu.insertSeparator(1);

      add(fileMenu);
    }
```

In order to launch a new browser, again, this method calls the static `showBrowser()` method of the `PhotoViewer` class.

```
    public void addLink(final URL link) {
      JMenuItem item = new JMenuItem(link.toString());
      item.addActionListener(new ActionListener() {
        public void actionPerformed(ActionEvent ae) {
          PhotoViewer.showBrowser(link);
        }
      });
      fileMenu.add(item);
```

```
    }
  }
}
```

PhotoPanel

The `PhotoPanel` class is a specially implemented `JPanel` subclass, designed purely to display images. It will scale images down to fit within the panel's size, but will always maintain the correct aspect ratio.

When a `PhotoPanel` is created for the first time, it calls the `getImage()` method, calling for a download of the image to be made:

```
package com.wrox.rapid.j2se.photoview;

import javax.swing.*;
import java.awt.*;
import java.awt.image.*;
import java.io.*;
import javax.imageio.*;
import java.util.*;
import java.net.*;
import javax.jnlp.*;

public class PhotoPanel extends JPanel {

  private BufferedImage photo;

  public PhotoPanel(URL location) {

    try {
      photo = PhotoViewer.getImage(location);
    } catch (Exception e) {
      e.printStackTrace();
    }
  }

  public BufferedImage getImage() {
    return photo;
  }

  public Dimension getPhotoSize() {
    return new Dimension(photo.getWidth(), photo.getHeight());
  }

  public void paint(Graphics g) {
```

```
    super.paint(g);
    double spaceWidth  = getWidth();
    double spaceHeight = getHeight();
    double height      = photo.getHeight();
    double width       = photo.getWidth();
    double aspect      = width / height;

    if (height > spaceHeight) {
      height = spaceHeight;
      width  = height * aspect;
    }
    if (width > spaceWidth) {
      width  = spaceWidth;
      height = width / aspect;
    }
    int horizSpace = (int) ((spaceWidth - width) / 2);
    int vertSpace  = (int) ((spaceHeight - height) / 2);
    g.drawImage(photo, horizSpace, vertSpace,
                (int) width, (int) height, this);
  }
}
```

PhotoFrame

The `PhotoFrame` class is a `JFrame` with a menubar, and a content pane set to be a `PhotoPanel`. The menu contains two options: Close, and Save....

```
package com.wrox.rapid.j2se.photoview;

import javax.swing.*;
import java.awt.*;
import java.awt.image.*;
import java.awt.event.*;
import java.io.*;
import javax.imageio.*;
import javax.imageio.stream.*;
import java.util.*;
import java.net.*;
import javax.jnlp.*;

public class PhotoFrame extends JFrame {

  private PhotoFrame theFrame;
  private String filename;
  private PhotoPanel photo;
```

When a PhotoFrame is created, it sets its title, stores away the filename, and configures a menubar. Then, it initializes a PhotoPanel, which as we said before always initiates an image download (remember that initiating an image download can have the side effect of populating the image's thumbnail).

```
public PhotoFrame(URL source) {
  setTitle(source.getPath() + " on " + source.getHost());
  filename = source.getPath();
  theFrame = this;
  setJMenuBar(new PhotoMenu());
  photo = new PhotoPanel(source);
  setContentPane(photo);
  setSize(photo.getPhotoSize());
}

public BufferedImage getImage() {
  return photo.getImage();
}
```

Now we have to define the menubar that's going to go on each window:

```
private class PhotoMenu extends JMenuBar {

  private JMenu fileMenu = new JMenu("File");

  public PhotoMenu() {
    JMenuItem saveMenuItem = new JMenuItem("Save...");
```

The following section is probably the most interesting part; it sets up the ActionListener for the **Save** menu item.

The save operation is performed via the JNLP FileSaveService's saveFileDialog() method, which has the following full signature:

```
public FileContents saveFileDialog(java.lang.String pathHint,
                                   java.lang.String[] extensions,
                                   java.io.InputStream stream,
                                   java.lang.String name)
                                   throws java.io.IOException
```

The parameters of the method are:

- pathHint – A hint from the application to the default directory to be used, which the JNLP client is free to ignore
- extensions – A list of default extensions (for example, txt, java) to show in the file chooser, which might be ignored by the JNLP client.
- stream – The contents of the file to save, represented as an InputStream

4 Clients and GUIs

- `name` – The suggested filename, which might be ignored by the JNLP client, and can anyway be overridden by the user.

The `stream` parameter is probably not the most helpful aspect of the JNLP API. Most of the time, if we have some data, and we want to write it out, we expect to do so by calling write operations on an `OutputStream`, pushing data down a pipe to a file. In this case, however, the JNLP client wants you to hand it an `InputStream` so that it can call read operations in order to pull data *out* of your program, and subsequently write it to a file.

Byte array streams are one great solution to this problem. The NIO buffers and channels, while capable of solving this problem, all seem a bit heavyweight, especially when we're trying to work between, on the one hand, the Image I/O API which wants to write data to an `OutputStream`, and on the other the JNLP API, which wants to read it from an `InputStream`. Even though these fantastic facilities we saw in Chapter 2 would be perfect for solving this problem, they would at the same time obfuscate the code beyond recognition.

So, we use the old-fashioned `ByteArrayOutputStream` to allow Image I/O to write out its data to a buffer. We use the statement, `ImageIO.write(photo.getImage(), "jpeg", imageOut)`, which takes our buffered image, and writes it to our byte buffer as a JPEG. You could also opt for GIF or PNG, and both formats would be supported by the J2SE 1.4 distribution (implementing a dialog box to let the user choose between these formats is left as an exercise for the reader). Then, we create a `ByteArrayInputStream` from the byte array created by our output operation, and give it to the JNLP environment.

At this point, a save dialog will open, and the user will be asked to choose a file to save to.

```
saveMenuItem.addActionListener(new ActionListener() {
  public void actionPerformed(ActionEvent ae) {
    try {
      ByteArrayOutputStream buffer =
         new ByteArrayOutputStream();
      ImageOutputStream imageOut =
        new MemoryCacheImageOutputStream(buffer);
      ImageIO.write(photo.getImage(), "jpeg", imageOut);
      byte[] bytes = buffer.toByteArray();
      ByteArrayInputStream imageStream =
        new ByteArrayInputStream(bytes);
      try {
        FileSaveService fss =
          (FileSaveService) ServiceManager
            .lookup("javax.jnlp.FileSaveService");
        fss.saveFileDialog("", new String[] { "jpg" },
                           imageStream, filename);
      } catch (Exception e) {
```

```
            System.out.println("JNLP failed to save");
          }
        } catch (Exception e) {
          e.printStackTrace();
        }
      }
    });
    fileMenu.add(saveMenuItem);
    fileMenu.insertSeparator(1);
```

By comparison, closing the window is simple. Calling `dispose()` frees up some of the resources associated with the window immediately, but doesn't guarantee all the resources will be cleaned up. But it also has the side effect of causing a window-close event to be fired, which is caught by our window-close handling code in the `PhotoViewer` class. This will dispose of any lingering references to this object, so that it can be garbage-collected, along with its image buffer.

```
    JMenuItem closeMenuItem = new JMenuItem("Close");
    closeMenuItem.addActionListener(new ActionListener() {
      public void actionPerformed(ActionEvent ae) {
        theFrame.hide();
        theFrame.dispose();
      }
    });
    fileMenu.add(closeMenuItem);
    add(fileMenu);
  }
 }
}
```

And that's actually the complete application. All that remains is to compile it, JAR it, and deploy it to a web server. The compilation step is as follows:

```
> javac -classpath %JNLP_HOME%\jnlp.jar; .
  com\wrox\rapid\j2se\photoview\*.java

> jar cvf photoview.jar
  com\wrox\rapid\j2se\photoview\*.class
```

Remember, you need the JNLP class files on your `classpath`, so either the `jnlp.jar` or `javaws.jar` file should be included.

Now, we need to set up a web site to host our application. This requires a web server. Any such server will do: Apache, Microsoft IIS or PWS, Jakarta Tomcat, or whatever other server you prefer. Almost any web server serves files from a particular directory on the filesystem, which we call the document root. For example, Microsoft servers use the folder `C:\inetpub\wwwroot` by default, Apache uses a directory called `htdocs` (although where it is mounted will vary from installation to installation), and Tomcat has a directory under its root directory called `webapps\ROOT`.

I'm going to pretend I'm setting this application up on a server called rapid.wrox.com, and in a directory called j2se/photoview/ under the web server root. That means I need to put the JAR file in the j2se/photoview directory under the web server document root, together with photoview.jnlp, the JNLP file we looked at earlier:

```
<?xml version="1.0" encoding="UTF-8"?>
<jnlp codebase="http://rapid.wrox.com/j2se/photoview/">
  <information>
    <title>PhotoView</title>
    <vendor>Wrox Press - J2SE 1.4</vendor>
    <icon href="PhotoView.jpg"/>
  </information>

  <resources>
    <j2se version="1.4.0+"/>
    <jar href="photoview.jar"/>
  </resources>

  <application-desc main-
class="com.wrox.rapid.j2se.photoview.PhotoViewer"/>
</jnlp>
```

I also need to include an icon, PhotoView.jpg, which will be displayed during the download by the Web Start client.

We're specifying that the JRE version must be 1.4.0+ (that is, 1.4.0 or later. If you're still running a pre-release version, such as 1.4.0-beta-b65, or 1.4.0-rc, they are counted as preceding 1.4.0, so you'll have to specify the version in full, explicitly, as it is stated when you run java -version at the command prompt.), because we used the Image I/O API that's only present in the current version.

In addition, we need an HTML page that hyperlinks to the JNLP file. index.html might look like this:

```
<html>
  <head>
    <title>J2SE 1.4 - Photo Viewer</title>
  </head>
  <body>
    <h1>Photo Viewer</h1>
    <img src="PhotoView.jpg"/>
    <a href="photoview.jnlp">Launch!</a>
  </body>
</html>
```

And that's it. All that remains is to add a pv_index.txt file and some images (don't forget to generate and add thumbnails for a couple, as well). The web site structure might look like this:

```
j2se/
  photoview/
    PhotoView.jpg
    photoview.jar
    photoview.jnlp
    index.html
    pv_index.txt
    m_street.jpg
    s_frisco.jpg
    S_frisco.jpg.thumb.jpg
    s_ggbridge.jpg
    s_ggbridge.jpg.thumb.jpg
    s_hill.jpg
    s_streets.jpg
```

With `pv_index.txt` containing:

```
m_street.jpg
s_frisco.jpg
s_ggbridge.jpg
s_hill.jpg
s_streets.jpg
```


Now, to run this application, I would navigate to http://rapid.wrox.com/j2se/photoview/ (you need to navigate to the appropriate URL you've deployed to – change the server name and path appropriately). You need to use the web browser on the machine you have Web Start running on, click the hyperlink, and the application will launch:

Trusted Execution

Let's look at how we would go about getting a JNLP application a trusted execution environment, which would enable us too use the full range of J2SE APIs without running into the security manager.

The first rule of JNLP is that you can't get a trusted environment unless your JAR files are signed. This might seem inconvenient, but it makes sense. If you receive an unsigned JAR over a network connection, even though you may think it comes from a reputable source, you have no way of knowing that it wasn't tampered with on the way, or created by someone else entirely. So, signed JARs are a pre-requisite. Obviously, if you sign the JAR with a key that has a certificate chain all the way up to a root certificate (such as the root certificates stored in the `cacerts`, certification authority certificates, keystore that ships with Java and Web Start) then anyone downloading your application can be certain that the code was created by you, and hasn't been altered since.

You can self-certify though, which doesn't provide as strong a guarantee as a certificate chain, but if you know someone, it should be adequate. As we saw in Chapter 3, keys generated with Java's `keytool` are also self-certified certificates. We can use them to sign JAR files with.

To set yourself up to self-certify JAR files, you first need a keystore and a public-private key pair, like the ones we used in the last chapter:

```
> keytool -genkey -alias jnlp-cert -keystore jnlp.key
```

This tells the `keytool` to generate a key (`genkey`) called `jnlp-cert`, in the keystore `jnlp.key`. If `jnlp.key` doesn't exist, it will be created. After a few questions (as we saw before), and a short time, the command will complete, and the keystore now contains a certificate. You can examine it using this command:

```
> keytool -list -v -alias jnlp-cert -keystore jnlp.key
Enter keystore password:  passwd
Alias name: jnlp-cert
Creation date: 27-Feb-2002
Entry type: keyEntry
Certificate chain length: 1
Certificate[1]:
Owner: CN=James Hart, OU=Rapid, O=Wrox Press, L=Birmingham, ST=West
Midlands, C=uk
Issuer: CN=James Hart, OU=Rapid, O=Wrox Press, L=Birmingham, ST=West
Midlands, C=uk
Serial number: 3c7d0821
Valid from: Wed Feb 27 16:24:01 GMT 2002 until: Tue May 28 17:24:01
BST 2002
Certificate fingerprints:
         MD5:  47:B4:8E:EB:C1:2D:C2:DC:E8:F8:B4:94:57:A1:1E:CA
         SHA1: 94:E9:21:10:D1:44:E3:7E:85:7D:13:86:25:F5:03:3D:
               79:36:C7:66
```

You can export this into a public certificate file:

```
> keytool -export -file jnlp.cer -alias jnlp-cert -keystore jnlp.key
Enter keystore password:  passwd
Certificate stored in file <jnlp.cer>
```

This file, `jnlp.cer`, can then be distributed to other people so they can use it to verify that JNLP applications signed with your private key are genuinely from you. The two sets of fingerprints on the above listing, which should distinguish your certificate from almost any other, will be obtainable from the certificate file, so if someone has received your certificate and wishes to verify that it's really yours, they can speak to you by telephone, or some other means, to confirm that the fingerprint on the certificate they have matches your original certificate's fingerprint. Within an organization, such as a corporate intranet, this is a great low-hassle means to set up clients to access trusted JNLP applications.

If they decide they trust you, they can place the certificate in the `cacerts` file of the Java Web Start directory. This is done with the `import` command. The default password on Sun's `cacerts` files is `changeit`, which is not only a password, it's also good advice.

```
> keytool -import -file jnlp.cer -alias james -keystore cacerts
Enter keystore password:  wibble
Owner: CN=James Hart, OU=Rapid, O=Wrox Press, L=Birmingham, ST=West
Midlands, C=uk
Issuer: CN=James Hart, OU=Rapid, O=Wrox Press, L=Birmingham, ST=West
Midlands, C=uk
Serial number: 3c7d0821
Valid from: Wed Feb 27 16:24:01 GMT 2002 until: Tue May 28 17:24:01 BST
2002
Certificate fingerprints:
         MD5:  47:B4:8E:EB:C1:2D:C2:DC:E8:F8:B4:94:57:A1:1E:CA
         SHA1: 94:E9:21:10:D1:44:E3:7E:85:7D:13:86:25:F5:03:3D:
               79:36:C7:66
Trust this certificate? [no]:  y
Certificate was added to keystore
```

Any JAR file signed using your self-certified key will now be considered just as trustworthy as one signed by a key certified by a reputable certificate authority.

Now, this is not to say that you have to distribute a public certificate to everybody who will use your JNLP application, only that in order for them to trust you, they may need to establish your identity, and one way to do so is through certificate distribution.

However, it is possible to allow a signed (but not certified trustworthy) JAR file unrestricted access to your system through JNLP – you simply have to agree to a dialog box.

You can sign JAR files using a certificate you've created using the `jarsigner` tool:

```
> jarsigner -keystore jnlp.key -signedjar trustedphotoview.jar
  photoview.jar jnlp-cert
Enter Passphrase for keystore: passwd
```

We specify the keystore containing our certificate, the filename we want to give the signed JAR file, the name of the JAR we want to sign, and the name of the key we want to use.

Now, if we make a change to the JNLP file and request full access to the client system:

```
<?xml version="1.0" encoding="UTF-8"?>
<jnlp codebase=" http://rapid.wrox.com/j2se/photoview/">
  <information>
    <title>PhotoView</title>
    <vendor>Wrox Press - J2SE 1.4</vendor>
    <icon href="PhotoView.jpg"/>
  </information>
  <security>
    <all-permissions/>
  </security>
  <resources>
    <j2se version="1.4.0+"/>
    <jar href="photoview.jar"/>
  </resources>
  <application-desc
    main-
class="com.wrox.rapid.j2se.photoview.PhotoViewer"/>
</jnlp>
```

When we access the application using Java Web Start, we see this screen:

The warnings are less severe (but still there) if a trusted certificate is used:

If I'd had my certificate signed by a genuine root CA, then you'd see their name in the dialog vouching for my identity. If, in either case, the user hits the Start button, the application gets full local access, as if it were run from the command line.

Conclusions

Java as a GUI and client development platform just keeps getting better. The support of complex frameworks like volatile memory, drag-and-drop, and Image I/O, help us achieve things that were extremely hazardous before. But the crowning achievement of this J2SE release may well yet turn out to be JNLP. By offering a rich user experience, and a breadth of choice to developers, it could well become an extremely widespread, networked deployment platform for the Internet, in exactly the same way that applets haven't. JNLP already ships as standard with Apple's Mac OS X (albeit running on J2SE 1.3.1 at the moment).

Getting a head start over Microsoft's planned .NET software rental model in this way is probably a shrewd move by Sun. With Microsoft concentrating on getting the server-side of its .NET Framework in place, and the client vision slipping further and further down the roadmap, this is one of the few chances Sun will ever have to win some desktop mindshare. By minimizing the hassle of installation and upgrades, JNLP could be a key enabling component for this, and it would be great to see a really powerful application deploy across JNLP – something like StarOffice, or NetBeans. That would really demonstrate some of the power that's in JNLP, and help kick start people's interest.

Java J2SE 1.4 Core Platform Update

XML

XML is almost certainly the biggest thing to happen to programming since the Web. It is revolutionizing the way people think about data, about networked applications, and about architectures, which, for something that started out as a plain-text markup language, is pretty impressive. Its success is built on the Internet, on the Web, and on ubiquitous and powerful computer technology. That sounds a lot like the basis on which Java was created, and sure enough, Java and XML do share a lot of similar goals. XML is cross-platform, universal data; Java is cross-platform, universal code. Are they a natural match then? Well, as we'll see, until now, that's not quite been true. Certainly, looking into the future, it's clear that XML will play an increasingly important role in the Java platform. This, then, is the first step down a long road.

In this chapter, we'll begin by looking briefly at what we can accomplish with XML, before moving on to describe the three primary functions JAXP provides: XML parsing, XML document creation, and XSLT transformation.

XML Applications

We're not going to explain in detail what XML is and what it's for here. Good introductions can be found on the web, and in books, and there's no point rehashing the basics. We've all encountered XML data in one form or another – here's a sample that we'll be using later in this chapter:

```
<?xml version="1.0" encoding="UTF-8"?>

<song writer="trad" title="Happy Birthday">
  <verse>
    <line>Happy birthday to you,</line>
    <line>Happy birthday to you,</line>
```

```
    <line>Happy birthday dear [name],</line>
    <line>Happy birthday to you.</line>
  </verse>
</song>
```

XML syntax is very intuitive, and easy for humans to read and write. Its power lies in the fact that it's also easy for computers to read. The purpose of XML is to use tags to describe structure within data, so obviously, what we have here is a song, containing a verse, containing four lines, the text of which is given in the file. There's also metadata about the song – we can see that the song is traditional (it has a writer attribute set to `trad`), and its title is `Happy Birthday`.

If we had a lot of similar files, all containing different songs, we could, perhaps, use them to create a repository of song lyrics on the Internet. We'd want to be able to easily access the `writer` and `title` attributes of each such song, so we could build a database people could use to search through our archive. We'd also need some way to extract the lines from the file, and format them using HTML. And this is where XML programming comes in. Using an XML parser, and other XML processing tools, we can develop applications quickly and easily to extract and handle data from XML documents. Using **XSLT** (the **Extensible Stylesheet Language for Transformations**), we can take data from an XML document and systematically format it as a new document.

You can store data in a file system in XML format, and use it as a data repository – like a directory or database. Or you can stream data formatted using XML across a network, so that a remote computer can process the data. XML has applications in persistence, in data storage and processing, and in communication and networking. The most significant current XML application is as the key enabling technology in web services architecture. Web services revolve around writing programs that interact entirely via XML data over the network. A program might receive an XML document, interpret its contents, take some action, and return another XML document to the originator containing the results of its actions. A whole framework is being developed that will enable applications to find a web service that can perform a particular task, learn how to communicate with that service, and then use the service, on the fly, as and when it is required.

Terminology

The following table defines the XML terminology we'll be using in this chapter, so that we can be clear that when we say "tag", we are talking about something distinct from an "element".

Term	Definition
Tag	An XML tag contains metadata about the content of an XML document. It consists of an open angle bracket, some data, and then a closing angle bracket. Opening tags look like this `<...>`, and closing tags look like this `</...>`. The opening and closing tag of an element both begin with the element's name. The opening tag may optionally contain attributes. There is a shorthand notation for an empty element (one with no content between the opening and closing tags), which uses a single tag, `<.../>`.

Term	Definition
Element	An XML element consists of an opening tag, the attributes contained in the opening tag, all the content between the opening tag and the closing tag, and the closing tag itself. Elements have two types of data: attributes and content. The content can be character data, other elements, or a mixture of both. If an element has no content, it can be written using the special empty element syntax.
Attribute	An attribute is a name-value pair, specified in the opening tag of an element.
Namespace	XML uses human-readable names for elements and attributes. This means that there are likely to be several different uses in different XML documents for the same words, such as "address" or "name". A namespace allows an XML document author to specify that when they use the word "address", they mean it in one particular sense, globally uniquely identified. A namespace is identified by a URI (Universal Resource Identifier) and the author simply uses this to declare that, within a certain document (or part of a document), names belonging to a particular namespace will be prefixed by a specified string called the **namespace prefix**. Prefixed names can then be interpreted correctly as belonging to a particular namespace, enabling a processing program to distinguish between two different kinds of "address" element. Alternatively, a default namespace can be declared for an element, and any un-prefixed names within that element or its content will be interpreted as belonging to that namespace.
DTD	A Document Type Definition is a set of definitions of element names, detailing what kinds of data are permitted in elements with that name. It can also declare entities. A particular document has either zero or one DTD, which may consist of an internal and/or an external subset. The internal subset consists of any declarations included in the document. The external subset consists of any declarations that were made in a separate file identified as containing DTD information. DTDs can contain `ELEMENT`, `ATTLIST` (attribute list), `ENTITY`, and `NOTATION` declarations. They may also contain references to parameter entities, which will be expanded and treated as a part of the DTD.
Schema	A Schema is, in general, any document that defines an XML vocabulary, such as a DTD. More specifically, this term is usually used to refer to a W3C Schema document, which conforms to an XML schema language defined by the W3C. The W3C Schema language specifies a more rigorous way of describing what content is allowed within an XML document than the DTD specification allows – it supports data typing so, for example, it allows you to restrict elements to contain only numerical data. An XML parser may provide W3C Schema support, but JAXP does not require the underlying parser to understand W3C Schema, only DTDs. Indeed, Crimson, the default JAXP parser, does not support W3C Schema.

Table continued on following page

Term	Definition
Entity	An entity is a shorthand notation, declared in a DTD, which when used in an XML document is interpreted by the parser, and replaced with a particular piece of data. Entities can be internal (completely defined by the declaration in the DTD) or external (contained in a resource identified by the DTD declaration). External entities can be either parsed (the entity can be referenced in the body of an XML document, and when it encounters such a reference, the parser should obtain the content of the entity and substitute it into the document), or unparsed (the entity can only be referenced from an attribute declared in a DTD to be of type `ENTITY`, and the parser should not attempt to load the entity anyway). There are also parameter entities, which are declarations of entities that can be used inside DTD definitions. Entities are generally expanded by the parser, and the process is transparent to the application that called the parser. The only exception is with external entities, where the parser may sometimes not be able to locate the entity, or may need more information to do so, for example if the entity is indicated with a relative URI.
Well-formedness	An XML document must conform to the basic criteria of being well-formed – it must begin with an XML declaration (`<?xml version="1.0" encoding="UTF-8"?>`) and contain exactly one root element. All elements must be correctly opened and terminated with a closing tag, and they must be properly nested within one another (you can't write `<a><b></a></b>` – only `<a><b></b></a>`. Attribute values must all be enclosed in quotation marks (either single or double).
Validity	An XML document is valid if, in addition to being well-formed, it has a DTD, and its elements all conform to the content model described by that DTD.
Schema-validity	An XML document is schema-valid if, in addition to being well-formed, it has a valid W3C schema, and its elements all conform to the content-model described by that schema.

XML Parsing

XML parsers serve one principal purpose: to read an XML document and present the data it contains in a manner that we can use programmatically. They handle the syntax of XML documents (all those angle-brackets and attribute declarations), resolve entity references within the XML, and perform whatever validation they support, and we request from them. This means we can delegate the task of understanding the complexities of XML syntax to a specialist piece of software, rather than having to code our own.

Two APIs are widely used to access the functionality of XML parsers: **SAX** and **DOM**.

SAX

The **Simple API for XML** is an event-driven API. By "event-driven", we mean that it uses callbacks or event notifications to tell our application what it is doing. As is typical for such an architecture, we have to create event-handling objects and pass them to the event generator in order to register our interest in hearing about certain events.

SAX defines an interface, `XMLReader`, which represents the parser itself. Then, there is a set of interfaces – `ContentHandler`, `DTDHandler`, `EntityResolver`, and `ErrorHandler` – that we implement and pass instances of to the `XMLReader`. When we subsequently call the `XMLReader`'s `parse()` method, specifying a document to read, the parser calls methods on our implementations of the handler objects. This allows our code to respond to the different events the parser encounters while reading the document.

SAX was developed as a standard parser API by David Megginson and the members of the `xml-dev` mailing list (now hosted at http://www.xml.org/xml/xmldev.shtml). They wanted to develop a way of interacting with XML at the lowest level. Proposals were underway for systems that would represent the structure of an XML document as an in-memory object graph, but the SAX discussions were focused on producing a lightweight standard, perhaps one that could serve as a basis for these heavier proposals that were being developed. DOM, the second API we'll be looking at, is the most standardized result of these heavyweight efforts.

The SAX interfaces are contained in the `org.xml.sax` package and its sub-packages. You can find out more about SAX at http://www.saxproject.org.

DOM

The **Document Object Model** is derived ultimately from the document manipulation features of DHTML. When the W3C was working on DHTML, a way of presenting the structure of the HTML document to scripts within the page was required. DOM is, ultimately, the result of this effort, subsequently adapted from HTML to generic XML applications. DOM presents an in-memory object graph, with each object representing a part of the XML document that the DOM models. DOM parsers will typically offer a method that takes a file as an argument, and returns a complete DOM `Document` object graph. This will consist of objects belonging to classes specific to the parser, but which implement the interfaces defined in the W3C DOM specification. We can then read and manipulate the data in the objects via the methods in those interfaces.

DOM is a large and complex standard, and although that doesn't mean it's hard to use, it does place a lot of demands on parsers. It also requires that a complete document be read into memory and turned into objects before we can even get at the first bit of it. So for some applications, it is extremely unwieldy. However, for many purposes, having the entire document in memory is a necessary step – for example, when performing complex transformation operations on the document. DOM representations of XML data also provide a convenient way to pass around an XML data structure within our code *without* having to write it out as XML, then parse it back in again.

XML in J2SE 1.4

The 1.4 release of the Java 2 Platform, Standard Edition, incorporates XML support for the first time. A compliant implementation of the J2SE must now provide an **XML parser** and an **XSLT transformation engine**, so Java code deployed to the 1.4 Platform will be able to rely on XML support being in place. This is a major improvement for applications such as applets, which in the past had been forced to include such tools in their download, increasing the size of the applet considerably. It is also important in server-side Java, in that it mandates the Java run-time environment to provide an XML parser, rather than leaving the ambiguous situation that, for example, J2EE 1.2 is currently in with some application servers providing XML parsers, and others requiring individual applications to supply their own.

Significantly, the API that the J2SE provides for accessing, parsing, and transformation functionality is the **Java API for XML Processing**, **JAXP 1.1**, about which more information can be found at http://java.sun.com/xml/xml_jaxp.html. This API is designed to provide a layer of separation between application code and parser implementations. This is necessary because, while XML parser vendors have developed standard APIs for handling XML data, they have not agreed a standard approach for accessing the parser initially. This means that the application developer must know precisely which class the application should instantiate at run time in order to access the standard APIs. Obviously, given that Java applications are meant to be written once and run anywhere, Java developers should be wary of making any assumptions about what will be present at run time beyond what is provided in the J2SE specification (or J2EE/ME, depending on the target platform, of course).

The following diagrams show the layers involved in writing an XML application without JAXP. Most parsers provide implementations of the SAX and DOM interfaces (defined, respectively, by David Megginson– http://www.megginson.com/SAX/index.html – and the members of the `xml-dev` mailing list, and the W3C, http://www.w3.org/DOM), and a parser-specific interface that is used to access these standard interfaces. In order to use SAX and DOM, the application needs to know the parser's API. Essentially, it needs to know the name of a class in the parser that has methods that can be called in order to perform a SAX or DOM parse. For example, here are the steps needed to perform a SAX parse using such a parser, in the absence of JAXP:

Figure 1

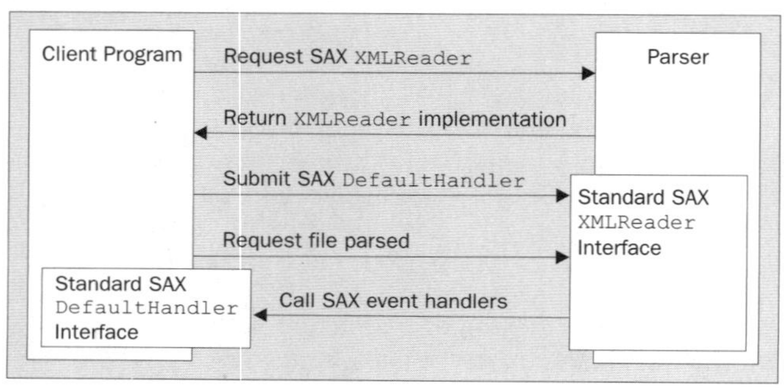

Figure 2

The first couple of steps require the use of non-standard, parser-specific APIs. Similarly, DOM parsing follows this procedure:

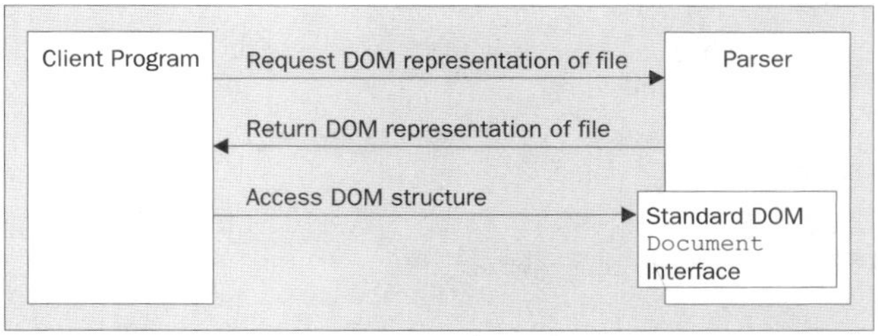

JAXP was first made available as a standard extension to the Java platform, with the intention that it would provide a means to access any JAXP-compliant parser, without making any design-time assumptions about the run-time environment. It provides a bridge that bypasses any vendor-specific access classes, allowing developers to access the standard DOM and SAX APIs without needing to know anything about the parser providing the implementation. JAXP is essentially a specification of a couple of abstract factory classes, and some interfaces, which must be implemented by a parser in order to become JAXP-compliant. In addition, JAXP mandates, and effectively incorporates, the SAX 2.0 and DOM Level 2 standards, so a JAXP-compliant parser must also implement these.

So, at design time, if we stick to using the JAXP, DOM, and SAX classes, we can be sure that at run time, whatever parser is provided by the machine to which our code is deployed, the code will still work as designed.

Figure 3 shows the layers involved in accessing SAX functionality with JAXP:

Figure 3

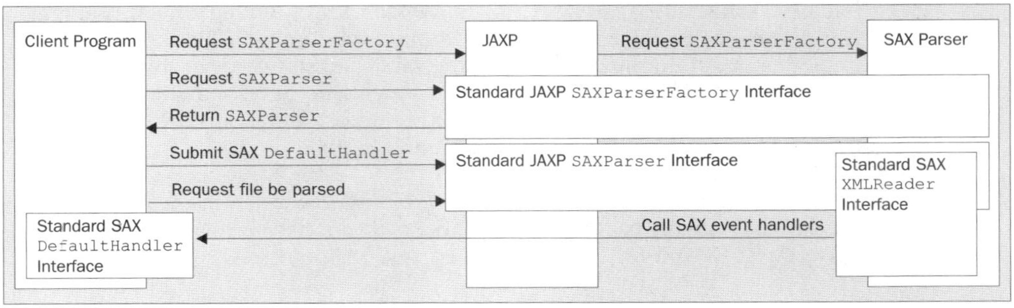

The parser now implements two standards: Dave Megginson's SAX standard, and also the Sun/Java Community Process-defined JAXP standard interface. Our application is completely isolated from the underlying parser.

Here is the equivalent process for accessing DOM functionality via the JAXP intermediary:

Figure 4

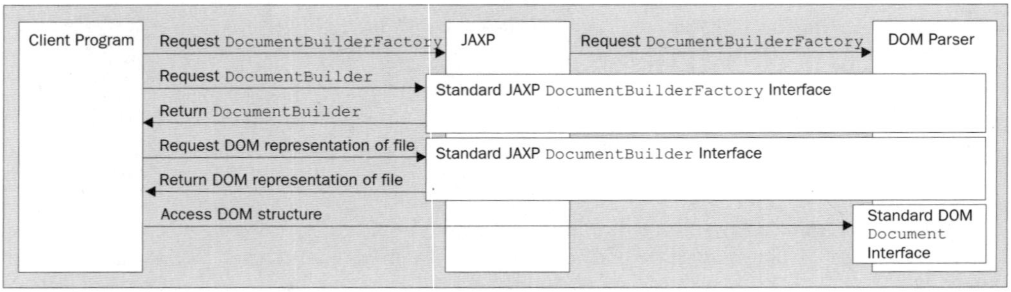

As you can see, in both cases, only one request is fired directly at JAXP. Other requests are made to objects implementing the JAXP interface, but which are in fact *provided by the underlying parser*. We'll see later how JAXP can identify and obtain a parser-specific instance of the required factory class (the step in the top-right of each of the diagrams).

The SAX classes are contained in the `org.xml.sax` package hierarchy, DOM in `org.w3c.dom` and its sub-packages, and JAXP in `javax.xml.parsers`.

JAXP 1.1 enhanced the original DOM and SAX APIs, but more importantly, introduced a new vendor-neutral API for accessing XSLT transformation engines: **TrAX** (the **Transformation API for XML**), with a similar bridging API that removes any need to know about the underlying XSLT implementation. In the absence of an established standard for this function like SAX or DOM, the TrAX interface is a welcome development, but its adoption by XSLT vendors would have been less than assured were it not for the fact that it is included in JAXP and now in J2SE 1.4.

TrAX and the JAXP classes to access it are both contained in the `javax.xml.transform` packages. This makes it harder to draw the line between TrAX and JAXP than between, say, SAX and JAXP.

In order to provide actual XML support, a J2SE 1.4-compliant runtime environment must include, as well as the JAXP, SAX, and DOM interface definitions, a JAXP-compliant parser and transformation engine. In the case of Sun's J2SE 1.4, these are **Apache Crimson** and **Apache Xalan**.

Crimson is derived from an XML parser project started at Sun by Rajiv Mordani under the codename Project X. The Project X parser was included with the JAXP 1.0 download, and supported SAX 1.0 and DOM Level 1, but JAXP 1.1 requires that parsers support SAX 2.0 and DOM Level 2. The next version of Project X, with experimental support for the enhanced functionality, was handed over to the Apache Software Foundation (ASF) as an open source project, named Crimson (http://xml.apache.org/crimson). The functionality was developed under the ASF's development process, and as a result, Crimson is now fully functional as a JAXP 1.1 parser. It now serves as Sun's reference implementation. The current version is 1.1.1, but it is version 1.1 that is included in J2SE 1.4.

The early-access release of JAXP 1.2 that is already available from Sun comes with another Apache project parser, Xerces, which originated as an IBM project called XML4J. Apache efforts are concentrated on taking the best bits from Crimson and incorporating them into Xerces, so it is likely that Crimson will wither, while Xerces will grow in terms of features and power. Xerces supports W3C Schema validation, for example, and schema support is a key feature enhancement in JAXP 1.2.

Xalan (http://xml.apache.org/xalan-j) had a similar journey, from its development at Lotus under the name LotusXSL, until it was handed over to the Apache XML Project, who renamed it. Xalan has, however, had a long development life as an open source project, and was not originally designed to work with JAXP. Like any XML transformation engine, it requires the support of an XML parser to provide it with the ability to read in documents for transformation, as well as the XSLT documents that contain transformation instructions. Originally, Xalan was tied to a specific XML parser, Xerces (because it is derived from the IBM XML4J parser that Scott Boag had used when writing LotusXSL), but Xalan 2 was designed to access its parser functionality via JAXP. It was during the development of Xalan 2 that what became the TrAX API began to develop. When JAXP 1.1 was first introduced, early drafts were only around twenty pages long, and featured no reference to XSL transformation. Suddenly, with the final draft, Xalan creator Scott Boag's name had been added, and fifty pages of material had appeared in the spec, detailing the TrAX API. TrAX, and therefore JAXP's transformation functionality, was developed more or less directly on top of the Xalan 2 sourcecode, so it was an obvious choice as an XSLT engine for inclusion in the Sun Java platform. However, Scott Boag did not develop TrAX entirely in isolation. Michael Kay, the author of the Saxon XSLT parser, among others, contributed to the specification. His homepage can be found at http://users.iclway.co.uk/mhkay.

Xalan 2 continues to develop at a pace, and the latest version (at time of writing) is a development release version of Xalan 2.3. The version distributed with J2SE 1.4 from Sun is a trimmed down version of an earlier Xalan 2 release. It lacks the current version's support for XSLT compilation and use of the Bean Scripting Framework to provide embedded scripting inside XSLT documents.

Endorsed Standards

SAX 2.0 and DOM Level 2 are standard APIs that are defined externally to the Java community process. Both specify interfaces (and in a few cases, classes) that an implementation must provide – so their incorporation into the J2SE standard requires J2SE to include these interfaces and classes.

There exist optional extensions to both of these APIs, which are required by some parsers. The SAX 2.0 extensions are included in the J2SE spec, but the DOM extensions aren't. In an interesting twist, Xalan, the supplied XSLT processor, actually brings along a lot of baggage with it, including the DOM Level 2 extension interfaces – all of which are therefore included in the J2SE 1.4 `rt.jar` file, even though there's no parser provided that can make use of them, and they're not officially part of the J2SE.

In addition, the supplied XML parser and XSLT processor, Crimson and Xalan, are open source products developed and distributed independently by the XML project of the Apache Software Foundation (http://xml.apache.org).

This adds some complexity to Java's class library, which we've touched on back in Chapter 1. It's especially acute for XML, because of the fact that SAX and DOM are widely adopted standards, and SAX and DOM class libraries are included in the JAR file of most XML parsers.

How could this cause problems? Well, imagine you have an XML-based application that was written against a prior version of J2SE. Not wanting to write all your own XML-parsing code, you downloaded an XML parser from the Internet. It shipped as a JAR file, which, following Sun's advice for software distribution, contained the `sealed` attribute in its manifest. JAR sealing is a way of telling the Java classloader that the JAR file contains all of the code that belongs in the packages it contains. Once a class has been loaded from a sealed JAR, the classloader should refuse to load any further classes into that package unless they also come from the same JAR file.

Unfortunately, as tends to be the common practice among XML parser distributions, this sealed JAR file also contains all of the DOM and SAX classes. This was fine, when the only place these classes existed was in the sealed JAR file, but now you come to run it against J2SE 1.4 you find that suddenly, the parser might try obtain some class, expecting it to be loaded from within the same JAR file, but find that the system classloader steps in and tries to load it from the standard `rt.jar` file, which always takes first place in the classloading queue. This might, in some circumstances, lead to a sealing violation, which will normally crash your application quite thoroughly.

This is only going to happen in the, admittedly rare, situation where the parser accesses some class it has in one of the included packages, that does not exist in the J2SE distribution. The situation is more likely to be the case with respect to one of the packages of a supplied component – in other words if the parser in question is a version of Crimson. Now, by default, Crimson JAR files obtained from the Apache group aren't sealed, but its availability under the Apache licence means that third parties can distribute it as part of their products. In such a situation, it's not unlikely that the two versions might contain different classes in the same packages.

A more dangerous problem, and one which is very likely to crop up, comes when you consider the situation where you want to write a program that uses a newer version of SAX or DOM, or indeed of Crimson or Xalan. DOM Level 3 is already well on its way through the W3C standards process, and Xalan adds features at every point release, so this certainly isn't idle speculation. Luckily for us, this is a problem that has been anticipated by Sun engineers, and we are now able to benefit from the new **Endorsed Standards Override Mechanism**. Basically, certain packages included in the J2SE release, including those making up Crimson and Xalan, and SAX and DOM, are now overridable. JAR files located in the `jre/lib/endorsed` directory of the Java platform folder are checked for newer versions of these endorsed standards.

For example, if you download Sun's early-access "JAX-Pack", which includes the early-access version of JAXP 1.2, you should place the `xerces.jar` and `xalan.jar` files (the XML parser and XSLT processors that ship with the JAX Pack) in the endorsed standards directory. The included versions of SAX and DOM, and of Xalan, will override those included in the J2SE release.

If you need classes of this sort, then installing them anywhere other than in the endorsed standards directory can lead to problems. One widely deployed application that might cause developers headaches with the new situation is the servlet engine Jakarta Tomcat (http://jakarta.apache.org). Because of its role as a web application server Tomcat has had to go to great lengths to separate out the classloading arrangements for individual web applications and different parts of the server itself. This caused particular problems with XML parsers, because of the proliferation of different versions of classes with the same names caused by parsers shipping with SAX and DOM classes included. Tomcat itself needs an XML parser that matches certain specifications, to read in configuration files. In addition, individual web applications may also need XML parsing functionality, specific to their needs. Additionally, any web application that uses JSP pages makes use of a part of Tomcat called Jasper, which processes JSP pages, and which always requires its own XML parser for processing configuration files as well.

Tomcat got around this with an ingenious arrangement of classloaders, and finally, with Tomcat 4.01, developers were able to deploy web applications with whichever XML-processing functionality they required reliably onto Tomcat. The way to do so was to include the JAR files of your chosen XML parser in the web application's `lib` directory.

Unfortunately, if you install the latest version of Tomcat onto J2SE 1.4, and deploy an application that incorporates its own XML parser, then access a JSP page within that application, something somewhere snaps, and Jasper is unable to compile JSP pages. This seems to be resolved by removing the offending parser JAR file from the web application (which makes sense, since if you're deploying an application onto J2SE 1.4, you don't need to bring your own parser). Naturally, this will only work if your application can make use of the J2SE XML functionality via JAXP, and doesn't rely on new or parser-specific features. If this is the case, you'll have to install the JAR files into the standard override directory – but of course, that will affect all applications run using the same JRE. If two different web applications have differing requirements, then they can't share the same run-time environment!

The situation still doesn't seem satisfactory for specialized cases such as Tomcat's, where individual applications have different requirements and can't rely on being able to change a JRE default.

The presence of these third-party, open source products in the J2SE 1.4 distribution also means that it's quite possible to compile and run programs that use some of the features of Xalan and Crimson directly. Xalan and Crimson do have published APIs (Xalan has a particularly strong set of classes to support XPath operations), but using them would be a mistake – you're depending on features that are part of the implementation of Sun's J2SE 1.4 distribution on a particular platform, not the J2SE 1.4 platform. One area to be particularly careful is in use of those DOM Level 2 extension classes, which belong to Xalan, not to the J2SE.

JAXP Architecture

JAXP uses **Abstract Factory Classes** (following the pattern described by the "Gang of Four" in the classic book *Design Patterns*, Gamma et al., published by Addison-Wesley, *ISBN 0-201-63361-2*) to provide us with a means to get at a parser without knowing its name. Essentially, for each of the types of parser object we need to access, JAXP provides an abstract class that has a static `newInstance()` method. Calling `DocumentBuilderFactory.newInstance()`, for example, causes the static method to locate an appropriate concrete subclass of `DocumentBuilderFactory` (remember, the factory class is abstract, so it can't be instantiated) provided by a parser's JAXP implementation, instantiate an object from that class, and return it to us. We now have an instance of an object of type `DocumentBuilderFactory` that comes from the parser, and which we can use to access the parser's DOM functionality.

JAXP provides three factory classes:

- `javax.xml.parsers.DocumentBuilderFactory` – For accessing DOM parsers
- `javax.xml.parsers.SAXParserFactory` – For accessing SAX parsers
- `javax.xml.transform.TransformerFactory` – For accessing XSLT processors

Their `newInstance()` methods all use the same technique to look for a concrete subclass provided by a parser or XSLT engine. They look in each of the following places for the name of a suitable class, and use the first one that results in a valid class name:

- A system property with a specific name is checked
- The property file `jaxp.properties` in the `JRE` directory is checked for a property of the same name
- The JAR services API is used to look for a JAR file on the `classpath` declaring that it provides a service with the same specific name
- A default class is tried

For each of the factories, the property name used to identify the provider class is the fully qualified name of the abstract factory class – one of:

- `javax.xml.parsers.DocumentBuilderFactory`
- `javax.xml.parsers.SAXParserFactory`
- `javax.xml.transform.TransformerFactory`

So, if we don't use any other means to specify a class, the default classes will be used. These are, for the J2SE 1.4 release from Sun obviously, the provider classes from Crimson and Xalan. If a JAR containing a relevant service declaration is present on the `classpath`, however, the class specified in its services directory will be used. If the `jaxp.properties` file is present and correct then the file specified there will be used.

We can override this behavior completely on the command line at run time, by declaring a system property on the `classpath`. For example, to use Xerces, the other XML parser developed by the Apache Software Foundation, for SAX parsing we might use the following command:

```
> java -Djavax.xml.parsers.SAXParserFactory=org.apache.xerces.jaxp.SAX
  ParserFactoryImpl -classpath xerces.jar Main.java
```

It's interesting to note that although the Crimson DOM parser does use an XML parser to provide a stream of events with which it can build a document object model, it doesn't obtain that SAX parser via JAXP, so this setting doesn't allow us to create a hybrid parser from Xerces and Crimson.

JAR Services

The JAR specification includes a little-known section explaining how JAR files can declare that they provide a concrete implementation of a service specification. However, while this is specified in the JAR standard, Java provides no tool or API support for locating such service implementations. Still, this is the system used by JAXP, so it might be interesting to at least understand how it works, and what it allows us to do. For example, a multimedia program could specify the interface for a codec (coder/decoder) service, but leave the implementation of codecs for different sound or video file formats up to other organizations. Those organizations could distribute codecs as JAR files conforming to the service's API, and the program would be able to locate all the available codecs at run time by searching for the appropriate service declarations.

Services are named after the class or interface that defines the service API. For example, the ACME multimedia company's codec service might be called `com.acme.mediaplayer.codec.CodecService`. A JAR file declares that it provides a class that implements a particular service by providing a file whose name is the name of the service, and whose contents are a single line containing the fully qualified name of the service provider class. This file must be located in the JAR file's `META-INF/services` directory.

So, if a company developed a new multimedia format called, say, MP4, it would write a class implementing the codec, which extends `com.acme.mediaplayer.codec.CodecService`. Let's say that its class is called `com.mp4.codecs.acme.CodecServiceImpl`. It would package up a JAR file containing the usual package hierarchy with the `CodecServiceImpl.class` file at the bottom, plus a `META-INF/services` directory, containing a file called `com.acme.mediaplayer.codec.CodecService`, containing the text `com.mp4.codecs.acme.CodecServiceImpl`. A user wishing to play MP4 files then simply has to place this JAR file somewhere on the `classpath` so that the ACME media player can find it.

Unfortunately, Java doesn't provide a simple `getService()` method somewhere that locates service implementations for you. This is largely because the logic that dictates which actual implementation you want to locate, where multiple matches exist, is application-specific. However, in the common situation where you simply want to locate the first match on the `classpath` (just as JAXP does), the approach is quite simple:

```
import java.io.*;

public class Service {

  public static Class forClass(Class service)
    throws ClassNotFoundException {

    Class impl = null;
```

XML

5

```
    try {
      String resourceName = "META-INF/services/" + service.getName();
      InputStream is =
        ClassLoader.getSystemResourceAsStream(resourceName);
      BufferedReader in = new BufferedReader(
        new InputStreamReader(is));
      String implName = in.readLine();
      in.close();
      impl = Class.forName(implName);
    } catch (Exception e) {
      throw new ClassNotFoundException(
                  "Unable to locate service implementation");
    }
    return impl;
  }
}
```

This utility class simply allows us to use code like this:

```
Class codecService = Class.forName(
                     "com.acme.mediaplayer.codec.CodecService")
Class codecClass   = Service.forClass(codecService));
CodecService cs    = (CodecService) codecClass.newInstance();
```

You'll need to catch a few exceptions around this code, but the essence is there.

The Simple API for XML

SAX, as we've said before, provides a lightweight event-driven API for accessing the contents of an XML document. As the parser reads through an XML file, it encounters several different situations that can trigger events of interest to an application: the start of an element, the end of an element, sections of character data, and so on. Using SAX, we can write classes that understand these events and register instances with the parser so that, when the events occur, our code is informed. JAXP supports version 2.0 of SAX, which supports namespaces, so that is the version we'll discuss here.

Essentially there is a three-step approach to using SAX 2.0:

- Implement the SAX 2.0 event-handling interfaces `org.xml.sax.ContentHandler`, `org.xml.sax.DTDHandler`, `org.xml.sax.EntityResolver`, and `org.xml.sax.ErrorHandler` by extending the convenience class `org.xml.sax.helpers.DefaultHandler`
- Use JAXP to obtain a concrete subclass of `javax.xml.parsers.SAXParser`, provided by the underlying parser

- Instantiate our `DefaultHandler` implementation, instantiate an `org.xml.sax.InputSource` object representing the data we want to parse, and pass them to the `SAXParser's` `parse()` method

This hands over control to the parser, which calls back into our event handlers.

Note that the capabilities that an XML parser provides may not be limited to the basic functionality of SAX 2.0. JAXP, via SAX 2.0, provides methods to discover the additional capabilities of a parser, and activate or deactivate them. For example, W3C Schemas are widely seen as a future replacement for XML DTDs, but are not supported by default by a SAX 2.0 parser. Crimson can't validate documents against schemas, but Xerces, another JAXP-compliant parser, can. If you use one of the techniques above to tell JAXP to use Xerces, not Crimson, then you can activate its schema-validation using the JAXP API. For more details about how to access advanced SAX functionality like this, take a look at the Java XML Programmer's Reference *(from Wrox Press, ISBN 1-861005-20-2).*

XML

5

The org.xml.sax.helpers.DefaultHandler Class

The `DefaultHandler` class provides a null implementation of all of the event-handling methods in SAX 2.0. By extending it, we can override only those methods we're interested in, resulting in a child class that provides a complete implementation of all four of the event-handling interfaces:

- `org.xml.sax.ContentHandler`
- `org.xml.sax.DTDHandler`
- `org.xml.sax.EntityResolver`
- `org.xml.sax.ErrorHandler`

The majority, and the most interesting, of these are generally the methods defined in `ContentHandler`, which unsurprisingly are related to the XML document's content. The following table details all the methods in `DefaultHandler`:

Method Name	Defined In	Event
`characters()`	`ContentHandler`	The parser encountered some character data.
`endDocument()`	`ContentHandler`	The parser has reached the end of the document.
`endElement()`	`ContentHandler`	The parser reached the end of an element.
`endPrefixMapping()`	`ContentHandler`	A namespace mapping previously introduced is no longer in force.

Method Name	Defined In	Event
`error()`	`ErrorHandler`	A recoverable error occurred. For example, the parser can continue if a document is not valid.
`fatalError()`	`ErrorHandler`	An unrecoverable error occurred. For example, the parser can't continue if a document is not well formed.
`ignorableWhiteSpace()`	`ContentHandler`	The parser encountered whitespace characters in a location where they do not have any significance to the meaning of the XML document, only its layout.
`notationDecl()`	`DTDHandler`	The parser came across a notation declaration while parsing a DTD.
`processingInstruction()`	`ContentHandler`	An XML-processing instruction was encountered.
`resolveEntity()`	`EntityResolver`	The parser needs assistance in obtaining access to an external entity required to parse the document.
`setDocumentLocator()`	`ContentHandler`	The parser is offering a reference to an object it provides, which can be used during subsequent event handlers to discover whereabouts in the XML document the event occurred. This object will implement the `Locator` interface.
`skippedEntity()`	`ContentHandler`	The parser is reporting that it came across an entity but didn't resolve it – perhaps because it is declared externally.
`startDocument()`	`ContentHandler`	The parser has begun to parse the document.
`startElement()`	`ContentHandler`	The parser has reached the start of an element.

Table continued on following page

Method Name	Defined In	Event
`startPrefixMapping()`	`ContentHandler`	The parser has come across a namespace mapping declaration.
`unparsedEntityDecl()`	`DTDHandler`	The parser encountered a declaration of an unparsed entity during DTD processing.

When the parser calls these methods, it passes our handler parameters containing information about the event. If there is no information needed, no parameter is passed. For example, `startDocument()` doesn't need any parameters. `startElement()`, on the other hand, receives much more information. In particular, it receives a lot of information about the name of the element. Let's look at precisely why:

An XML element's name is basically the string that immediately follows the opening angle bracket of its opening tag. So, for the element:

```
<foo bar="baz"></foo>
```

The element's name is `foo`.

However, things are complicated by the existence of XML namespaces. We can qualify the `foo` element by telling the XML parser that it belongs to a specific namespace, say `http://www.foobar.com/`. There are two ways we can explain to the parser that this association exists. The first is to declare a default namespace, using the `xmlns` attribute. For example:

```
<foo bar="baz" xmlns="http://www.foobar.com/"></foo>
```

Alternatively, we can specify a namespace using a namespace prefix:

```
<foobar:foo bar="baz"
xmlns:foobar="http://www.foobar.com/">
</foobar:foo>
```

In both cases, the element's name is still `foo`, but its full name is "`foo` as defined by the namespace `http://www.foobar.com/`", much as my name is James, but my full name is James Hart. To distinguish me from other people called James, we use a namespace qualifier, a family name. I am "James as defined by the family called Hart", to use similar terms. So, both parts of this element's name are of interest to us in distinguishing it from other elements with similar names. If we encounter an element called `foo`, with a different namespace name, we know it's a different kind of `foo` altogether.

In the latter case, however, the element not only has its local name (`foo`), and its namespace name (`http://www.foobar.com/`), it also has a nickname, `foobar:foo`. This is in much the same way that around the office, I'm known as James H, to distinguish me from others who work here, like James R. It's a shorthand for specifying my full family name. The namespace prefix on a qualified XML element name provides a similar function – it qualifies the element, without having to specify its full namespace prefix each time.

So, three parts make up the name of an element:

- Its qualified name – the name actually used in the document to refer to it, with the qualifying prefix if there is one
- Its local name – the name that distinguishes it within its namespace
- Its namespace name – the name of the namespace to which the element belongs

So, the `element()` method is called by the SAX parser with four parameters:

- The namespace URI
- The local name
- The qualified name
- An `Attributes` collection containing all of the attributes specified on the element

Now, since a parser can be configured to be namespace-aware or not, then it is important to realize that the parser will not always be able to work out all of these different parts.

So, if a namespace-aware parser encountered the following element:

```
<song writer="trad" title="Happy Birthday"
 xmlns="http://www.wrox.com/song">
  Happy birthday to you,
  Happy birthday to you,
  Happy birthday dear [name],
  Happy birthday to you.
</song>
```

our handler's `startElement()` method would be called with the following arguments:

- The namespace URI `http://www.wrox.com/song`. The element has no prefix, so it belongs to the default namespace, as declared in the `xmlns` attribute.
- The local name of the element, `song`, which is the name of the element within its namespace, without any prefixes.
- The qualified name. The parser may return to us the qualified name of the element, or may not, depending on the implementation. In this case, the qualified name is the same as the local name – `song`.
- An `Attributes` object containing the `writer` and `title` attributes. The `xmlns` attribute is ignored, since it is intended for the parser, not for us.

In order to find out what the `song` element contains, we need to wait for the parser to call our handler's `characters()` method.

Event-Driven Parsing

Let's look at how SAX really works by building an event-reporting handler class. Then, we can build a test framework into which we can pass XML documents to see what events are fired.

Our handler class will simply override all of the methods of the `DefaultHandler` class, providing implementations that output all of the information available to the method.

The test framework will be a command-line tool, which will take a filename as an argument, and will run the parser with namespace awareness and DTD validation either turned on or off.

The handler class, `EventReporter`, is simple, but quite long:

```
import org.xml.sax.*;
import org.xml.sax.helpers.*;

public class EventReporter extends DefaultHandler {
```

The first thing to do is to provide some support for `Locators`. Remember, a SAX parser may provide us with a `Locator` object, which we can query during subsequent events to discover where the particular event took place. Some parsers may not provide a locator, so we shouldn't rely on it being present. This code shows an example of how to write some code that uses a locator if one is provided, but still functions properly if one isn't. We'll store a locator, if one is provided, in a private data member, where it can be accessed during the processing of later events. We'll also write a convenience method that returns a string representing the current location, if a locator is available. If there is no locator, it returns an empty string. That way, we can include a location in our event reports easily.

```
  private Locator locator;

  private String location() {
    if (locator != null) {
      return locator.getSystemId() + ", "
        + locator.getLineNumber() + ": ";
    } else {
      return "";
    }
  }
```

The location string we return consists of two parts:

- The system ID, which is XML-speak for the path to the source file
- The line number

Public IDs and System IDs

You'll often come across the term **system ID** in XML applications, and it always simply refers to a URL indicating where a file is located. It can be a relative URL, or an absolute one. The other kind of ID XML also uses is a **public ID**, which is a URN, rather than a URL, and represents a globally unique name by which a certain resource is known. A public ID provides no information about where the document can be located – the assumption is that the recipient of a document containing a public ID knows what it means.

Tracking Document Location

Now we can implement the first of the `ContentHandler` methods, `setDocumentLocator()`. If the SAX parser decides to provide us with a locator, it will call this method, and it's up to us to store the locator for future reference. We'll report that we've been given a locator on standard out, and then store a reference to it in our private field.

```
public void setDocumentLocator(Locator locator) {
  System.out.println(location() +
                         "ContentHandler: received a Locator");
  this.locator = locator;
}
```

It's worth noting that `org.xml.sax.Locator` is in fact an interface, not a class. What we're actually passed is an object belonging to one of the SAX parser's classes, which we can access using the `Locator` interface.

Implementing EntityResolver

Now, before we implement the rest of `ContentHandler`, let's quickly implement the smaller interfaces. First, `EntityResolver`, which has just one method:

```
public InputSource resolveEntity(String publicId,
                                 String systemId)
throws SAXException {
  System.out.println(location() +
                         "EntityResolver: ResolveEntity\n\t"
                         + publicId + " " + systemId);
  return null;
}
```

`resolveEntity()` is called whenever an XML document or DTD contains a reference to an external entity that the parser needs to load in order to continue. As discussed briefly under *Public IDs and System IDs* above, an entity can be identified by a public ID, a system ID, or both. A system ID gives the resource's location, and a public ID gives its globally unique name, if it has one. An XML parser can generally resolve entities described using a system ID, provided that it is either an absolute URL, or it is a relative URL but the XML parser knows the URL from which the XML document was obtained. The XML document's source URL is referred to as the system ID of the document, naturally. However, regardless of whether the XML parser can resolve the entity unaided, it will call this method to see if our program wants to override this behavior. If the XML parser is unable to resolve the entity on its own, then it relies on our code here to provide it with an `InputSource` object representing the entity. We'll come back to `InputSource` objects later on, when we come to initialize and run the parser.

Our handler, unfortunately, doesn't know any more than the XML parser does about where entities are located, so we return the programmatic equivalent of a shrug of the shoulders – `null`. Before doing so, however, we report the event to standard output, including the information the parser gave us about what entity it was interested in.

Implementing DTDHandler

Next, we implement the `DTDHandler` interface's two methods:

```
public void notationDecl(String name, String publicId,
                         String systemId) throws SAXException {
  System.out.println(location()
                    + "DTDHandler: NotationDecl\n\t" + name
                    + " " + publicId + " " + systemId);
}

public void unparsedEntityDecl(String name, String publicId,
                               String systemId,
                               String notationName)
throws SAXException
{
  System.out.println(location()
                    + "DTDHandler: UnparsedEntityDecl\n\t"
                    + name + " " + publicId + " " + systemId + " "
                    + notationName);
}
```

There aren't methods for every declaration made in a DTD. DTDs can contain ELEMENT, ATTLIST, ENTITY, and NOTATION declarations, and we'll only be informed about NOTATIONs and unparsed entities – ENTITYs that are declared as NDATA (not XML data). The reason for this is that everything else in a DTD is intended as an aid to the parser in understanding the document, and it will handle resolution of everything else that the DTD contains (with the help of our EntityResolver). Unparsed entities and their associated notations are intended for the application using the parser though, so information about them is passed on through to us. We'll look at notations and unparsed entities in our last XML file example later.

Implementing ContentHandler

Now we're ready to implement the ContentHandler methods that actually handle content. We'll take them in pairs:

```
public void startDocument() throws SAXException {
  System.out.println(location() + "ContentHandler: StartDocument");
}

public void endDocument() throws SAXException {
  System.out.println(location() + "ContentHandler: EndDocument");
}
```

startDocument() is guaranteed to be called before any of the other content methods are called, so it makes a good place to put initialization code. Note that the setLocator() method might already have been called.

endDocument() will be the last content method called, so it is the place to put code that should execute when the document has completed parsing.

```
public void startPrefixMapping(String prefix,
                               String uri) throws SAXException {
  System.out.println(location()
                     + "ContentHandler: StartPrefixMapping\n\t"
                     + prefix + " " + uri);
}

public void endPrefixMapping(String prefix) throws SAXException {
  System.out.println(location() +
                     "ContentHandler: EndPrefixMapping\n\t"
                     + prefix);
}
```

The PrefixMapping methods relate to the namespace declarations made in the document. They will only be activated if the parser has namespace awareness activated, which we'll see how to do later on. You'll only need to use them if you want to keep track of what local prefix mappings the original document author used, since the parser keeps track itself, and the namespace URI for each element and attribute will be reported to you at the time it is encountered.

```java
public void startElement(String uri, String localName,
                         String qName, Attributes attributes)
throws SAXException {
  System.out.println(location() + "ContentHandler: StartElement\n\t"
                     + uri + " " + localName + " " + qName);

  int attCount = attributes.getLength();
  for (int a = 0; a < attCount; a++) {
    System.out.println("\t\t" + attributes.getURI(a) + " "
                       + attributes.getQName(a) + " "
                       + attributes.getLocalName(a) + " "
                       + attributes.getValue(a));
  }
}

public void endElement(String uri, String localName,
                       String qName) throws SAXException {
  System.out.println(location() + "ContentHandler: EndElement\n\t"
                     + uri + " " + localName + " " + qName);
}
```

These are the two key methods for processing XML data. Most of the time, it is the element and attribute structure that we're interested in. As we mentioned earlier, elements are identified in terms of three strings:

- The URI of the namespace they belong to
- The name of the element within that namespace
- The qualified name, which is the name actually used within the XML document to identify the element, including a prefix, where one is provided

Typically, if our program is looking for an element belonging to a particular namespace, and the parser is namespace-aware, we will use the namespace URI and local name provided by the parser. If we're interested in namespaces, but not using the parser's namespace support, we'll use the qualified name, extract the prefix ourselves, and look it up against a previously declared prefix-mapping. If we're not interested in namespaces ourselves, we should look at the qualified name.

A parser with namespace support active must return a namespace URI (if the element has one) and a local name. If it isn't supporting namespaces, it must return a qualified name. Whether it passes any other parameters depends on the implementation.

The final parameter passed in is an `Attributes` object. The `Attributes` object presents a hash-table-like interface, which allows you to obtain access to any attributes declared in the element's opening tag. You can access them by name, by qualified name, or by index, and, using each method, retrieve any of the other attributes, the namespace URI, or the value of the attribute. The full list of methods to obtain information about an attribute is as follows:

- `int getIndex(String qName)`
- `int getIndex(String uri, String localPart)`
- `String getLocalName(int index)`
- `String getQName(int index)`
- `String getType(int index)`
- `String getType(String qName)`
- `String getType(String uri, String localName)`
- `String getURI(int index)`
- `String getValue(int index)`
- `String getValue(String qName)`
- `String getValue(String uri, String localName)`

There is also a single method that tells you how many attributes were defined:

- `int getLength()`

In our code, we simply find out how many attributes there are, and then iterate through the attribute indexes (starting from zero), obtaining the URI, local name, and qualified name of the attribute in question.

No guarantee is made about the order in which attribute names will be returned. The only guarantee is, each attribute on a given element will be given a unique serial ID number, from zero up, so we know each attribute will be returned once.

Note also that an `Attributes` object is useless as soon as we've returned from our method handler, and the return values of its methods are undefined if they are accessed later. It is quite possible, for example, for the parser to use the same instance each time it calls our methods. If we want to store the attributes for later reference, we must do so ourselves.

The next couple of event handlers are related to the content between the tags in XML:

```
public void characters(char[] ch, int start,
                       int length) throws SAXException {
  System.out.println(location() + "ContentHandler: Characters\n\t"
                     + String.copyValueOf(ch, start, length));
}

public void ignorableWhitespace(char ch[], int start,
                                int length) throws SAXException {
  System.out.println(location()
```

```
              + "ContentHandler: IgnorableWhiteSpace\n\t"
              + length
              + " characters");
}
```

When a parser is aware of the contents of a DTD (not necessarily because it is in validating mode – a DTD-aware parser may choose to use the information in a DTD, where present, even if it is not validating the document against it) it can tell the difference between elements that allow element-only content, elements that allow mixed content, and elements that allow only character data content. Where an element only contains elements, document authors are allowed to use whitespace to lay out the elements neatly in the document, through indenting, line breaks, and so on. This whitespace isn't actually part of the document's content, since the element isn't allowed to contain textual content in this position. It is therefore classified as ignorable whitespace, and parsers may (at their discretion) choose to report it via the `ignorableWhiteSpace()` method.

Otherwise, all data within elements should be reported via the `characters()` method. There's no guarantee that the `characters()` method will be called only once, even for a single contiguous run of character data, so it is best to store away the characters in a buffer and process them when the `endElement()` method is called, if we're interested in processing all of the data inside a particular element. The only guarantee given is that each character in the original XML will be reported once and once only, in order, through one or other of these methods.

Both of these methods pass us the data not as a `String` or `StringBuffer`, but as a character array, together with two `int`s: a `start` index and a `length`. The characters we should read are the next `length` characters, beginning with the `start` index. Any other characters passed to us in the array outside these limits are not guaranteed to have any particular significance, so they should never be read.

Conveniently, there is a static method for `String`s, `String.copyValueOf()`, that takes precisely these three arguments – a `char` array, a start point, and a length – and returns a `String` object constructed from the specified characters. Alternatively, you may want to use a New I/O `java.nio.CharBuffer`, particularly if the data you are reading could be long.

The last two content-handling events relate once more to the XML parser passing on responsibility for dealing with something to the client application, because it isn't equipped to deal with it alone. The first is activated when a processing instruction is encountered. **PI**s (**Processing Instructions**) are instructions embedded in XML documents that are intended for applications other than the parser. They consist of a target specifier, and then an instruction. An application should check to see if it is the specified target (or knows where to find it), and if so, interpret the instruction appropriately.

The second of these relates to entity references for which the parser was unable to make a substitution. This will typically be the case for an external entity that cannot be located. It will only be called when the parser is not in validating mode.

```
public void processingInstruction(String target,
                                  String data) throws SAXException {
  System.out.println(location()
                     + "ContentHandler: ProcessingInstruction\n\t"
                     + target + " " + data);
}

public void skippedEntity(String name) throws SAXException {
  System.out.println(location()
                     + "ContentHandler: SkippedEntity\n\t"
                     + name);
}
```

Implementing ErrorHandler

Finally, we implement the three methods of the `ErrorHandler` interface, which deal with errors of steadily increasing significance. The least significant is a **warning**; this signifies a condition that, while it does not mean the document can not be processed in its entirety, means the application needs to be made aware that all has not gone to plan. An **error** signifies a genuine problem with the document being processed. A parser in validating mode should report violations of the validity constraints as errors. Again, document processing may continue, but the application may, at its discretion, terminate the process. In order to do so – in fact, in order to do so from within any SAX event-handler – you should throw a `SAXException`. This will bubble up through the parser and be thrown out of the original method call your code made to the `SAXParser's parse()` method.

This is the approach used to process a **fatal error**. Fatal errors are conditions that preclude further processing of the document – the SAX parser will be in an unstable state, and further event reports may not be accurate. This is the case if it encounters some data that fails the well-formedness criteria. To ensure that further parsing doesn't take place, we throw an exception.

All of the methods take an exception generated by the parser as an argument.

```
public void warning(SAXParseException e) throws SAXException {
  System.out.println(location() + "ErrorHandler: Warning\n\t"
                     + e.getMessage());
}

public void error(SAXParseException e) throws SAXException {
  System.out.println(location() + "ErrorHandler: Error\n\t"
                     + e.getMessage());
```

XML

5

```
  }

  public void fatalError(SAXParseException e) throws SAXException {
    System.out.println(location() + "ErrorHandler: FatalError\n\t"
                        + e.getMessage());
    throw e;
  }
}
```

And that concludes our EventReporter class.

SAX Parsing

Now, we need to create a class that will parse a document using an object of this class as an event handler. We'll write a simple command-line program, VerboseSAXParser, which takes an XML document as an argument, and also has a couple of command-line switches that can be used to turn on validation and namespace awareness. We'll turn them off by default.

```
import javax.xml.parsers.*;
import org.xml.sax.helpers.*;
import java.io.*;

public class VerboseSAXParser {

  public static final String VALIDATING = "-v";
  public static final String NAMESPACE = "-n";
  public static final String USAGE =
    "Usage: java VerboseSAXParser [-n] [-v] <filename>";

  public static void main(String[] args) {
    boolean namespace = false;
    boolean validating = false;

    if (args.length < 1) {
      System.out.println(USAGE);
      System.exit(1);
    } else if (args.length > 1) {
      for (int a = 0; a < (args.length - 1); a++) {
        if (args[a].equalsIgnoreCase(VALIDATING)) {
          validating = true;
        } else if (args[a].equalsIgnoreCase(NAMESPACE)) {
          namespace = true;
        } else {
          System.out.println(USAGE);
          System.exit(1);
        }
```

```
    }
  }

  String filename = args[args.length - 1];
```

The first part of the main method simply parses the args list. If there are no arguments, or if there is more than one but any argument other than the last one isn't a command-line switch we recognize, we quit with a usage message. Otherwise, we read out the switches and set the `namespace` and `validating` variables to `true` or `false` appropriately. The final argument is assumed to be the filename. The real parsing work starts here:

```
  SAXParser parser = null;

  try {
    SAXParserFactory spf = SAXParserFactory.newInstance();
    spf.setNamespaceAware(namespace);
    spf.setValidating(validating);
    parser = spf.newSAXParser();
  } catch (Exception e) {
    e.printStackTrace();
  }
```

We use the static method of the abstract `SAXParserFactory` to obtain a `SAXParserFactory` instance. If we're using the default J2SE 1.4 installation, this is actually an instance of the `org.apache.crimson.jaxp.SAXParserFactoryImpl` class.

We set the factory's namespace awareness and validation parameters; this sets the default state for all `SAXParsers` we create using this factory. Next, we call the factory's `newSAXParser()` method, which returns an instance of a subclass of the abstract JAXP `SAXParser` class. Again, in the case of the default J2SE 1.4 system, this will really be an `org.apache.crimson.jaxp.SAXParserImpl` instance.

Now we need to run the actual parsing process. First, we have to instantiate an event-handler – our `EventReporter` class.

```
  EventReporter handler = new EventReporter();

  System.out.println("*** Validating: "
                     + (parser.isValidating() ? "on" : "off")
                     + ", Namespaces: "
                     + (parser.isNamespaceAware() ? "on" : "off")
                     + " ***");
  try {
    FileInputStream fis = new FileInputStream(filename);
    parser.parse(fis, handler, filename);
  } catch (Exception e) {
```

```
            e.printStackTrace();
        }
    }
}
```

Now, having printed out the options we're using for this parse, we open an input stream from the file, then call the parser's `parse()` method.

`SAXParsers` have a number of different `parse()` methods, all of which revolve around finding different ways to provide the SAX parser with the three pieces of information it needs:

- A source of data to parse
- An event-handler to pass parsing events to
- A system ID for the data source, which will be used to resolve relative URIs

As we've seen, a SAX parser can cope without knowing the system ID of the document it is parsing, since it can rely on an entity resolver, and in any case, there may not be any relative URIs in the document. In our case, the system ID we provide is simply the filename passed to the command line; this may in itself be a relative URI, and thus not adequate for resolving relative references. If you pass in a document that contains relative URIs, you will need to specify the path to the document as an absolute path.

The available `SAXParser` `parse()` methods are as follows:

- `parse(File f, DefaultHandler dh)`
- `parse(InputSource is, DefaultHandler dh)`
- `parse(InputStream is, DefaultHandler dh)`
- `parse(InputStream is, DefaultHandler dh, String systemId)`
- `parse(String uri, DefaultHandler dh)`

A `File` object provides the parser with an absolute path to the XML file, which can serve as a system ID as well, obviously, as the means to read the data. An `InputSource` is a SAX object that wraps a stream or reader object together with an optional system ID. An input stream doesn't itself provide any clue as to the location from where the data originates, so there are two versions of the `parse()` method that take `InputStreams` – one with a system ID argument, and one without. The final version simply takes the URI as an argument, and leaves it up to the SAX parser to open up a connection and read the data from the URI.

So, to get back to our example, we've called the `parse()` method. The flow of execution now is that the SAX parser begins its parse and, as it encounters events, calls into the methods of our handler class. This happens completely sequentially. Only after all of the events have been handled will the `parse()` method return. Alternatively, if any fatal errors occur in the course of the parse, a `SAXException` will be thrown.

Using the VerboseSAXParser to Examine SAX Events

If you've used JAXP in the past it is important to note that, since JAXP is now built into the platform, you no longer need to include `jaxp.jar` and `crimson.jar` on the `classpath` when compiling or running this code. That's a huge headache out of the way and if, like me, you used to juggle XML parsers frequently, making sure that JAXP picked the right one out of your `classpath` was a pain.

At this point, we need an XML document to parse. Here's a slightly modified version of a document we saw earlier on:

```
<?xml version="1.0" encoding="UTF-8"?>

<song writer="trad" title="Happy Birthday">
  <verse>
    <line>Happy birthday to you,</line>
    <line>Happy birthday to you,</line>
    <line>Happy birthday dear [name],</line>
    <line>Happy birthday to you.</line>
  </verse>
</song>
```

There's no DTD, so, while the document is well-formed, it isn't valid; a validating parser will generate errors when parsing it. There are no namespace declarations, so activating namespace awareness will have a negligible effect on the parsed data. Let's look at `VerboseSAXParser`'s output without namespace awareness or validation turned on:

```
> java VerboseSAXParser test.xml
*** Validating: off, Namespaces: off ***
ContentHandler: received a Locator
test.xml, 1: ContentHandler: StartDocument
test.xml, 3: ContentHandler: StartElement
          song
                 writer  trad
                 title  Happy Birthday
test.xml, 3: ContentHandler: Characters


test.xml, 3: ContentHandler: Characters


test.xml, 4: ContentHandler: Characters
```

XML

5

```
test.xml, 4: ContentHandler: StartElement
          verse
test.xml, 4: ContentHandler: Characters
            .
            .
            .
```

This continues for some time. As you can see, we're getting characters reported for each line break and indent. We're also only getting the qualified name (the literal name in the document) reported for each element and attribute.

Let's look at what happens if we use validation:

```
> java VerboseSAXParser -v test.xml
*** Validating: on, Namespaces: off ***
ContentHandler: received a Locator
test.xml, 1: ContentHandler: StartDocument
test.xml, 3: ErrorHandler: Warning
        Valid documents must have a <!DOCTYPE declaration.
test.xml, 3: ErrorHandler: Error
        Element type "song" is not declared.
test.xml, 3: ErrorHandler: Error
        Attribute "writer" is not declared for element
"song".
test.xml, 3: ErrorHandler: Error
        Attribute "title" is not declared for element
"song".
test.xml, 3: ContentHandler: StartElement
          song
                 writer  trad
                 title  Happy Birthday
test.xml, 3: ContentHandler: Characters
            .
            .
            .
```

Immediately, you can see that the validator starts to complain about the need for a DTD, and then also sends us an error message for each undeclared element and attribute. However, the parse does continue, and we still receive the same content-handling events.

Let's look at an example with namespaces. Here's the same document, but with a couple of trivial namespace declarations added to it:

```
<?xml version="1.0" encoding="UTF-8"?>

<lyric:song writer="trad"
            title="Happy Birthday"
            xmlns:lyric="http://www.wrox.com/song"
            xmlns:struct="http://www.wrox.com/song/structure">
  <struct:verse>
    <lyric:line>Happy birthday to you,</lyric:line>
    <lyric:line>Happy birthday to you,</lyric:line>
    <lyric:line>Happy birthday dear [name],</lyric:line>
    <lyric:line>Happy birthday to you.</lyric:line>
  </struct:verse>
</lyric:song>
```

And here's what happens if we run the parser with namespace awareness on:

```
> java VerboseSAXParser -n test1.xml
*** Validating: off, Namespaces: on ***
ContentHandler: received a Locator
test1.xml, 1: ContentHandler: StartDocument
test1.xml, 6: ContentHandler: StartPrefixMapping
        lyric http://www.wrox.com/song
test1.xml, 6: ContentHandler: StartPrefixMapping
        struct http://www.wrox.com/song/structure
test1.xml, 6: ContentHandler: StartElement
        http://www.wrox.com/song song lyric:song
                 writer writer trad
                 title title Happy Birthday
test1.xml, 6: ContentHandler: Characters

test1.xml, 6: ContentHandler: Characters

test1.xml, 7: ContentHandler: Characters

test1.xml, 7: ContentHandler: StartElement
        http://www.wrox.com/song/structure verse
struct:verse
            .
            .
            .
```

XML

5

Notice that the `startElement()` method doesn't receive the namespace declarations as attributes. We do receive all three pieces of name information for each element though: the URI, the local name, and the qualified name. Although we have followed a widely used XML convention – that attributes within a namespace-qualified element belong to that same namespace unless otherwise qualified by a prefix – we'll have to apply that convention ourselves in processing the data, since the parser is making no such assumption. Our un-prefixed attributes are passed on without a namespace URI.

The next example has an internal DTD, and a slightly less complex namespace system:

```
<?xml version="1.0" encoding="UTF-8"?>

<!DOCTYPE song [
  <!ELEMENT song (verse+)>
  <!ELEMENT verse (line+)>
  <!ELEMENT line (#PCDATA)>
  <!ATTLIST song
     writer CDATA #REQUIRED
     title  CDATA #REQUIRED
     xmlns  CDATA #FIXED "http://www.wrox.com/song"
  >
]>
<song writer="trad" title="Happy Birthday"
                   xmlns="http://www.wrox.com/song">
  <verse>
    <line>Happy birthday to you,</line>
    <line>Happy birthday to you,</line>
    <line>Happy birthday dear [name],</line>
    <line>Happy birthday to you.</line>
  </verse>
</song>
```

Running with validation and namespace awareness, we get the following:

```
> java VerboseSAXParser -n -v test2.xml
*** Validating: on, Namespaces: on ***
ContentHandler: received a Locator
test2.xml, 1: ContentHandler: StartDocument
test2.xml, 13: ContentHandler: StartPrefixMapping
        http://www.wrox.com/song
test2.xml, 13: ContentHandler: StartPrefixMapping
        http://www.wrox.com/song
test2.xml, 13: ContentHandler: StartElement
        http://www.wrox.com/song song song
                 writer writer trad
                 title title Happy Birthday
```

```
test2.xml, 14: ContentHandler: IgnorableWhiteSpace
        0 characters
test2.xml, 14: ContentHandler: IgnorableWhiteSpace
        1 characters
test2.xml, 14: ContentHandler: IgnorableWhiteSpace
        2 characters
test2.xml, 14: ContentHandler: StartElement
        http://www.wrox.com/song verse verse
            .
            .
            .
```

Now, we're getting all those line breaks and indents reported as ignorable whitespace, which is what they really are.

Finally, let's look at an example with a much more complex DTD. Here's our new `test3.xml` document:

```
<?xml version="1.0" encoding="UTF-8"?>
<!DOCTYPE song SYSTEM "file:///C:/song.dtd" [
  <!ENTITY happybday SYSTEM "file:///C:/happybirthday.wav" NDATA wav>
]>

<song writer="trad" title="Happy Birthday" tune="happybday"
                    xmlns="http://www.wrox.com/song">
  <verse>
    <line>Happy birthday to you,</line>
    <line>Happy birthday to you,</line>
    <line>Happy birthday dear &name;,</line>
    <line>Happy birthday to you.</line>
  </verse>
</song>
```

The DTD references an external DTD subset, `song.dtd`. It also identifies an external unparsed entity, a sound file, which is given the name `happybday`. Also, we've changed `[name]` into an entity reference, `&name;`. We'll see where that gets declared later on. Here's `song.dtd`:

```
<!ELEMENT song (verse+)>
<!ELEMENT verse (line+)>
<!ELEMENT line (#PCDATA)>
<!ATTLIST song
   writer CDATA #REQUIRED
   title  CDATA #REQUIRED
   tune   ENTITY #IMPLIED
   xmlns  CDATA #FIXED "http://www.wrox.com/song"
>
```

```
<!NOTATION wav PUBLIC "audio/wav">

<!ENTITY % name SYSTEM "file:///C:/name.dtd">

%name;
```

This file contains the DTD element declaration we used before, with the addition of an attribute of type `ENTITY` to the `song` element. We also declare a notation, `wav`, which is used to identify the MIME type of a WAV file. This notation is referenced in the external unparsed entity declaration above. Finally, we include a parameterized external entity, which refers to the `name.dtd` file. We then include the contents of that file in the DTD using the `%name;` parameter entity notation. `name.dtd` contains a single declaration of an external *parsed* entity:

```
<!ENTITY name SYSTEM "file:///C:/name.txt">
```

This is the entity that is referenced in the XML document above, so when that entity reference is encountered, it will be replaced with the contents of the file `name.txt`. In my case, the contents of that file is simply the word `James`.

It's not really possible to make an XML document that's much more complicated than this, in terms of using external entities, DTDs, and so on. However, as we'll see, all of this complexity can be handled by the XML parser itself. Here's the output of the program with validation and namespace awareness turned on, if we deactivate the output of ignorable whitespace (comment the whitespace-reporting method out in the code and recompile):

```
> java VerboseSAXParser -n -v test3.xml
*** Validating: on, Namespaces: on ***
ContentHandler: received a Locator
test3.xml, 1: ContentHandler: StartDocument
test3.xml, 3: DTDHandler: UnparsedEntityDecl
        happybday null file:///C:/happybirthday.wav wav
test3.xml, 4: EntityResolver: ResolveEntity
        null file:///C:/song.dtd
file:/C:/song.dtd, 10: DTDHandler: NotationDecl
        wav audio/wav null
file:/C:/song.dtd, 14: EntityResolver: ResolveEntity
        null file:///C:/name.dtd
test3.xml, 7: ContentHandler: StartPrefixMapping
         http://www.wrox.com/song
test3.xml, 7: ContentHandler: StartPrefixMapping
         http://www.wrox.com/song
test3.xml, 7: ContentHandler: StartElement
        http://www.wrox.com/song song song
                  writer writer trad
```

```
                title title Happy Birthday
                tune tune happybday
test3.xml, 8: ContentHandler: StartElement
        http://www.wrox.com/song verse verse
test3.xml, 9: ContentHandler: StartElement
        http://www.wrox.com/song line line
test3.xml, 9: ContentHandler: Characters
        Happy birthday to you,
test3.xml, 9: ContentHandler: EndElement
        http://www.wrox.com/song line line
test3.xml, 10: ContentHandler: StartElement
        http://www.wrox.com/song line line
test3.xml, 10: ContentHandler: Characters
        Happy birthday to you,
test3.xml, 10: ContentHandler: EndElement
        http://www.wrox.com/song line line
test3.xml, 11: ContentHandler: StartElement
        http://www.wrox.com/song line line
test3.xml, 11: ContentHandler: Characters
        Happy birthday dear
test3.xml, 11: EntityResolver: ResolveEntity
        null file:///C:/name.txt
file:/C:/name.txt, 1: ContentHandler: Characters
        James
test3.xml, 11: ContentHandler: Characters
        ,
test3.xml, 11: ContentHandler: EndElement
        http://www.wrox.com/song line line
test3.xml, 12: ContentHandler: StartElement
        http://www.wrox.com/song line line
test3.xml, 12: ContentHandler: Characters
        Happy birthday to you.
test3.xml, 12: ContentHandler: EndElement
        http://www.wrox.com/song line line
test3.xml, 13: ContentHandler: EndElement
        http://www.wrox.com/song verse verse
test3.xml, 14: ContentHandler: EndElement
        http://www.wrox.com/song song song
test3.xml, 14: ContentHandler: EndPrefixMapping

test3.xml, 14: ContentHandler: EndPrefixMapping

test3.xml, 14: ContentHandler: EndDocument
```

The DTDHandler and EntityResolver methods get a thorough workout this time. We receive the notation and unparsed entity declarations, and get asked to help resolve each external entity reference. Notice the information coming from the locator – this tells us which file is being read when each event is generated. We learn for example, that the notation declaration is on line 10 of song.dtd.

We also see that characters events within one element can come from different files. Inside the third line, we see three separate characters events – one each side of the entity reference, and one for the content of the entity itself. Together, they make the line read as intended, as Happy birthday dear James,.

As an XML application author, it's important to remember that we get all of this functionality free of charge. All we really need to understand are elements, attributes, and characters, and our application can handle anything from a simple single XML file with an internal DTD to a complex multi-file document, full of external entity references. The parser will do most of the hard work for us.

The Document Object Model

The DOM, in its XML incarnation, is a general object model capable of representing all of the items that make up an XML document. So, it contains interfaces with names like Element, Attribute, ProcessingInstruction, and so on, and instances of classes implementing these interfaces are created by a parser to represent each item in a particular document. All of these interfaces extend the base interface, Node, which provides methods that allow you to navigate through a parent-child relationship, from node to node. As such, it can be thought of as an object graph that maps to the original tree hierarchy of the document. However, thinking in terms of strict trees can be misleading when dealing with the DOM, so you need to be careful.

DOM Level 2, as supported by JAXP 1.1, includes support for exactly the same range of features as SAX 2.0: namespaces and DTD validation. Again, these facilities can be turned on and off before parsing a document.

There is a three-stage approach to using DOM to parse a document with JAXP:

- Obtain a concrete subclass of JAXP's abstract DocumentBuilderFactory via the newInstance() method
- Obtain a DocumentBuilder object from the factory with the newDocumentBuilder() method
- Call one of the DocumentBuilder's parse() methods to obtain a Document object representing the document you want to parse

Having obtained a Document object, you have a handle on one of the points in the node structure. A Document is a node, just as each element and attribute is a node. The full set of node types, each represented by a different interface that extends org.w3c.dom.Node, is as follows:

org.w3c.dom Interface	Value returned by getNodeType()	Represents
Attribute	Node.ATTRIBUTE_NODE	An attribute of an element
CDATASection	Node.CDATA_SECTION_NODE	A CDATA section, used to include literal unparsed content in an XML document
Comment	Node.COMMENT_NODE	An XML comment
DocumentFragment	Node.DOCUMENT_FRAGMENT_NODE	A document fragment represents a subsection of an XML document
Document	Node.DOCUMENT_NODE	An entire XML document
DocumentType	Node.DOCUMENT_TYPE_NODE	The document type declaration of a document
Element	Node.ELEMENT_NODE	An element
Entity	Node.ENTITY_NODE	An entity declaration in a DTD
EntityReference	Node.ENTITY_REFERENCE_NODE	A reference to a parsed entity
Notation	Node.NOTATION_NODE	A notation declaration in a DTD
Processing Instruction	Node. PROCESSING_INSTRUCTION_NODE	An XML processing instruction
Text	Node.TEXT_NODE	Some text content within an element

From the `Document` object we can navigate to any other point in the structure. Nodes have the following basic navigation methods:

- `boolean hasChildNodes()`
- `NodeList getChildNodes()`
- `Node getFirstChild()`
- `Node getLastChild()`
- `Node getNextSibling()`
- `Document getOwnerDocument()`
- `Node getParentNode()`
- `Node getPreviousSibling()`

They're all reasonably self-explanatory, and will return `null` if there is no other suitable response. As you can see, the general child-parent-sibling methods return `Node` objects, or collections of nodes. Some nodes can only have certain types of nodes as children (for example, an element can't contain a document node), but for a general `Node`, there is no way of predicting what type of `Node` any of these methods will return. So, if you have an arbitrary `Node` object, how can you find out what type it really is? `Node` provides the general method `getNodeType()`, which returns a `short` – a set of constants defined in the `Node` interface should be used to determine exactly what the significance of the value is. These are listed in the above table.

The `Node` interface also defines several methods that are relevant to a lot of nodes, and are generally the most used. If you call these methods on a type of node for which they are meaningless, you will get a `null` value in return. They are:

- `String getLocalName()`
- `String getNamespaceURI()`
- `String getNodeName()`
- `String getNodeValue()`
- `String getPrefix()`
- `boolean hasAttributes()`
- `NamedNodeMap getAttributes()`

Obviously, not all nodes have a name or attributes. If you check what kind of node you're handling, and know what to do with the data returned from them, it can save some awkward casting to specific subtypes.

Let's implement a DOM equivalent of our `VerboseSAXParser`. We'll parse in an XML document, and then we'll take a look at the returned document object and try to print out as much data as we can about it.

The opening is very familiar:

```
import javax.xml.parsers.*;
import org.w3c.dom.*;
import java.io.*;
import java.util.*;

public class VerboseDOMParser {

  public static final String VALIDATING = "-v";
  public static final String NAMESPACE = "-n";
  public static final String USAGE =
    "Usage: java VerboseDOMParser [-n] [-v] <filename>";

  public static void main(String[] args) {
    boolean namespace = false;
    boolean validating = false;

    if (args.length < 1) {
      System.out.println(USAGE);
      System.exit(1);
    } else if (args.length > 1) {
      for (int a = 0; a < (args.length - 1); a++) {
        if (args[a].equalsIgnoreCase(VALIDATING)) {
          validating = true;
        } else if (args[a].equalsIgnoreCase(NAMESPACE)) {
          namespace = true;
        } else {
          System.out.println(USAGE);
          System.exit(1);
        }
      }
    }

    String filename = args[args.length - 1];
```

Here's where and how we use the JAXP DOM API to parse in a document to a DOM model:

```
    Document doc = null;

    try {
      DocumentBuilderFactory dbf =
        DocumentBuilderFactory.newInstance();
      dbf.setNamespaceAware(namespace);
      dbf.setValidating(validating);
```

```
    DocumentBuilder parser = dbf.newDocumentBuilder();

    FileInputStream fis = new FileInputStream(filename);
    doc = parser.parse(fis, filename);
  } catch (Exception e) {
    e.printStackTrace();
  }
```

The DocumentBuilder has several parse() methods, which match the range of functionality the SAXParser has. The signatures only differ in not requiring a DefaultHandler, naturally (since the DOM is not an event-driven API), and in that they return a Document object.

- Document parse(File f)
- Document parse(InputSource is)
- Document parse(InputStream is)
- Document parse(InputStream is, String systemId)
- Document parse(String uri)

Having said that DOM is not event-driven, it is worth noting that DocumentBuilder also has these two methods:

- void setEntityResolver(EntityResolver er)
- void setErrorHandler(ErrorHandler eh)

Just like a SAX parser, a DOM parser will sometimes need a helping hand with those non-absolute URIs, and also in deciding what to do if something goes wrong. This is a sensible way to solve this problem, since behind every DOM parser is, typically, a SAX parser feeding events into a special ContentHandler that is building the DOM object model.

Now, having obtained a Document, we need to examine it and print out what we find. So, we pass it to a generic Node-examining routine, nodeWalk(), along with an integer representing how far text about this node should be indented.

```
  nodeWalk(doc, 0);
}
```

nodeWalk() is a recursive routine. In analyzing a node, we come across other nodes. When we do so, we call nodeWalk(), and tell it to print out the details of that node, indented an extra couple of character spaces. At this stage, let's make nodeWalk() as simple as possible – just looking at what we can find out about a node using methods in the Node interface itself. First we print out the node name, because that's guaranteed to exist (even if it's pretty meaningless in some cases) for all nodes. We'll also print out a string representation of the node type. Then we print out whatever's available of the other values – local name, namespace URI, namespace prefix, and value. Finally, we move on to the child nodes.

```
private static void nodeWalk(Node n, int i) {
  println(n.getNodeName() + " ["
          + nodeTypeAsString(n.getNodeType()) + "]", i);
  printNameValue("Local Name", n.getLocalName(), i + 2);
  printNameValue("Namespace URI", n.getNamespaceURI(), i + 2);
  printNameValue("Prefix", n.getPrefix(), i + 2);
  printNameValue("Value", n.getNodeValue(), i + 2);

  if (n.hasAttributes()) {
    nodeMapWalk("Attributes", n.getAttributes(), i + 2);
  }

  if (n.hasChildNodes()) {
    nodeListWalk("Children", n.getChildNodes(), i + 2);
  }
}
```

We've got a couple of routines that print out data for us, formatted the way we want. One, `println()`, simply prints the given text with the given indent. The other prints a name and a value at the given indent, but only does so if the value is not `null`. A lot of node types return `null` for values that they don't have, so this will prevent us outputting extraneous data. Here they are:

```
private static void println(String s, int i) {
  indent(i);
  System.out.println(s);
}

private static void indent(int i) {
  char[] indent = new char[i];
  Arrays.fill(indent, ' ');
  System.out.print(indent);
}

private static void printNameValue(String name, String value, int i)
{
  if (value != null) {
    println(name + ": " + value, i);
  }
}
```

The iteration occurs inside one of two routines, which will either walk through the members of a `NodeList` (a DOM collection representing an ordered set of nodes) or a `NamedNodeMap` (a DOM collection of uniquely-named items – a sort of half-set, half-map). `NodeList` has two methods – one to determine the size of the list, and one to retrieve items by index from the list. For each item in the list, we call `nodeWalk()`. Conveniently, `NamedNodeMaps` have both of these same methods, so the code is identical. They have some other methods to retrieve items by name, but we're not concerned about those here.

```
private static void nodeListWalk(String name, NodeList nl, int i) {
  println(name + ":", i);
  int count = nl.getLength();
  for (int a = 0; a < count; a++) {
    nodeWalk(nl.item(a), i + 2);
  }
}

private static void nodeMapWalk(String name, NamedNodeMap nnm, int i)
{
  println(name + ":", i);
  int count = nnm.getLength();
  for (int a = 0; a < count; a++) {
    nodeWalk(nnm.item(a), i + 2);
  }
}
```

The last method is a convenience method, which returns a string representing the type of a node, which we output in square brackets after the node name:

```
private static String nodeTypeAsString(short n) {
  String nodeType = null;
  switch (n) {
  case Node.ATTRIBUTE_NODE:
    nodeType = "Attribute";
    break;
  case Node.CDATA_SECTION_NODE:
    nodeType = "CDATA Section";
    break;
  case Node.COMMENT_NODE:
    nodeType = "Comment";
    break;
  case Node.DOCUMENT_FRAGMENT_NODE:
    nodeType = "Document Fragment";
    break;
  case Node.DOCUMENT_NODE:
    nodeType = "Document";
```

```
      break;
    case Node.DOCUMENT_TYPE_NODE:
      nodeType = "Document Type";
      break;
    case Node.ELEMENT_NODE:
      nodeType = "Element";
      break;
    case Node.ENTITY_NODE:
      nodeType = "Entity";
      break;
    case Node.ENTITY_REFERENCE_NODE:
      nodeType = "Entity Reference";
      break;
    case Node.NOTATION_NODE:
      nodeType = "Notation";
      break;
    case Node.PROCESSING_INSTRUCTION_NODE:
      nodeType = "Processing Instruction";
      break;
    case Node.TEXT_NODE:
      nodeType = "Text";
      break;
    }
    return nodeType;
  }
}
```

That's it for a simple example. Here are the edited highlights of its output for our final, complex, multi-document XML document from the SAX section:

```
> java VerboseDOMParser -n -v test3.xml
#document [Document]
  Children:
    song [Document Type]
    song [Element]
      Local Name: song
      Namespace URI: http://www.wrox.com/song
      Attributes:
        writer [Attribute]
          Local Name: writer
          Value: trad
        title [Attribute]
          Local Name: title
          Value: Happy Birthday
        tune [Attribute]
          Local Name: tune
```

```
        Value: happybday
      xmlns [Attribute]
        Local Name: xmlns
        Namespace URI: http://www.w3.org/2000/xmlns/
        Value: http://www.wrox.com/song
    Children:
      #text [Text]
        Value:
      #text [Text]
        Value:
      #text [Text]
        Value:
      verse [Element]
        Local Name: verse
        Namespace URI: http://www.wrox.com/song
        Children:
          #text [Text]
            Value:
          #text [Text]
            Value:
          #text [Text]
            Value:
          line [Element]
            Local Name: line
            Namespace URI: http://www.wrox.com/song
            Children:
              #text [Text]
                Value: Happy birthday to you,
                .
                .
                .
          line [Element]
            Local Name: line
            Namespace URI: http://www.wrox.com/song
            Children:
              #text [Text]
                Value: Happy birthday dear James,
                .
                .
                .
```

So it's possible, using only the Node methods, to access pretty much all of the data in the document. We have to know whether the particular data we're after is the name, value, or local name of a particular node, but the information is there. Also, all of the complexity of this document set is hidden from us. It's worth noting that the DOM specification allows parsers not to fully resolve a text node that contains an entity reference. We might have seen:

```
          line [Element]
            Local Name: line
            Namespace URI: http://www.wrox.com/song
            Children:
              #text [Text]
                Value: Happy birthday dear
              name [Entity Reference]
                Children:
                  #text [Text]
                    Value: James
              #text [Text]
                Value: ,
```

This means we have to be careful if we assume that a particular element contains only a single text node; it's possible that somebody will include an entity reference like this in a document, and we need to be prepared for that.

To access *all* of the data in the DOM of this document, we need to add some conditional code that can detect what sort of node we're dealing with:

```
  private static void nodeWalk(Node n, int i) {
    println(n.getNodeName() + " ["
            + nodeTypeAsString(n.getNodeType()) + "]", i);
    printNameValue("Local Name", n.getLocalName(), i + 2);
    printNameValue("Namespace URI", n.getNamespaceURI(), i + 2);
    printNameValue("Prefix", n.getPrefix(), i + 2);
    printNameValue("Value", n.getNodeValue(), i + 2);

    switch (n.getNodeType()) {
    case Node.DOCUMENT_TYPE_NODE:
      DocumentType dt = (DocumentType) n;
      nodeMapWalk("Entity declarations", dt.getEntities(), i + 2);
      nodeMapWalk("Notation declarations", dt.getNotations(), i + 2);
      printNameValue("System ID of external DTD subset",
                     dt.getSystemId(), i + 2);
      printNameValue("Public ID of external DTD subset",
                     dt.getPublicId(), i + 2);
      printNameValue("Available internal DTD subset",
                     dt.getInternalSubset(), i + 2);
      break;
    case Node.ENTITY_NODE:
      Entity ent = (Entity) n;
      printNameValue("System ID", ent.getSystemId(), i + 2);
      printNameValue("Public ID", ent.getPublicId(), i + 2);
      printNameValue("Notation", ent.getNotationName(), i + 2);

      break;
```

```
    case Node.NOTATION_NODE:
      Notation not = (Notation) n;
      printNameValue("System ID", not.getSystemId(), i + 2);
      printNameValue("Public ID", not.getPublicId(), i + 2);

      break;
    }

    if (n.hasAttributes()) {
      nodeMapWalk("Attributes", n.getAttributes(), i + 2);
    }

    if (n.hasChildNodes()) {
      nodeListWalk("Children", n.getChildNodes(), i + 2);
    }
  }
```

The added code interprets the `DocumentType` node that appears at the top of our printout. Two collections – `NamedNodeMaps` of entity declarations and notation declarations – can be accessed by casting this node to the `DocumentType` interface, and calling its `getEntities()` and `getNotations()` methods. Then, to get the full details about notation and entity declaration nodes, we need to cast them to appropriate types in order to obtain the system and public URIs if they're available. The resulting output now includes the following:

```
#document [Document]
  Children:
    song [Document Type]
      Entity declarations:
        happybday [Entity]
          System ID: file:///C:/happybirthday.wav
          Notation: wav
        name [Entity]
          System ID: file:///C:/name.txt
      Notation declarations:
        wav [Notation]
          Public ID: audio/wav
      System ID of external DTD subset: file:///C:/song.dtd
           .
           .
           .
```

XML 5

It's important to notice though that, in this structure, not every node is related to another node by a parent-child relationship. Attribute nodes are not children of the element they belong to – they are accessed through a different collection. Similarly, entity and notation declarations aren't children of the document type node – they are in separate collections. They're all nodes, and all of them belong to the ancestor document, but their attachment to the nodes that own them is not through the child link.

This is because the set of children a node has is governed by different rules, for example, from the set of attributes an element has. A node's children are an ordered set of arbitrary nodes, which are therefore uniquely identified by their position in the list, not their name. An element's attributes are an unordered set of named nodes, where each name must be unique within that set. For this reason, attributes cannot be represented as children of an element node.

Document Building

DOM has another capability that makes it more powerful than SAX for some applications. The in-memory representation of the DOM tree is not immutable – we can add, delete, and move nodes around.

We can create new nodes by calling the following methods of the `Document` object:

- `Attr createAttribute(String name)`
- `Attr createAttributeNS(String namespaceURI, String qualifiedName)`
- `CDATASection createCDATASection(String data)`
- `Comment createComment(String data)`
- `DocumentFragment createDocumentFragment()`
- `Element createElement(String tagName)`
- `Element createElementNS(String namespaceURI, String qualifiedName)`
- `EntityReference createEntityReference(String name)`
- `ProcessingInstruction createProcessingInstruction(String target, String data)`
- `Text createTextNode(String data)`

These create free-floating nodes of the appropriate type, which we can then attach to the document's structure. Note that only nodes created from a specific document's `create()` methods can be attached to nodes in that document. This prevents us from mixing up nodes belonging to two different DOM implementations.

We can add nodes as children by using these methods of the `Node` interface:

- `Node appendChild(Node newChild)`
- `Node insertBefore(Node newChild, Node refChild)`
- `Node replaceChild(Node newChild, Node oldChild)`

These methods can all throw a `DOMException` if we try to add a child that is not suitable for a particular node (such as trying to add an attribute as a child, or add a document type definition to an element, or anything as a child of an attribute).

To add nodes in any other relationship, we can use the methods of the `NamedNodeMap` interface, which is used to ensure that only one node with a particular name exists in a given node map. The methods of interest are:

- `Node setNamedItem(Node arg)`
- `Node setNamedItemNS(Node arg)`

These will replace any existing node with the same name with the supplied node.

Since setting attributes is one of the most commonly required tasks for a DOM builder, convenience methods exist in the `Element` interface, as follows:

- `void setAttribute(String name, String value)`
- `void setAttributeNS(String namespaceURI, String qualifiedName, String value)`
- `Attr setAttributeNode(Attr newAttr)`
- `Attr setAttributeNodeNS(Attr newAttr)`

Again, a `DOMexception` can be thrown if we can't add the attribute we want to.

Transformations with XSLT and TrAX

XSLT, the **eXtensible Stylesheet Language for Transformations**, is a stylesheet language with a declarative syntax, which can even be used as a functional programming language that is expressed in an XML format. XML tags may not seem like the most logical syntax for expressing programming constructs, but XSLT was created as a way to describe a mapping of one XML document to another, so the decision to use XML as the format for the language itself was made to ensure that the same parsers could be used for the input and the language.

XSLT can be used to extract data from an XML document, format it, sort it, perform calculations on it, and generally re-arrange it, into a completely different piece of XML or HTML data. This allows us to turn raw data described in XML into presentable data described using HTML, or take data described using one XML vocabulary of element names, and translate it into a different vocabulary.

An XSLT stylesheet describes a set of templates, which will be used to format parts of an input XML document into a different output document. A template can be applied to almost any specified subset of XML elements in the source document, and the content of the template can make use of any of the data available in the element to which it is being applied. For example, here is an XSLT stylesheet:

```
<?xml version="1.0" encoding="UTF-8"?>
<xsl:stylesheet xmlns:xsl="http://www.w3.org/1999/XSL/Transform"
                version="1.0"
                xmlns:wrox="http://www.wrox.com/song">

  <xsl:template match="wrox:song">
    <song>
      <writer><xsl:value-of select="@writer" /></writer>
      <title><xsl:value-of select="@title" /></title>
    </song>
  </xsl:template>
</xsl:stylesheet>
```

When applied to our last XML document, this generates the following output:

```
<?xml version="1.0" encoding="UTF-8"?>
<song><writer>trad</writer><title>Happy Birthday</title></song>
```

We've pulled out the contents of the song element's two attributes, and turned them into elements. How? Well, the key is the `xsl:template` element, which defines what output should be made whenever an element matching the specification in its `match` attribute is encountered. The specification in the `match` attribute here is that any element called `song`, belonging to the `http://www.wrox.com/song` namespace, should be replaced with the enclosed template.

Within this template, we output a new element called `song`, containing two elements, `writer` and `title`. The content of these elements is provided by the `xsl:value-of` elements, which specify what part of the matched element should be used. The `@writer` notation, for example, is the specification for the attribute called `writer`, belonging to the matched element.

We can perform this transformation using the TrAX API. Here's a short class that will do it for us:

```
import java.io.*;
import javax.xml.transform.*;
import javax.xml.transform.stream.*;
```

```
public class TrAX {

  public static final String USAGE =
    "Usage: java TrAX <source-file> <xslt-file>";

  public static void main(String[] args) {

    if (args.length != 2) {
      System.out.println(USAGE);
      System.exit(1);
    }

    String in = args[0];
    String xslt = args[1];

    try {
      StreamSource inSource =
        new StreamSource(new FileInputStream(in), in);
      StreamSource xsltSource =
        new StreamSource(new FileInputStream(xslt),xslt);
      StreamResult outResult = new StreamResult(System.out);

      TransformerFactory tf = TransformerFactory.newInstance();
      Transformer trans = tf.newTransformer(xsltSource);
      trans.transform(inSource, outResult);
    } catch (Exception e) {
      e.printStackTrace();
    }
  }
}
```

After extracting the two required arguments from the command line, we construct two source objects, and one result.

`Source` and `Result` are abstract classes defined in the TrAX API to encapsulate different types of input and output for a transformation process. Subclasses exist that map to a DOM object model, to a stream of SAX events, and to byte or character streams, which are what we're using.

Here are the constructors for `Source` objects:

- `javax.xml.transform.stream.StreamSource(File f)`
- `javax.xml.transform.stream.StreamSource(InputStream inputStream)`
- `javax.xml.transform.stream.StreamSource(InputStream inputStream, String systemId)`

XML

5

- `javax.xml.transform.stream.StreamSource(Reader reader)`
- ```
  javax.xml.transform.stream.StreamSource(Reader reader,
                                          String systemId)
  ```
- `javax.xml.transform.stream.StreamSource(String systemId)`
- `javax.xml.transform.dom.DOMSource(Node n)`
- ```
  javax.xml.transform.dom.DOMSource(Node node,
                                    String systemID)
  ```
- ```
  javax.xml.transform.sax.SAXSource(
                                 InputSource inputSource)
  ```
- ```
  javax.xml.transform.sax.SAXSource(XMLReader reader,
                                 InputSource inputSource)
  ```

And here are the Result constructors:

- `javax.xml.transform.stream.StreamResult(File f)`
- ```
  javax.xml.transform.stream.StreamResult(
                                 OutputStream outputStream)
  ```
- `javax.xml.transform.stream.StreamResult(String systemId)`
- `javax.xml.transform.stream.StreamResult(Writer writer)`
- `javax.xml.transform.dom.DOMResult(Node node)`
- ```
  javax.xml.transform.dom.DOMResult(Node node,
                                    String systemID)
  ```
- `javax.xml.transform.sax.SAXResult(ContentHandler handler)`

In order to perform a transformation, we must create a `Transformer` object from a `Source` object that will provide an XSLT document. Then we must call that transformer's `transform()` method, passing in a `Source` (representing the document we want to transform), and a `Result` (representing where we want the transformation results to end up). We make `StreamSource` objects out of `FileInputStreams` from the two filenames supplied on the command line. We make a `StreamResult` object out of `System.out`.

We can now easily perform XSLT transformations on XML files, and output the result to the console. Here's another example XSLT stylesheet. This one outputs HTML:

```
<?xml version="1.0" encoding="UTF-8"?>
<xsl:stylesheet xmlns:xsl="http://www.w3.org/1999/XSL/Transform"
                version="1.0"
                xmlns:wrox="http://www.wrox.com/song">
```

```
  <xsl:output method="html"/>

  <xsl:template match="wrox:song">
    <html>
      <head>
        <title><xsl:value-of select="@title"/></title>
      </head>
        <body>
          <h1><xsl:value-of select="@title"/></h1>
          <h3><xsl:value-of select="@writer"/></h3>
          <xsl:apply-templates/>
        </body>
    </html>
  </xsl:template>

  <xsl:template match="wrox:verse">
    <p>
      <xsl:apply-templates/>
    </p>
  </xsl:template>

  <xsl:template match="wrox:line">
    <xsl:value-of select="text()"/>
    <br/>
  </xsl:template>

</xsl:stylesheet>
```


This stylesheet includes an instruction to the XSL processor that the output should be treated as HTML. This means that certain elements will be treated specially, no XML processing instruction will be included at the start, and so on. Then, the sheet contains three templates, one for song elements, one for verses, and one for lines. In the song template, we use the same technique as before to pull out the values of the `title` and `writer` attributes. Then, having output them both inside HTML heading elements, we use a new element, `xsl:apply-templates`. This tells the processor to look at the contents of the matched element and see if any other templates match. `song` elements contain `verse` elements, so the next template will match the contained `verse`. This template outputs a paragraph element, and again applies templates to get the contents. The last template matches `lines`, and outputs the contents of the matched line (obtained with the function `text()`) followed by a `br` tag.

Running this stylesheet, we get the following output on our console:

```
<html xmlns:wrox="http://www.wrox.com/song">
<head>
<META http-equiv="Content-Type" content="text/html;
charset=UTF-8">
```

```
<title>Happy Birthday</title>
</head>
<body>
<h1>Happy Birthday</h1>
<h3>trad</h3>

<p>
    Happy birthday to you,<br>
    Happy birthday to you,<br>
    Happy birthday dear James,<br>
    Happy birthday to you.<br>

</p>

</body>
</html>
```

A browser would display this as follows:

The same stylesheet will produce similar output for any document conforming to the song DTD.

XPath

As you can probably see, the real power of XSLT is in defining which elements a particular template matches, and in selecting pieces of data to output using the `value-of` element. There's a lot more to XSLT besides these techniques, but both of them make use of an expression language called **XPath**.

XPath allows us to select nodes in a document tree. Unfortunately, and it has to be said fairly predictably for a W3C standard, the XPath document tree is not exactly the same as the DOM document tree. An XPath is a specification of a set of nodes on one of these trees, relative to a starting node.

An XPath expression consists of a number of steps, separated by slashes (/). Each step is effectively a selection operation that chooses a set of nodes, based on the set of nodes selected by any previous steps. Each step selects a node set by first of all selecting a set of nodes for consideration, applying a test to each of those nodes, and then applying a further filter called a **predicate** to the remaining nodes. The nodes that pass all the tests are the resulting node set.

Like a filesystem path, an XPath can be either relative or absolute. An absolute XPath starts with a `/`, but a relative XPath doesn't. A relative XPath passes a node set containing just the current node, called the **context node**, to the first selection operation in the path. An absolute XPath passes a node set containing just the **root node** (a container node analogous to a DOM `Document` node).

The possible candidate node sets relative to a particular node are called its axes. For each node, you can select the child axis (the node set containing all of a node's children), the parent axis (the node set containing the node's parent, if it has one), and so on. The XPath axes are as follows:

Axis	Selects
`ancestor`	Any node that is above the context node in the node tree
`ancestor-or-self`	The context node itself, plus all of the nodes in the ancestor axis
`attribute`	All of the attribute nodes belonging to the context node
`child`	All of the direct child nodes of the context node
`descendant`	All of the nodes below the context node in the node tree
`descendant-or-self`	The context node itself, plus all of the nodes in the descendant axis
`following`	See below
`following-sibling`	The next child of the context node's parent
`namespace`	Any namespace nodes that are attached to the context node
`parent`	The context node's parent node
`preceding`	See below
`preceding-sibling`	The previous child of the context node's parent
`self`	The context node

Following and preceding node sets are a little harder to describe. The following diagram shows slightly more clearly how the nodes in a tree relate to the five core axes:

- `self`
- `descendant`
- `ancestor`
- `following`
- `preceding`

Figure 5

The letters in each node cell represent which of the five key axes the nodes lies on:

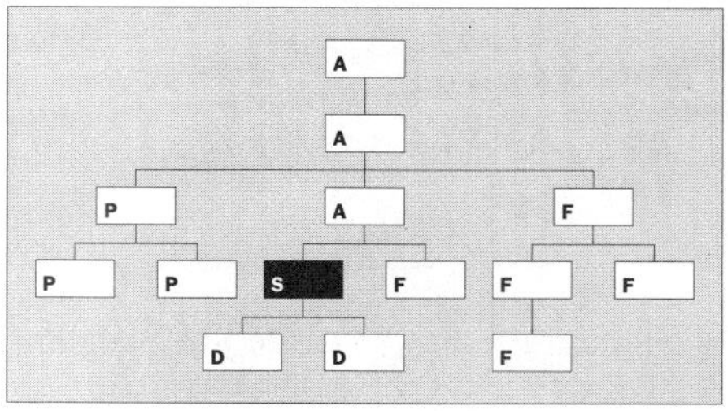

- The **black** cell is the context node
- A represents ancestor nodes
- D represents descendants
- F is for following
- P for preceding
- S is the self axis

As you can see, all the nodes in the document fall on exactly one of these five axes. In the context of an XML document, `ancestor` nodes are those that contain the context node; `descendant` nodes are those that the context node contains; `preceding` nodes are nodes outside the context node, which do not contain it, and which come completely before the context node in the document; `following` nodes are the same, but come after the context node in the document.

Having specified an axis, we then have to specify a test that should be applied to each node in the candidate node set (the set of nodes on the axis) to see if they should be eliminated from the set. The complete specification is written as:

```
<axis>::<node-test>
```

One type of node test is to specify a node type. Nodes that are not of a matching type will be eliminated from the node set. This is done using the following tests:

Node test	Matches
`attribute()`	Attribute nodes
`namespace()`	Namespace nodes
`text()`	Text nodes

Table continued on following page

Node test	**Matches**
`comment()`	Comment nodes
`processing-instruction()`	Processing instruction nodes
`processing-instruction("name")`	Processing instruction nodes whose target is `name`
`node()`	Any node

In addition, the node test can simply be a string. In this case, the node test succeeds if the node is an element or an attribute whose name matches the string. Alternatively, you can specify an asterisk (*) character for the node test, in which case it acts as a wildcard, and will match any element or attribute node.

So, based on this, here are some example XPaths:

XPath	**Specifies**
`child::node()`	All of the nodes that are direct children of the context node.
`child::node()/attribute::foo`	All of the attribute nodes called `foo` that belong to nodes that are direct children of the context node.
`/self::node()`	The root node.
`/child::element()`	All of the elements that are direct children of the root node. If the document being processed is well-formed XML, then there will only be one – the document's root element.
`/descendant-or-self::text()`	All of the text nodes in the entire document.

Finally, we can specify an optional predicate after the node test. It is written in square brackets immediately after the node test, and is a Boolean test carried out on each node passing the node test to further qualify the node set. Within a predicate, we can use various functions to perform tests. For example, the `position()` function returns the index of the node being tested. The function `last()` returns the index of the last node in the current node's context. To select the last node from a node set, we can simply add the predicate `[position() = last()]`, which will test as `true` for the last node, but as `false` for all the others.

So, an XPath consists of a series of selection steps, separated by slashes, each of which consists of an axis, a node test, and an optional predicate. None of the expressions in any of our stylesheets look like that though – what's going on? Well, we've been using XPath's abbreviated syntax. The XPaths we used in the first XSLT document were as follows:

- The `xsl:template` element's match attribute specified the XPath `wrox:song`
- Within this template, we used `value-of` to insert the text values specified by the XPaths `@title` and `@writer`

These are all relative XPaths, consisting of just one selection step (since they don't begin with a slash, or contain any slashes). So, they are all selecting nodes based on the context node, not based on the root node. The first XPath, `wrox:song`, consists simply of a string. A selection step consisting of just a string is interpreted as meaning `child::<string>`. So, our XPath is really `child::wrox:song`, which we've said will select all child nodes of the context node whose name is `wrox:song`.

The second two paths both begin with the `@` character. This is equivalent to specifying the attribute axis, so these XPaths are the equivalent of the XPaths `attribute::title` and `attribute::writer`.

Some other useful XPath abbreviations are as follows:

Abbreviation	Expansion	Effect
`.`	`self::node()`	Selects the context node. Useful for making the context of a relative XPath obvious, as in: `./wrox:song`.
`..`	`parent::node()`	Selects the parent node. Use just like the `..` path in UNIX and DOS file paths.
`<node-test>`	`child::<node-test>`	Selects any child nodes that pass. `<node-test>`. This allows us to simply specify a string as a step in an XPath.
`//`	`/descendant-or-self::node()/`	Applies the following selection operation at every level of a node's children, rather than just at the node itself. For example: `.//line` selects all of the line elements anywhere in the context node's descendant tree, regardless of how many containing elements intervene.
`@<string>`	`attribute::<string>`	Selects the attribute with the given name.
`[<number>]`	`[position() = <number>]`	Acts like an array index, selecting the `<number>`th member of a node set – as in: `./verse[3]` This will select the third element named `verse` from the context element's children.

Table continued on following page

XPath is a powerful expression language in its own right, and we have covered the basics here. For extracting data of interest from within an XML document, XPath is easily as capable as SQL is at doing the same from a relational database.

For complete coverage of XSLT, XPath, and TrAX, take a look at Michael Kay's *XSLT Programmer's Reference (Second Edition)*, ISBN 1-861005-06-7, and *Java XML Programmer's Reference*, ISBN 1-861005-20-2, by Akif et al., both from Wrox Press.

Through the addition of TrAX to JAXP, Java developers now have access to the capabilities of two more languages: XSLT and XPath. Unfortunately, JAXP currently doesn't provide us with the ability to simply execute XPath queries on a document, and retrieve the resulting node set for processing. This is basically down to the fact that no standard interface exists for examining an XPath node set, and as we said before, it isn't directly compatible with the widely used DOM node model. Instead, we are forced to write XSLT documents containing the XPath logic required to extract the relevant information, which transform the original document into a different XML document containing the information we want. In spite of this limitation, this does provide us with some powerful capabilities for XML processing.

DOM Level 3, currently working its way through the W3C standards process, includes an extension that allows XPath queries to be made on DOM nodes.

Conclusions

The inclusion of JAXP in the J2SE is a huge benefit to developers looking to deploy any application that reads or writes XML data. It removes the necessity to include your own parser with the distribution, and provides a clear standard to program against. Crimson and Xalan are two very powerful programs in their own right, and their inclusion as standard in the run-time environment ensures that the XML parsing and XSLT processing functionality provided will be first class.

There's a great deal more to programming XML applications than we've been able to cover here. These APIs, in themselves, provide a relatively low-level access to the data in XML documents. For more advanced approaches to XML programming, largely made possible by building libraries on top of JAXP, DOM, and SAX, you may want to look at *Professional Java XML*, by Ahmed et al. from Wrox Press, *ISBN* 1-861004-01-X. This covers the possibilities opened up by XML for communication between computers, for storing data, and for accessing web services.

Java J2SE 1.4 Core Platform Update

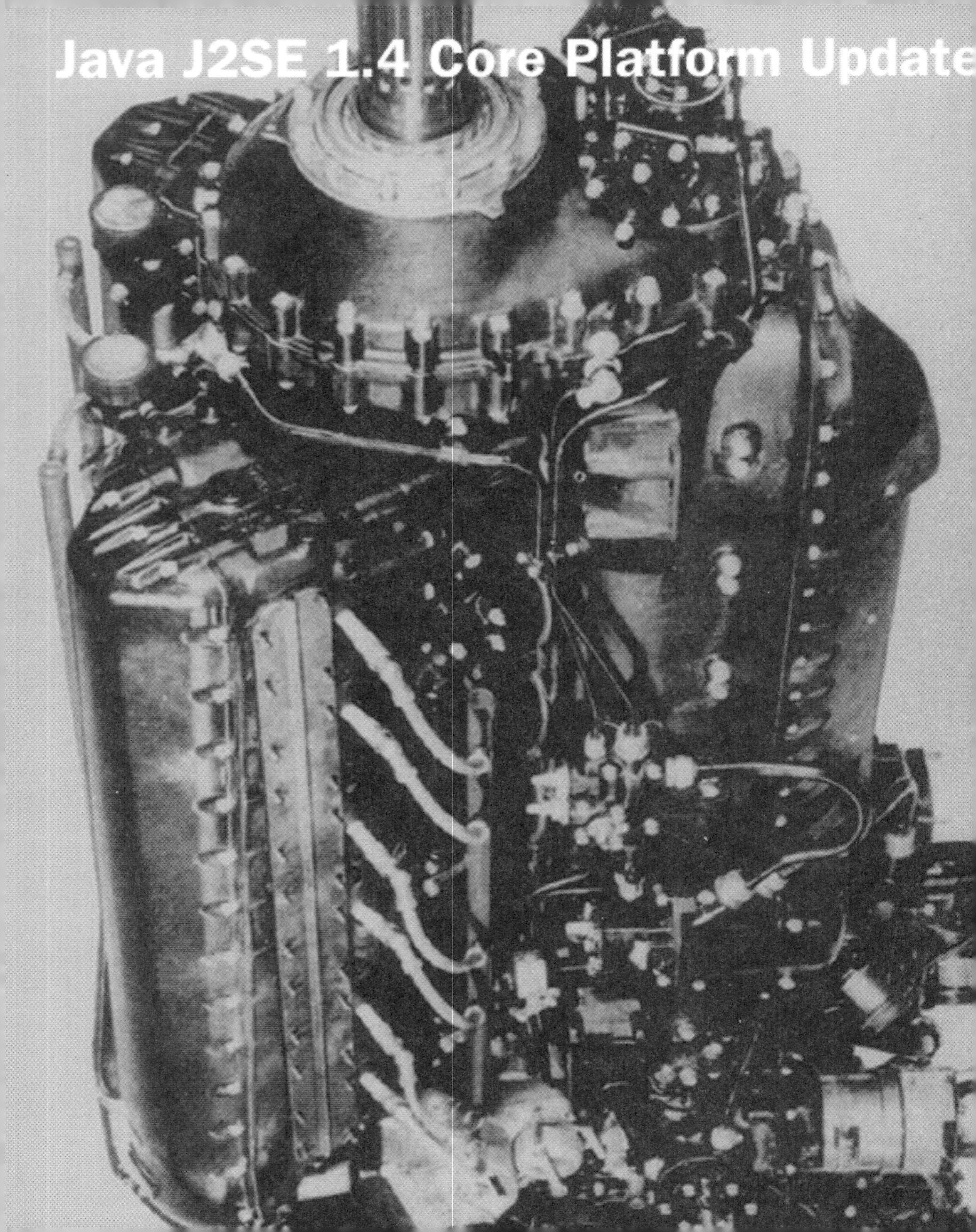

Utilities

One of the most important package hierarchies in the Java runtime is `java.util`. It brings localization support, property files, string handling, JAR and ZIP file support, timers, events, and, of course, collections. These classes touch on almost every aspect of Java programming. In J2SE 1.4, three significant new APIs have been added to the utility package hierarchy:

1. **Preferences**
2. **Logging**
3. **Regular expressions**

In addition, there have been some minor changes to collections, and a minor improvement to localization.

Preferences

The **preferences system** is a brand new API intended largely to replace the use of old-style properties files. The release notes for the preferences API have this to say about using property files to store preferences:

1. There is no standard place to keep application properties, user preferences, or properties for libraries.
2. The lack of policies for naming and placement of property files makes name conflicts between applications, or elements of applications, a real possibility.
3. The property `file` system is reliant on files – it is wedded to the filesystem, and so property file access is predicated on filesystem access. Not to mention that on some platforms, such as telephones or set-top boxes, there is no filesystem.

4. The diversity of locations in which property data is stored makes it hard to back up and restore user preferences, or move them between machines.

The alternative to using the property file approach is to use **JNDI**, which is a heavyweight approach to storing a few pieces of lightweight information about what color someone prefers for their menu bars. JNDI does at least provide a storage-neutral solution. The preferences API sets out to provide a lightweight facility with the same back-end neutrality, while also providing a clear set of policies that, if followed, should prevent namespace conflicts and ensure that all of a user's preferences are conveniently collected together.

Logging

The **logging architecture** is a centrally provided service, designed to be accessed from all points in an application, through which events can be reported, sorted, filtered, and fired off to any of a number of different types of storage. This system enables anything from classic file-based logging of significant application events, with the usual customizable logging levels to change the granularity of events that are logged, to complex custom logging systems for distributed applications, which gather information from a number of networked machines, detect alarm conditions, and fire off the necessary message to a system administrator's pager.

Logging systems are one of the most frequently home-baked Java components, so the inclusion of a full-blown logging system in the Java platform should eliminate the need for a lot of duplicated effort.

Regular Expressions

If Java has one serious weakness, it has got to be text processing. With the exception of the existing `java.util.StringTokenizer`, most fundamental Java classes treat strings as either solid chunks of data that can't be broken up, or as simple character arrays. Strings are often much more complex than that though; they carry meaning, which is not communicated by treating them as a simple array of characters. Different types of character have different types of meaning, according to context. Whitespace, for example, might be a word separator, a paragraph indent, the column separator in a data file, or it might be the thousand-separator in a European financial report. A dollar sign could signify a currency, or the start of a shell variable, or the separator between the name of a class and its inner class in the name of a Java class file. Extracting data from within characters with such diverse meanings typically involves writing complex string-matching logic, using verbose character-handling code. We need a way to bridge the gap between what characters make up an expression, and what the expression means.

Regular expressions go a long way to bridging that gap. They provide a concise expression language for describing the structure of a particular type of string, for example an e-mail address, or an XML tag. This makes it possible to identify and extract the parts of those strings that are of interest because of their semantic value and ignore those parts that are not interesting, such as whitespace. For example, regular expressions make it trivial to extract the domain names from a list of e-mail addresses, perhaps in order to produce statistics on subscriptions to a mailing list by domain.

Regular expressions are a widely used text-processing tool in the UNIX command-line world, and are probably the single most important core feature of the Perl programming language. Java's new **regex support** opens up some fantastic possibilities for simplifying the code needed to perform what should be simple text manipulation tasks, and for making possible tasks that you would previously have never considered attempting in Java.

Collections

The Java **Collections API**, on the other hand, is one of the Java platform's finest features. It's a model of polymorphism, extensibility, choice, and power. Even something as fine as this needs the occasional refurbishment though, and J2SE 1.4 has introduced a few new collection classes. Two new types of `HashMap`, and a new `HashSet`, have been added. One of the `HashMaps` is a specialized map that uses reference equality, rather than the `equals()` method, when looking up keys. This has a few specialized uses, generally to do with tracking instance references in order to perform serialization of an object graph, and since it explicitly does not behave the way a `Map` is supposed to behave, its use is only advised if you know you need its special functionality. The other `HashMap`, `LinkedHashMap`, is based on the new `HashSet`, `LinkedHashSet` (a `Map` is basically a `Set` of `Map.Entry` objects under the covers). `LinkedHashSet` contains a doubly-linked list running through all of its entries, which enables an `Iterator` to read out the entries in a fixed and repeatable order (something not guaranteed by standard sets). This adds another option when choosing a set or map implementation, offering *some* of the predictability benefits of a `TreeSet` or `TreeMap`, without the performance penalty incurred by maintaining the tree structure.

Four new static methods have been added to the `Collections` utility class, to handle operations such as rolling a list round to a different start point. A new marker interface, `RandomAccess`, has been added to mark lists that provide constant-time random access, as opposed to providing sequential access, which requires a different search time to locate elements different distances from the start point. This is intended to provide a clue to sort or search algorithms so they can modify their behavior to be optimal for the particular list being handled.

These are a fairly specialized set of tool changes, so we won't look into them further here – the JavaDoc should provide a fairly thorough explanation of the new capabilities (http://java.sun.com/j2se/1.4/docs/guide/collections/changes4.html).

Localization

J2SE 1.4 includes a new class called `java.util.Currency`. It's an interesting little class that provides the facility to discover the currency symbol, international currency code, and customary number of decimal fraction digits to use when reporting amounts in the currency, for a given locale.

Localized currency formatting has in fact been present in the `java.text.NumberFormat` class for some time, and this existing functionality seems to know more about correct local currency formatting conventions (should the symbol precede or follow the amount, does the currency have denominations less than 1000 units, and so on) than can be ascertained using the new class. The old `NumberFormat` also seems to know the currency symbols for most common currencies, whereas the new class often just returns the ISO currency code, rather than the symbol in everyday use. On the other hand, it does seem to be able to provide the international currency codes for a lot more countries than the `NumberFormat` recognizes.

However limited its ability to provide detailed formatting information is, this new class does provide a means to find the currency symbol for a specific locale. This could be useful in performing automatic lookups of currency conversion rates, perhaps to provide a user with localized pricing. With currency conversion rates available in real time via web services (see http://www.xmethods.com for examples), and with ISO currency codes as the standard parameters, this is an exciting possibility.

For formatting, I'd still recommend using `NumberFormat.getCurrencyInstance().format(float f)`, or `NumberFormat.getCurrencyInstance(Locale l).format(float f)`, rather than trying to build a format out of the elements returned by the `Currency` class.

Changes in currency support are definitely afoot so, if this were a function that you need, you would do well to watch the evolution of the `Currency` class in subsequent releases of the J2SE platform.

The Preferences API

The main objective of the Preferences API is to provide applications with a storage system for simple primitive data preferences, which basically allows the application to put a piece of data away, and then retrieve it either later in the same session, or in a different session. It provides mechanisms for storage of user-specific and application-wide settings, a namespace management system, change-notification support, and an import/export mechanism that transfers preferences information to or from XML.

One of the design decisions of the Preferences API is that the storage system should be completely invisible to the application developer. From the developer's perspective, we simply ask the JRE to store the piece of data for us under a certain key, and then trust that when we next ask for it, we'll probably get the same piece of data back. It's a lot like having a large, persistent hash-table that can only store primitive data. Whenever we request a piece of preference information, we must also provide a default value, which will be returned if no preference exists, or if the storage system is for some reason not available. Preferences should only be used for data that isn't critical to an application's functionality – they are there to provide an enhanced, personalized user experience, *not* to store crucial pieces of information that the application needs to run.

If the store is like a giant hash-table, how do we specify keys to associate with the values we are interested in? The Preferences API accomplishes this by using a directory-like structure. Each piece of preference information is stored under a named key, at a node in a conceptual "preferences tree". It is therefore identifiable by a unique path – just like the unique path that identifies every unique file in a hierarchical filesystem – which specifies the names of all the node's parents, together with the key name. This path functions as a unique key to identify each group of preference data, and the key provides a unique name for a preference within the group. How does the API expect to avoid name conflicts in this system? Well, this is done in the same way that we avoid conflicts of Java class names, or indeed, conflicts between preferences files stored in the file system. The idea is that a class should store its preferences in nodes below the node whose path is equivalent to its fully qualified name. For example, a `com.wrox.ea.j2se.Sample` class might store its preferences in the node `/com/wrox/ea/j2se/Sample`. We might want to store preferences that relate to several of our classes in the package node – perhaps `/com/wrox/ea/j2se`. If we have some preferences we want the user to be able to persist across several applications, we could go even further up the tree, to `/com/wrox`. The trick is to store preferences only in bits of the namespace we control.

This storage system is modeled very closely on the framework used by the Windows registry, and has just about the same problems, risks, and dangers of abuse. We'll try to identify the main danger areas as we go through the API.

It's worth noting, for example, that the preferences system has very coarse-grained security; if a `SecurityManager` is running, the single run-time permission `preferences` is checked before some operations can be performed, but once passed, it allows complete access to all preferences. The preferred security model might have been to have a property-permission-like system that could permit preferences access on a package-tree basis, to force applications running under a security manager to follow the package naming convention.

The preferences system provides two separate preference node trees:

- **System tree** – Provides a global store for application settings applicable to all users on a system
- **User tree** – Provides a separate set of preferences for each user

The actual storage provision for these trees is completely implementation-dependent, and shouldn't affect us as developers. On Windows, for example, the implementation provided with J2SE 1.4 uses the Windows registry to store the preferences information (in a key hierarchy under `HKEY_LOCAL_MACHINE/Software/JavaSoft/Prefs` and `HKEY_CURRENT_USER/Software/JavaSoft/Prefs`, if you're interested – you can browse them using the `regedit` utility included with Windows). On UNIX, it uses an invisible file (one whose name begins with a '`.`') in the user's home directory, or a common file in the system's preferences storage space (usually `/etc`).

The preferences specification is deliberately uninterested in back-end storage, in particular:

- It doesn't require that preferences should propagate to the persistent store immediately (however, even though preferences have not been persisted, subsequent requests to read preference data should return the value that is being cached)
- It doesn't define behavior if multiple VMs are accessing the same preferences simultaneously
- It doesn't mandate any particular medium for storage
- It requires that we supply a valid default value whenever we perform a retrieve operation, so that our code will function smoothly if the store is not available for some reason (this avoids the need for us to check for `null` return values, or catch an exception)

Using Preferences

The preferences classes are all contained in the package `java.util.prefs`. The most important class is the `Preferences` class, which represents a node in one of the preference trees. To access a preference node, the first thing we need to do is obtain the appropriate `Preferences` object. The following methods all return `Preferences` objects:

- `static Preferences systemNodeForPackage(Class c)`
- `static Preferences systemRoot()`
- `static Preferences userNodeForPackage(Class c)`
- `static Preferences userRoot()`
- `Preferences node(String pathName)`
- `Preferences parent()`

The first four static methods provide a route into the system and user node trees, and are the way to initially obtain a `Preferences` object. The `systemRoot()` and `userRoot()` methods return the node with the name `/`, or root, from the respective tree. `systemNodeForPackage()` and `userNodeForPackage()` return the appropriate node for the package containing the class passed in (but not the node for the object's fully-qualified name). This is likely to be used in the form `Preferences.userNodeForPackage(Foo.class)` or `Preferences.userNodeForPackage(this.getClass())`.

Once you have a node in one of the trees, you can navigate to other nodes using the `parent()` and `node()` methods. Use `parent()` to navigate up the node tree (towards the root), and `node()` to navigate either down (using a relative path to a node further down the hierarchy) or to an arbitrary different node in the same tree (using an absolute path). A relative path, just as with the filesystem, is interpreted relative to the current node. Relative paths are distinguished because they don't begin with `/`. Any path that does is an absolute path (one relative to the root node).

You can navigate to a node whether preferences exist there or not, but simply doing so will create any necessary entries in the persistent store. Calling something arbitrary, like `node("/foo/bar/baz/bat/bam")` will always succeed, and return a valid `Preferences` object, whether or not such a package hierarchy exists. Bear in mind that doing so does create entries in the system. To test if a node already exists, you can use `nodeExists("/foo/bar/baz/bat/bam")`, which returns a Boolean `true` if the node is there.

So, having obtained the node we want to use to store our preferences, or to read preferences from, how can we do so? The following methods in the `Preferences` class are provided for storing preferences in a node:

- `void put(String key, String value)`
- `void putBoolean(String key, boolean value)`
- `void putByteArray(String key, byte[] value)`
- `void putDouble(String key, double value)`
- `void putFloat(String key, float value)`
- `void putInt(String key, int value)`
- `void putLong(String key, long value)`

And the equivalent methods to read data are:

- `String get(String key, String def)`
- `boolean getBoolean(String key, boolean def)`
- `byte[] getByteArray(String key, byte[] def)`
- `double getDouble(String key, double def)`
- `float getFloat(String key, float def)`
- `int getInt(String key, int def)`
- `long getLong(String key, long def)`

Note that you must provide a default value, which will be returned if you try to read a preference that hasn't been set, or if the backing store is missing. This should be a sensible default that will allow the program to continue to function acceptably.

Whenever you build a program that uses local preferences, you should always build it in such a way that, if the preferences aren't available, the program uses a sensible default value. This preferences API literally forces you to do so.

So, each node can store any number of uniquely named preferences, of any primitive type or as strings. Key lengths are limited to a maximum of 80 characters, and `String` and `byte[]` value lengths are "limited" to 8192 characters (which, it has to be said, should be more than adequate, and if you plan to store 8 KB of data, you shouldn't be trusting it to the preferences system). These values are available in the `MAX_KEY_LENGTH` and `MAX_VALUE_LENGTH` public static variables.

To remove a key completely from the node, you can use the `void remove(String key)` method. To remove a node and all of its children completely (wiping out an entire preferences sub-tree), use the `void removeNode()` method. This renders the `Preferences` object on which it is called more-or-less obsolete; it no longer belongs to a node tree, so can't even be used for navigation to other nodes.

A User Preferences Application

Here is a quick Swing application that illustrates the basic principles of preferences. It defines a preferences form, which looks like this:

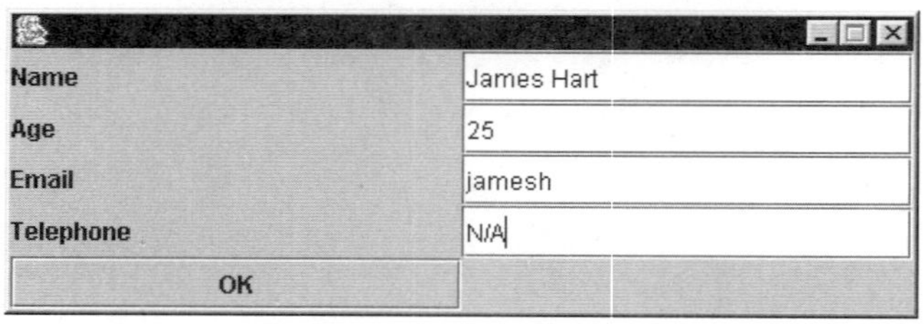

Obviously, this form is designed to be nicer to code than it is to look at. The form stores a user's personal details in a preference node on the user tree. The settings are stored when the OK button is clicked, and the application closes. On subsequent occasions when the application is run, the fields are initialized with the settings the user gave before.

```
package com.wrox.j2se.utilities;

import javax.swing.*;
import java.awt.*;
import java.awt.event.*;
import java.util.prefs.*;

public class PreferencesForm extends JFrame {

  private Preferences userPrefs;

  public static final String NAMEPREF = "name";
```

```
public static final String AGEPREF = "age";
public static final String EMAILPREF = "email";
public static final String PHONEPREF = "phone";
```

It is always best to store the keys for preferences you wish to use in some fixed fashion, like in `static final String` variables. This ensures that you are always using exactly the same string key when writing and reading the preferences.

```
public static void main(String args[]) {
  new PreferencesForm().show();
}
```

The `main()` method simply creates an instance of this class, which extends `JFrame`, and shows it. The constructor does all of the work:

```
public PreferencesForm() {
  super();
  userPrefs = Preferences.userNodeForPackage(PreferencesForm.class);
```

We obtain the user preferences node for this package, which will be the node `/com/wrox/ea/j2se/utilities`, and store it in an instance variable. This makes it easy to access the user's preferences from anywhere in the class.

Now, we need to do some Swing housekeeping to make sure our window behaves as expected:

```
  this.setResizable(false);
  this.setDefaultCloseOperation(EXIT_ON_CLOSE);
  this.setLocationRelativeTo(null);
```

Next, it is time to initialize the components. We have four `JLabels`, four `JTextFields`, and a `JButton`. The `JLabels` are each initialized with a name, and an alignment property. The `JTextFields` are initialized with the `String` value for the appropriate user preference. If the user has not set any preferences before, the fields should be empty, so we pass the default value of an empty string to the preferences node's `get()` method.

```
  final JLabel nameLabel = new JLabel("Name", JLabel.LEFT);
  final JTextField nameField =
    new JTextField(userPrefs.get(NAMEPREF, ""), 20);
  final JLabel emailLabel = new JLabel("Email", JLabel.LEFT);
  final JTextField emailField =
    new JTextField(userPrefs.get(EMAILPREF, ""), 20);
  final JLabel ageLabel = new JLabel("Age", JLabel.LEFT);
  final JTextField ageField =
    new JTextField(userPrefs.get(AGEPREF, ""), 20);
  final JLabel phoneLabel = new JLabel("Telephone", JLabel.LEFT);
  final JTextField phoneField =
    new JTextField(userPrefs.get(PHONEPREF, ""), 20);
  final JButton OKButton = new JButton("OK");
```

Clearly, this style of code is a very tidy way to obtain values in-line. We don't need to obtain the preference value, store it, check that the value isn't `null`, and substitute a suitable default if it is – we can just call `get()` and use the value returned, knowing that it will always either be the user's preference, or our own default value.

You should exercise caution in using any data that comes from the Preferences API; it comes from your user's machine, so it might not necessarily be the data you originally stored. If you pull a user name in from a preferences file, and send it to a server to be looked up in a database, at some point you should definitely check that the string hasn't been tampered with by the user to contain potentially malicious SQL code. The fact that on Windows systems, the data is stored in the public registry makes us particularly vulnerable, since it is a common point of attack by viruses. You should take a leaf out of the server-side programmers' books: never trust data that comes from the client.

One solution is to ensure that you can verify the integrity of any data you retrieve, say by storing a checksum, or MD5 hash in the registry as well, or even encrypting all data you send. But that complicates things quite considerably.

The next task is to create an `ActionListener` that stores all of the user preferences when the **OK** button is pressed. This is simply a case of calling the preference node's `put()` method for each value we want to store.

```
ActionListener okListener = new ActionListener() {
  public void actionPerformed(ActionEvent evt) {
    userPrefs.put(NAMEPREF, nameField.getText());
    userPrefs.put(AGEPREF, ageField.getText());
    userPrefs.put(EMAILPREF, emailField.getText());
    userPrefs.put(PHONEPREF, phoneField.getText());
    System.out.println("Preferences stored");
    System.exit(0);
  }
};
```

The final task is to put all of the components into a `GridLayout` and pack the frame.

```
OKButton.addActionListener(okListener);

Container content = getContentPane();
content.setLayout(new GridLayout(5, 2));

content.add(nameLabel);
content.add(nameField);
content.add(ageLabel);
```

```
    content.add(ageField);
    content.add(emailLabel);
    content.add(emailField);
    content.add(phoneLabel);
    content.add(phoneField);
    content.add(OKButton);

    pack();
  }
}
```

The result is an application that persists its state across invocations, with no tricky I/O or database operations. Unlike almost any other storage solution, there's not a single `try...catch` block in sight. So we're definitely getting a lot of usability in return for those security compromises.

Detecting Changes

The preferences system also includes the ability to register a listener to detect changes in preference settings. Here's a quick modification of the above application to use `PreferenceChangeListeners`. We are going to create a form that detects changes in our user preferences and displays them in another `JFrame`, similar to the one we just built, only with `JLabels` instead of `JTextFields`:

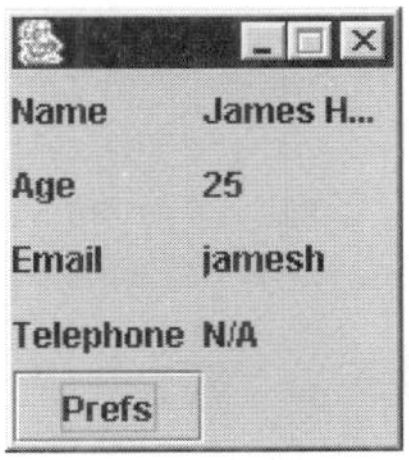

Clicking the **Prefs** button will bring up a modified version of our `PreferencesForm`, `PreferencesInspector`, which allows us to change our preferences and see the effects instantly propagate to the listening form.

Here are the changes needed to turn `PreferencesForm` into `PreferencesInspector`:

```
package com.wrox.j2se.utilities;

import javax.swing.*;
import java.awt.*;
import java.awt.event.*;
import java.util.prefs.*;

public class PreferencesInspector extends JFrame {

  private Preferences userPrefs;

  public static final String NAMEPREF = "name";
  public static final String EMAILPREF = "email";
  public static final String AGEPREF = "age";
```

```
public static final String PHONEPREF = "phone";

// public static void main(String args[]) {
//   new PreferencesForm().show();
// }

public PreferencesInspector() {

  super();

  userPrefs =
    Preferences.userNodeForPackage(PreferencesInspector.class);

  this.setResizable(false);
  this.setDefaultCloseOperation(HIDE_ON_CLOSE);
  this.setLocationRelativeTo(null);

  final JLabel nameLabel = new JLabel("Name", JLabel.LEFT);
  final JTextField nameField =
    new JTextField(userPrefs.get(NAMEPREF, ""), 20);
  final JLabel emailLabel = new JLabel("Email", JLabel.LEFT);
  final JTextField emailField =
    new JTextField(userPrefs.get(EMAILPREF, ""), 20);
  final JLabel ageLabel = new JLabel("Age", JLabel.LEFT);
  final JTextField ageField =
    new JTextField(userPrefs.get(AGEPREF, ""), 20);
  final JLabel phoneLabel = new JLabel("Telephone", JLabel.LEFT);
  final JTextField phoneField =
    new JTextField(userPrefs.get(PHONEPREF, ""), 20);
  final JButton applyButton = new JButton("Apply");
  final JButton OKButton = new JButton("OK");

  ActionListener applyListener = new ActionListener() {
    public void actionPerformed(ActionEvent evt) {
      userPrefs.put(NAMEPREF, nameField.getText());
      userPrefs.put(AGEPREF, ageField.getText());
      userPrefs.put(EMAILPREF, emailField.getText());
      userPrefs.put(PHONEPREF, phoneField.getText());
      System.out.println("Preferences stored");
    }
  };     /* apply button identical to OK button, but
            doesn't hide window */

  ActionListener okListener = new ActionListener() {
    public void actionPerformed(ActionEvent evt) {
```

Utilities

6

```
        userPrefs.put(NAMEPREF, nameField.getText());
        userPrefs.put(AGEPREF, ageField.getText());
        userPrefs.put(EMAILPREF, emailField.getText());
        userPrefs.put(PHONEPREF, phoneField.getText());
        System.out.println("Preferences stored");
        // System.exit(0);
        hide();   // don't exit
      }
    };

    applyButton.addActionListener(applyListener);
    OKButton.addActionListener(okListener);

    Container content = getContentPane();
    content.setLayout(new GridLayout(5, 2));

    content.add(nameLabel);
    content.add(nameField);
    content.add(ageLabel);
    content.add(ageField);
    content.add(emailLabel);
    content.add(emailField);
    content.add(phoneLabel);
    content.add(phoneField);
    content.add(applyButton);
    content.add(OKButton);

    pack();
  }
}
```

This changes the window so it doesn't control the application. It has no `main` method, and doesn't exit the application when it's closed. It is now a floating window in another application.

That application is `PreferenceListener`, and it looks like this:

```
package com.wrox.j2se.utilities;

import javax.swing.*;
import java.awt.*;
import java.awt.event.*;
import java.util.prefs.*;

public class PreferencesListener extends JFrame
  implements PreferenceChangeListener {
```

We are going to implement the one method in PreferenceChangeListener at the end of this class definition. First, we have to set up some instance variables. We want one instance of the PreferencesInspector frame to associate with the application, so we keep it in an instance variable. It will start off hidden, and we can show() it when we want to. We also need to store some of the window components in instance variables (rather than local final variables as were used in the previous frames), so they can be accessed in more than one method. These four JLabels will display the values of properties as they are changed.

```
PreferencesInspector inspector = new PreferencesInspector();

private JLabel name;
private JLabel email;
private JLabel age;
private JLabel phone;

public static void main(String args[]) {
  new PreferencesListener().show();
}
```

Again, the constructor does all the hard work. The first task is to register this class as a PreferenceChangeListener for the package preference node. This means we will receive event notifications if any of the preferences in that exact node are changed (we won't receive notifications for the equivalent system node, or for child nodes of this node). We are only *guaranteed* to receive notification if preferences are changed from within this Virtual Machine – the API does not require the implementation to watch the back-end store, and notify us of any changes made to it from other processes, although it is allowed to if it's possible. Normally, we'll only receive notification when such events happen because some part of the application has called a put() method on this node.

```
public PreferencesListener() {
  super();

  Preferences.userNodeForPackage(PreferencesListener.class)
    .addPreferenceChangeListener(this);

  this.setResizable(false);
  this.setLocationRelativeTo(null);
  this.setDefaultCloseOperation(EXIT_ON_CLOSE);
  inspector.setLocationRelativeTo(this);
```

We initialize the labels that will display our preferences with blank labels.

```
  name = new JLabel("", JLabel.LEFT);
  email = new JLabel("", JLabel.LEFT);
  age = new JLabel("", JLabel.LEFT);
```

Utilities

6

```
    phone = new JLabel("", JLabel.LEFT);

    final JLabel nameLabel = new JLabel("Name", JLabel.LEFT);
    final JLabel emailLabel = new JLabel("Email", JLabel.LEFT);
    final JLabel ageLabel = new JLabel("Age", JLabel.LEFT);
    final JLabel phoneLabel = new JLabel("Telephone", JLabel.LEFT);
    final JButton prefsButton = new JButton("Prefs");
```

The **Prefs** button simply has to show the inspector:

```
    ActionListener prefsListener = new ActionListener() {
      public void actionPerformed(ActionEvent evt) {
        inspector.show();
      }
    };

    prefsButton.addActionListener(prefsListener);
```

Again, we finish construction by packing our components into a grid layout.

```
    Container content = getContentPane();
    content.setLayout(new GridLayout(5, 2));

    content.add(nameLabel);
    content.add(name);
    content.add(ageLabel);
    content.add(age);
    content.add(emailLabel);
    content.add(email);
    content.add(phoneLabel);
    content.add(phone);
    content.add(prefsButton);

    pack();
  }
```

Now we must implement the method required by `PreferenceChangeListener`:

```
  public void preferenceChange(PreferenceChangeEvent evt) {
```

We are passed a `PreferenceChangeEvent` object, which can be queried for the key of the preference changed, the value it was changed to, and the node that initiated the event. We simply examine the key to determine what was changed, and then change the text of the appropriate label to match the new value.

```
    String key = evt.getKey();
    String val = evt.getNewValue();

    if (key.equals(PreferencesInspector.NAMEPREF)) {
      name.setText(val);
    } else if (key.equals(PreferencesInspector.EMAILPREF)) {
      email.setText(val);
    } else if (key.equals(PreferencesInspector.AGEPREF)) {
      age.setText(val);
    } else if (key.equals(PreferencesInspector.PHONEPREF)) {
      phone.setText(val);
    }
  }
}
```

It is interesting to note that, if you run this application after running the previous application, the same preferences are loaded in. This is because they are stored in the package node, and are therefore shared by both applications. To use different sets of preferences for each application, we would need to put them in different packages, or use `Preferences.userNodeForPackage(this).node("appName")` to obtain a child node of the package node.

Preferences Conclusions

The Preferences API is a very simple, lightweight persistence API, but it does have a lot of basic limitations. The security model is probably the biggest worry, because of the danger of using it to store preferences for a network client (such as a JNLP program) and relying on the data stored as preferences. There's no reason to assume that the value you read from the preferences store is one you put there yourself. However, for non-essential preference information (colors, window positions, and so on), it provides a useful quick-and-easy option.

The Logging API

The logging system provides a framework of classes that can be quickly used to add logging functionality to any application. While logging is most immediately useful in a server environment, there is no reason to think that a client or desktop application should not need to perform logging operations. There's no need to think of logging purely in terms of writing event reports out to a file, either. The logging system also provides a generally useful infrastructure for an application to report on its activities, and for those activity reports to make their way to any number of different destinations: log files, the console, a network socket, or an in-memory buffer for later output as an error report. A logging handler could even be written to send an e-mail, message a pager, generate a web page and post it, and so on, when certain events occur.

The Logging API consists of five core object types:

- **Loggers** – A `Logger` is an object that presents a number of logging methods, which can be used to pass in messages for logging.
- **LogRecords** – A `LogRecord` is an object representing a logging message inside the logging system. `LogRecords` are created by `Loggers`. They carry all the information about a logging event; where it originated, what time it occurred, what level of importance or granularity it carries, and so on.
- **Handlers** – A `Handler` is an object that knows how to write a log file to a particular output destination – a file, a database, a memory buffer, and so on.
- **Formatters** – A `Formatter` is an object that helps a `Handler` to write out a `LogRecord`. `Formatters` can perform message localization, selection of which parts of a message to log, and formatting of the selected data into string form.
- **Filters** – A `Filter` is an object that helps a `Logger` to decide whether to pass a message on to a handler, or to ignore it, or helps a `Handler` decide whether to format and output a message, or ignore it.

The logging system can be used in a number of ways. We can create loggers, handlers, and filters and stick them together to make a custom logging-framework like this:

Figure 1

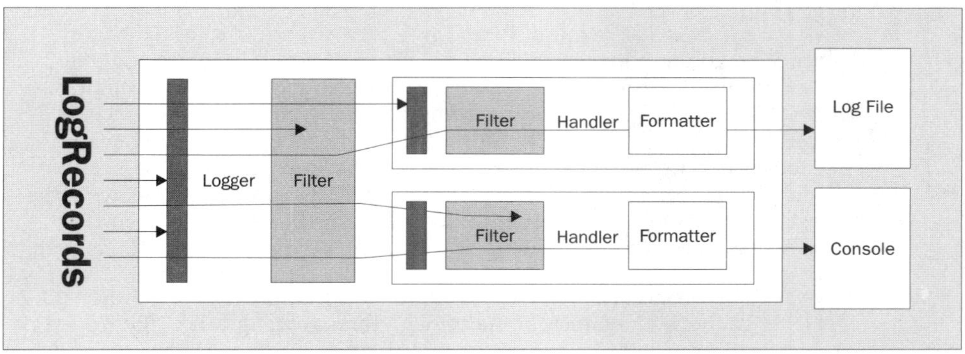

Messages are passed to the logger, make their way through the logging system, and ultimately come out of the end into files or to the console, or wherever we want the information to go. On the way, various filters can intercept and discard messages that are not of interest.

Utilities

6

The logger has a set of handlers (we can add as many as we need). Each handler can have its own filter, in addition to the logger's filter. The dark bars on the above diagram represent the built-in lightweight log-level filters. In addition to the heavyweight filtering provided by `Filter` objects, loggers and handlers have a property that sets the minimum log-level of messages that they are interested in processing. A level is an indication of the importance of a message, so some loggers may only be interested in high-importance messages, while others might be interested in messages of all importance levels. All messages carry a logging level described by a `Level` object – by default, one of the following predefined `static final` members of the `Level` class:

- `Level.SEVERE`
- `Level.WARNING`
- `Level.INFO`
- `Level.CONFIG`
- `Level.FINE`
- `Level.FINER`
- `Level.FINEST`

We normally don't need to worry about these constants in our code; we simply use the provided logging methods on the `Logger` class, and the appropriate `Level` object is attached to the resulting `LogRecord`. If we set the log-level filter on either a `Handler` or a `Logger`, they will silently discard any messages whose level is below that threshold.

It is possible to create and use our own `Levels` by creating a sub-class of `Level`, and defining a new set of `Level` objects appropriate to our particular application.

The process in the above diagram is as follows: Our code calls a logging method on the `Logger` object, passing in a message, which results in a `LogRecord` with a specific `Level` being created. The logger immediately performs a simple check on the message's level and decides whether to proceed or discard the message. If it decides to proceed and if a `Filter` is present, the message is passed to it for approval. If approval is received, the `Logger` then passes the message on to each `Handler` that has been registered with it.

When a `LogRecord` arrives at a `Handler`, the same procedure is followed. The level is checked against the `Handler`'s threshold, and then the record is passed to any assigned `Filter` (which could be sensitive to an error code, specific words in a message, or anything else you like) for approval. If approval is given, then the record is passed to a `Formatter`, and then the localized, formatted string is written out or stored in whatever manner the handler uses.

Note that this lifecycle can take place asynchronously, on a relatively low priority thread – the call to the initial logging method should almost certainly return before any data is written out to a file.

The LogManager

The above type of logger is called an **anonymous logger** (you can obtain one by calling `Logger.getAnonymousLogger()`). It exists in isolation, with its own set of handlers. We can make a logger like this available to different classes in our application by passing it around via parameters, or perhaps by creating it in a central location and then having other objects request a reference to it. This permits the sharing of a single logger among a few classes, but when a large application is being developed, logging requirements could be considerably more complicated. You might have several different error logs, all for different subsystems, a connection log for a socket subsystem, and a console log for severe warning conditions. Making all these different logging systems available, and managing their different levels, filters, and handlers, could grow to be quite a headache. To provide a simpler solution to these complex logging needs, the Logging API provides the `LogManager` class. `LogManager` is a singleton, a reference to which is obtained by calling `LogManager.getLogManager()`, and through this one global instance, provides four services:

- It manages a pool of named `Loggers` (typically named with package syntax after the package of classes that use the logger). Request a logger by name, and if one already exists for that name, it will be returned. If it doesn't, one will be created.
- It manages hierarchical relationships between these loggers. If they are configured to do so, loggers send messages not only to their own handlers, but also to those of their parent, and their parent's parent, and so on. Similarly, loggers inherit features from their parents, such as the granularity of logging events they should allow.
- It can load a set of preferences that will set up an initial pool of loggers and handlers in a certain configuration.

The key method on the `LogManager` is this one:

- `Logger getLogger(String name)`

Remember that before you can call it, you must obtain a reference to the `LogManager` singleton, by calling:

- `static LogManager getLogManager()`

One specific logger in the managed pool is the **global logger**. It is obtained by asking the `LogManager` to return the `Logger` called `global`, and it provides a simple means to quickly access logging functionality.

Logging Messages

There are a bewildering number of methods in the `Logger` class. This is because in addition to carrying a simple `String` message, `LogRecords` can carry information about how to localize a particular resource, an optional array of objects, known as **log record parameters**, which can be used by filters and formatters to provide more information about a logged event than a text message alone. If it is reporting an error condition, it can also contain an exception (or, more accurately, a `Throwable`), which can provide useful information to a formatter as well. Here is a summary of the methods that exist.

Raw Logging Methods

The most basic methods allow us to specify the `Level` object for the message ourselves, or to provide a complete `LogRecord` object we've already constructed. There are four main types. The first type are used to simply log a message:

- `void log(Level level, String msg)`
- `void log(Level level, String msg, Object param1)`
- `void log(Level level, String msg, Object[] params)`
- `void log(Level level, String msg, Throwable thrown)`

The second are direct equivalents of these, used to log a message, but also to specify the source class and method that generated the logging request:

- `void logp(Level level, String sourceClass, String sourceMethod, String msg)`
- `void logp(Level level, String sourceClass, String sourceMethod, String msg, Object param1)`
- `void logp(Level level, String sourceClass, String sourceMethod, String msg, Object[] params)`
- `void logp(Level level, String sourceClass, String sourceMethod, String msg, Throwable thrown)`

If we don't specify these ourselves, then the logging system will attempt to work out the source for us. It can do so by creating an `Exception` and tracing the stack, provided the object isn't passed into a separate thread for processing. In some circumstances, the logging system will therefore be unable to create this information when it needs it, so if we must know where the log message was sent from, we should include the information ourselves.

The final group of methods is again directly equivalent to the first group, but these associate a resource bundle with the log record, which can be used to generate localized logging output:

- ```
  void logrb(Level level, String sourceClass,
             String sourceMethod,
             String bundleName, String msg)
  ```
- ```
  void logrb(Level level, String sourceClass,
             String sourceMethod,
             String bundleName, String msg, Object param1)
  ```
- ```
  void logrb(Level level, String sourceClass,
             String sourceMethod,
             String bundleName, String msg, Object[] params)
  ```
- ```
  void logrb(Level level, String sourceClass,
             StringsourceMethod,
             String bundleName, String msg, Throwable
             thrown)
  ```

The last method simply takes a `LogRecord` object that we have already constructed:

- `void log(LogRecord record)`

These different parameters make up the full range of options open to us in specifying a logging event, and we can actually generate any log result we wish using just these methods. However, a number of convenience methods that provide shorthand for common logging tasks exist. We'll look at these in groups.

Level-Based Logging Methods

Shorthand methods for creating logging events at each of the standard log levels are provided. They are as follows:

- `void severe(String msg)`
- `void warning(String msg)`
- `void info(String msg)`
- `void config(String msg)`
- `void fine(String msg)`
- `void finer(String msg)`
- `void finest(String msg)`

These are probably the most clearly usable logging methods the class has to offer.

Method Activity Logging Methods

The final five convenience methods generate `FINER`-level log messages, and can be used to provide a debugging trace of program activity, down to the level of which methods are accessed in what order, with what parameters, and returning what values. They are as follows:

- `void entering(String sourceClass, String sourceMethod)`
- `void entering(String sourceClass, String sourceMethod, Object param1)`
- `void entering(String sourceClass, String sourceMethod, Object[] params)`
- `void exiting(String sourceClass, String sourceMethod)`
- `void exiting(String sourceClass, String sourceMethod, Object result)`
- `void throwing(String sourceClass, String sourceMethod, Throwable thrown)`

The idea of this part of the API is that you write your methods like this:

```
import java.util.logging.*;

public class MethodLogging {

  public String fullName(String firstName, String lastName)
    throws IllegalArgumentException {

    Logger log = Logger.getLogger("MethodLogging");
    log.entering("MethodLogging", "fullName", new Object[] {
      firstName, lastName
    });

    if ((firstName.indexOf(' ') > 0) || (lastName.indexOf(' ') > 0)) {
      IllegalArgumentException e =
        new IllegalArgumentException("names cannot contain spaces");
      log.throwing("MethodLogging", "fullName", e);
      throw e;
    }

    String result = firstName + " " + lastName;

    log.exiting("MethodLogging", "fullName", result);
    return result;
  }
}
```

OK, so it doesn't lend itself to readability, turning a trivial two-line method into a relatively huge monstrosity, but if you have a hard-to-trace bug that only shows up on the production system, preventing you from using a debugger on it, perhaps this might be a useful tool. As it is, you might want to look into writing a script that inserts the necessary logging calls into your code, since doing so by hand is laborious, and probably a sure-fire way to introduce even more bugs into the system.

Using the Logging Framework

So, now we've got a good understanding of how the logging framework hangs together, let's look at how we actually use it in a program.

By default, the logging framework sets up two global handlers. One, an instance of `FileHandler`, stores log entries in an XML file in a system temporary directory. The other, a `ConsoleHandler`, outputs log messages to `System.err`. Both have their level threshold set to `INFO`. This means that any log message we fire with a level of `INFO` or higher will appear on the console, and in that log file, unless we tell our `Logger` not to use the global handlers, or remove the global handlers that were set up for us.

The `logging.preferences` file in the `jre/lib` directory dictates the precise configuration that the Logging API configures for us on startup. This file is read by the `LogManager` object when it is first instantiated, which basically happens when we first use almost any of the logging classes. This file is in standard Java properties format, and can be used to configure handlers, default settings for handlers and loggers, and the default level for newly created logger and handler objects (the standard distribution sets this to `INFO`). Details about the configuration syntax can be found in the Logging API documentation,
http://java.sun.com/j2se/1.4/docs/guide/util/logging/index.html.

Here's a quick demonstration of logging, using, naturally, a song about logging:

```
import java.util.logging.*;

public class Logging {

  public static void main(String[] args) {
    Logger log = Logger.getLogger("global");

    log.finest("I'm a lumberjack and I'm okay,");
    log.finer("I sleep all night and I work all day.");
    log.fine("He's a lumberjack and he's okay,");
    log.config("He sleeps all night and he works all day.");
    log.info(
      "I cut down trees, I eat my lunch, I go to the lavatory.");
    log.warning("On Wednesdays I go shoppin',");
```

```
    log.severe("And have buttered scones for tea");
  }
}
```

This will generate the following output:

```
> java Logging
22-Feb-2002 11:03:04 Logging main
INFO: I cut down trees, I eat my lunch, I go to the
lavatory.
22-Feb-2002 11:03:05 Logging main
WARNING: On Wednesdays I go shoppin',
22-Feb-2002 11:03:05 Logging main
SEVERE: And have buttered scones for tea
```

Those messages are in fact coming to `System.err`, not `System.out`. Notice that the logging system has established the correct class and method (`Logging main`, written after the timestamp for each entry), without us telling it.

If we look in our system-specific temporary files folder, we'll find a file containing XML details of each logging event, something like the following:

```
<?xml version="1.0" standalone="no"?>
<!DOCTYPE log SYSTEM "file:logger.dtd">
<log>
    .
    .
    .
<record>
  <date>2001-08-23T00:47:50</date>
  <millis>998524070390</millis>
  <sequence>1</sequence>
  <logger>com.wrox.ea.j2se.utilities.Logging</logger>
  <level>WARNING</level>
  <class>Logging</class>
  <method>main</method>
  <thread>10</thread>
  <message>On Wednesdays I go shoppin',</message>
</record>
    .
    .
    .
</log>
```

There will be more records than that, but this should give you some idea. Again, only the last three lines will have been logged, thanks to the level limit of `INFO`.

Custom Logging Behavior

The logging system provides five `Handler` implementations. These are:

- `MemoryHandler` – A memory buffer that keeps a rolling store of the last *n* (by default, 1000) log messages, and forwards them to another `Handler` when it receives a message at a certain trigger level (by default, `SEVERE`). It performs no formatting itself, and keeps records in `LogRecord` form.
- `StreamHandler` – An implementation that provides the base functionality for handlers that output logging information to a byte or character stream.
- `ConsoleHandler` – A `StreamHandler` that writes to `System.err`.
- `FileHandler` – A `StreamHandler` that writes to a file.
- `SocketHandler` – A `StreamHandler` that writes to a socket.

Custom `Handlers` are also relatively easy to implement, especially by extending the existing classes.

We can register instances of any kind of `Handler` with individual `Loggers`. Remember that a handler will get any logging messages intended not only for the logger for which it is registered, but also for any children in the managed pool. Let's look at the common types.

MemoryHandler

A `MemoryHandler` is a buffer that holds on to a store of recent log messages, until an event of higher level than its `pushLevel` occurs – at which point, it forwards all the messages it is storing to another nominated handler. This enables us, for example, to buffer fine-grained logging information, but only output it to a log file if an error condition occurs. We can create a `MemoryHandler` with the following constructor:

- `public MemoryHandler(Handler target, int size, Level pushLevel)`

StreamHandler

A `StreamHandler` can be constructed from any `OutputStream` object. It simply writes inbound messages to the stream, using a formatter to generate `String` data from the `LogRecord` objects it is passed. Two formatters are provided with the Logging API:

- `SimpleFormatter` – Generates the shorthand logging information we've seen above
- `XMLFormatter` – Generates the verbose XML formatted data

Utilities

6

Custom formatters can be used to include information interpreted from a LogRecord's parameter objects. For example, an HTTP server might forward a Request object as a parameter to a logging message, which reaches a custom formatter that extracts the information needed to write out a server connection log entry.

StreamHandler has the following constructor:

- public StreamHandler(OutputStream out, Formatter formatter)

FileHandler

FileHandler is the workhorse log file writer. It has a couple of tricks up its sleeve though, which are worth noting. First, it can write to a single file, or to a group of size-limited files. In the second case, it will rotate log files whenever a pre-determined size limit is reached, and start writing to another file. Second, it allows the log filename to be specified using a pattern, rather than an absolute filename. This pattern is a String that may contain the following meta-characters:

Symbol	Expansion
/	The file path separator on the present system
%t	A directory suitable for storing temporary files, such as the system temporary directory
%h	A directory suitable for storing user-specific files, such as the current user's home directory, or a system-wide directory on a single-user system
%g	A log generation number, for use where the handler is managing a rotating set of logs
%u	A number that makes the filename unique
%%	A literal percent sign

The FileHandler will use this pattern to generate a candidate filename for the log file, initially substituting a zero into the pattern in place of the %u meta-character, if it is used. If a file with the chosen name is already open, and the pattern contains the %u meta-character, the handler will then try increasing the number it substitutes, until it finds a number that makes the name for a file that's not open. This ensures that separate processes running the same application can co-exist on the same system at the same time. So, the following pattern would make a log file in the system temporary directory:

```
%t/com/wrox/lumberjack.%u.log
```

We'd expect to find log files with paths like:

```
/var/tmp/com/wrox/lumberjack.0.log
C:\TEMP\com\wrox\lumberjack.3.log
```

```
C:\Documents and Settings\Joe\Local Settings\Temp\com\wrox\
lumberjack.2.log
```

The two constructors for `FileHandlers` are:

- `public FileHandler(String pattern)`
- `public FileHandler(String pattern, int limit, int count)`

The second specifies a rotating set of `count` files, whose size is limited to `limit` bytes.

SocketHandler

`SocketHandler` is actually very simple. It transmits log records over a network connection, to a specified IP address and socket. Its constructor is self-explanatory:

- `public SocketHandler(String host, int port)`

The default behavior is for it to use an `XMLFormatter`. This enables the logging information to be reconstructed at the other end of the socket connection.

Logging Conclusions

The logging system is a formidably versatile architecture. Its extensibility and configurability is quite astounding, although I'm not sure which way people will go with their use of the logging framework. Firing logging messages off to the central handlers, and allowing whoever uses your application to configure their own logging parameters, offers very little control to the application over what information it releases, and the kind of logging you want to make available at development time is, no doubt, very different to the kind of information you want to let your customers log at run time. Server applications will clearly benefit most from the Logging API, since they often have to track the activities of multiple simultaneous users, as well as keeping global centralized logs of server activity, errors, and accesses. An application server, potentially hosting multiple server applications at once, each with its own complex logging requirements, will be able to use the logging framework to make available an individualized log manager for each application. For client-side development, there are rarely going to be times when you need more than a single log file.

We'll make more use of logging in an extended example in the next section, once we've examined the regular expression syntax.

The Regular Expression API

The regular expression system consists of just two new classes and a new exception, but its power doesn't come from its classes. The power is in the regular expression language, which we use to specify textual **patterns**. These patterns, regular expressions, or **regex**es to their friends, are simply a way of describing the defining characteristics of a particular set of strings. The expression can then be compared to a candidate string, to see if the string is in the set (in other words, if it **matches**) or not. Alternatively, the candidate string can be searched from beginning to end to see if it contains any sub-strings that match. Or, the string can be split into a set of sub-strings, by searching for matches, and retrieving the strings *between* the matches – an advanced version of the character-based splitting provided by `java.util.StringTokenizer`. The key to this power lies in regular expressions' ability to concisely define the precise characteristics of the strings we want to match, which distinguishes such strings from those we don't want to match.

For example, here is a regular expression:

```
^Professional [A-Z]{3}
```

This expression matches a significant proportion of the book titles in the Wrox Press back-catalog. In particular, it matches all of these:

Professional XML	Professional WAP
Professional ASP	Professional ASP 2.0
Professional ASP 3.0	Professional JSP
Professional JSP Second Edition	Professional ASP Databases
Professional PHP Programming	Professional ATL COM
Professional MFC6	

It doesn't match:

Professional Java Server Programming	Professional Jini
Professional C#	Professional IE4 Programming
Beginning XML	Beginning Java 2
ASP 2.0 Programmer's Reference	Early Adopter J2SE 1.4

So, it provides us with a way to select strings out of a set that share some particular characteristics – in this case, Professional books about topics whose name is a three-letter acronym. We'll look at exactly how that expression works later.

With that in mind, let's quickly look at those two new classes, so we can build a simple toy that will allow us to experiment with regular expressions. The classes are `java.util.regex.Pattern`, and `java.util.regex.Matcher`.

Conceptually, a `Pattern` is an object representing a compiled regular expression. Before we can use a regular expression, we must first compile it into a `Pattern` object, using the `Pattern.compile(String regex)` static method. This is where the new exception class comes in; a checked `java.util.regex.PatternSyntaxException` is thrown if we try to compile an invalid pattern.

A `Pattern` object will generate a `Matcher` object when we call its `matcher(String candidateString)` method. A `Matcher` is an inspector that we can use to determine the results of matching the compiled regex against the candidate string.

The other way to use a `Pattern` object is to call its `split(String input)` method, or its `split(String input, int limit)` method, which return an array of the strings found between successive matches of the compiled regex in the `input` string. If a `limit` is specified, this is the number of splits that will be sought (any subsequent matches won't be used to split the string).

A `Matcher` can perform a number of different match tests of the pattern on the candidate string. It can provide a Boolean `true` or `false` answer to the simple question, "Does the expression match the entire candidate string?" through the `matches()` method. The `lookingAt()` method answers the similarly simple question, "Does the candidate string start with a string that matches the expression?"

The `find()` method is a little more powerful. It starts looking through the candidate string from the beginning, looking for a sub-string that matches the expression. If it finds one, it returns `true`, but it also sets a marker at the end of the sub-string that it matched. The next time it is called, it starts looking from the character after this mark, rather than from the beginning. So, sequential calls to `find()` will find each successive matching sub-string of the candidate string. If there are no matches in the remainder of the string, the method returns `false`.

If any of these methods has successfully matched (it returned `true`), we can use the `start()` and `end()` methods to find the index of the beginning and end of the sub-string within the candidate string. We can also use the `group()` method to retrieve the actual sub-string that matched.

Regular expressions can specify sub-expressions, by grouping part of the expression in parentheses, `(...)`. We can retrieve the sub-sub-strings that matched these sub-expressions, and their start and end points, by providing the integer index of the sub-expression we want to retrieve as a parameter to the `start()`, `end()`, and `group()` methods.

The `Matcher` class also provides a couple of methods for performing intelligent replacement of a matched sub-string, which we'll look at a little later on.

For now, we're ready to implement a quick little tool to allow us to play with regular expressions. It's basically a greatly simplified version of the UNIX command line tool, `grep`. In its basic mode, `grep` takes as its command-line arguments a regular expression and an optional list of filenames. If no filenames are specified, it processes standard in; if filenames are specified, it reads them and processes them in sequence.

This processing is simple. For each line of input, it attempts to match the regular expression. If the line contains a matching sub-string, then it is output, unchanged, to standard out. If it doesn't, then the line is discarded.

We can perform this same task pretty simply by using the Java regex framework as follows:

```
import java.util.regex.*;
import java.io.*;

public class Grep {

  public static void main(String args[]) {
    String regex = "";
    InputStream in = System.in;
```

The first task is to parse the command-line arguments. We need at least one argument – the regular expression. If we have more than one argument, we assume the second is a filename we should process:

```
    switch (args.length) {
    case 0:
      System.err.println("Error: no regular expression specified");
      System.exit(1);
      break;
    case 1:
      regex = args[0];
      break;
    default:
      regex = args[0];
      try {
        in = new BufferedInputStream(new FileInputStream(args[1]));
      } catch (IOException e) {
        System.err.println("Error: could not find file");
        System.exit(1);
      }
      break;
    }
```

The next job is to compile the `Pattern` object representing the regular expression:

```
    Pattern p = null;

    try {
      p = Pattern.compile(regex);
    } catch (PatternSyntaxException e) {
      System.err.println("Error: invalid regular expression " +
regex);
      System.exit(1);
    }
```

If we have gotten this far, we need to open a reader so we can obtain the input data line by line:

```
    BufferedReader buff =
      new BufferedReader(new InputStreamReader(in));

    try {
      String a;
      for (a = buff.readLine(); a != null; a = buff.readLine()) {
```

For each line read, we retrieve a `Matcher`, and call the `find()` method. This will return `true` if there is a sub-string of the line that matches the regular expression. If it does, we print the line. Otherwise, we do nothing.

```
        Matcher m = p.matcher(a);
        if (m.find()) {
          System.out.println(a);
        }
      }
    } catch (Exception e) {
      e.printStackTrace();
    }
  }
}
```

And that's it. We can now use this as a command-line `grep` tool.

Note that the flavor of regular expression understood by the Java regex engine is not identical to that understood by the `grep` utility on POSIX UNIX systems (although there is even variation among different POSIX implementations). There is a great deal of subtlety in the more extreme applications of regular expressions, and while the Java version builds on the widely understood Perl 5 regular expression syntax, these "standards" are not documented as standards, they are simply reference implementations. Regular expressions should always be tailored to the particular engine they are to run on.

Using Regular Expressions the Easy Way

So, now that we've seen the role of the `Pattern` and `Matcher` classes, let's look at how we can actually use regular expressions without even worrying about them.

The `java.lang.String` class now has a whole bunch of regular expression methods built in to it, which mask behind-the-scenes calls to `Pattern` and `Matcher`, of course. The full set of regex methods is as follows:

String Method	Underlying Semantics
`boolean matches(String regex)`	`Pattern.matches(regex, this)`
`String replaceAll(String regex, String replacement)`	`Pattern.compile(regex).matcher(this).replaceAll(replacement)`
`String replaceFirst(String regex, String replacement)`	`Pattern.compile(regex).matcher(this).replaceFirst(replacement)`
`String[] split(String regex)`	`Pattern.compile(regex).split(this)`
`String[] split(String regex, int limit)`	`Pattern.compile(regex).split(this, limit)`

Note that the given semantics show simply what the meaning of the method call is equivalent to, not the actual implementation of the method.

These can all throw a `PatternSyntaxException`, but since this is an unchecked exception, if we're using hard-coded regular expressions we can call these methods with impunity, without cluttering our methods up with `try...catch` blocks. So, you can easily drop into your code lines like this:

```
import java.util.regex.*;

public class OptionChecker {
  public static void main(String[] args) {
    if (args.length > 0) {
      if (!args[0].matches("^-[atvd]$")) {
        System.out.println("Invalid option specified - " +
                           "must be -a, -t, -v, or -d");
      }
    }
  }
}
```

Regular Expression Syntax

In case you aren't familiar with regular expressions, we'll try to give you a lightning tour here.

Let's create a file of sample words we can use as a test bed for some regular expression experimentation. This is `words.txt`:

```
an
ant
can
man
tan
ban
mañana
banana
canned
banned
manned
tanned
Canada
Canadian
fandango
mango
tango
dingo
flamingo
```

Now, we can use our Java `Grep` tool to search through this file for lines that match any regular expression we choose.

Regular expressions are just strings. They contain two kinds of character; **literal characters**, and **meta-characters**. The simplest regular expression is one that consists of just literal characters:

```
> java Grep "an" words.txt
an
ant
can
man
tan
ban
mañana
banana
canned
banned
manned
tanned
```

Utilities

6

```
Canada
Canadian
fandango
mango
tango
```

> *I recommend that you get into the habit of writing quote characters around regular expressions on the command line – it stops the command shell from stepping in and interpreting characters for you, and also allows your expressions to contain space characters. If you use double quotes, as shown above, a UNIX shell may still step in and perform environment variable substitution, so you should use the more emphatic single quotes, which tell the shell to completely ignore the contents of the string. Double quoted strings should be used on Windows, although they are still subject to shell variable substitution – a string `%FOO%` will be substituted with the contents of the environment variable `FOO`, if it exists.*

Here, the regular expression is `an`. It matches every line that contains the literal two-character string `an`. Note that the lines containing `dingo` and `flamingo` were not output. In order to better understand the way regular expressions work, however, you need to stop thinking about the whole string, and instead consider them one character at a time. In a regular expression, a literal character, like `a`, means something to the effect of *a character that is an* `a`. So, the regular expression `an` is a regex that matches if it finds *a character that is an* `a`, followed immediately by *a character that is an* `n`.

While for most characters we can specify a literal character to match it just by writing that character, there are a lot of characters for which that approach is not convenient or even possible. There are a number of other ways of specifying a single specific literal character:

Notation	Character literal
`\\`	The backslash character
`\0n`	The character with octal value `0n` (0 <= `n` <= 7)
`\0nn`	The character with octal value `0nn` (0 <= `n` <= 7)
`\0mnn`	The character with octal value `0mnn` (0 <= `m` <= 3, 0 <= `n` <= 7)
`\xhh`	The character with hexadecimal value `0xhh`
`\uhhhh`	The character with hexadecimal value `0xhhhh`
`\t`	The tab character (`\u0009`)
`\n`	The newline (line feed) character (`\u000A`)
`\r`	The carriage return character (`\u000D`)
`\f`	The form feed character (`\u000C`)
`\a`	The alert (bell) character (`\u0007`)
`\e`	The escape character (`\u001B`)
`\cx`	The control character corresponding to `x`, usually written as `^x`

Note that while these expressions are similar, they are *not* the escape sequences used in Java string literals. If I write the Java String `"\\"`, I am specifying the literal string '\'. If I write the Java String `"\u221E"`, I am actually specifying the literal string '∞', an infinity character. When we talk about these codes being valid within regular expressions, we're talking about them being valid when specified in a literal string. So, the Java String `"\\u221E"` specifies the literal string `"\u221E"`, which is the regular expression that matches the literal character '∞'.

For example, we can match the character `ñ` in `mañana` by specifying the character code `\u00F1`:

```
> java Grep "\u00F1" words.txt
mañana
```

Character Classes

The first kind of meta-character is the character class. A character class is a special character, or character sequence that, instead of matching just one specific character, matches a character that is part of its character class – a set of characters that share some property. The following are the main character classes specified in Java's regular expression language:

Notation	Character class
`.`	Any character
`\d`	A digit
`\D`	A non-digit
`\s`	A whitespace character (space, tab, newline, form feed, carriage return)
`\S`	A non-whitespace character
`\w`	A word character (a letter, number, or underscore)
`\W`	A non-word character
`{lower}`	A lowercase alphabetic ASCII character
`{upper}`	An uppercase alphabetic ASCII character
`{alpha}`	An alphabetic ASCII character
`{alnum}`	An ASCII alphanumeric character
`{punct}`	ASCII Punctuation. One of `!"#$%&'()*+,-./:;<=>?@[\]^_`{|}~`
`{graph}`	A visible ASCII character (alphanumeric or punctuation)
`{print}`	A visible ASCII characters, or an ASCII space
`{blank}`	An ASCII space or tab
`{xdigit}`	A hexadecimal digit (a digit, or a character (uppercase or lowercase) from A to F)

We can also define our own character classes. We do this by specifying the characters we want in our character class, inside a pair of square brackets, `[]`. For example, to specify a character class that will match an uppercase `C` and a lowercase `c`, we can write the character class `[Cc]`. We can try this out:

```
> java Grep [Cc] words.txt
can
canned
Canada
Canadian
```

Alternatively, we can specify a range of characters in a character class. For example, the character class `[a-z]` will match any lowercase character from `a` to `z`. This is equivalent to the predefined character class `{lower}`.

We can mix together specifications of ranges and individual characters within a character class, and the resulting character class is the union of all the characters and ranges that make it up. For example, to match any consonant, we could specify the character class `[b-df-hj-np-tv-z]`. Remember, though, that this will match only lowercase consonants.

We can also specify a character class that will match any character that is not listed. To do so, we place a caret (^) character at the beginning of the character set. To match any character other than a lowercase vowel, we could use the character class `[^aeiou]`. This is not the same as our consonant class, though. For example, a space is not a lowercase vowel, so it would match this character class, but it isn't a consonant, so it wouldn't match the previous class.

It is also possible to specify a character class by taking one character class, and subtracting the members of another character class from it. To do so, we write the minus sign, followed by the character class we wish to subtract at the very end of the character class. For example, `[a-zA-Z-[AEIOUaeiou]]` specifies the set of letters, minus the set of vowels. This is probably the best way to write a character class that matches consonants.

Due to the special meaning of the minus sign/hyphen character in a character class, if you want to specify a character class that will match hyphens, the hyphen must be the first character in the class.

We use character classes, whether specified by us, or by the regex language, in exactly the same way as we use literal characters. Reading them in the same way as we read literal characters, a character class means *a character that is a member of the set.* So, the regular expression `d[aeiou]` means *a character that is a* `d`*, followed by a character that is an* `a`*,* `e`*,* `i`*,* `o`*, or* `u`.

Testing this yields:

```
> java Grep "d[aeiou]" words.txt
Canada
Canadian
fandango
dingo
```

Quantifiers

The next meta-characters, and the ones which give regular expressions so much of their power, are called **quantifiers**. A quantifier qualifies the previous character's significance, by adding the concept of quantity to it. Following a character with a quantifier is like replacing the phrase *...a character...* in our descriptions of the meaning of characters so far, with the phrase *...between* `a` *and* `b` *characters...*, where `a` and `b` are defined by the quantifier.

The basic quantifiers are as follows:

Quantifier	Min (*a*)	Max (*b*)	Effect
`?`	0	1	Makes matching the previous character optional
`+`	1	unlimited	Requires that the previous character be present at least once, but allows it to be repeated indefinitely
`*`	0	unlimited	The previous character is optional, but if present, can be repeated indefinitely
`{x}`	x	x	The previous character must occur exactly *x* times
`{x,}`	x	unlimited	The previous character must occur at least *x* times
`{x,y}`	x	y	The previous character must occur at least *x* times, but no more than *y* times

You can quantify a character, a character class, or a sub-expression in this way. A sub-expression is a section of the regular expression that is enclosed in parentheses. If a sub-expression is followed by a quantifier, then a sub-string matching the complete sub-expression must occur the requested number of times. So, for instance, the next example means *look for a character that is an* `a`, *followed by one or more characters that are an* `n`, *followed by a character that is an* `e`:

```
> java Grep "an+e" words.txt
canned
banned
manned
tanned
```

And the following expression means *look for at least two characters that are either an* `a`, *an* `e`, *an* `i`, *an* `o`, *or a* `u`:

```
> java Grep "[aeiou]{2,}" words.txt
Canadian
```

Utilities 6

Canadian matches, because it contains the sequence ia. Both the i and the a are members of the character class, so the expression matches.

Here's an example with a sub-expression:

```
> java Grep "(a[\u00F1n]){2}" words.txt
mañana
banana
```

This expression means, look for a sub-string that matches the expression a[\u00F1n] exactly twice. The sub-expression simply says, look for a character that is an a, followed by a character that is either an ñ or an n.

Choice

We can specify a sub-expression that will match one of a range of possible patterns. This is like a slightly broader from of character class – almost an expression class. We do so by dividing the alternative patterns up within the sub-expression using bar (|) characters. Here's an example:

```
> java Grep "(ta|di)ngo" words.txt
tango
dingo
```

Position Markers

We can also demand that certain sequences occur in a certain position, in relation to the string being matched. For example, the expression ^c means *the start of a line, followed by a character that is a* c:

```
> java Grep "^c" words.txt
can
canned
```

So, the caret character (^) doesn't actually match a particular character in the candidate string. It matches the space before the start of the line, anchoring the regular expression to the beginning of the line.

The $ character can be used to provide a similar anchor to the end of a line.

```
> java Grep "d$" words.txt
canned
banned
manned
tanned
```

Escaping Characters

The characters `.`, `*`, `+`, `|`, `[`, `{`, and `\` all have special meaning within a regex, as we've seen. If we want to write a regex that matches one of these characters, we can do so by writing the escape sequence for that character literal. To escape a character, precede it with a backslash, `\`. The escape sequence for an asterisk character, then, is `\*`. For a backslash character it is `\\`.

More Information

That covers the basics of regex syntax. There's a good syntax guide included in the Javadoc for the `Pattern` class. For a really through coverage of the topic, the seminal work on regular expressions is *Mastering Regular Expressions*, by Jeffrey Friedl, published by O'Reilly and Associates (*ISBN 1-56592-257-3*). With regex support built into Java, this book is sure to find its way onto the shelves of a lot of Java programmers in the near future.

Using Regular Expressions

One common use for regular expressions is validating user entry. A regular expression can be written that describes exactly how a piece of data must be structured in order to be valid. For example, we might want to ensure that a user has entered a valid e-mail address; we can do so by seeing if it matches the regular expression:

```
[-A-Za-z0-9_.]+@[-A-Za-z0-9_.]+\.[A-Za-z]{2,}
```

To quickly go through what this expression does, it matches one or more characters that are either alphanumeric, underscores (`_`), periods (`.`), or hyphens (`-`), followed by an at sign (`@`), then again one or more characters that are either alphanumeric, underscores, periods, or hyphens, followed by a literal period (indicated by the `\.`), then two or more alphabetic characters, signifying the top-level domain. This allows multi-part domains, like `wrox.co.uk`, or similar.

The final `{2,}` quantifier is there because a valid e-mail address must end in, at minimum, a two-letter country code (like `.uk`, `.ca`, or `.de`), or failing that a full top-level domain (like `.com`, `.org`, or, nowadays, a four character name like `.info`, or even the recently approved TLD `.museum`). Demanding at least two characters should deter casual attempts to circumvent your validation by typing nonsense addresses like `a@b.c`. Unfortunately, the more persistent troublemaker who types `qeqeqw@qweqweq.ewqeqw` will get past even our more rigorous check.

We can use this technique to modify our user preferences application to ensure that only valid data is entered. To perform validation, we can use Swing's `InputVerifier` system. We can implement our own `InputVerifier` class, and register it with a text field component. Whenever the user attempts to change focus, the input verifier is called for the component the user is trying to leave, and the focus change is only allowed if the `InputVerifier` approves it. An `InputVerifier` must implement just one method, `public boolean verify(JComponent input)`.

Here is the code for a regular expression `InputVerifier`, `RegexVerifier.java`:

```
package com.wrox.j2se.utilities;

import javax.swing.*;
import java.util.regex.*;
import java.awt.Color;
import java.util.*;
import java.util.logging.*;

public class RegexVerifier extends InputVerifier {
  private HashMap regexes = new HashMap();
  private static Logger log =
    Logger.getLogger("com.wrox.j2se.utilities");

  public boolean addRegexForComponent(JTextField comp, String regex) {
    Pattern pat;
    try {
      pat = Pattern.compile(regex);
    } catch (PatternSyntaxException e) {
      log.finer("Could not add requested regex validator " + regex
              + " for component " + comp.toString());
      return false;
    }
    log.finer("Adding regex validator " + regex + " for component "
            + comp.toString());
    regexes.put(comp, pat);
    comp.setInputVerifier(this);
    return true;
  }

  public void removeRegexForComponent(JTextField comp) {
    log.finer("Removing regex validator for component "
            + comp.toString());
    regexes.remove(comp);
    comp.setInputVerifier(null);
  }
```

```
  public boolean verify(JComponent input) {
    log.finer("Verifying content of " + input.toString());
    boolean valid = true;
    if (!(input instanceof JTextField)) {
      return true;
    }
    JTextField subject = (JTextField) input;
    Pattern p = (Pattern) regexes.get(subject);
    if (p != null) {
      if (!p.matcher(subject.getText()).matches()) {
        subject.setForeground(Color.RED);
        log.fine("Invalid value " + subject.getText() + " in field "
                  + input.toString() + " rejected");
        valid = false;
      } else {
        subject.setForeground(Color.BLACK);
      }
    }
    return valid;
  }

  public boolean verifyAll() {

    log.fine("Verifying all registered components");

    Iterator i = regexes.keySet().iterator();
    while (i.hasNext()) {
      if (!verify((JComponent) i.next())) {
        return false;
      }
    }
    return true;
  }
}
```

RegexVerifier is designed so that one instance can be shared between multiple components. We register a regular expression for each component we want the verifier to perform validation on, and it compiles it and stores it away in a HashMap. Compiling the regular expression at this stage saves us the effort of compiling it each time it's needed, and also flags up any errors in the regular expression early. The verifier then registers itself with the component to act as its InputVerifier. When a component that has this verifier registered loses the focus, the verify() method is called, the appropriate compiled expression is extracted, and matched against the component's value. If we don't have an expression registered for a particular component, we return true as a safe default that allows the focus change to take place.

I've also included logging support in this class. All its messages are logged at either FINE or FINER level, since the verifier is likely to be called very frequently.

I also have to admit to being a bit naughty: the verify() method of an InputVerifier is supposed to be side effect-free, but I am guilty of tweaking the color of the component's text from within the method. In a more complex UI, this might get us into trouble, but it'll work fine here. This is probably going to get me sent to programmer hell, but I feel it's worth it for the user feedback it creates. Of course, in the real world, we would separate the layers of business logic and user interface, but for the purposes of the example, this is simpler.

Now, let's modify the PreferencesInspector class from earlier in the chapter to use the RegexVerifier to validate user input. We'll also add logging to it as we go.

```
package com.wrox.j2se.utilities;

import javax.swing.*;
import java.awt.*;
import java.awt.event.*;
import java.util.prefs.*;
import java.util.logging.*;

public class ValidatingLoggingPreferencesInspector extends JFrame {

  private Preferences userPrefs;
  private static Logger log =
    Logger.getLogger("com.wrox.j2se.utilities");

  public static final String NAMEPREF = "name";
  public static final String EMAILPREF = "email";
  public static final String AGEPREF = "age";
  public static final String PHONEPREF = "phone";
```

We store the regular expression for each of the text fields in a private static final String. Let's take each of them in turn:

```
  private static final String NAMEREGEX =
    "((Dr|Miss|Mrs|Ms|Mr)\\.? )?([A-Za-z]+[- ])*[A-Za-z]+";
```

A valid name consists of an optional title (which might or might not end in a dot), followed by zero or more first or middle names (which are a set of one or more letters followed by a space) or name prefixes (which are a set of one or more letters followed by a hyphen), followed by a last name (which consists of one or more letters). The following are all valid names under this scheme:

- George W Bush
- Hillary Rodham-Clinton

- `Dr. Frasier Crane`
- `Miss LeAnn Rimes`
- `Louis XIV`
- `Prince`
- `Q`

Notice that when we specify the regular expression inside a Java string-literal, we have to use a backslash to escape the backslash character. This means that to specify a literal `.` character (such as after the title in the above expression), we have to write `\\.` for Java's benefit, so that it creates a string containing the literal characters `\.`, which the regex engine can interpret as meaning a literal `.` character.

If our regex were to contain the regular expression backslash escape character, `\\`, we would have to write `\\\\` in the Java string literal.

> *When composing regular expressions in Java String literals, remember that you must encode any backslash or quotation mark characters so that Java can generate the correct literal regular expression.*

```
private static final String AGEREGEX = "[0-9]+";
```

An age is simply a number – one or more digit characters. We don't allow people to specify their age in hexadecimal digits. A stricter restriction might be to not allow people to claim ages over 200, perhaps using the expression `1?[0-9]{1,2}`, but we want our code to be future-proof, and we don't know what medical advances the new millennium may bring.

```
private static final String EMAILREGEX =
  "[-A-Za-z0-9_.]+@[-A-Za-z0-9_.]+\\.[A-Za-z]{2,}";
```

We've seen the e-mail regular expression. Again, note the use of the Java backslash escape character.

```
private static final String PHONEREGEX = "\\+?([0-9]+-)+[0-9]+";
```

The International Telecommunications Union (the ITU) recommends that telephone numbers be written as a series of numbers separated by hyphen characters. If an international country code is included on the beginning of the telephone number, it should be prefixed with a plus sign. This regular expression rigorously enforces these restrictions.

The final bit of housekeeping to be added to this class is to create a single instance of a `RegexVerifier` to use with all our components.

```
private RegexVerifier regexVerifier = new RegexVerifier();

public ValidatingLoggingPreferencesInspector() {
```

```
super();

log.fine("Creating preferences inspector");

userPrefs =
  Preferences.userNodeForPackage(
    ValidatingLoggingPreferencesInspector.class);

this.setResizable(false);
this.setLocationRelativeTo(null);

final JLabel nameLabel = new JLabel("Name", JLabel.LEFT);
final JTextField nameField =
  new JTextField(userPrefs.get(NAMEPREF, ""), 20);
final JLabel emailLabel = new JLabel("Email", JLabel.LEFT);
final JTextField emailField =
  new JTextField(userPrefs.get(EMAILPREF, ""), 20);
final JLabel ageLabel = new JLabel("Age", JLabel.LEFT);
final JTextField ageField =
  new JTextField(userPrefs.get(AGEPREF, ""), 20);
final JLabel phoneLabel = new JLabel("Telephone", JLabel.LEFT);
final JTextField phoneField =
  new JTextField(userPrefs.get(PHONEPREF, ""), 20);
final JButton applyButton = new JButton("Apply");
final JButton OKButton = new JButton("OK");
```

Here's where we register our components, and their regular expression restrictions, with the verifier.

```
regexVerifier.addRegexForComponent(nameField, NAMEREGEX);
regexVerifier.addRegexForComponent(ageField, AGEREGEX);
regexVerifier.addRegexForComponent(emailField, EMAILREGEX);
regexVerifier.addRegexForComponent(phoneField, PHONEREGEX);

ActionListener applyListener = new ActionListener() {
  public void actionPerformed(ActionEvent evt) {
    log.fine("Apply button clicked");
```

Clicking a button does not force a focus change, so the verifier is not called before the Apply or OK buttons receive the click action. This means we have to force a verification operation before we can trust the settings in all of the text fields.

```
    if (regexVerifier.verifyAll()) {
      userPrefs.put(NAMEPREF, nameField.getText());
      userPrefs.put(AGEPREF, ageField.getText());
      userPrefs.put(EMAILPREF, emailField.getText());
```

```
        userPrefs.put(PHONEPREF, phoneField.getText());
        log.info("Preferences stored");
      }
    }
  };

  ActionListener okListener = new ActionListener() {
    public void actionPerformed(ActionEvent evt) {
      log.fine("OK Button clicked");
      if (regexVerifier.verifyAll()) {
        userPrefs.put(NAMEPREF, nameField.getText());
        userPrefs.put(AGEPREF, ageField.getText());
        userPrefs.put(EMAILPREF, emailField.getText());
        userPrefs.put(PHONEPREF, phoneField.getText());
        log.info("Preferences stored");
        hide();
      }
    }
  };

  applyButton.addActionListener(applyListener);
  OKButton.addActionListener(okListener);

  Container content = getContentPane();
  content.setLayout(new GridLayout(5, 2));

  content.add(nameLabel);
  content.add(nameField);
  content.add(ageLabel);
  content.add(ageField);
  content.add(emailLabel);
  content.add(emailField);
  content.add(phoneLabel);
  content.add(phoneField);
  content.add(applyButton);
  content.add(OKButton);

  pack();
  log.fine(
    "Preferences inspector components initialization completed");
  }
}
```

The final changes need to be made to the `PreferencesListener` class. We need to initialize the logging system, as it is our application's main class. No other changes are really needed, since the class is only loosely coupled to the preferences inspector via the change-listener relationship. We just need to create an instance of our new preferences inspector, in place of the old one. We'll also add logging to this class, while we're at it:

```
package com.wrox.j2se.utilities;

import javax.swing.*;
import java.awt.*;
import java.awt.event.*;
import java.util.prefs.*;
import java.util.logging.*;

public class LoggingPreferencesListener extends JFrame
  implements PreferenceChangeListener {

  ValidatingLoggingPreferencesInspector inspector =
    new ValidatingLoggingPreferencesInspector();
  private static Logger log =
    Logger.getLogger("com.wrox.j2se.utilities");

  private JLabel name;
  private JLabel email;
  private JLabel age;
  private JLabel phone;

  public static void main(String args[]) {
```

We need to initialize the logging system. First, we obtain a reference to the `LogManager`, and open up the level valves on all loggers created in the `com.wrox` package hierarchy. Next, we create a new global handler class with a very fine-level filter, and register it with the `LogManager`:

```
    LogManager lm = LogManager.getLogManager();

    try {
      FileHandler fileLog = new FileHandler("%h/com.wrox.j2se.%u.txt");
      fileLog.setFormatter(new SimpleFormatter());
      fileLog.setLevel(Level.ALL);

      lm.getLogger("com.wrox.j2se").addHandler(fileLog);
    } catch (Exception e) {
      log.log(Level.WARNING, "Could not create log file", e);
    }
```

```
    log.info("Application starting up");
    new LoggingPreferencesListener().show();
  }

  public LoggingPreferencesListener() {
    super();
    log.fine("Created new LoggingPreferencesListener");
    Preferences.userNodeForPackage(
                                  LoggingPreferencesListener.class)
                                  .addPreferenceChangeListener(this);

    this.setResizable(false);
    this.setLocationRelativeTo(null);
    this.setDefaultCloseOperation(EXIT_ON_CLOSE);
    inspector.setLocationRelativeTo(this);

    name = new JLabel("", JLabel.LEFT);
    email = new JLabel("", JLabel.LEFT);
    age = new JLabel("", JLabel.LEFT);
    phone = new JLabel("", JLabel.LEFT);

    final JLabel nameLabel = new JLabel("Name", JLabel.LEFT);
    final JLabel emailLabel = new JLabel("Email", JLabel.LEFT);
    final JLabel ageLabel = new JLabel("Age", JLabel.LEFT);
    final JLabel phoneLabel = new JLabel("Telephone", JLabel.LEFT);
    final JButton prefsButton = new JButton("Prefs");

    ActionListener prefsListener = new ActionListener() {
      public void actionPerformed(ActionEvent evt) {
        log.fine("Prefs button clicked");
        inspector.show();
      }
    };

    prefsButton.addActionListener(prefsListener);

    Container content = getContentPane();
    content.setLayout(new GridLayout(5, 2));

    content.add(nameLabel);
    content.add(name);
    content.add(ageLabel);
    content.add(age);
    content.add(emailLabel);
    content.add(email);
```

```
    content.add(phoneLabel);
    content.add(phone);
    content.add(prefsButton);

    pack();
    log.fine(
      "finished creating LoggingPreferencesListener components");
  }

  public void preferenceChange(PreferenceChangeEvent evt) {

    String key = evt.getKey();
    String val = evt.getNewValue();

    log.fine("Preference change event detected: " + key + ":" + val);

    if (key.equals(ValidatingLoggingPreferencesInspector.NAMEPREF)) {
      name.setText(val);
    } else if (key
        .equals(ValidatingLoggingPreferencesInspector.EMAILPREF)) {
      email.setText(val);
    } else if (key.equals(
                 ValidatingLoggingPreferencesInspector.AGEPREF)) {
      age.setText(val);
    } else if (key
        .equals(ValidatingLoggingPreferencesInspector.PHONEPREF)) {
      phone.setText(val);
    }
  }
}
```

That's it. Running the application now, once you have opened the preferences inspector you will not be able to change the preferences to any value that doesn't match the regular expressions we've specified.

In addition, a log of all actions will be stored in your home directory.

Regular Expression Conclusions

Regular expressions are a long overdue piece of advanced text-handling functionality for the Java language. The implementation is certainly powerful, although performance is probably going to be the biggest issue – how well optimized is the 100 percent pure Java regular expression engine?

You can use regular expressions in almost any kind of application – they are a true utility API. From parsing data out of files, to input validation, to text search and replace, to data filtering, regexes are going to transform the way people program with strings in Java.

Conclusions

This has been a whistle-stop tour of the expanded functionality of the `java.util` package hierarchy in J2SE 1.4. Utility classes are there to be used in any kind of application – hopefully we've seen some of the versatility that exists in the APIs.

The preferences system has its shortcomings, but it will no doubt prove useful as a quick-and-dirty place to store handy little pieces of information. In that sense, it is more like using cookies in a web application than it is like using a database, and there's always going to be a use for a place to persist little pieces of data. The security model is its real downfall, not being fine-grained enough to permit restricted access. The all-or-nothing approach means that a lot of applications that could benefit from a little local storage, like applets, are not necessarily going to be able to benefit from this facility.

Logging is a comprehensive system, with all the advantages and disadvantages that usually go along with being flexible and extensible. It runs the risk of being too complex for trivial use. Although it is very easy to use it to send a few information messages to the system log, configuring anything from within an application opens up a large can of worms. However, as an architecture for logging in a multi-application, multi-user environment, it is certainly well equipped to serve as a good basis for reliable logging on server systems.

Regular expressions are probably the most welcome of the three new systems. Their existence makes a lot of things that were once difficult or impossible, simple or at least possible. Regex syntax can be a tricky beast to get to grips with, but once you *get* it, expressions come naturally, and they seem like the logical solution to all manner of problems. I've often found myself writing argument parsers in a `main()` method, wishing that the arguments had just come in as a single `String` I could parse with a regular expression. A little work with a `StringBuffer` now, and this is possible. If that's the only Java annoyance regexes solve, they'll have justified their place in the platform.

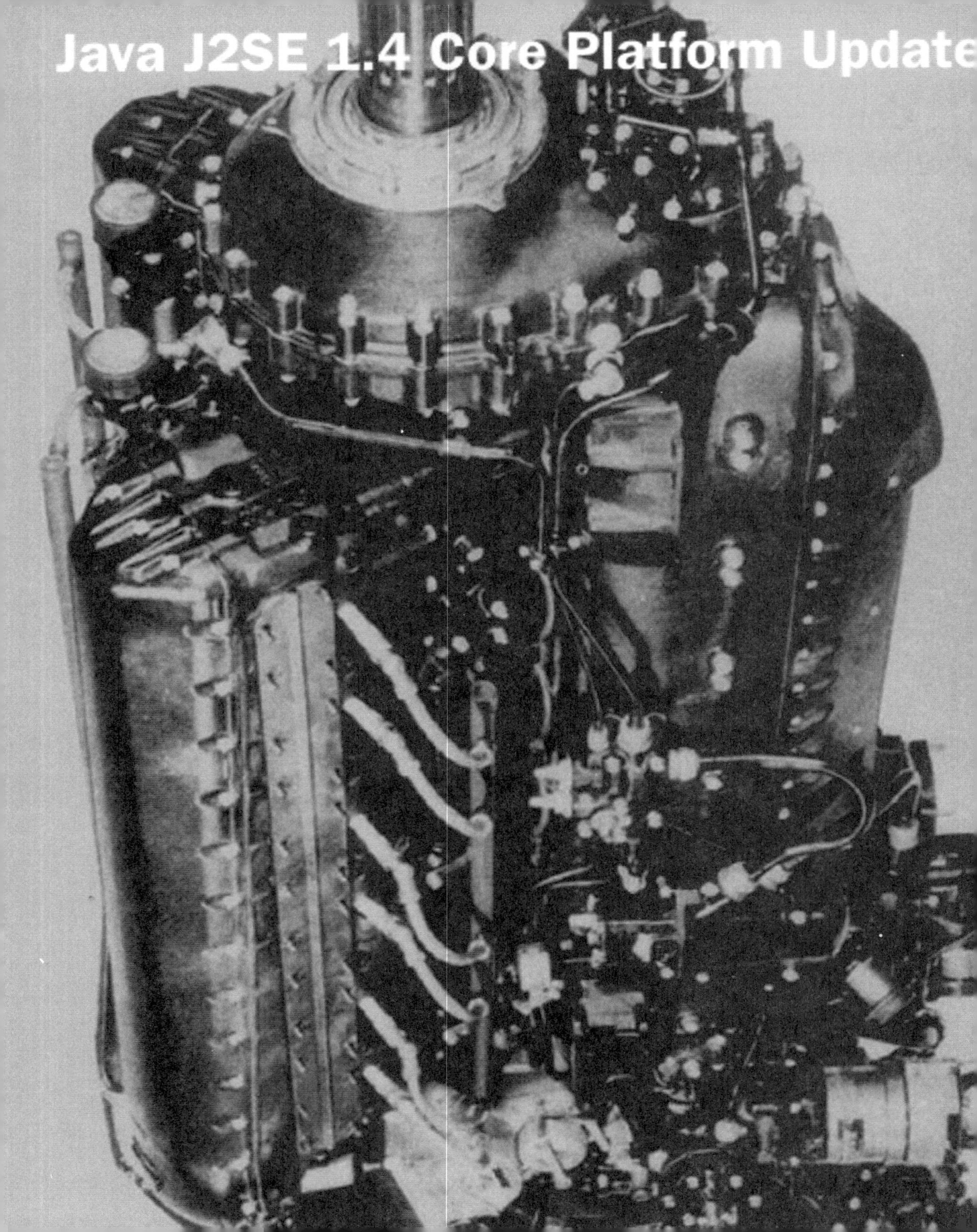
Java J2SE 1.4 Core Platform Update

Language

The Java programming language has remained pretty stable since its creation. Java 1.1 was the biggest linguistic shakeup, adding inner and anonymous classes, the `transient` keyword, object initializers, the `@deprecated` tag and the literal syntax for initializing arrays. Then, right through to J2SE 1.3.1, the only change to the language specification was to amend the way floating-point numbers were handled to better map onto real hardware platforms (introducing the `strictfp` keyword), and this came in with the original Java 2 release. Most of the functionality of the Java language was already in place in version 1.0. Given this historical conservatism, and an ever-increasing body of legacy code, which nobody wants to break by making incompatible changes, requests for serious amendments to the Java language have been contentious to say the least. There are two effects that language changes can have that need to be taken into account when they are considered: sourcecode compatibility, and byte-code compatibility.

A sourcecode-compatible change to the Java language is a change such that all Java code that was correct before the language change was made is *still* correct Java code after the language change is made. For example, when object initializer blocks were added in Java 1.1, the language specification was changed, but code that was written before they were introduced would still compile; this is a compatible change. However, at the same time, the `transient` keyword was added to the language. Any code written previous to this change that used the word `transient` as a variable or class name would now no longer compile; this is an incompatible change to the Java language.

Any change to the Java language necessitates a change to the Java compiler, `javac`. It needs to be amended so that it can understand the new syntax structures. However, the job of the Java compiler is to convert the concepts expressed by the Java syntax structures into concepts expressed in Java byte-code. If it is possible to express the new concepts in terms of existing byte-code constructs, then the compiler will generate byte-code compatible `.class` files. That is, the class files generated from sourcecode that uses the new syntax will still run on older, existing Java Virtual Machines. However, if a language change introduces a new concept that really can't be expressed in terms of existing byte-codes, then the change is byte-code incompatible and resulting code won't necessarily run on existing virtual machines. In other words, a change to the Java language always necessitates a change to the compiler, but not necessarily to the virtual machine. In addition, the modified compiler may or may not be able to understand Java source written for older versions of the language.

J2SE 1.4 takes a bold step of introducing a new language feature, and breaking source (but not byte-code) compatibility. This chapter is, predominantly, devoted to looking at that change – the introduction of the simple assertion facility to the Java language.

In addition, changes have been made to the default or optional behavior of the Java compiler or JVM that affect the way code is executed. We'll also take a look in this chapter at a small but useful change to the `javac` program.

A form of language change that is rarely considered, but a language change nonetheless, is a change in the formatting of Javadoc comments. J2SE 1.4 introduces some major changes to Javadoc, so we'll examine those at the end of this chapter.

Requests for Enhancements

In spite of the side effects risked by any language change, few people are entirely satisfied with Java's capabilities as it stands. That is not a criticism of Java – it doesn't seek to provide everybody's favorite language feature, instead finding virtue in simplicity and syntactic purity.

But right now is an interesting time in object-oriented language development. Microsoft's .NET strategy has introduced a new language, C#, which shares many goals and, it has to be said, syntactic similarities with Java. C# provides most of the facilities of Java (it is fundamentally built around single implementation and multiple interface inheritance, with classes containing static and instance methods and fields, and static inner classes – it even has a similar exception mechanism), but it adds a plethora of new facilities. It supports a compact syntax for properties (the equivalent of JavaBean getter and setter methods), collection indexing, the ability to define custom value types, type-safe enumerations, and a system for creating pointers to methods, called delegates (if you've ever programmed in Visual J++, you've probably encountered them). It also provides for operator overloading, and has a number of subtle syntactic differences – making method overriding a more explicit process than it is in Java, for example.

Few people want to turn Java into C#, but certainly some Java developers would like to have some of those facilities. There are four language changes that constantly end up at the top of most wish lists, some of which C# has, others it doesn't:

- **Operator overloading**
- **Type-safe enumerations**
- **Generics**
- **Assertions**

In addition, a Java Specification Request called **Concise Object Array Literals** is currently under development, and was originally intended for inclusion in J2SE 1.4. It aims to provide a means for writing methods that take an arbitrary number of parameters. We'll look at the work that's been done on this issue shortly.

While it's true that of these, only an assertion facility has been introduced in J2SE 1.4, it's interesting to look at the field of common requests from which it was selected. It's also worth keeping an eye on what else is out there on the wish-list, because it looks like language changes in the future are not going to be limited to just this one new feature. Generics are already slated for 1.5. Let's look at what these different requests would involve:

Operator Overloading

This is the ability to define new uses for Java operators, or possibly even to define your own operators. It is mostly requested by scientific developers, who need to create classes representing mathematical entities such as complex numbers or matrices, and want to write more natural code than method syntax allows. For example, currently the Java code to add two complex numbers might look like this:

```
ComplexNumber a = new ComplexNumber(4, -5);
ComplexNumber b = new ComplexNumber(-3, 4);
ComplexNumber c = a.add(b);
```

With operator overloading, this could be changed to:

```
ComplexNumber a = new ComplexNumber(4, -5);
ComplexNumber b = new ComplexNumber(-3, 4);
ComplexNumber c = a + b;
```

This could be achieved by writing an operator-overloading declaration within the `ComplexNumber` class, which would basically be the same code as is required for the `add()` method used in the first example. It would simply require a syntax to indicate that, when a `ComplexNumber` was followed by a + sign and another `ComplexNumber`, the result would be a `ComplexNumber`, and the declaration would contain code to return a new `ComplexNumber` instance with the correct value.

Many languages provide operator overloading, notably C++, but it has as many detractors as supporters. James Gosling, one of the original creators of the Java language, has a section of his web site, http://java.sun.com/people/jag/FP.html, describing a syntax that would allow this kind of operator overloading in a quite natural, Java-like fashion. Since the underlying implementation would be to map the operations to method calls, there wouldn't necessarily need to be any changes to the byte-code specification. However, many people regard unrestricted operator overloading as one of the worst causes of unreadable and unmaintainable code (the temptation is to attach frequently used methods to operators to save on typing, and the proliferation of symbolic operators instead of descriptive method names destroys readability), and it has been regarded as a low priority for the Java language, since it is principally used in academic computing. Java, as we know, is intended for commercial and enterprise environments, where complex numbers are a lot less common. Operator overloading is not planned for future versions of Java at this time.

Type-Safe Enumerations

One Java programming idiom that we all use every now and then is to write code like this:

```
public class Quark extends SubatomicParticle {

  /*
   * A quark is a sub-atomic particle. A Proton, for example,
   * is made up of three quarks. There are six flavors of
   * quark, each of which come in three colors.
   */

  // Flavors
  public static final int UP = 1;
  public static final int DOWN = 2;
  public static final int TOP = 3;
  public static final int BOTTOM = 4;
  public static final int CHARMED = 5;
  public static final int STRANGE = 6;

  // Colors
  public static final int RED = 1;
  public static final int GREEN = 2;
  public static final int BLUE = 3;

  private int flavor;
  private int color;

  public Quark(int flavor, int color) {
```

```
    this.flavor = flavor;
    this.color = color;
  }
}
```

Now, we can construct quarks using lines like this:

```
Quark p = new Quark(Quark.UP, Quark.GREEN);
```

However, there is nothing at all to stop us from accidentally writing code like this:

```
Quark p = new Quark(Quark.RED, Quark.BOTTOM);
```

This is a hard bug to spot, and the compiler won't flinch at it, even though we've actually created an up quark of a non-existent color, rather than the red, bottom quark we thought we were creating. This is because we're really passing around `int`s, not type-safe colors and flavors.

The classic way to get around this problem in Java is to write classes like this:

```
public final class Flavor {

  public static final Flavor UP = new Flavor();
  public static final Flavor DOWN = new Flavor();
  public static final Flavor TOP = new Flavor();
  public static final Flavor BOTTOM = new Flavor();
  public static final Flavor CHARMED = new Flavor();
  public static final Flavor STRANGE = new Flavor();

  private Flavor() {
  }

}
```

```
public final class Color {

  public static final Color RED = new Color();
  public static final Color GREEN = new Color();
  public static final Color BLUE = new Color();

  private Color() {
  }

}
```

Since these classes have private constructors, and are not subclassable or serializable, the only instances of them that exist are those we create within the class definitions themselves. So, there are only three distinct `Color` objects in existence, and only six `Flavors`. The `Quark` class can then be written in a type-safe manner:

```
public class Quark extends SubatomicParticle {

  /*
   * A quark is a sub-atomic particle. A Proton, for example,
   * is made up of three quarks. There are six flavors of
   * quark, each of which come in three colors.
   */

  private Flavor flavor;
  private Color color;

  public Quark(Flavor flavor, Color color) {
    this.flavor = flavor;
    this.color = color;
  }
}
```

This time, the accidental typo:

```
Quark p = new Quark(Color.RED, Flavor.BOTTOM);
```

Is picked up by the compiler.

However, these kinds of classes, which define a set of what are known as **enumerated constants**, are slightly limited. You can't use them in several ways that would seem to make sense. For example, we can't write a method like this in our type-safe `Quark` class:

```
public String getFlavorString() {
  switch (flavor) {
    case Flavor.UP:
      return "Up";
      break;
    case Flavor.DOWN:
      return "Down";
      break;
    case Flavor.TOP:
      return "Top";
      break;
    case Flavor.BOTTOM:
      return "Bottom";
      break;
```

```
    case Flavor.STRANGE:
      return "Strange";
      break;
    case Flavor.CHARMED:
      return "Charmed";
      break;
  }
  return "Unknown";
}
```

This is because Java's `switch` statement will only operate on `int`s, `byte`s, and `char`s. We could have written this sort of code using the earlier version of `Quark`, which stored its flavor as an `int`.

Similarly, it is difficult to iterate through all of the possible values for an enumerated constant class such as our `Color` or `Flavor` classes, whereas iterating through a series of `int`s is quite simple.

The idea behind the requests for Java to introduce a type-safe enumeration syntax would be to combine the flexibility of `static final int`s with the type-safety of enumerated constant classes. Different proposals recommend different degrees of power in enumerations, from relatively weak `int` wrappers (similar to C `typedef`s), to Pascal-style enumerations, which enforce completeness in switch statements (failure to handle all possible values is a compile-time error).

To get an idea of what syntax might be like, Microsoft's Java-like language, C#, has a syntax for defining an enumeration type, like this:

```
enum Flavor {Up, Down, Top, Bottom, Strange, Charmed};
```

A variable of type `Flavor` can then only contain one of these values. It's also possible to switch on values of this type, and to iterate through the set.

Many see this sort of syntactic nicety as an unnecessary overhead for Java, hence it has been dismissed repeatedly by Sun, which says there's no need to bloat the language with new ways of doing things you can already do, and that the workaround is to use an enumerated constant class. This view has considerable merit, but it doesn't seem to stop people constantly calling for a language construct for enumerations.

Generics

Often, we need to write a class that can handle objects of an arbitrary type. Java's solution to this problem is typically **polymorphism** – define a class that handles objects belonging to a certain class, and it can handle objects belonging to all its subclasses as well. Unfortunately, if the different objects you need to handle are not related by inheritance, you're left handling the lowest common denominator: the `Object` class. A typical example is in the collections framework, where, for example, the `List` class's `add()` method takes an `Object` argument, and the `get()` method returns an `Object`. If we write all of the code around a list, we may well be absolutely certain that we only ever put in objects of a type `Foo`, so we know that we'll only ever get out `Foo` objects. Java doesn't know this though, and forces us to cast the returned object to type `Foo` whenever we use one of the list's methods. In fact, we can't be certain that all the objects in the list are of type `Foo`; if we make a programming error and put in an object of type `Bar` by accident, there is no compiler check that will warn us we've made a mistake. The first we'll know about it is when our code pulls out the `Bar` object, tries to cast it to type `Foo`, and fails.

Generics is the name for a programming construct that would get around this. If Java supported generics, then when we instantiated our `List` object, we could specify what types it should hold – we could create a list of `Foo`s, for example, by creating an object of type `List<Foo>`. The compiler would remember we had said that the list was a `Foo`-only list, and check that all the objects we passed in were of the correct type. It would also allow us to assume that all the objects we got out were already of type `Foo`, so we wouldn't have to cast them.

Generics is a powerful concept, common to several other programming languages, notably Eiffel, and similar capabilities are provided by C++ templates, and it's slated for inclusion in J2SE 1.5. There is a technology preview available now though, which enables you to develop generic classes. This can be found at http://www.jcp.org/aboutJava/communityprocess/review/jsr014/index.html. It also provides a completely generic collections library. We'll take a look at the preview in Chapter 8, *The Future*.

Concise Object Array Literals

Not widely regarded as a must-have feature for the Java language, this language proposal has been under development under the Java Community Process as Java Specification Request 65. The initial drive behind this JSR came out of the development of the NIO API, which was to include a simple print-formatter. Print formatting is common to C and C++, and many other languages (although it has to be said, better ways of achieving the same results already exist). The idea is that in order to include some programmatic data in a printable string, we simply call a method that takes a string, and a series of pieces of data as arguments. The string contains formatting codes, which are then replaced, from left to right, with the pieces of data from the argument list. For example, we might use the C `printf` print formatting command:

```
printf("%s account balance: $%f.2", name, income - expenditure);
```

The % characters introduce formatting instructions. This string uses two: %s, which means output the corresponding argument as a string, and %f.2, which means output the corresponding argument as a floating-point value with two decimal places.

As you can see, the printf() function in C is very flexible. It can take arguments of any primitive type, and format them as strings, decimal numbers, hexadecimal numbers, floating-point values (with specified precision), and so on. In order to do so, it has to be able to take an unlimited number of arguments of any type.

NIO was to introduce similar functionality (although it's not entirely clear whether it was wise to do so, and the functionality was not developed in time). However, Java has no way of writing a method that takes some arbitrary mixture of primitive arguments, and no way of writing a method that takes an unlimited number of arguments. The only approach that works is to write the method to take an object array (a parameter of type Object[]), and then force the user to box up the data they want to pass to the method. If the user will be passing in primitive types, such as floats and ints, this is going to be very tedious:

```
formatter.fmt("%s account balance: $%f.2", new Object[] {name,
                                  new Float(income - expenditure)});
```

The proposal of JSR 65 is simply to allow Object arrays (and only Object arrays) to be initialized with values of any type, with primitives being automatically boxed into their equivalent wrapper type. This should allow the above line to be written:

```
formatter.fmt("%s account balance: $%f.2",
                                       {name, income - expenditure});
```

There is probably a good chance that this change will make it into the Java language at some point, since it is, so it seems, completely sourcecode and byte-code compatible. However, it does somewhat fall into the category of "syntactic sugar", which has prevented a lot of previous language changes being accepted, so it may yet not make it.

Assertions

Assertions are a facility that provides developers with the ability to encapsulate their assumptions about the state of the computer program at any given point into Boolean statements, and abort program execution if something which should be true, turns out to be false. Typically, well-commented source is full of bits of code like this:

```
  if (connectionPool.isEmpty()) {
    connectionPool.add(new Connection());
  }
```

```
// connectionPool is not empty
Connection conn = connectionPool.get();
// conn is not null
```

This comment is a statement the programmer is making about the state the program should be in. In this case, the programmer is using a `connectionPool` object, possibly to manage database connections, and is stating the assumption that one of two things has happened up to that point in the code; either the pool was initially not empty, or the pool was initially empty. In the latter case, the `add()` method was called, which should have led to the pool acquiring a new member. Either way, at this point, the pool should no longer be empty. This means it should be safe to call the `get()` method and retrieve one of the connections from the pool. Therefore further code should be able to proceed on the assumption that `conn` contains a `Connection` object, not `null`.

It is important to remember that bugs in the implementation of the connection pool, false assumptions about the way that the connection pool functions, or programmatic misuse of the class containing this code (for example, perhaps this class should never be used in a multi-threaded environment) could lead to the statements not holding. However, the programmer believes that they will always be true, and is developing the application on those assumptions, so if they prove false, they will pinpoint the source of a programming error.

Assertions allow those statements to be encapsulated in a way that tells the run-time environment what the programmer believes is going on. If this turns out not to be the case, the run-time environment can stop the process. So, the above could be rewritten with assertions as:

```
if (connectionPool.isEmpty()) {
  connectionPool.add(new Connection());
}
assert (!connectionPool.isEmpty());
Connection a = connectionPool.get();
assert a != null;
```

The same effect could be achieved, of course, with a simple run-time exception:

```
if (connectionPool.isEmpty()) {
  connectionPool.add(new Connection());
}
if (connectionPool.isEmpty()) {
  throw new RuntimeException(
        "Connection Pool did not behave as expected");
}
Connection a = connectionPool.get();
if (a == null) {
  throw new RuntimeException(
        "Connection Pool did not behave as expected");
}
```

However, unlike these `if` statements, assertion-checking can be switched on and off at run time as required, without changing the sourcecode or recompiling. Assertions might be used during the test phase for a product, and then switched off for production deployment. In addition, their syntax is considerably easier to understand and maintain.

Assertions, unlike the other wish-list items, have in fact been added to the J2SE 1.4 version of the Java Language Specification. In the next part of this chapter, we'll look at what facilities assertions provide, how they should be used, and how they can be used in a real development environment.

The Java Assertion Facility

Assertions are enabled principally by the introduction into the Java language of a new keyword, `assert`. An `assert` statement can be placed anywhere in a Java class where you could normally place an executable statement – within methods, constructors, or initializer blocks. It has two forms:

```
assert boolean_expression;
```

And:

```
assert boolean_expression: any_expression;
```

In both cases, if assertions are enabled, the Boolean expression is evaluated. If it evaluates to `false`, then a `java.lang.AssertionError` object is created and thrown. If the second syntax is used, then if the assertion fails, the second expression is evaluated and passed to the `AssertionError`'s constructor. `AssertionError` has constructors for all of Java's basic types, including the `java.lang.Object` type, and each constructor converts whatever value was passed in into a string that serves as the error message.

If the Boolean expression evaluates to `true`, then execution passes on to the next line, and the second expression, if present, is not evaluated.

It's important to note that, since you cannot be certain at design time whether your code will be run with assertions enabled or not, you must be careful to ensure that the expressions evaluated in the course of processing assertions do not have any side effects. By side effects, we mean changes to the state of the program. The result of executing the program should be no different whether assertions are enabled or not, so the contents of an `assert` statement should never make changes to the values stored in local, instance, or class variables, or otherwise alter the state of the system.

An assertion can call methods that contain more complex Boolean tests, but particular care should be taken to avoid side effects. Calling methods on other classes can lead to all kinds of changes happening that you are not aware of, and could lead to some real difficulty reproducing bugs which only occur when asserts are disabled.

Since the result of an assertion failure is a thrown error, this will propagate up through the call stack, triggering any `finally` clauses attached to `try` or `catch` blocks during which the assertion failure occurs. Although it is possible to catch throwables of type `Error` (such as `AssertionError`), this isn't recommended, since the point of an assertion failure is to inform you that the program is no longer in a state anticipated by the programmer, so continued execution could be dangerous.

Using Assertions

Naturally, since assertions introduce a new keyword into the Java language, one which was never reserved, there is the possibility that existing code exists that contains the word `assert`. Anybody who rolled their own assertion mechanism and used a method of that name to provide the functionality, for example, is going to have a problem compiling that code on the J2SE 1.4 compiler.

For this reason, `javac` defaults to **compatible mode** if you write some code using `assert` statements like those shown above, similar to this:

```
public class AssertFailure {
  public static void main(String[] args) {
    assert (2 + 2) == 5;
    System.out.println("2 + 2 is 5");
  }
}
```

You'll get the following error:

```
> javac AssertFailure.java
AssertFailure.java:3 warning: as of release 1.4, assert is a keyword,
and may not be used as an identifier
      assert (2 + 2) == 5;
      ^
AssertFailure.java:3 not a statement
      assert (2 + 2) == 5;
                     ^
1 error
1 warning
```

To enable the compiler's awareness of the `assert` keyword, we need to tell it that this sourcecode file uses the 1.4 language feature:

```
> javac -source 1.4 AssertFailure.java
```

To enable assertion support in the compiler, you need to use the `-source 1.4` flag.

The code will now compile without any errors or warnings. It should be anticipated that later versions of `javac` will change the default behavior so that 1.4 (or later) source is assumed, unless the `-source` flag specifies otherwise. The addition of the `assert` keyword does not cause any problems with existing binaries (`.class` files) that use `assert` identifiers.

Now, when this code is executed, again, the default behavior is to ignore asserts. To enable assertion checking, we have to use either the `-ea` or `-enableassertions` flag when we call the Java program:

```
> java -ea AssertFailure
Exception in thread "main" java.lang.AssertionError
        at AssertFailure.main(AssertFailure.java:1)
```

The assertion fails, obviously, because the program states that at the start of the `main()` method, it is working on the assumption that two plus two is five – a pretty dangerous assumption on which to proceed. Quite rightly, the assertion failure causes the program to stop executing.

If we don't enable assertions, this happens:

```
> java AssertFailure
2 + 2 is 5
```

Without assertion checking in place, the program is allowed to continue executing based on its faulty assumptions, and is therefore quite happy to spread dangerous rumors about arithmetic. The assertion is included so that the fault is discovered during testing, fixed, and then not present in the final release, thus avoiding this sort of blunder.

Assertions can be disabled using the `-da` flag, although since they are disabled by default, there is very little reason why you would need to use this flag.

Enabling Assertions Selectively

Assertions are not simply on or off for the entire virtual machine. Assertion status is in fact a property of each class, and it is set at the time the class is loaded. Once set, it can't be changed for that class while it is deployed in the VM. So generally, enabling and disabling of assertion checking is handled by class loaders. When we specify `-ea` or `-enableassertions` on the command line, we are setting the default assertion status for all classes loaded by any class loader, other than the system class loader, to `true`. We can do the same for the system class loader by specifying `-esa` or `-enablesystemassertions`. At the moment, there really aren't many assertions in Sun's Java source files (although there's a lot of comments suggesting where assertions might be added); only `BigDecimal`, the new `URI` class, and the NIO buffer implementations actually use asserts. Of course, if they've been used correctly, and there's nothing wrong with Sun's Java implementation, we shouldn't see any assertion errors resulting from running with system assertions turned on, since if we misuse any of these classes, we should see exceptions, not assertion errors being thrown.

Class loaders can be more discriminating, however, in setting the assertion status of classes as they load them. We can specify on the command line that we're actually only interested in assertions in a specific class, or package, or indeed that we aren't interested in assertions in specific classes or packages.

We can add a package or class name as an argument to the `-ea` or `-enableassertions` switch by following it with a colon, and the fully qualified name of the class, or the package name followed by `"..."`. You can include multiple assertion-enabling switches in the same command. For example:

```
> java -ea:AssertFailure -ea:java.lang... AssertFailure
```

The package identifier `"..."` is used for two reasons. Firstly, because an asterisk in a command line will often be interpreted by the command shell as meaning that the word containing it should be interpreted as a wildcarded filename, the `import`-style syntax cannot be used. Secondly, because it actually means this package *and all its sub-packages*. So, `java.lang...` refers also to `java.lang.reflect` and `java.lang.ref`. If you use the switch `-ea:...`, assertions will be enabled for the default package – that is, for classes that do not contain a `package` statement.

The `-disableassertions` and `-da` switches can be used to switch off assertion checking for a class or package previously switched on by a more general assertion-enabling switch. So, for example, to enable assertion checking for all classes except our own class, we could use the sequence:

```
> java -ea -da:AssertFailure AssertFailure
```

Assertion Idioms

So, now that we've been given asserts to use in our code, what should we, as developers, use them for? Essentially, asserts should be used by programmers to say, "If my code does what I think it does, this is what will have happened." Here are some typical situations where assertions are a useful aid to debugging and testing.

Algorithm Verification

Probably the most common use of asserts is to codify what the result of running an algorithm should be, if the algorithm is implemented correctly. It's often possible to write a test that verifies an algorithm's result is right even before the algorithm itself has been implemented, essentially coding a functional requirement into the application. A simple example:

```
public int biggest(int a, int b) {
  int result;

  // insert algorithm which puts the larger of a and b into result
```

```
  assert (result == a && a >= b) || (result == b && b >= a);

  return result;
}
```

We're now free to experiment with different algorithms, and if we accidentally write one that doesn't work, the assertion will fail (although only if you test enough input conditions that you come across the combination of inputs that breaks your algorithm – it's important to come up with a good set of test cases that will stretch the algorithm).

This is a form of **design-by-contract post-condition**. Design-by-contract is a more formal way of using assertions to precisely describe the behavior of methods and classes.

Design-by-Contract

Design-by-contract is a software design methodology originating in the work of Bertrand Meyer, particularly on the Eiffel programming language. Design-by-contract attempts to force individual developers working on separate modules to ensure that their code's behavior is completely predictable. The concept of a "contract" implies that two parties promise to do certain things for one another, in a reciprocal fashion. In a design contract, the developer of a module, such as a method, makes the promise to any developers who use the module that it will do certain things, and return certain values, provided that those using it uphold their half of the bargain, and only use the module in certain ways, and pass in certain values. If the developer using the module breaks their half of the deal, the module is allowed (in fact expected) to behave unpredictably. If the module itself doesn't fulfill its half of the bargain, the client code cannot be expected to continue to function as designed.

The purpose of any design-by-contract system is to detect breaches of the design contract, and prevent further program execution. This is done by providing a means for the developer to tell the execution environment what the program should have done, so that it can check if it has done so, and call a halt if it hasn't.

In a practical sense, a contract relating to a specific method consists of three things:

- **Pre-conditions**
- **Post-conditions**
- **Invariants**

A **pre-condition** is a condition that must be met before the method is executed. It may relate both to the environment in which the method is executing, and to the parameters passed to the method. It is the responsibility of any code calling the method to meet any pre-conditions the method lays out.

A **post-condition** is a condition that must be the case after the method has completed execution. It can relate, again, both to the execution environment as a whole, and to the return value the method produces. It is the responsibility of the method to ensure that the post-conditions are met.

An **invariant** is something that is always true. More precisely, it is something which any module of code can always rely on being true when it starts executing, and must ensure is still true when it finishes executing. It is the responsibility of any relevant piece of code to ensure that invariant conditions are met. Typically, these will be internal class invariants (properties which are always true of an object of a certain class), which describe the conditions that govern what internal states are valid for an object.

The general contract, then, is as follows: if a piece of code calls a method, having met all of its pre-conditions, and all invariants are true, it can always assume that when the method returns, the post-conditions have been met, and the invariants are still true.

Assertions and Design-by-Contract

Assertions are not, in themselves, a design-by-contract mechanism. However, they can be used to meet some of the requirements of one. Other Java mechanisms already enforce some contracts in a design-by-contract manner. For example, strong typing ensures that methods can always be assured that, if they expect a parameter to be an `int`, the compiler will not allow code to be built that tries to pass in anything else. Exceptions provide a mechanism for methods to say, "If you don't provide valid input, I won't complete execution, and I'll throw an exception. It will then be your responsibility to clean up the mess." One example of this behavior is the constructor for a `java.net.URL` object, which will throw a `MalformedURLException` if you pass it bad data.

A design-by-contract approach to Java programming can make use of asserts, but should not use them at the expense of using these existing mechanisms.

Pre-conditions

As noted above, Java does some work in enforcing pre-conditions already. Our methods are guaranteed to be passed data of the correct type, for a start. If we want to be more specific than Java's typing system allows though – we want to allow only positive integers, or we need an array of exactly three strings, or we expect to be handed an object whose `init()` method has already been called – the compile-time check is of no use to us. In addition, pre-conditions can relate to other parts of the execution environment as well. Our method might only want to be called once, or it might be necessary to have called another method first. It might be that our method is designed to run only on Christmas Day. If the method in question is public, then the correct programming practice is always to check that the system status and input matches our criteria, and if it doesn't, to throw a specific, named exception. The exceptions our code can throw form part of our method's public interface, and they serve to make the client developers aware that they must meet our input criteria, however esoteric they may seem. Throwing a `NotChristmasDayException` may seem harsh, but if this is the `getPresent()` method, perhaps it is justified.

Remember, an assertion is a statement that the programmer believes to be true. When you are entering a public method, you have no idea where the input data originated, so there is nothing you can usefully assert to be true about that data. You could, in principle, write assertions like this:

```
public void foo(int a, String b) {
  assert a < Integer.MAX_VALUE && a > Integer.MIN_VALUE :
    "Java has breached the laws of integer arithmetic";
  assert b instanceof String || b == null :
    "Java's type system is broken";
}
```

However, this doesn't help us much, since if any of these assertions prove false, we've got much bigger problems than a design-by-contract breach – like a broken virtual machine, for example.

However, if the method has private, or package-private access, then we might want to assume that our own code is slightly better behaved. In these situations, rather than throwing checked exceptions, and forcing our code to become cluttered with `try...catch` blocks whenever we try to access our own internal methods, an acceptable alternative is to use assertions.

For example, we might have a package-private class whose lifecycle needs to be managed by calling its `init()`, `start()`, and `destroy()` methods, exactly once each, and in that order. We know that if the methods aren't called in sequence, it is because of a bug in our own code, not some external developer playing fast and loose with our specified interface. So, rather than throwing an `InvalidStateException` if the methods are called in the wrong order (as we would on a public class), we can use assertions to halt program execution if this happens.

This is a valid use of assertions, because in this context, we know where the method call originated, and it is therefore, possible for us to make assertions about the state of the program when the method is called.

Assertions may be used to perform pre-condition checks on private or package-private classes, but should not be used to do the same on public methods.

When we are about to make a call to a method that has a documented set of pre-conditions, which we believe we have satisfied, we *could* use an assertion to capture that belief, stating that we believe we know what the method's preconditions are, and that we think we have met them. However, it seems unnecessary to make checks such as these, when the method we are calling is almost certainly going to make the same checks itself, and throw an exception if we have, in fact, not met its preconditions. In that case, we can more efficiently assert that the exception will never be thrown – a technique we'll meet in a moment.

Post-conditions

As we saw above, a post-condition is a verification that the result of executing the method is what was expected. Since responsibility for meeting post-conditions lies with the method author, and post-condition checks can be executed at the end of the method, just before it returns, assertions are a logical choice.

The algorithm example above is a trivial one, but it shows the sort of statement it is possible to make about how a method's result should relate to its input. Obviously, if your algorithm does something complex, such as calculate the first 1000 digits of pi, then there's little point in having an assertion at the end of the method that verifies it by calculating the same 1000 digits in the same manner. An assertion is there to check if your algorithm has done what it claims to do. So, we might perform a simple sanity check that the value is in an expected range, say between 3.1 and 3.2. In many cases though, we can perform an accurate test that the result is the expected one, without having to do the same sum again; a sorting algorithm could be followed by an assertion that checks that the elements of an array are in fact now in ascending order. It could also perform a check that all the original elements are each present exactly once.

Again, a post-condition can involve external state as well. A method that is supposed to open a connection to a specified URL might want to verify that the connection is indeed open before passing it back to the client.

It doesn't make any difference if the method is public or private – if it reaches the point of performing post-condition checks, then it will have passed all its pre-condition checks. The program is in a known state, and as a programmer, we can make assertions about what we have done to it over the course of the method's execution. Assertions are therefore a good choice for making post-condition statements in any method.

Post-condition checks can be performed using asserts in any kind of method.

Invariants

Some classes might have certain rules that govern their internal state. It is the job of the class's methods, in manipulating that state, to ensure that those rules are not broken. To give an example, a `Person` class might specify private instance variables `firstName`, `surname`, and `fullName`. The `fullName` string should always be exactly `firstName + " " + surname`, regardless of what happens in the course of (possibly public) methods being called on the object. This property is a class invariant.

Class invariants like this, where all access to the data members representing the state is handled through accessor methods, can be stated as assertions, which should be performed at the end of every method in the class. It makes sense, since the same code is repeated in this way, to bundle the logic into a private method, which returns a `boolean` value indicating whether the class's state is consistent, and call this method from an assert statement before each `return` statement or end of a method in the class.

If an object's state should be subject to some invariant rule, but access to the object's state is not handled entirely through mutation methods, but through direct member access, then that is a sign of a badly designed class, and design-by-contract can't help you there.

Class invariants that relate to private object state can be stated as assertions.

Impossibilities

There are often situations in code where you know something will never happen. For example, in the following code:

```
public String chooseColor() {

  int color = new java.util.Random().nextInt(3);

  switch (color) {
    case 0:
      return "Red";
    case 1:
      return "Green";
    case 2:
      return "Blue";
  }
}
```

The fact is, we know that `color` contains zero, one, or two. We know that it's not possible for this code to continue executing after the `switch` statement, since one of our cases is guaranteed to match. Java doesn't know this though, and it will, unfortunately, insist that it is possible for this method to complete without us having returned anything. For that reason, it won't compile. That means we must include a dummy `return` statement at the end of the method. If that happens though, it means one of our assumptions about how `Random.nextInt()` works is incorrect, so the program should stop executing, as it is in an unpredictable state. This is exactly what assertions are for: to capture that assumption programmatically.

We can use assertions to state that we believe a particular point in the code can never be reached. We simply write an `assert` statement that always fails. This way, if code execution does reach that point, execution will be halted. So, we can write the above method as follows:

```
public String chooseColor() {

  int color = new java.util.Random().nextInt(3);

  switch (color) {
    case 0:
```

```
      return "Red";
    case 1:
      return "Green";
    case 2:
      return "Blue";
  }

  assert false;
  return null;

}
```

Other similar situations include having a loop iterate across a list, and returning when a certain value is found. If you know for a fact that the value is in the list being searched, then the return will always happen – the code will never continue after the loop. So, again, we just `assert false`, and `return null`.

The reason both lines are required is that the compiler does not assume that assertions will always be executed, so can't assume the `assert false` will terminate the method. We have to provide a statement that will exit the method even if assertions are disabled. You could, equally (if you so choose), replace this combination with the equivalent `throw new AssertionError();` statement – it has the effect of providing a way out of the method whether assertions are enabled or not (so the compiler is happy), and if your assumption is correct and the line is never reached anyway, it will never get thrown, even if assertions aren't turned on.

Another classic example of this "we should never end up here" use of assertions occurs if you're calling a method that declares that it throws an exception, but you know there is no way the input you are giving it could result in that exception being thrown. Instead of simply putting a `try...catch` block around it, with an empty `catch` clause containing a comment saying "will never be thrown", this is another case for `assert false`. For example:

```
java.net.URL u = null;
try {
   u = new java.net.URL("http://www.wrox.com/");
} catch (MalformedURLException e) {
   assert false; // the URL isn't malformed
}

return u;
```

Again, a little care is required. The compiler will not be satisfied with this code if we don't ensure that when we reach the `return u` statement, we have initialized `u` at some point. We get around it by initializing it to `null`, but we could equally do so by including a `return null` after the `assert false` statement.

You do need to be careful using this technique. `javac` is moderately intelligent and knows some situations where lines in a method can never be reached, and it won't let you put any statements there, even `assert false`. For example, if a method contains a single `if...else` statement, then it knows that one or other half of the statement will execute. If there is a `return` statement in both halves, then no code after the closing brace of the `else` clause will be reachable.

No Side Effects

One useful assertion to make, at the end of a method that took an object as its input, is that the object is unchanged at the end of the method's execution. This is often particularly important with arrays, since they are reference types that are often used in contexts where value semantics are desirable. In order to do this, the Java documentation suggests we should take a copy of the object as soon as it arrives, and then assert at the end of the method that the original object is the same as this copy. However, we probably don't want to copy an entire object if asserts are turned off. We can accomplish this by making the copy operation take place within an `assert` statement as well, but ensuring that that `assert` statement always succeeds. Here's an example:

```
public void processArrayData(Object[] array) {

  Object[] arrayCopy = null;
  assert (arrayCopy = (Object[]) array.clone()) != null;

  // ... array processing functionality ...

  assert arrayCopy.equals(array);

}
```

The first `assert` statement creates a copy of the array (breaking the golden rule that assertions must have no side effects). The last `assert` statement checks that both copies of the array match.

If you have to monitor several variables in this way, you might want to use an inner class to store the clones. Here's the above example translated to use this technique:

```
public void processArrayData(final Object[] array) {

  class Data {

    private Object[] arrayCopy;

    Data() {
      arrayCopy = (Object[]) array.clone();
    }
```

```
    boolean unchanged() {
      return arrayCopy.equals(array);
    }

  }

  Data data = null;
  assert (data = new Data()) != null;

  // ... array processing functionality ...

  assert data.unchanged();

}
```

Another technique which is not 100 percent guaranteed but is also quite effective is to make use of the `hashCode()` method.

```
public void processArrayData(Object[] array) {

  int hash = array.hashCode();

  // ... array processing functionality ...

  assert hash == array.hashCode();

}
```

This isn't entirely guaranteed because the contract defined for the `hashCode()` method does not guarantee that different hash codes will be returned for objects with different values (different, as in, not the same according to the `equals()` method). In other words, it is possible for some objects that, if we have changed the object's state, the resulting hash code won't actually be different. If we know that for the objects we're handling, a change to their state will be reflected in the hash code, then this technique will work.

You can also use the first two techniques to perform other similar checks that the resulting data is related to the incoming data in some specific way, other than that it is identical. This would enable you to implement the tests we described for a post-condition for a sort algorithm, that the resulting array contained all the original values, just arranged in ascending order.

Assertions in the Development Process

So, having written some code full of assertions, what do you do with them? Obviously you can enable them during debugging, and your program will screech to a halt whenever one of your assumptions proves to be misguided (or, perhaps, poorly expressed). You can enable them during any formal testing phase, or beta program. Most people would say that once you're satisfied all your assumptions hold, and the code follows the rules, you should deactivate assertion checking and release the product – the performance overheads of assertion checking should after all, by now, be obvious, so you would want to run your production code with assertions disabled.

There is a school of thought, however, which says that mission-critical code should always be run with assertions enabled – you can never have tested every possible scenario, and an assertion failure is a good fail-fast mechanism for detecting that something has gone wrong, and the application is operating outside expected parameters. Enabling assertion checking on a selective class or package basis may be the best compromise between these approaches.

Controlling Assertions Programmatically

You can actually control the default assertion status that new classes loaded into the JVM will have programmatically. This has been accomplished by adding several methods to the `ClassLoader` class:

Method	Description
`setDefaultAssertionStatus (boolean enabled)`	Sets the default assertion status for the class loader. This setting may be overridden on a per-package or per-class basis.
`setPackageAssertionStatus (String packageName, boolean enabled)`	Sets the package default assertion status for the named package or any of its sub-packages.
`setClassAssertionStatus (String className, boolean enabled)`	Sets the assertion status for the named top-level class in the class loader and any nested classes contained therein. This setting takes precedence over the class loader's default assertion status, and over any applicable per-package default.
`clearAssertionStatus()`	Sets the default assertion status for the class loader to `false` and discards any package defaults or class assertion status settings associated with the class loader.

These work in much the same way as the command-line flags. The first sets the default assertion status, which will be used for classes for which no other instructions exist, then the package and class variants can override the default status for a particular package or class. The last method resets the class loader's behavior to the defaults set by the JVM.

The settings will only apply to classes that the class loader has not yet loaded into the virtual machine, so you can never use these methods to set the assertion status for your program's main class. To change the default for every other class in your application, you'll have to move fast to ensure that your instructions reach the class loader before it loads anything else in. The first thing to get called in any class loaded into the system is a `static` initializer block. However, it's difficult to get at anything directly from within that piece of code. The following trick gets you a reference to the `ClassLoader` that loaded your class:

```
public class MainClass {

  static {
    ClassLoader.getSystemClassLoader().setDefaultAssertionStatus(true);
  }

  public static void main(String[] args) {

    assert "black" == "white";

    AssertFailure.main(args);

  }
}
```

Running this code without enabling asserts on the command line doesn't make any difference; the assertion in `AssertFailure`, (`2 + 2 = 5`, if you remember) is tested, and fails, leading to the program terminating. However, our assertion in `MainClass` that black equals white is not tested; the class is already loaded, and assertions are not enabled for it, and so this dangerous assumption goes unchallenged. Assertions are only enabled for classes loaded after the static initializer has run.

Setting the class loader's assertion status in this way does not provide a real guarantee that all classes will be loaded with assertions enabled. If a different class loader loads them, or if the class loader manages to load some other classes before we can get to it, assertions might not be activated on a class where we need them. If you really want to ensure that some code doesn't execute without assertion checking, you can use the following precondition idiom:

```
boolean assertsEnabled = false;
assert assertsEnabled = true;
if (!assertsEnabled) {
  throw new RuntimeException("Assertions must be enabled");
}
```

Compiler Changes

In addition to the `-source` switch that has been added to `javac` to support the simple assertion facility, Sun's J2SE 1.4 compiler has another little feature enhancement: a switch has been added to tell the compiler to emit a warning if it detects a fall-through `case` statement (one without a `break`).

It's a non-standard option (it doesn't have to be supported by other vendor's virtual machines), but it's potentially useful for eliminating annoying bugs. The switch is `-Xswitchcheck`, and it simply checks that each case in a switch statement is properly terminated, emitting a warning if it encounters a situation where this is not the case. Obviously, there are situations where a fall through is deliberate, but compiling with this switch will tell you if there's a fall through anywhere you aren't expecting one.

In addition, an undocumented feature that has in fact been supported by `javac` in the past has now been documented. Previous Java documentation stated that it was possible to specify a list of files for compilation, using an `@` directive on the `javac` command line. It's not a very well known feature, so I'll run through the details quickly.

If we want to compile `Foo.java`, `Bar.java`, and `FooBar.java`, we can do so using the command:

```
> javac Foo.java Bar.java fooBar.java
```

Alternatively, we can create a file, called say `sourcefiles`, containing the text:

```
Foo.java
Bar.java
FooBar.java
```

Then we can compile them using the command:

```
> javac @sourcefiles
```

Now, what wasn't made clear in the documentation before was that the same applied to compilation options. So, for example, we could enable both new J2SE 1.4 compilation features – assertion compilation and switch-checking – by creating a file containing the options. Let's call the file `1.4`.

```
-Xswitchcheck
-source 1.4
```

Now we can compile code with these options enabled, simply using a command like this:

```
> javac @1.4 Foo.java
```

Javadoc in J2SE 1.4

The J2SE 1.4 release has provided an opportunity to clear up a lot of little bugs in Javadoc, and in the standard doclet. Some serious enhancements have been made to usability as well. In fact, the Javadoc tool has been completely rewritten. At the same time, a new facility for adding your own Javadoc tags has also been introduced.

Here's a simple example of how Javadoc has been improved: generating Javadocs for a large program used to require entering the names of all the individual packages you wanted to document. Now, using the new `-subpackages` switch, you can request documentation generation on an entire package tree.

Let's look at the significant features that have been added in Javadoc 1.4.

Bug Fixes

A lot of the changes fall into the category of bug fixes. Some fix things that either Javadoc or the standard doclet did wrong, others fix things that they did right, by their own standards, but that were really annoying.

Most importantly, Javadoc now reports class structures correctly. It used to make a few mistakes, particularly when handling inner classes. It would occasionally get spoofed into generating inappropriate documentation by the way the compiler interprets certain language features (such as `static` initializers), and would occasionally report members as having the wrong access level. These bugs have been eradicated. Some problems related to incorrect interpretation of inherited documentation comments have been cleaned up by introducing a new system for documentation inheritance (although the inaccurate reporting of static methods in the "methods inherited from..." box is still present).

Chief in the "annoyances" category has to be that Javadoc used to refuse to generate documentation if the target directory (specified with the `-d` option) didn't exist. Since Javadoc generates a complete directory tree to contain the resulting documentation, this always seemed unnecessarily petty, so it's great to see that the 1.4 version will now create a target directory if it doesn't already exist.

Another "annoyance" is the inconsistent behavior of Javadoc when interpreting comments in different locales. Javadoc uses the first sentence of any documentation comment to generate a summary sentence for use in tables of contents and so on. The original Javadoc was not locale-sensitive, and used its own algorithm to extract the text that constitutes the first sentence, using loose English grammar rules. While support for other locales has been added since J2SE 1.2, the old algorithm was maintained for English language comments, for purposes of backward compatibility, and this algorithm has certain limitations. For example, it will incorrectly determine that the first sentence of the following comment is "Implements a K.L.F.".

```
/** Implements a K.L.F. decreasing flux density algorithm
 * over an inverse macrobiotic Fourier function (using the
 * method described by Dr. K. Zoidberg).
 */
```

The new algorithm is more advanced, and will interpret the sentence as "Implements a K.L.F. decreasing flux density algorithm over an inverse macrobiotic Fourier function (using the method described by Dr. K. Zoidberg)". So that's an improvement, if not a complete success.

The new algorithm is not the default for Javadoc yet, but it will be in the future, and you can check what your Javadoc documentation will look like when interpreted with the new algorithm by activating the new algorithm using the `-breakiterator` option. This tells Javadoc to use the `java.text.BreakIterator` class to establish sentence breaks in a language-independent manner, even if the locale is set to English.

Even if you don't enable the break iterator mode, Javadoc will generate warnings when it encounters comments that will differ when interpreted with the new algorithm.

Documentation Inheritance

In the past, if you omitted any part of the Javadoc comment for a method that overrode a method in a superclass, then that part of the superclass's documentation comment would be inherited. Unfortunately, it's rarely desirable to completely override a documentation comment. While it makes sense to provide your own comment on an overriding method, there are usually reasons why you might want to incorporate at least elements of the documentation you're overriding. For example, the return value and parameters usually have exactly the same semantics, even if the implementation documentation changes. After all, that's what polymorphism is for. Most importantly, the convention that run-time (unchecked) exceptions that can be thrown by a method should be declared using an `@throws` Javadoc tag causes problems with inheritance. The reason is that such run-time exceptions are generally very closely tied to the implementation. If an overriding method is implemented in a way that means it won't throw a run-time exception that might be thrown by the superclass, then you don't want to inherit the `@throws` tag from the parent.

So the new system is more careful. If you declare a `@throws` tag in an overriding Javadoc, for a run-time exception that is similarly declared in the superclass, then you can inherit the documentation from the superclass, by not including a comment. On the other hand, if you don't explicitly declare the `@throws` clause, no such documentation will be inherited.

Any element of a Javadoc comment can include the documentation from a parent class, by including the inline tag `{@inheritDoc}`. In a main body comment, this will include the parent comment. In a `@param` or `@returns` tag, it will include the parent text from the equivalent tag. This allows you to include, and add to, documentation from the parent class. Think of it like a documentation call to `super`.

Well, that's the theory, anyway – unfortunately, this functionality is broken in version 1.4.0 at the moment, so we'll have to wait for a working implementation to arrive in a later release of the 1.4 platform.

Custom Tags

The standard doclet supports a couple of new mechanisms for developers to implement their own custom tags. We can specify simple formatting for our tags using the doclet's `-tag` option. In addition, we can code special classes that provide complex formatting, using a new taglet API. We tell the doclet about taglets we want to use using the `-taglet` and `-tagletclasspath` options.

Simple Tags

Let's look at simple formatting first. Suppose we're implementing a framework where concurrency issues are likely to be important. We can add comments on the concurrency implications of each method using our own tag, say: `@concurrency`. We might write a class comment like this:

```
/**
 * An <code>account</code> represents a user's order, payment,
 * and credit history. It contains a list of transactions the
 * user has undertaken, and a list of open orders, and due payments.
 * @author James Hart
 * @version 1.0
 * @concurrency All public methods on this class are
 *     synchronized against the instance on which they are called.
 *     Users of this class in a multithreaded environment should
 *     ensure that if they plan to query the account status, and
 *     then perform some account operation based on that query,
 *     they must enclose both operations in a block synchronized
 *     on the account instance to ensure no concurrent modification
 *     occurs between the operations.
 */
```

Now, we can request that the standard doclet simply outputs this special concurrency information in its normal documentation style, under a heading of our choice, simply by using the `-tag` option when we call Javadoc.

A tag specification is of the following form:

`-tag` *`tagname`*`:`*`flags`*`:"`*`heading`*`"`

The *`tagname`* is the name of the tag, as used in our documentation comments. In our case, it's `concurrency`.

Language

7

The *flags* are a set of characters, signifying where tags of the specified type are valid, and also whether or not the content of these tags should be output in this documentation run. Whether you want the output or not, you *must* specify all custom tags that occur in your source code using -tag or -taglet options, or the Javadoc parser will choke on them. The flags are made up of a combination of the following letters:

- X – suppress output of this tag
- a – allow the tag anywhere
- o – allow the tag in overviews
- p – allow the tag in package documentation
- t – allow the tag in type (class or interface) documentation
- c – allow the tag in constructor documentation
- m – allow the tag in method documentation
- f – allow the tag in field documentation

The heading is a string that will be output in Javadoc pages where the tag occurs, followed by the documentation comment. So, we can enable output of our concurrency documentation by adding a -tag option to a Javadoc call, like this:

```
> javadoc -tag concurrency:a:"Threading issues:" Account.java
```

Now, if we regularly use a lot of these tags, it's quickly going to become tiresome typing in the options every time. So it's just as well that, like the Java compiler, Javadoc supports the previously undocumented ability to specify a file containing arguments. So, we can create a list of all the tags we support in a file (call it tags):

```
-tag concurrency:a:"Threading issues:"
-tag changes:a:"Changes in this version:"
```

And we can add these to our command line very easily using the @-notation:

```
> javadoc @tags Account.java
```

Taglets

The most interesting new doclet feature is the introduction of a new API for developing custom tags: taglets.

Taglets, as you would expect if you've been keeping up with all of Java's little Xlets over the years, are classes that implement the Taglet interface – com.sun.tools.doclet.Taglet, to be precise (you'll find the interface in tools.jar, so you'll have to ensure that's on your classpath when you compile a taglet, or run Javadoc using one).

Taglets allow you more control over the final appearance of documentation generated from the original documentation tag than the simple tags shown above. In addition, as well as writing standalone tags that appear after the main comment, under their own heading, we can code inline tags, that can be included within the text of the main body comment, or even other tags.

Taglets are easy to write. Most of the methods we have to implement are to provide a way for the doclet to find out where the tag we're coding is valid (the programmatic equivalent of the flags we provided before). The one tricky element is that we have to provide a static method with a special signature that the doclet can use to obtain an instance of our taglet. This method must have the signature:

```
public static void register(java.util.Map tagletMap)
```

This is called by the doclet, and it is our responsibility then to initialize a taglet instance and place it into the map, indexed with a string key, containing the exact name of the tag, as used in Javadoc comments (without the preceding `@` sign). The documentation of the taglet API demands that you remove from the map any taglets that have previously been registered under the same name – although conventional map semantics suggest this is unnecessary, since a map can only contain one item matching each key. I've had no problems simply putting the taglet I've created into the map.

The work of the class is done in these two methods:

```
public String toString(com.sun.javadoc.Tag tag)
public String toString(com.sun.javadoc.Tag[] tags)
```

Each time the doclet encounters a tag matching the name under which this taglet was registered, one of these methods is called. A `Tag` object, as passed in to these methods, represents the tag that was written into the Javadoc comment. It's our responsibility to return an HTML string suitable for inclusion in the output HTML.

The first method is called if the content of the tag is simple – just plain text. We can access the text using the tag's `text()` method. The second is called if the tag body contains other inline tags that need to be evaluated. Some of the "tag" objects in the tag array may actually represent plain text, others inline tags. We can obtain the text value of all of them using the same `text()` method. If we're interested in finding out the name of any of the tags, we can do so using the `name()` method.

So let's get on and develop a simple taglet class. This taglet provides a `@usage` tag, which can be used to provide a code example to support a particular piece of documentation. It formats the provided text as code, using HTML `<pre>` tags. Let's step through the code:

```
import com.sun.tools.doclets.Taglet;
import com.sun.javadoc.*;
import java.util.Map;
```

```
/**
 * This simple standalone Taglet provides the Javadoc tag
 * <code>@usage</code>. This tag can be used in Javadoc
 * anywhere in a class file to include an example of a particular
 * piece of functionality in use.
 * @usage
 * &#047;&#042;&#042;
 *  &#042; &#064;usage
 *  &#042; Foo foo = new Foo();
 *  &#042; foo.bar();
 *  &#042;&#047;
 * @author James Hart
 * @version 1.0
 */
```

The class Javadoc comment, naturally, uses the tag itself to provide an example of its own usage. Once we've compiled the class, we'll use it to generate its own Javadoc. Let's get on to the main class definition:

```
public class UsageTaglet implements Taglet {

  private static String NAME = "usage";
  private static String HEADER = "Usage:";

  public static void register(Map tagletMap) {
     tagletMap.put(NAME, new UsageTaglet());
  }
```

The first method is the static access point. We've used a simple implementation here that instantiates this class and registers it in the map. It's possible to imagine more complex registration schemes, with a class registering instances of other taglet classes at the same time – creating whole taglet families, perhaps – or registering the same instance under several different names, allowing it to be used for a number of similar purposes.

Now, let's get on to the meaty `toString()` methods. The first simply defers to the second:

```
  public String toString(Tag tag) {
      return toString(new Tag[] {tag});
  }

  public String toString(Tag[] tags) {
      if (tags.length == 0) {
          return null;
      }
      StringBuffer result = new StringBuffer("<DT><B>" +
```

```
                                                       HEADER + "</B><DD>");
    result.append("<pre>");
    for (int i = 0; i < tags.length; i++) {
        if (i > 0) {
            result.append(", ");
        }
        result.append(tags[i].text());
    }
    result.append("</pre>\n");
    return result.toString();
}
```

The methodology is trivial – create a string buffer, build the header and prefix, and then iterate through the tag array, appending text. When we've finished, append a suffix, and return the result.

Now, we simply need to pad out the implementation with the methods the doclet will call to find out about this taglet. We need to provide our name on demand, then we need to answer yes or no as to whether the tag is valid in a variety of documentation contexts. This tag is valid anywhere except inlined.

```
public String getName() {
    return NAME;
}

public boolean inField() {
    return true;
}

public boolean inConstructor() {
    return true;
}

public boolean inMethod() {
    return true;
}

public boolean inOverview() {
    return true;
}

public boolean inPackage() {
    return true;
}

public boolean inType() {
    return true;
```

```
    }

    public boolean isInlineTag() {
        return false;
    }
}
```

So, that's our taglet. We can compile it with a command like this:

```
> javac -classpath %JAVA_HOME%\lib\tools.jar;. UsageTaglet.java
```

And then we can use it to document itself, like this:

```
> javadoc -tagletpath . -classpath %JAVA_HOME\lib\tools.jar -taglet
UsageTaglet UsageTaglet.java
```

The class documentation will now include a nice little section of code illustrating a Javadoc comment with a `@usage` tag.

Inline tags are written similarly, except that they must, obviously, return `true` from the `isInlineTag()` method, and they needn't worry about handling composite tag content – an inline tag can't contain nested tags.

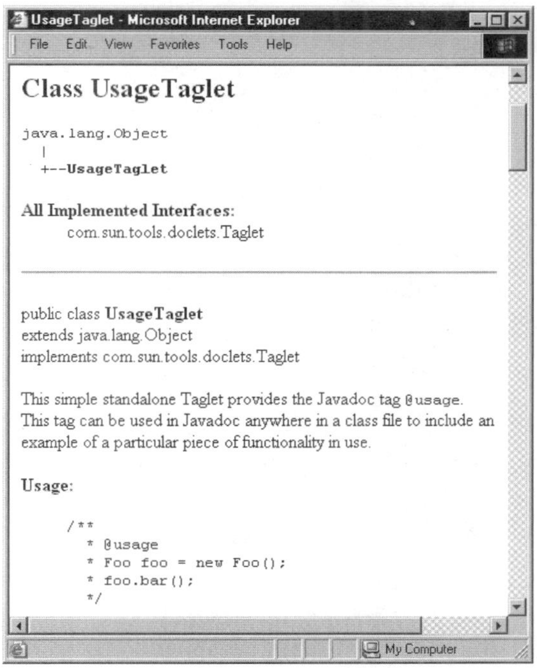

Here's a quick example of an inline tag implemented with a taglet. This provides an `{@rfc}` inline tag that conveniently provides links to the IETF's repository of RFCs online at http://www.ietf.org/rfc.

```
import com.sun.tools.doclets.Taglet;
import com.sun.javadoc.*;
import java.util.Map;

/**
```

```
 * This simple inline Taglet provides the tag
 * <code>{&#064;rfc}</code>. This tag can be used in Javadoc
 * anywhere in a class file to include a link to the
 * <a href="http://www.ietf.org/">IETF</a> provided
 * online version of the RFC. Links look like this: {@rfc 2026}
 * @usage
 * &#047;&#042;&#042;
 *  &#042; HTTP 1.1: {&#064;rfc 2616}
 *  &#042;&#047;
 * @author James Hart
 * @version 1.0
 */

public class RFCTaglet implements Taglet {
  private static String NAME = "rfc";

  public static void register(Map tagletMap) {
    tagletMap.put(NAME, new RFCTaglet());
  }

  public String toString(Tag tag) {
    return "RFC <a href=\"http://www.ietf.org/rfc/rfc"
           + tag.text() + ".txt\">" + tag.text() + "</a>";
  }

  public String toString(Tag[] tags) {
    return "";
  }

  public String getName() {
    return NAME;
  }

  public boolean inField() {
    return true;
  }

  public boolean inConstructor() {
    return true;
  }

  public boolean inMethod() {
    return true;
  }
```

Language

7

```
  public boolean inOverview() {
    return true;
  }

  public boolean inPackage() {
    return true;
  }

  public boolean inType() {
    return true;
  }

  public boolean isInlineTag() {
    return true;
  }
}
```

We can compile and run the taglet on its own documentation as follows:

```
> javac -classpath %JAVA_HOME%\lib\tools.jar;. RFCTaglet.java
> javadoc -tagletpath . -classpath %JAVA_HOME\lib\tools.jar -taglet
UsageTaglet -taglet RFCTaglet RFCTaglet.java
```

Here's the output:

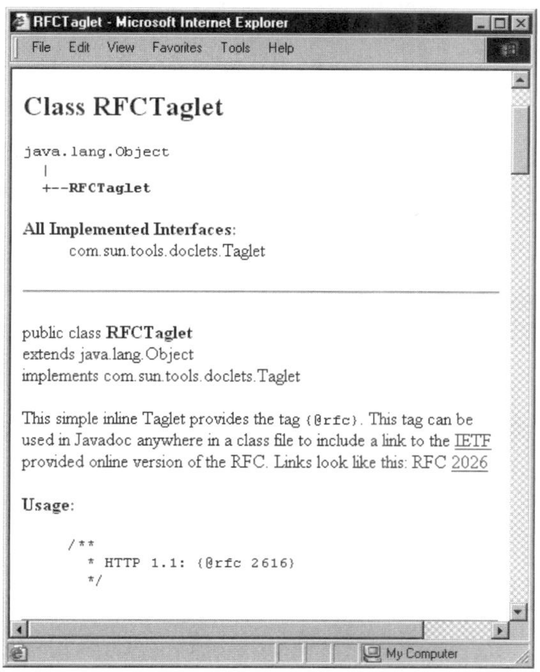

New Output Options

A few new options have been added to Javadoc, enabling us to integrate new information into the generated documentation. One new feature that can't be disabled is that a page is generated containing constant field values – any `final static` fields that are accessible at the level the documentation is covering are listed on the page, together with their literal value.

Optional features that we can enable selectively include the following:

Source Code Linking

If we specify `-linksource` on the command line, an HTML version of each documented source file will be generated, and hyperlinks will be created from the documentation into this sourcecode. It's a simple, tidy feature, and it works exactly as you'd hope.

Fully-qualified Package-names Configurable

We can instruct Javadoc not to generate fully qualified package names for all classes outside the package being documented, whenever they are mentioned in the documentation. For example, it is generally unnecessary to include the package identifier `java.lang`. A package that builds on a particular well-known package may wish to omit the package identifiers where they should be obvious.

The instruction is, again, a command-line option, `-noqualifier`. We can either specify `-noqualifier all`, or `-noqualifier` followed by a colon-separated list of packages that should be omitted.

Easy Documentation of Package Hierarchies

Package hierarchies can be complex. For example, generating Javadoc for the JAXP XML classes of J2SE, requires the inclusion of a number of packages in the `javax.xml` hierarchy. Previously, you would have had to write a command like this:

```
> javadoc javax.xml.parser javax.xml.transform
javax.xml.transform.stream javax.xml.transform.dom
javax.xml.transform.sax
```

It's easy to accidentally forget a key package, or to include a node in the directory hierarchy that in fact contains no classes. With Javadoc 1.4, you can simply type:

```
> javadoc -subpackages javax.xml
```

Now all classes in the package hierarchy, for which source is available on the source path, will be documented.

If we aren't interested in the stream classes, we can exclude them from the hierarchy using the `-exclude` option.

```
> javadoc -subpackages javax.xml -exclude javax.xml.transform.stream
```

Conclusions

Assertions provide a mechanism for capturing the implicit assumptions we make in writing code in a form that can be tested at run time. We've looked in this chapter at the mechanics of the assertion mechanism J2SE 1.4 has introduced. We've seen how to write assertion statements, how to compile code that contains assertions, and how to enable assertion checking at run time, both from the command line, and using calls to the new `ClassLoader` methods.

We looked at some idiomatic use of `assert` statements in Java code. We examined several situations where assertions can be a useful tool, and in particular looked at how they can be used as part of an informal design-by-contract framework.

Javadoc 1.4 presents some powerful new facilities to developers documenting their code. The source-linking facility is fantastic, and will benefit a great many projects directly. Taglets represent an interesting way to add functionality to Javadoc without writing a complete doclet yourself. One thing to beware of, though, is that while it is trivial to include taglets into a custom documentation run, if you distribute your sourcecode to somebody who doesn't have those taglets, they won't be able to generate documentation.

Java J2SE 1.4 Core Platform Update

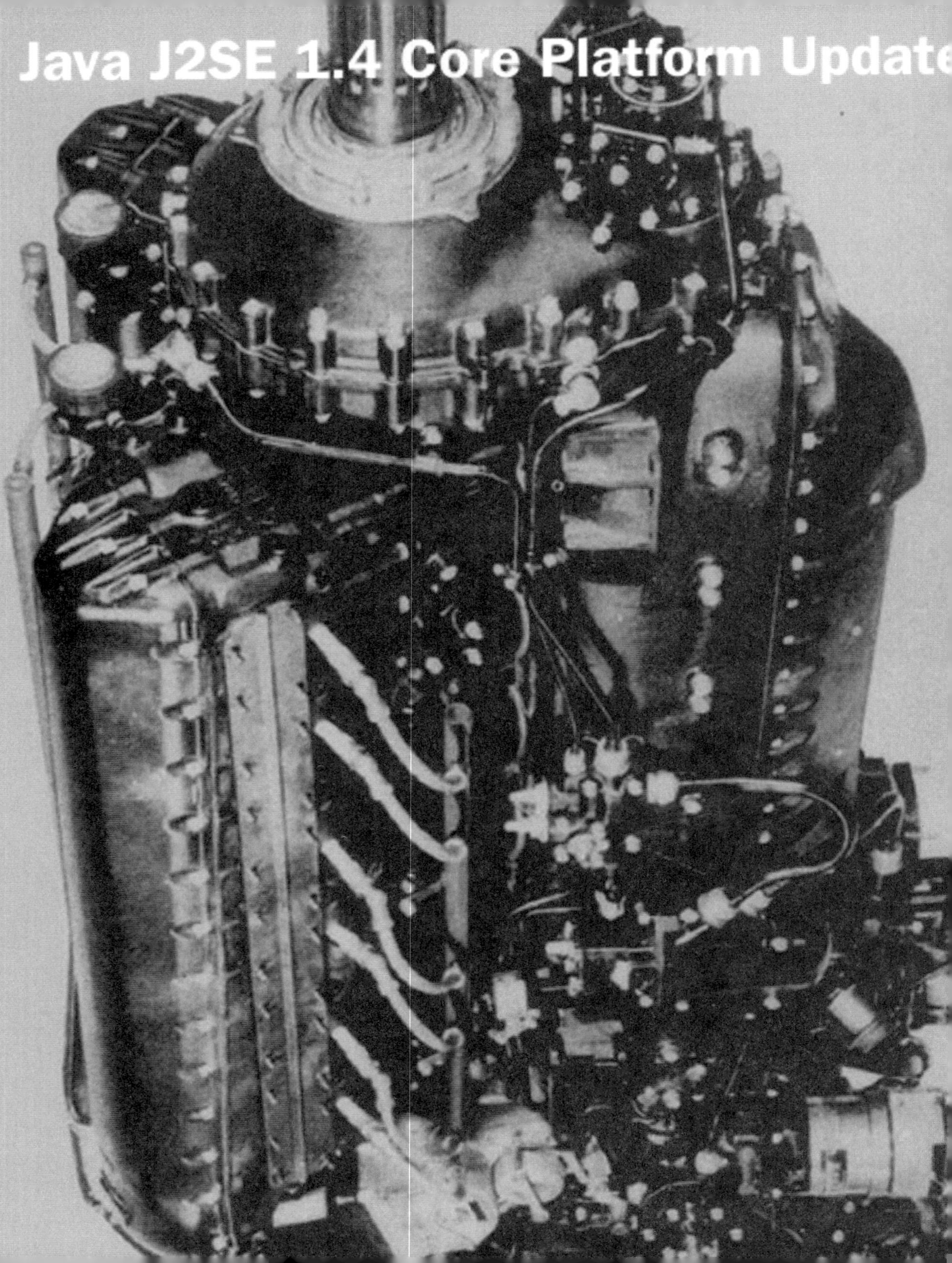

The Future

So, with J2SE 1.4 out of the way, what can we expect to see in the future of the Standard Edition? Well, there are a few APIs that didn't quite make it into the 1.4 release, and there are already some plans for what will be included in J2SE 1.5, the project codenamed **Tiger**. Tiger is not due for release until mid 2003, so what can we expect in the future of the Standard Edition?

Well, when Merlin was announced, the full feature list was a little larger than the final J2SE 1.4 release specification. It was set to include an overhaul of the File APIs to go with the NIO architecture discussed in Chapter 2, *I/O*, but it was dropped because of time constraints. A print formatting API to match the formatting functionality of C-style `printf` and `sprintf` commands was also supposed to be included. There should have been full support for the **Java Architecture for XML Binding**, **JAXB**, but that was dogged by delays and missed the deadline for inclusion.

At the same time, one feature that has been on the horizon for a long while, but was never scheduled for Merlin, is **generics**. This is a major language enhancement, intended for inclusion in Tiger, but already available as an early-access release.

In this final chapter, we'll take a quick look down the list of **Java Specification Requests (JSRs)** that are on the horizon for the Standard Edition, and examine the technology previews of JAXB and generics, which can be downloaded from the **Java Developer Connection** at http://developer.java.sun.com.

JSR Watching

JSRs are the main vehicle for change in the Java platforms. A JSR can be proposed by any participant in the **Java Community Process** (the **JCP**), and its progress towards becoming an actual standard is then controlled by the JCP. A JSR goes through the following stages in its life:

Stage	Final Product
Expert Group	First Draft
Community Review	Public Draft
Public Review	Proposed Final Draft
Executive Committee	Final Draft

The first two phases involve members of the Java Community Process only. Organizations, companies, and individuals can become members of the Java Community (for a $5000 fee), and thus become eligible to participate in expert groups, and in the community review of all specifications. Individual experts may participate in specific expert groups without full membership. Only in the public review phase is the specification made available to the general public.

You can examine all publicly announced JSRs at http://www.jcp.org.

Here is a list of some of the more interesting ones being considered for the J2SE platform, with their descriptions taken from the JCP web site:

JSR No.	Title	Description	Status
12	Java Data Objects (JDO) Specification	The JDO specification provides for interface-based definitions of data stores and transactions, and selection and transformation of persistent storage data into native Java programming language objects.	PFD
14	Add Generic Types to the Java Programming Language	Extending the Java programming language with generic types (a.k.a. parameterized types) .	PR
31	XML Data Binding Specification	A facility for compiling an XML schema into one or more Java classes that can parse, generate, and validate documents that follow the schema.	EG

JSR No.	Title	Description	Status
38	Application Installation API Specification	This proposal is to develop a set of Java APIs that will enable cross-platform installation and de-installation of Java applications as well as platform-specific applications.	CD
65	Concise Object Array Literals	A minor extension to the Java programming language that will support a concise notation for automatically-boxing object-array literals.	EG
67	Java APIs for XML Messaging (JAXM)	JAXM provides an API for packaging and transporting business transactions using on-the-wire protocols being defined by ebXML.org, Oasis, W3C, and IETF	PFD
80	Java USB API	This specification provides a Java API for communicating with devices that are attached via the USB (Universal Serial Bus). It will allow Java applications to communicate with and manipulate USB devices attached to the bus.	PR
83	Multi-Array Package	This JSR proposes a package implementing true rectangular multi-dimensional arrays for the Java platform.	EG
92	Localizable Text	Localizable Text is the infrastructure necessary to translate language-neutral information (in an object) from anywhere in a distributed network. When the object is formatted the locale, time zone, and language-neutral information is sent to a server where the translated text is assembled from resource bundles.	EG
96	Java Daemons	The Java Daemon API supplies a small container framework for developing and deploying independently running services in order to fill the gap caused by different handling on existing native platforms.	CR

Table continued on following page

JSR No.	Title	Description	Status
102	JDOM 1.0	JDOM is a way to represent an XML document for easy and efficient reading, manipulation, and writing.	EG
108	Units Specification	The Java Units package supports programmatic unit handling via an abstract `Unit` class, run-time checking and conversion, unit arithmetic, unit parsing and formatting, and a units database.	EG
121	Application Isolation Specification	An API for initiating and controlling computations isolated from each other to varying degrees. Some API semantics are similar to those of `ThreadGroup`.	EG
134	Java Game Profile	Defines a Java 2 Micro Edition Profile for the purposes of game development targeting high-end consumer game devices and desktops.	EG
163	Java Platform Profiling Architecture	A mechanism and APIs for extracting time and space profiling information from a running Java™ Virtual Machine.	EG
166	Concurrency Utilities	The JSR proposes a set of medium-level utilities that provide functionality commonly needed in concurrent programs.	EG

Here are the meanings of the entries in the **Status** column:

- **EG** – **E**xpert **G**roup formed
- **PR** – **P**ublic **R**eview underway
- **CD** – **C**ommunity **D**raft published
- **PFD** – **Pr**oposed **F**inal **D**raft published

The status shown for the JSR numbers was correct as of February 2002.

The following is a short analysis on the possible uses of the JSRs shown in the table:

- **JDO Specification** – JDO promises a much more object-centric, rather than SQL-centric, view of relational data than JDBC offers. For applications that deal with databases only to store a limited range of data, JDO could present a powerful alternative to embedded SQL in code.

- **Generic Types** – We will look at this later on in this chapter. Briefly though, this offers the potential to vastly decrease the number of potentially risky casting operations in code, by creating classes that handle generic specified types of data, rather than arbitrary `Objects`.
- **XML Data Binding** – Again, we will examine this later in the chapter. Briefly, this promises a similar object-centric view of XML documents that JDO offers of relational data.
- **Application Installation API** – While the JNLP platform offers a powerful new technology to developers for deploying networked applications, it isn't really suited to the deployment of standalone code. An installation API would allow applications to write one installer program, rather than a series of platform-specific batch scripts or executables, to perform complex installations of large applications.
- **Concise Object Array Literals** – Essentially, this offers a means for writing methods that take an unlimited number of parameters, and easily accessing them. Designed to benefit APIs such as NIO's print formatting, and some aspects of the logging API.
- **JAXM** – The Java API for XML Messaging will provide the Java platform with support for SOAP and ebXML messaging – transmitting objects and remote method invocations as XML documents.
- **Java USB APIs** – The `java.comm` extension has provided Java developers with a means to access serial peripheral devices for some time, but nothing has existed for the modern equivalent of the old nine-pin or PS/2 port – USB.
- **Multi-Array Package** – Java's multi-dimensional arrays are really just arrays of arrays, and the collection APIs are resolutely one-dimensional. This JSR proposes a proper API for creating multi-dimensional collections. (Note that the detail of the proposal makes it clear that it is a package-based API, not a language change that is proposed. This isn't a proposal to add C#-style `int[5,5]` arrays).
- **Localizable Text** – This API offers an interesting means for deploying localized applications to a corporate network infrastructure. Instead of localizing each installation individually, the localization is performed across the entire network.

- Java Daemons – Java programs typically operate within a container. The most common are the J2SE command-line application and applet containers, and the J2EE servlet and EJB containers. There is also the less well-known J2EE client container. JNLP defines a new container environment. This JSR proposes a new container, for Java programs that should function as extensions to an operating system, running in the background from system startup to shutdown. This is most obviously of use to servers.

- JDOM 1.0 – JDOM is an interesting API to make JSR. The product of the work of two authors of O'Reilly Java-series books, Jason Hunter and Brett McLaughlin, it attempts to provide a more naturally object-oriented approach to representing arbitrary XML documents as Java objects than W3C's DOM (as incorporated into JAXP) provides. In the process, it also offers a parser-abstraction layer (somewhat like JAXP). Curiously, it does succeed in offering something different. With JAXB on the horizon as well though, it seems likely JDOM will remain an optional extension. Incidentally, JDOM isn't an acronym.

- Units Specification – An interesting utility API, this could provide some useful tools for handling, printing, and parsing values that are expressed in the standard SI unit system, as well as in various locally understood traditional units systems, providing some powerful new localization tools.

- Application Isolation – This proposal essentially builds an architecture to allow multiple Java applications to execute in isolation within a single Java Virtual Machine. This would enable a system to simply spawn a single JVM, and launch all Java applications into the same environment, saving on resources, but without compromising on security.

- Game Profile – The proposal is to develop a J2ME profile that can be targeted by games developers, which can be implemented by dedicated games consoles, and desktop computers. It would encompass 3D and 2D graphics, sound, media streaming, and access to game controller devices.

- Platform Profiling – This proposal would add capabilities for accessing information about the performance of a running JVM process.

- Concurrency utilities – A proposal from author and threading guru Doug Lea, offering several high-level utilities for managing concurrent-threaded applications.

As you can see, there is a wide range of platform enhancements under consideration: language changes, amendments to the core APIs, new extension APIs, and new container environments. Not all of these are intended to make changes to the platform itself (in the case of proposed extension APIs, for example), but some would have far-reaching implications should their implementation be included in the J2SE specification. Some of these specifications will never emerge, but others will almost certainly be part of the J2SE 1.5 release.

One thing that *is* clear is that XML is set to take on an ever-more significant role in the Java platform, and in particular in terms of support for web services. There are in fact thirteen APIs currently in the JCP that are directly related to supporting the use of XML and web services for one purpose or another:

- ebXML CPP/A APIs for Java
- Implementing Enterprise Web Services
- Java API for XML Registries (JAXR)
- Java APIs for WSDL
- Java APIs for XML-based RPC (JAX-RPC)
- Java APIs for XML Messaging (JAXM)
- JDOM
- Web Services Security Assertions
- XML Data Binding Specification (JAXB)
- XML Digital Encryption APIs
- XML Digital Signature APIs
- XML Transactioning API for Java (JAXTX)
- XML Trust Service APIs

That's all, remember, in addition to the two that were completed and introduced into J2SE 1.4 (The Java API for XML Processing, JAXP, to which we devoted Chapter 5, and Long-Term Persistence for JavaBeans, which we looked at in Chapter 4, *Clients and GUIs*, and uses an XML syntax).

We can also see that application deployment is still a key concern, even with JNLP in place, with proposals for facilities such as the Java Daemon container, and the Application Installation API Specification. Scientific applications have led to a number of JSRs, including multi-dimensional arrays, and scientific units, although the one feature scientists have been desperate to add to Java for years, operator overloading, has not made it to the JCP yet.

Two technologies almost certain to make it into J2SE 1.5 are **XML binding** and **generics**. Early access releases of each of these are currently available from the JDC at http://developer.java.sun.com:

- JAXB – http://developer.java.sun.com/developer/earlyAccess/xml/jaxb
- Generics – http://developer.java.sun.com/developer/earlyAccess/adding_generics

We'll take a look at them both now.

The JDC site requires you to register in order to obtain the downloads we will be using.

Java Architecture for XML Binding

Project Adelard was announced almost three years ago, and its release has been anticipated for all that time. It has undergone a couple of name changes; it became known as Databind for a while, then it was registered with the JCP as JSR-31. Then, in Spring 2001, Sun announced the Sun ONE plan – an ambitious project to create a platform for development and deployment of web services, widely seen as Sun's response to the Microsoft .NET platform. A key part of that announcement was the announcement of the JAX API family, and a new name for Databind/Adelard – **JAXB**, the Java Architecture for XML Binding.

Adelard's goals have shifted a few times as well in those two years, but the fundamental point of the XML binding facility was always there; to provide a seamless transition between the data in XML documents and the data in Java objects.

XML processing from within object-oriented languages is frequently unsatisfactory. The lowest-level XML API, SAX, doesn't feel object-oriented at all – its callback mechanisms feel like something C programmers would be comfortable with, but to most Java programmers it feels somehow inverted, awkward, and messy. DOM was developed as a "proper" object-based approach to XML. It provides neatly encapsulated classes that represent entities in the XML world – elements, attributes, documents, and so on. The problem with this view of the world though, is that most developers, when they're handling XML documents, aren't really interested in writing a program that knows about elements, attributes, and documents. Instead, most developers are interested in the data they are actually trying to read from, or encode into, the XML document in the first place.

Back in Chapter 5, *XML*, we used a file similar to the following XML document, `song.xml`, to illustrate XML parsing using DOM and SAX:

```
<?xml version="1.0" encoding="UTF-8"?>
<!DOCTYPE song SYSTEM "song.dtd">
<song writer="trad" title="Happy Birthday">
  <verse>
    <line>Happy birthday to you,</line>
```

```
    <line>Happy birthday to you,</line>
    <line>Happy birthday dear [name],</line>
    <line>Happy birthday to you.</line>
  </verse>
</song>
```

The thing is, when writing a program to process documents like this, it doesn't seem natural to have to extract the first child node of the document node, check that it's called `song`, as expected, then ask that node to give us its attributes, and finally extract the attribute called `title`, just to obtain the string `Happy Birthday`. This XML document represents a real-world song entity, so why is it not represented in the Java world with a `Song` object? It should be possible to write code like this:

```
Song song = new Song("song.xml");
System.out.println(song.getTitle());
```

That's the sort of code we'd like to write, naturally. And it is possible to do so, if we create a custom `Song` class that knows how to access an XML parser, parse in documents of a certain type, and make their data available through convenient accessor methods. Doing so every time you encounter a new type of XML document though, is tedious, repetitive, and presumably therefore, automatable.

Here is a DTD, `song.dtd`, for song documents like the `song.xml`:

```
  <!ELEMENT song (verse+)>
  <!ATTLIST song
    writer CDATA #REQUIRED
    title  CDATA #REQUIRED
  >
  <!ELEMENT verse (line+)>
  <!ELEMENT line (#PCDATA)>
```

An XML parser can use this document to validate the `song.xml` document and ensure that it only contains elements that are allowed, in the right context. There's something about this DTD, though, that is somewhat reminiscent of a class definition. For example, the first line says that elements of type `song` have one or more `verse` elements. The `ATTLIST` declaration says that `song` elements also have two attributes, one called `writer`, and one called `title`. It's not that hard to imagine turning this DTD declaration into the following class definition:

```
class Song {
  Verse[] verseArray;
  String writer;
  String title;
}
```

Now, if we also included a constructor, or a class method that could instantiate a `Song` object and populate its data members with the data from an XML file, and another method that could write out the data members of such an object to XML, we'd have a really simple, natural way to programmatically handle XML documents conforming to that DTD.

The goal of JAXB is to automatically generate this sort of class from DTD files. This has proven to be more difficult than it sounds, and JAXB has only recently reached a stage where the specification was publishable. The working draft of the JAXB specification currently available is version 0.21, and was published in May 2001. At the same time, the early-access release of the JAXB compiler and runtime version 1.0 was made available for evaluation, and it is now also included in Sun's XML and web services toolkits, the JAX-Pack and the Web Services Pack.

The classes JAXB generates are a little more complex than our trivial example suggests. It draws a distinction between the elements described by a DTD that have **complex content**, and those that have **simple content**. In this sense, by simple content, we mean that an element has no attributes, and contains only character data (`CDATA` in the DTD).

JAXB's DTD compiler, `xjc`, generates one class for each type of element that has complex content (it doesn't generate classes for elements that have simple content, since these are easily represented by an existing class, `String`). An instance of such a class will represent an occurrence of an element of that type in a document. So, for our `song.xml` example, a `Song` class will be used to represent `song` elements, and one instance of this class will represent the root element of `song.xml` once it is parsed in. The class will define methods, so that we can ask this `Song` object for its title, its writer, and its verses.

An element with complex content has two types of data associated with it: attributes, which are unordered, uniquely-named strings that can be represented as named properties, and child nodes, which are an ordered list of objects that can be either character-data nodes or named element nodes. If they are character data, they can be represented by a `String`. If they are an element node, they are either complex, and therefore represented by another object, or simple, and therefore represented by a `String`. All elements have names, but their name may not necessarily be unique among the children of the parent node; it is their position in the list of child elements that distinguishes them from other elements.

JAXB classes all use mutator methods to access and manipulate the content of their data members (attributes, elements, and character data). They also have `marshal()` and `unmarshal()` methods, which can be used, respectively, to write out the object's state to XML, and read state in from XML. In addition, they have two validation methods. One, `validateThis()`, performs a local validation, ensuring that all of the immediate data members of the element the object represents meet the DTD's validity requirements – that is, all required attributes have values, all required children are present and ordered correctly, no illegal children are present, and so on. The other, `validate()`, performs a global validation, which ensures that the entire data structure of the document would generate valid XML if it were output in its current state.

Validation on demand, rather than on the fly, allows us to perform operations such as removing all of an element's children and replacing them in a different, valid order, without having to ensure that each intermediate step is also valid (which may well be impossible in many cases).

Where multiple elements are allowed, such as in our song example, the elements are stored in a `java.util.List` object. In fact, it uses a special list class, which ensures that only objects of a certain type can be put into the list (generics, as we'll see later, would really help here, but JAXB uses a bit of a hack to get around it, and enforce its rule at run time by throwing exceptions if the wrong kind of object is added to the list).

So, we should expect running JAXB's `xjc` compiler on `song.dtd` to produce one class for the `song` element, and one for the `verse` element. It shouldn't produce one for `line`, since each line is simply a `String`. The class for the `song` element will have properties for the `song`'s `title` and `writer`, and a `List` of objects representing `verses`. The `verse` objects will just have a list of `Strings` representing `line` elements.

The JAXB early-access release unzips to contain a `lib` directory holding two JAR files, `jaxb-rt-1.0-ea.jar` and `jaxb-xjc-1.0-ea.jar`. These are, respectively, the **JAXB runtime**, and the **JAXB XML-Java compiler**, `xjc`. The compiler is a tool that can be used to generate Java sourcecode from XML DTDs. It can be run on a UNIX platform using the `xjc` script in the EA release's `bin` directory, or simply using the command:

```
> java -jar jaxb-xjc-1.0-ea.jar
```

To compile a DTD, we simply need to run the compiler with the `-roots` flag, followed by the names of any elements defined in the DTD, which can be root elements of documents (separated by commas), followed by the name of the DTD file. For example, to compile `song.dtd`, from above, we need to type:

```
> java -jar %JAXB_HOME%\lib\jaxb-xjc-1.0-ea.jar -roots song song.dtd
.\Song.java
.\Verse.java
```

Or, on UNIX:

```
> $JAXB_HOME/bin/xjc -roots song test.dtd
./Song.java
./Verse.java
```

Why `-roots`, and not `-root`? Well, while any particular XML document can only have one root element, it is not the case that a DTD can only define the grammar for one type of document. In fact, any element defined in a DTD `ELEMENT` tag can serve as a root element in an XML document. An XML document declares which element is to serve as its root by naming it in its `DOCTYPE` declaration. JAXB recognizes that a DTD can define more than one grammar in this way, and so allows us to generate more than one set of classes from a single DTD.

As you can see, in either case, the output is two Java source files, `Song.java` and `Verse.java`. We can now compile them, ensuring the runtime JAR file is on the classpath:

```
> javac -classpath %JAXB_HOME%\lib\jaxb-rt-1.0-ea.jar Song.
java Verse.java
```

Let's look at `Verse` class first. `Verse` has, among others, the following methods:

- `public Verse()`
- `public java.util.List getLine()`
- `public void deleteLine()`
- `public void emptyLine()`

`getLine()`, `deleteLine()`, and `emptyLine()` are all slightly misleadingly named. They all refer not to an individual line element, but to a `List` object containing the lines that make up the verse. `deleteLine()` completely deletes this element's lines, and stores `null` in their place. `emptyLine()` deletes all the lines, replacing them instead with a new empty `List` object. `getLine()` simply gets you a reference to the `List` object.

The equivalent methods on the `Song` class are as follows:

- `public Song();`
- `public java.lang.String getWriter();`
- `public void setWriter(java.lang.String writer);`
- `public java.lang.String getTitle();`
- `public void setTitle(java.lang.String title);`
- `public java.util.List getVerse();`
- `public void deleteVerse();`
- `public void emptyVerse();`

In addition to the same list-handling methods for the song's verses, there are getter and setter methods for each of the song's two attributes, `writer` and `title`.

Naming Conventions

It's worth noting that JAXB does an impressive job of understanding and adhering to the naming conventions of Java and XML. XML elements typically begin with lowercase letters, and if they consist of more than one word, they are often hyphenated. Java names, on the other hand, are written in `camelCase`, in the case of methods and variable names, and in the case of classes, the same but with an initial capital, sometimes called `PascalCase`. Constants are written in all uppercase, with underscores as word separators. These rules are broken, however, when acronyms are included in a name, such as in the `URLConnection` class.

Things are further complicated by the fact that XML and Java are in fact both Unicode-compliant, and allow names to be specified in many different character sets, all of which have different ideas of what constitute uppercase, lowercase, and word-separating characters. XML is particularly flexible in this regard.

The JAXB specification devotes several pages to describing the algorithms it uses to convert between XML and Java naming conventions, and it makes interesting reading for those intrigued by internationalization issues. For the most part, though, you just need to know that JAXB is happy to convert XML names into Java method and class names, and will generate an API that feels natural in the Java world, from names that feel natural in the XML world.

Validation

So, the methods for examining and changing the structure of the objects have been generated; both classes also have a set of validation, marshaling, and unmarshaling methods. You'll almost certainly only call the marshaling methods on the root element class, in this case, `Song`. They are present in both, since the marshaling and unmarshaling process is handled recursively. The full set of such standard methods is as follows, and they are present in (or inherited by) every class generated by the JAXB 1.0 EA release:

- ```
  public void validateThis()
          throws javax.xml.bind.LocalValidationException;
  ```

- ```
  public void validate()
          throws
            javax.xml.bind.StructureValidationException;
  ```

- ```
  public void marshal(java.io.OutputStream os)
          throws java.io.IOException;
  ```

- ```
  public static Song unmarshal(java.io.InputStream is)
          throws javax.xml.bind.UnmarshalException;
  ```

- ```
  public static Song unmarshal(javax.xml.marshal.
                                      XMLScanner x)
          throws javax.xml.bind.UnmarshalException;
  ```
  ```

We've mentioned the validation methods. The key marshaling and unmarshaling methods are `marshal(java.io.OutputStream os)`, `unmarshal(java.io.InputStream is)`, and `unmarshal(javax.xml.marshal.XMLScanner x)`. The uses of these marshaling and unmarshaling methods are shown in the next two sections.

Unmarshalling

The simplest way to unmarshal a JAXB object from an XML file is using the `unmarshal (java.io.InputStream is)` method. Simply open a `FileInputStream`, and call the method:

```
import java.io.*;

public class Unmarshal {

  public static void main(String[] args) {

    try {
      FileInputStream fis = new FileInputStream(args[0]);
      Song song = Song.unmarshal(fis);
      System.out.println(song.getTitle());
    } catch (Exception e) {
      e.printStackTrace();
    }
  }
}
```

To run this example, and those that follow, you need to ensure that the runtime JAR for JAXB is available on the classpath, so the compile command looks like this (note that it should appear as a single line entry):

```
> javac -classpath %JAXB_HOME%\lib\jaxb-rt-1.0-ea.jar Song.
java Verse.java Unmarshal.java
```

Now, we can run this as follows:

```
> java -classpath .;%JAXB_HOME%\lib\jaxb-rt-1.0-ea.jar
Unmarshal song.xml
Happy Birthday
```

Marshaling

The `marshal` method accepts an `OutputStream`. The following code writes out a new XML document to a file. We build up the document object by creating instances of the JAXB-generated classes, and accessing their data structure through the generated methods:

```
import java.io.*;
import java.util.List;

public class Marshal {

  public static void main(String[] args) {

    try {
      Verse verse1 = new Verse();
      List lines = verse1.getLine();

      lines.add("Hickory dickory dock,");
      lines.add("The mouse ran up the clock,");
      lines.add("The clock struck one,");
      lines.add("The mouse ran down,");
      lines.add("Hickory, dickory dock.");

      Song song = new Song();

      List verses = song.getVerse();
      verses.add(verse1);

      song.setWriter("anon");
      song.setTitle("Hickory Dickory Dock");

      song.validate();

      FileOutputStream fos = new FileOutputStream(args[0]);

      song.marshal(fos);
    } catch (Exception e) {
      e.printStackTrace();
    }
  }
}
```

As usual, we can compile the classes using:

```
> javac -classpath %JAXB_HOME%\lib\jaxb-rt-1.0-ea.jar Song.
java Verse.java Marshal.java
```

and run the code like so:

```
> java -classpath .;%JAXB_HOME%\lib\jaxb-rt-1.0-ea.jar
Marshal song2.xml
```

Now, `song2.xml` contains:

```
<?xml version="1.0" encoding="UTF-8"?>

<song writer="anon" title="Hickory Dickory Dock">
  <verse>
    <line>Hickory dickory dock,</line>
    <line>The mouse ran up the clock,</line>
    <line>The clock struck one,</line>
    <line>The mouse ran down,</line>
    <line>Hickory, dickory dock.</line></verse></song>
```

Interesting, perhaps, that no `DOCTYPE` declaration has been included. This seems like an oversight, which may well be corrected in a future release.

Before attempting to marshal the document, it is important to call the `validate()` method. JAXB won't allow you to write out a document that has not been validated. Separating the validation and stream operations allows us to place appropriate error handling code around each operation more efficiently.

As you can see, the code we're writing to handle the objects is quite natural. Compare the above example to the JAXP DOM code required to generate the same XML document:

```
import javax.xml.parsers.*;
import javax.xml.transform.*;
import javax.xml.transform.dom.*;
import javax.xml.transform.stream.*;
import org.w3c.dom.*;
import java.io.*;
import java.util.List;

public class DOM {

  public static void main(String[] args) {

    try {
      DocumentBuilderFactory dbf =
        DocumentBuilderFactory.newInstance();
      DocumentBuilder db = dbf.newDocumentBuilder();

      Document song = db.newDocument();

      Element line1 = song.createElement("line");
      line1.appendChild(song.createTextNode("Hickory dickory dock,"));
      Element line2 = song.createElement("line");
      line2.appendChild(
        song.createTextNode("The mouse ran up the clock,"));
```

```
      Element line3 = song.createElement("line");
      line3.appendChild(song.createTextNode("The clock struck one,"));
      Element line4 = song.createElement("line");
      line4.appendChild(song.createTextNode("The mouse ran down,"));
      Element line5 = song.createElement("line");
      line5.appendChild(song.createTextNode(
                              "Hickory, dickory dock."));

      Element verse = song.createElement("verse");
      verse.appendChild(line1);
      verse.appendChild(line2);
      verse.appendChild(line3);
      verse.appendChild(line4);
      verse.appendChild(line5);

      Element songElem = song.createElement("song");
      songElem.appendChild(verse);

      songElem.setAttribute("writer", "anon");
      songElem.setAttribute("title", "Hickory Dickory Dock");

      song.appendChild(songElem);

      Transformer nullTransformer =
        TransformerFactory.newInstance().newTransformer();

      Result out = new StreamResult(new FileOutputStream(args[0]));
      Source dom = new DOMSource(song);

      nullTransformer.transform(dom, out);
    } catch (Exception e) {
      e.printStackTrace();
    }
  }
}
```

This class is compiled simply by using the standard `javac` command:

```
> javac DOM.java
```

And we can run it on the command line supplying it an argument to name the outputted XML file:

```
> java DOM test.xml
```

The XML file is generated as expected:

```
<?xml version="1.0" encoding="UTF-8" ?>
<song writer="anon" title="Hickory Dickory Dock">
  <verse>
    <line>Hickory dickory dock,</line>
    <line>The mouse ran up the clock,</line>
    <line>The clock struck one,</line>
    <line>The mouse ran down,</line>
    <line>Hickory, dickory dock.</line>
  </verse>
</song>
```

DOM is suited to writing code that can handle arbitrary XML documents, because its objects are built to represent arbitrary things, which are found in all XML documents, whereas JAXB is designed to provide us with objects that relate specifically to the things in a certain type of XML document. For developing code that deals with specific data, JAXB is infinitely more suitable.

Customizing JAXB Mappings

JAXB also allows us a degree of control over the classes it generates from DTDs. A **binding schema** is an XML document that supplements the information in the DTD to provide the `xjc` program with more information about how to translate elements and attributes into classes, supplementing its default behavior described earlier. You can do any and all of the following using a binding schema:

- Specify that data in an attribute or element should be interpreted as some type other than `String`. You can specify translation methods that will perform the conversion if the type you specify is not primitive, or not an object that has a `String` constructor and usable `toString()` method.
- Specify that some of the elements in the DTD all implement a certain interface. For example, if two elements both have a `name` attribute, you might specify that they implement a `named` interface, which specifies the `name` property. The interface will also be generated.
- Specify type-safe enumerations, which can be used for attributes that only allow one of several fixed values.
- Specify that the different elements allowed in a mixed content model element (one that can contain elements of more than one type) all implement a certain interface, so they can be handled in a type-safe manner.

This enables richer APIs to be developed, which consist of more useful classes and interfaces that can be used to access and manipulate the data in an XML document, in a type-safe fashion. This is instead of treating all elements as just elements, as the DOM does, or all data as just `String`s.

The intention of JAXB is to support W3C schemas at some point in the future. This schema language has a lot more type-oriented capabilities than the DTD schema language, so will allow the writing of schemas that incorporate most of this information directly. The delays in the development of the W3C schema standard are one of the key reasons for the delay in the release of JAXB.

Additionally, it is interesting that similar work is being done in the JAXM specification to generate automatic translators between SOAP data types and Java classes – a process that also requires translation from XML Schema data types to Java types.

JAXB Conclusions

XML binding looks like it will revolutionize Java XML development. By enabling data classes to be compiled from pure data descriptions written in the XML DTD language it eliminates a lot of typically tedious getter and setter coding, and equally eliminates a lot of possibilities for errors. The fact that the generated classes are guaranteed to always produce XML data that fits the DTD from which the class was generated, and can be constructed from XML data on an `InputStream`, takes many of the headaches out of XML I/O. In addition, the binding schema seems powerful and versatile, although W3C schema support would seem to be essential to ensure success. In addition, incorporating DTD compilation into the build process for a project could prove tricky without good tools support. We need to start thinking of DTDs as sourcecode, now. For more information, you should read the JAXB user's guide, which can be downloaded from the JAXB page at http://java.sun.com/xml/jaxb.

Generics

Generics are a proposed modification to the Java type system, which by definition would have far-reaching consequences. By far the most ambitious change to the Java language ever considered, they present some fantastic possibilities by eliminating most of the irritating situations where you are forced to make an explicit cast. They also present some fantastic opportunities for confusion, creating code that's hard to read and maintain, and for generally scaring off new developers.

A **generic class** is basically a class that can handle any kind of object. At the moment, generic classes are written using the `Object` type as a parameter or return type, so that they can polymorphically process absolutely any kind of object. The classic example is a collection class. If you have a `List` object, you can pass it any object to add, since its `add()` method takes `Object` parameters; and when you get an object back out of the list, you are forced to make an explicit cast back to the type of the object you put in, since the return type of the method is `Object`.

Parameterizable and Parameterized Types

Generics add the ability to write a class like a `List`, but parameterize it so that if somebody creates a `List` that is parameterized to accept only `Strings`, then not only does it only accept `Strings`, but it returns them as well. What's more, this type-checking is performed at compile time, not at run time. If you're familiar with C++, then you may well have come across templates, which provide similar functionality, although you should be wary assuming that Java generics are the same thing, or carry the same disadvantages. Eiffel also has a similar facility.

Let's see what a **parameterizable class** looks like:

```
public class Store<A> {

  private A storage;

  public void store(A newValue) {
    storage = newValue;
  }

  public A read() {
    return storage;
  }
}
```

The new notation here is the angle-bracketed suffix to the class name. In this context, it is saying that this class is **parameterizable**; we're going to allow people to create instances of the `Store` class, which are specifically typed to work with objects of a certain class. The letter `A` is a **type parameter**; within the class definition, we can refer to the parameter using this letter. As you can see, we are able to declare a variable as being of type `A`, and to declare methods whose parameters and return types are of this mysterious type `A`. So, this defines a class that can store objects of type `A`. It has a type `A` instance variable, which is set when an object of type `A` is passed to the `store()` method. The `read()` method returns an object of type `A`, by reading the stored value. The crucial thing is, we only specify what type `A` is actually going to be when we use this class elsewhere in our code.

To appreciate what power this gives us, let's look at an example of this class in use:

```
public class UseGenerics {

  public static void main(String[] args) {

    Store<String> stringHolder = new Store<String>();
    Store<Integer> integerHolder = new Store<Integer>();
```

```
    stringHolder.store("Hello");
    integerHolder.store(new Integer(42));

    stringHolder.store(integerHolder.read());    //compile-time error
  }
}
```

We create two different **parameterized instances** of the Store class in this code, parameterized with two different specific types. You need to think of the parameterized types, Store<String> and Store<Integer>, as completely separate compile-time types – as if they were different classes. In this context, when we write something between the angle brackets after the class name, we are specifying the type that should be substituted for A in the class definition. We can pass a String to the first object's store() method, and an Integer to the second. When we call the integerHolder's read() method though, the compiler detects that the return type should be an Integer, and that Integer is not compatible with the stringHolder's read() method. A compile-time error is then detected on that line.

How does the compiler know this? Well, remember that integerHolder's type isn't Store – it is Store<Integer>. If you substitute Integer for A throughout the Store<A> class definition, you discover that the read() method returns an Integer. At the same time, stringHolder is of type Store<String>. Substitute String for A, and we see that store() takes a String as an argument. So, there's a type mismatch, and the compiler will fail.

What we've done, in writing a parameterizable class, is create a whole swath of possible classes, which will actually be virtually generated as and when they are needed. So, we wrote the Store<Integer> and Store<String> classes, as well as all possible future Store<Foo>, Store<Bar>, and so on classes, all by writing one class: Store<A>.

The Generics Early-Access Release

To see this in action for yourself, you'll have to download the generic compiler modification from the JDC at http://developer.java.sun.com/developer/earlyAccess/adding_generics in the same way you obtained the early-access release of JAXB (the generics download is small, less than a megabyte). This early access release works in combination with the standard Java compiler, by running the compiler with a special classpath, bootstrapping its classes in place of some of the classes in the standard Java compiler.

To run it, you need to take the following two steps:

1. **Common for UNIX and Windows** – Set the two environment variables, J2SE13 and JSR14DISTR. JSR14DISTR should point to the directory containing the generics technology preview. J2SE13 should be the path to your J2SE directory (don't be misled by the 13 on the end – it will work fine if you set this variable to point to J2SE 1.4).

2. **For UNIX** – Use the `javac` shell script to compile your Java code. The `javac` script is provided in the `scripts` directory of the generics download. You may find it useful to create a link to this script, under a name like `gjavac`, from a directory on your path, using something like `ln -s javac /usr/bin/gjavac`.
   For Windows – Create a batch file, named say `gjavac.bat`, containing the following lines:

```
@echo off
%J2SE13%\bin\javac -J-Xbootclasspath/p:%JSR14DISTR%\javac.jar
-bootclasspath %JSR14DISTR%\collect.jar;%J2SE13%\jre\lib\rt.jar %1 %2
%3 %4 %5 %6 %7 %8 %9
```

The second line should contain no breaks. By the way, in case the notation is unfamiliar to you, the `%1 %2 %3` and so on at the end ensure that any parameters specified on the command line are passed on to the `javac` program.

Having put the `gjavac` script on your path, you can now use the `gjavac` command exactly as you use the `javac` command. The only difference being that you can now compile code containing generic syntax, such as the two classes shown above (although you should remember that, as we said, the `UseGenerics` program contains a deliberate compile-time error).

The generic syntax is an entirely compile-time implementation; the generated byte-code is completely compatible with an unmodified virtual machine. The compiler checks that the types match up correctly, then compiles classes that really operate on `Object`-type instances, and inserts casts wherever they will be needed. This means that to run the above code, you only have to type `java UseGenerics`.

One of the biggest problems with C++ templates is that the compiler generates a new class, based on the template, each time we specify a parameterized type in our code. Use the template a lot, and your compiled code will bloat as if you wrote a load more classes. The Java implementation doesn't suffer from this problem, since the compiler only generates a single class for each generic type, and generates modified code that works with the generic class every time we interact with it. This is why the Java implementation is called generics, not templates.

The difference between these compiler-inserted casts, and our own casting operations, is that the compile-time type checking guarantees that compiler casts will succeed. This means that if somebody wants to write code to inter-operate with your generic classes using a non-generic compiler, they can do so, but will have to perform their own casts. If they get it wrong, and pass in the wrong data type, or get a cast wrong, then they'll cause the usual run-time `ClassCastException`. In addition, their compiler won't be able to understand the sourcecode of your classes, only the binary `.class` files. Similarly, to compile generic code against a generic class library, your compiler needs access to the sourcecode to discover the original generic specifications.

The generics preview includes a set of class stubs (that is, mock-ups which share the same names and interfaces, but have no implementation) for generic versions of the collections classes. These classes can be used to create parameterized versions of normal collection objects. By compiling against these using the generic-capable compiler, the generics compiler allows you to write code without casts, and ensures you are completely type-safe. Your compiled code, however, contains all the necessary casts, and so can be run against the normal collections library at run time.

The Power of Parameters

As well as creating parameterized classes, like the one shown above, it is possible to create parameterized interfaces. For example, here's an interface for a generic object lifecycle manager:

```
public interface Manager<B> {
  public B create();
  public boolean validate(B obj);
  public void reset(B obj);
}
```

This defines an interface for a "manager" of objects of type `B`. If we come across an object of type `Manager<String>`, we can expect its `create()` method to return a `String`, and its `validate()` method to take a `String` as an argument. Before we can get an object of that type though, we need a concrete class definition to go with the interface. There are two ways this can be done.

We can write a normal, non-parameterizable class like this one:

```
public class WidgetManager implements Manager<Widget> {

  public Widget create() {
    return new Widget();
  }

  public boolean validate(Widget w) {
    return w.isConsistent();
  }

  public void reset(Widget w) {
    w.reset();
  }
}
```

This is not a parameterizable class. If we create an instance of `WidgetManager`, we don't have to specify what sort of widget it manages, the decision has been made at the level of this implementation – a `WidgetManager` is a `Manager` of `Widgets`. So, this class is a valid implementation of the `Manager<Widget>` interface; all places in the `Manager<B>` interface where the identifier `B` is used have been replaced with `Widget`, and the class implements all of the methods correctly.

Alternatively, we could implement the interface by writing a new, parameterizable class, like this:

```
import java.util.List;

public class ListManager<C> implements Manager<List<C>> {
  public List<C> create() {
    return new List<C>();
  }

  public boolean validate(List<C> list) {
    return list != null;
  }

  public void reset(List<C> list) {
    list.clear();
  }
}
```

The class type declares that `ListManager` objects can be parameterized, and declares the parameter variable `C`. The `implements` statement then uses this parameter variable to parameterize `java.util.List`, and then uses *this* type to parameterize `Manager`. This means that an object, for example, of type `ListManager<String>` must implement `Manager<java.util.List<String>>`. That means that its `create()` method returns a `List<String>` object, and its `reset()` method requires a `List<String>` type as an argument.

So, as you can see, it's possible to parameterize a parameterizable type using any type – including a parameterized one! The only restriction is that the parameter must be an object and not a primitive type.

It's also possible to specify more then one parameter for a type. For example:

```
public interface Converter<A,B> {
  public A convertUp(B b);
  public B convertDown(A a);
}
```

We can now write classes that implement `Converter<String, Date>` or similar, and the compiler will ensure that we provide methods with the appropriate signatures and return types.

Any number of parameters may be specified in this manner. The generic collections classes that ship with the early-access generics preview use this technique to enable us to specify the acceptable types for keys and values of a Map:

```
Map<String, Integer> map = new HashMap<String, Integer>();
map.put("One", new Integer(1));
map.put("Two", new Integer(2));
map.put(new Integer(3), "Three"); // compile-time error
```

Generic Methods

In addition to parameterized types, the generics system also supports generic methods. These allow you to have the return-type of a method depend in some way on one of the method's parameters, or otherwise have a method handle arbitrary types. You must specify a parameter list, inside angle brackets, immediately before the method's return type. You should then specify these parameter variables in one of the types of the method's argument list – this will then be used to determine the type for the parameter. Here's an example:

```
import java.util.*;

public class ListTool {

  public <A> List<A> singleItemList(A item) {
    List<A> list = new ArrayList<A>();
    list.add(item);
    return list;
  }
}
```

Now, the following will work:

```
import java.util.*;

public class ListToolTest {

  public static void main(String[] args) {
    ListTool lt = new ListTool();

    int a = lt.singleItemList("Hello").get(0).length();
    int b = lt.singleItemList(new Integer(5)).get(0).intValue();

    if (a == b) System.out.println("success!");
  }
}
```

We've basically got the ability to instantly overload a method so it can handle any number of different object types, and return safely typed objects back to our code. Notice that, in spite of the fact that we're pulling objects out of the returned `Lists` without casting them, we're able to immediately call class-specific methods on them. Generics enable us to write code that, like the above, is intuitively correct, natural to read, and also completely type-safe. In standard Java, the first of the above generic method calls would look like this:

```
int a = ((String) (lt.singleItemList("Hello").get(0))).length();
```

As well as being ugly and hard to debug, this version lacks compile-time type-safety. Currently, there's no way around this, so hopefully this provides some justification for generics coming to Java.

Covariant Return Types

As a side effect of the language changes introduced with generics, it is possible to compile classes with methods that override those in their superclass, and provide a covariant return type.

*If we say that a method, `a()`, has a return type that is **covariant** with the return type of another method, `b()`, then we are saying that the value returned by `a()` could be used in the place of the value returned by `b()`. It is a little like saying 'equivalent', except that it's a one-way correspondence. There is no reciprocal guarantee that the return type of `b()` is covariant with that of `a()`. On the other hand, we can say that `b()`'s return type is **contravariant** with `a()`'s return type.*

Take a look at these two classes, which won't compile:

```
public class Foo {
  String id;
  String getID() {return id; }
}
```

```
public class Bar extends Foo {
  Integer id;
  Integer getID() {return id; }
}
```

Obviously, there's a simple reason they won't compile – the `Bar` class's implementation of the `getID()` method doesn't make any sense. If we have a reference to a `Foo` object, and we call `getID()`, we're expecting to receive a `String` object, but a `Foo`-type variable can hold a `Bar`-type object (since it's a subclass), and if we called `getID()` on such an object, we'd get an `Integer` in return, which would be both unexpected and undesirable. This is why the compiler will prevent you from compiling `Bar.java`.

However, there is one specific situation that deserves special attention:

```
public class Foo {
  Number id;
  Number getID() {return id; }
}
```

```
public class Bar extends Foo {
  Integer id;
  Integer getID() {return id; }
}
```

Here, the return type of the `getID()` method in `Bar` is a subclass of the return type in `Foo` – `Bar.getID()` is *covariant* with `Foo.getID()`. If we called the `getID()` method on a `Foo`-type variable, expecting the result that comes back to be a `Number`, we would not have a problem, since the type that comes back would be a subclass of `Number`.

However, Java won't allow you to compile the above example, even though it is completely type-safe. In order to prevent the previous kind of problem, the compiler simply rejects any overriding method whose return type doesn't match the original.

The generic Java compiler will happily compile the second example, while complaining about the first, just as things should be.

The best example of why covariant return types are needed in Java, and why it's a pain that they're not there, is the `clone()` method. This method is defined in the `Object` class, and as a result, its return type is specified as `Object`. Other classes are encouraged, of course, to override the `Object` `clone()` method and provide their own implementation, but the return type of these clone methods is still `Object`, forcing us to write code like the following:

```
Integer i = new Integer(12);
Integer j = (Integer) i.clone();
```

The cast operation adds nothing, semantically, to the clone operation. We know that when we call `clone()` on an `Integer` object, we're going to see an `Integer` object returned, so why do we have to perform the cast?

The generic compiler's acceptance of covariant return types means that it's possible to write `clone()` methods in your classes that don't return `Object` – they return the type of the class itself. And you can write code that uses these `clone()` methods without having to perform that annoying cast back to the correct type. Be careful, though: until this makes it into the official Java language specification, this style of code (which is really only a side effect of generics) is not correct Java, even if it should be.

Generic Engineering

Let's create a more substantial example than the trivial code we saw just now. We created an interface earlier for an object lifecycle manager. This interface can form part of a generic framework for the pooling of objects of an arbitrary type. Here it is again:

```
public interface Manager<B> {
  public B create();
  public boolean validate(B obj);
  public void reset(B obj);
}
```

We can implement this interface to create a manager for any kind of object, from database connections, to server threads, to objects representing aliens in a computer game. We can't create a generic class to manage objects of an arbitrary type for the simple reason that it's not possible to construct objects belonging to the parameter type of a class (we can't write a method body for the `create()` method that reads `return new B()` – the compiler can't guarantee that for all classes, there is an accessible constructor with that signature). By creating an interface like this though, which provides a factory method for a generic class, we can build a dynamic object pool.

The basic principles of our object pool are based on the example by Thomas E Davies, published in the June 1998 edition of *JavaWorld* and available online at http://www.javaworld.com/javaworld/jw-06-1998/jw-06-object-pool.html.

Here's `Pool.java`:

```
import java.util.*;

public class Pool<A> {
```

The pool stores objects of its parameterized type in two `HashSets`. We naturally use the generic `HashSet` classes to create `HashSets` that will hold objects of the right type. In addition, we'll need a `Manager` object that manages objects of the parameterized type. The constructor simply initializes these three instance variables:

```
  private HashSet<A> checkedOut;
  private HashSet<A> checkedIn;
  private Manager<A> manager;

  public Pool(Manager<A> manager) {
    checkedOut = new HashSet<A>();
    checkedIn = new HashSet<A>();
    this.manager = manager;
  }
```

We call the checkOut() method to take an object out of the pool. The method looks through the set of checked-in objects, and asks the manager whether each one is valid. This facility allows us to decommission objects once they've been used too many times, or after a timeout has expired. Notice we're using a parameterizable version of the Iterator class, as well. There are no explicit casts anywhere in this section.

If the manager tells us the object is valid, we remove it from the checked-in set, add it to the checked-out set, and then return a reference to it. If it says the object is no longer valid, we just remove it from the checked-in set.

```
public synchronized A checkOut() {

  A target;

  if ( checkedIn.size() > 0 ) {
    // There are checked in objects. Let's find a valid one
    Iterator<A> i = checkedIn.iterator();

    while ( i.hasNext() ) {
      target = i.next();

      if ( manager.validate(target) ) {
        // Found a valid object, so check it out, and return it
        i.remove();
        checkedOut.add(target);
        return(target);
      } else {
        // Found an invalid object, so dispose of it
        i.remove();
      }
    }
  }
```

If we reach this point in the code, we didn't manage to find a suitable object in the pool – either it was already empty, or it only contained invalid objects. So, we need to add another object to the pool. We do this using the manager's create() method.

```
  // no usable objects in pool, create a new one
  target = manager.create();
  checkedOut.add(target);
  return target;
}
```

The checkIn() method is nowhere near as complex. It simply calls the manager's reset method, which should prepare the object to be returned to the pool, removes it from the checkedOut set, and puts it in the checkedIn set.

```
  synchronized void checkIn(A target) {
    manager.reset(target);
    checkedOut.remove(target);
    checkedIn.add(target);
  }
}
```

We can now create `Pool` classes to handle any type of object. Pools are an effective resource management technique for any class where creation is more expensive than reuse (although Java is very efficient at creating objects that only use internal data storage, so pooling shouldn't be used too liberally). This pool doesn't manage object proliferation in order to reduce resource usage, although such an addition would be fairly simple. It would involve setting an upper limit on the number of objects in the pool, and keeping track of the object count as they are created. Then when an object is requested, but none are available and no more can be created, you would need to wait and block until an object had been put back into the pool (obviously, only an effective strategy in a multi-threaded program).

Generics Conclusions

Clearly generics will be a huge change to the way we think about typing in Java. Parameterized types should eliminate from code a lot of common annoying bugs that don't show up until run-time, by detecting mismatched types far more readily at compile time. The overhauled Collections API is intuitive, simple, and it just works the way you want it to. Generics open up the language to a lot of interesting new patterns and interface designs, and the chances are that once they're introduced into the language specification, you won't be able to get very far as a Java programmer unless you embrace and exploit their power.

How much of a barrier to entry this ends up presenting remains to be seen. When you have to understand generics in order to use something as fundamental as collections, perhaps they are a dangerous complication to the simplicity and shallow learning curve Java presents at the moment. Generics could represent the first step on a slippery slope into C++-level complexity in the Java language.

Beyond Merlin

So, over the course of this book, we've seen how J2SE is being enhanced as a GUI application and rich client-development platform, with an emphasis on ease of deployment, power, and networking. We've also seen how support for XML will be a defining feature of the Java language, going forward. Tiger looks, for now at least, like it will provide more of the same; extending the existing APIs, adding a few new features like JAXB, and, of course, the minor matter of a complete overhaul of the type system. Obviously, there's a long way to go yet, and a great deal can happen between now and the release of J2SE 1.5.

In spite of calls from a lot of Java developers for a reduction in the size of the Java runtime, it seems that the number of classes that make up Java must continue to increase. But in which direction? Well, J2SE 1.3 saw the introduction of the JavaSound API into the Standard Edition, so perhaps some other multimedia APIs will follow. Java3D, speech synthesis and recognition, enhanced 2D rendering, support for media playback and streaming media formats, are all possible candidates for future Java standard APIs. As the range of needs the platform seeks to meet expands to cover every possible interest though, size does begin to matter more and more.

However, one of the possibilities offered by the **Java Network Launching Protocol (JNLP)** and **Web Start** (a reference implementation of JNLP) is automated on-demand downloading and installation of standard extensions. This could make it possible for the Java platform to be cut back to a much smaller subset even of its current self, but with a huge range of possible extension APIs available instantly online. If this capability is expanded and exploited properly in the run up to the next Java release, we could instead see it effect a reduction, or at least a halt in the growth, of the size of the core platform.

Of course, the future of the J2SE is also tied to future developments in the role and power of home and office computers. While mobile devices continue to get more powerful, with ever better network access and user interfaces, and at the same time information appliances start to become a common Internet access platform in the home, Java 2 is finding itself deployed on an ever broader range of devices, from mobile phones to the PlayStation 2. The J2SE target platform is a shrinking part of the Java universe, and the key to what will happen to J2SE is probably going to depend very much on the parallel changes in the J2ME mobile and embedded world.

Java J2SE 1.4 Core Platform Update

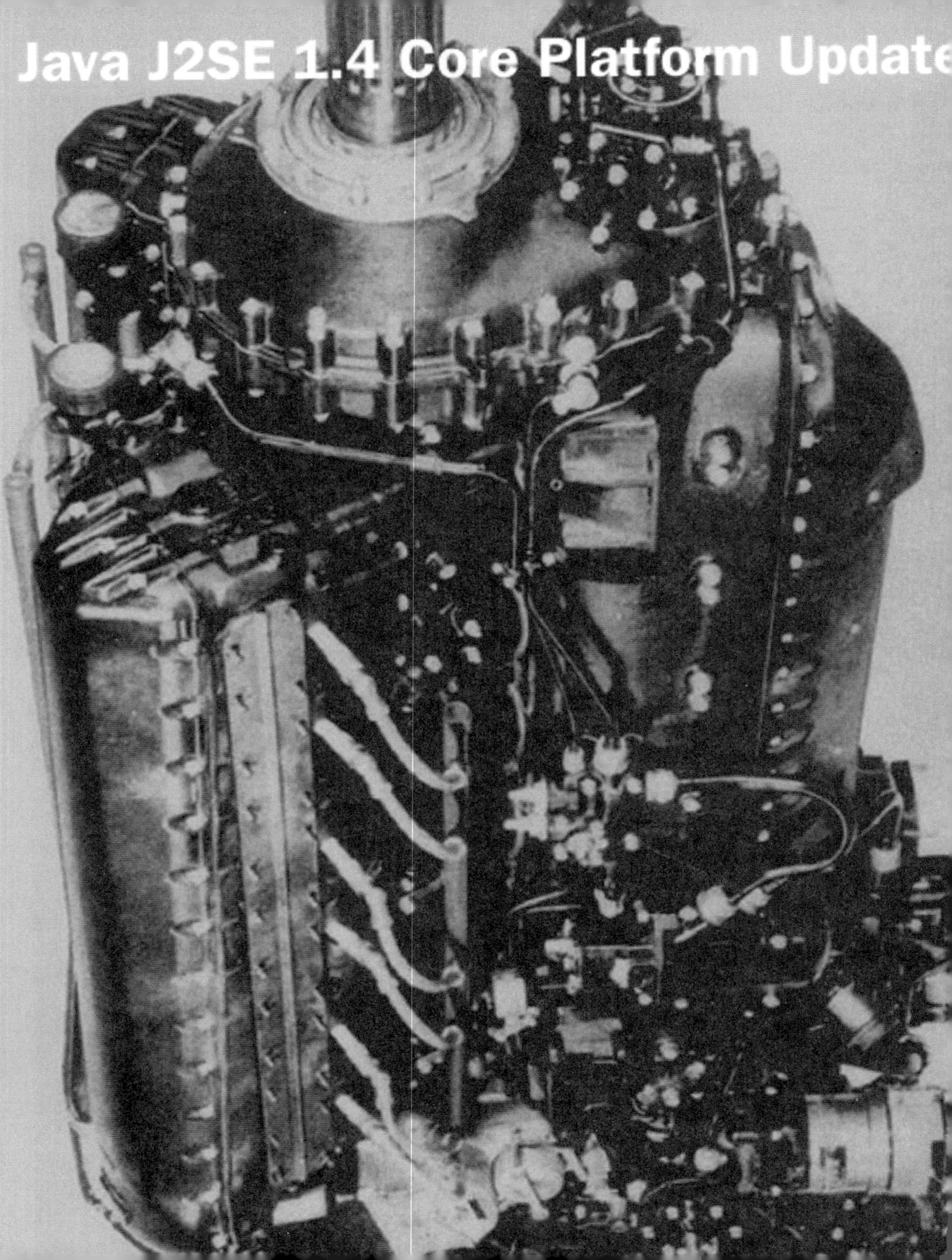

Support and Code Download

We always value hearing from our readers, and we want to know what you think about this book: what you liked, what you didn't like, and what you think we can do better next time. You can send us your comments, either by returning the reply card in the back of the book, or by e-mailing us at feedback@wrox.com. Please be sure to mention the book title in your message.

Downloading the Code for this Book

When you log on to the Wrox site, http://www.wrox.com/, simply locate the title through our fast code download finder facility or by using one of the title lists. Click on Download in the Code column or on Download Code on the book's detail page.

The files that are available for download from our site have been archived using WinZip. When you have saved the archive to a folder on your hard-drive, you may need to extract the files using WinZip or a compatible tool (such as the `jar` utility that ships with the Java SDK). Inside the zip file will be a folder structure and an HTML file that explains the structure and gives you further information.

Errata

We've made every effort to ensure that there are no errors in the text or in the code. However, no one is perfect and mistakes can occur. If you find an error in one of our books, like a spelling mistake or a faulty piece of code, we would be very grateful for feedback. By sending in errata, you may save another reader hours of frustration, and of course, you will be helping us provide even higher quality information. Simply e-mail the information to support@wrox.com, your information will be checked and, if correct, posted to the errata page for that title.

Appendix

To find errata on the web site log on to http://www.wrox.com/earlyadopter and simply locate and click on the title on that page. Click on the Book Errata link on the book's detail page.

E-Mail Support

If you have a problem using any of the code or techniques shown in the book, and wish to discuss it with an expert who knows the book in detail, then e-mail support@wrox.com with the title of the book and the last four numbers of the ISBN in the subject field of the e-mail. A typical e-mail should include the following things:

1. The title of the book, the last four digits of the ISBN, and the page number of the problem in the Subject field
2. Your name, contact information, and the problem in the body of the message

For this book, the title is *Java J2SE 1.4 Core Platform Update*, and the last four digits of the ISBN are 7272.

We won't send you junk mail. We need the details to save your time and ours. When you send an e-mail message, it will go through the following chain of support:

1. **Customer Support**
   Your message is delivered to our customer support staff. They have files on most frequently asked questions and will answer anything general about the book or the web site immediately.
2. **Editorial**
   More in-depth queries are forwarded to the technical editor responsible for that book. The editor has experience with the programming language or particular product, and is able to answer detailed technical questions on the subject. Once an issue has been resolved, the editor can post the errata to the web site.
3. **The Authors**
   Finally, in the unlikely event that the editor cannot answer your problem, the editor will forward the request to the author. We do try to protect the author from any distractions to their writing (or programming); however, we are quite happy to forward specific requests to them. All Wrox authors help with the support on their books. They will mail the customer and the editor with their response, and again all readers should benefit.

The Wrox Support process can only offer support to issues that are directly pertinent to the content of our published title. Support for questions that fall outside the scope of normal book support, is provided via the community lists of our http://p2p.wrox.com/forum.

p2p.wrox.com

For author and peer discussion join the P2P mailing lists. Our unique system provides Programmer to Programmer™ contact on mailing lists, forums, and newsgroups, all in addition to our one-to-one e-mail support system. Be confident that the many Wrox authors and other industry experts who are present on our mailing lists are examining any queries posted. At http://p2p.wrox.com/, you will find a number of different lists that will help you, not only while you read this book, but also as you develop your own applications.

To subscribe to a mailing list just follow this these steps:

1. Go to http://p2p.wrox.com/
2. Choose the appropriate category from the left menu bar
3. Click on the mailing list you wish to join
4. Follow the instructions to subscribe and fill in your e-mail address and password
5. Reply to the confirmation e-mail you receive
6. Use the subscription manager to join more lists and set your mail preferences

The Early Adopters Page

The Early Adopters series and its page were created in response to the demand from programmers for information about the potential effect of upcoming technologies; the Early Adopter team is always on the lookout for new programming ideas, new standards, new libraries, new ways to do old tricks, and new versions of old technologies. Early Adopter books provide information on the most important technologies as well as a realistic, programmer's perspective on when they are going to change.

For more information about Early Adopters, or to contact the Early Adopter team with new ideas, you can visit the Early Adopter site at http://www.wrox.com/earlyadopter.

Java J2SE 1.4 Core Platform Update

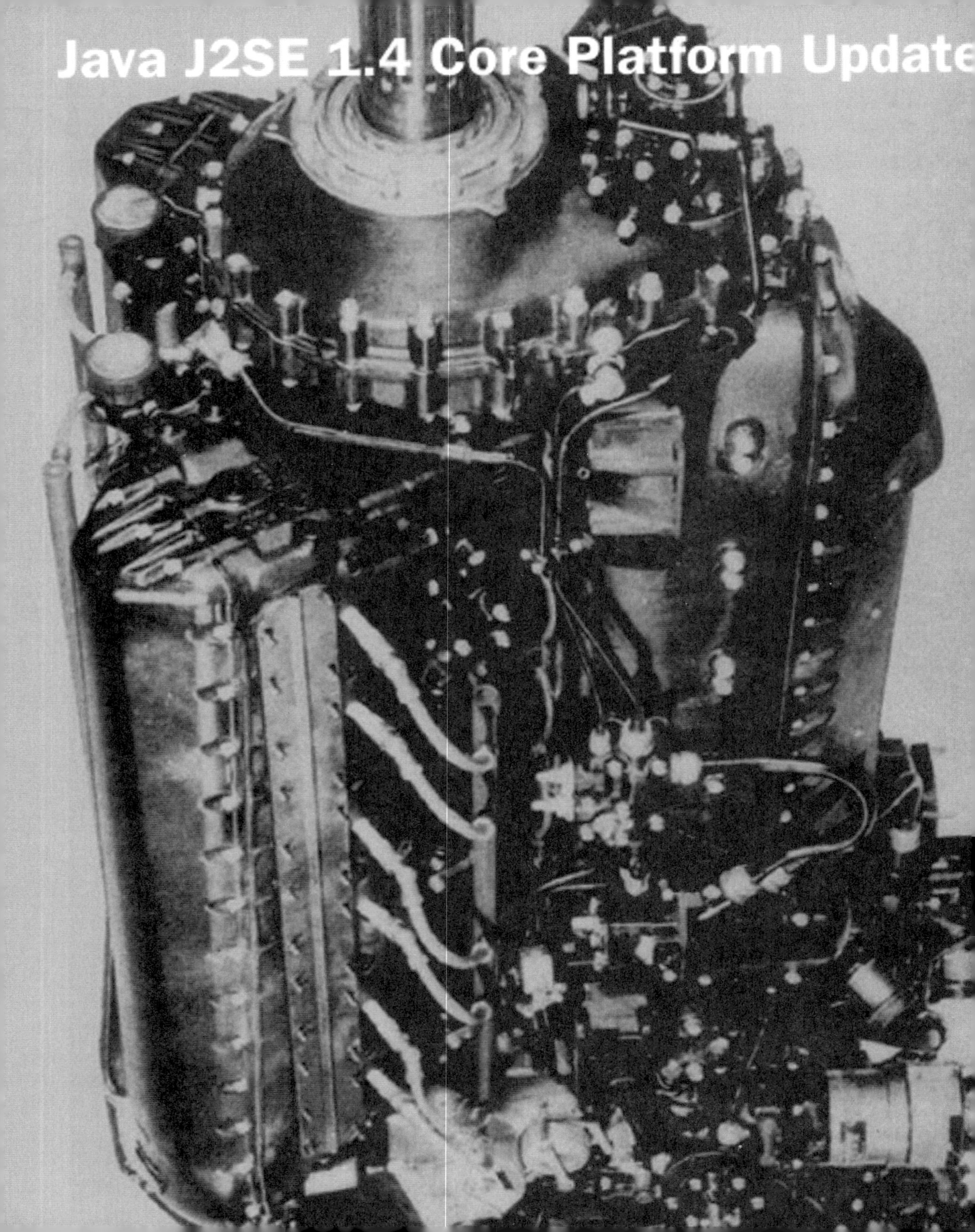

Index

A Guide to the Index

The index covers the numbered chapters but not the Appendix. It is arranged in word-by-word alphabetical order (so that New York would appear before Newark), with symbols preceding the letter A. Acronyms have been preferred to their expansions as main entries and asterisks (*) indicate variant endings.

Symbols

A

B

C

D

E

F

G

H

I

J

K

L

M

N

O

P

Q

R

S

V

W

X

Z

Wrox

Programmer to Programmer™

Wrox writes books for you. Any suggestions, or ideas about how you want information given in your ideal book will be studied by our team. Your comments are always valued at Wrox.

Free phone in USA 800-USE-WROX
Fax (312) 893 8001

UK Tel.: (0121) 687 4100 Fax: (0121) 687 4101

Java J2SE 1.4 Core Platform Update – Registration Card

Name ______________________

Address ______________________

____

____

____

City __________ State/Region __________

Country __________ Postcode/Zip __________

E-Mail ______________________

Occupation ______________________

How did you hear about this book?

- ❒ Book review (name) ______________
- ❒ Advertisement (name) ______________
- ❒ Recommendation ______________
- ❒ Catalog ______________
- ❒ Other ______________

Where did you buy this book?

- ❒ Bookstore (name) __________ City __________
- ❒ Computer store (name) ______________
- ❒ Mail order ______________
- ❒ Other ______________

What influenced you in the purchase of this book?

❒ Cover Design ❒ Contents ❒ Other (please specify):

____

How did you rate the overall content of this book?

❒ Excellent ❒ Good ❒ Average ❒ Poor

What did you find most useful about this book? ______________

____

____

What did you find least useful about this book? ______________

____

____

Please add any additional comments. ______________

____

____

What other subjects will you buy a computer book on soon?

____

What is the best computer book you have used this year?

____

Note: This information will only be used to keep you updated about new Wrox Press titles and will not be used for any other purpose or passed to any other third party.

Programmer to Programmer™

Note: If you post the bounce back card below in the UK, please send it to:

Wrox Press Limited, Arden House, 1102 Warwick Road,
Acocks Green, Birmingham B27 6HB. UK.

Computer Book Publishers

NO POSTAGE
NECESSARY
IF MAILED
IN THE
UNITED STATES

BUSINESS REPLY MAIL

FIRST CLASS MAIL PERMIT#64 CHICAGO, IL

POSTAGE WILL BE PAID BY ADDRESSEE

WROX PRESS INC.
29 S. LA SALLE ST.
SUITE 520
CHICAGO IL 60603-USA